------------------------------------------

**Citizens and Subjects:**
**The Netherlands, for example**
A Critical Reader

------------------------------------------

**Dutch Pavilion**
52nd International Art Exhibition
La Biennale di Venezia 2007

------------------------------------------

------------------------------------------

# Citizens and Subjects:
# The Netherlands,
# for example

Edited by Rosi Braidotti, Charles Esche and Maria Hlavajova

Citizens and Subjects:
The Netherlands, for example

This critical reader has been published as part of the project *Citizens and Subjects*, the Dutch contribution to the 52nd International Art Exhibition – La Biennale di Venezia, commissioned by the Mondriaan Foundation. The three-part project consists of new work and installation by artist Aernout Mik in the Dutch Pavilion in Venice, 10 June–21 November 2007, this publication and an 'extension' of the Pavilion taking place in the Netherlands in autumn 2007.

www.citizensandsubjects.nl

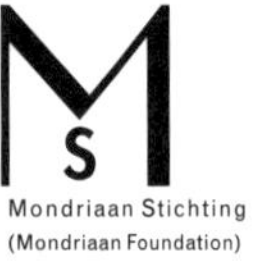

Mondriaan Stichting
(Mondriaan Foundation)

Mondriaan Foundation
Jacob Obrechtsstraat 56
NL-1071 KN Amsterdam
T: +31 (0)20 6762032
F: +31 (0)20 6762036
info@mondriaanfoundation.nl
www. mondriaanfoundation.nl

**bak**  **basis voor actuele kunst**

**jrp|ringier**

Concept and Curator:
Maria Hlavajova
Editors: Rosi Braidotti, Charles Esche, Maria Hlavajova
Associate Editor: Jill Winder
Copy Editor: D'Laine Camp
Research: Suzanne Tiemersma, Jill Winder
Transcription: Nadine Orth, Suzanne Tiemersma
Design: Kummer & Herrman, Utrecht
Printing/Lithography: Die Keure, Bruges
Binding: Hexspoor, Boxtel
Printed in the EU

© 2007 the artists, authors, BAK, basis voor actuele kunst and JRP|Ringier



ISBN: 978-3-905770-73-5

Published by:
BAK, basis voor actuele kunst
Postbus 19288
NL–3501 DG Utrecht
T +31 (0)30 2316125
F +31 (0)30 2300591
info@bak-utrecht.nl
www.bak-utrecht.nl

and

JRP|Ringier
Letzigraben 134
8047 Zürich
Switzerland
T +41 (0)43 3112750
F +41 (0)43 3112751
info@jrp-ringier.com
www.jrp-ringier.com

JRP|Ringier books and DVDs are available internationally at selected bookstores and from the following distribution partners:

Switzerland:
Buch 2000, AVA Verlagsauslieferung AG, Centralweg 16,
CH-8910 Affoltern a.A.,
buch2000@ava.ch, www.ava.ch

Germany and Austria:
Vice Versa Vertrieb,
Immanuelkirchstrasse 12,
D–10405 Berlin,
info@vice-versa-vertrieb.de
www.vice-versa-vertrieb.de

France:
Les Presses du réel, 16 rue Quentin
F–21000 Dijon,
info@lespressesdureel.com
www.lespressesdureel.com

UK:
Cornerhouse Publications,
70 Oxford Street,
UK–Manchester M1 5NH,
publications@cornerhouse.org,
www.cornerhouse.org/books

USA:
D.A.P./Distributed Art Publishers,
155 Sixth Avenue, 2nd Floor,
USA–New York, NY 10013,
dap@dapinc.com, www.artbook.com

Other countries:
IDEA Books, Nieuwe Herengracht
NL–1011 RK Amsterdam,
idea@ideabooks.nl,
www.ideabooks.nl

For a list of our partner bookshops or for any general questions, please contact JRP|Ringier directly at info@jrp-ringier.com, or visit our homepage www.jrp-ringier.com for further information about our program.

**Images**

14–103    **Aernout Mik, *Training Ground*, 2007**
two-channel video installation, courtesy carlier | gebauer,
Berlin and The Project, New York

104–213    **Aernout Mik, *Convergencies*, 2007**
two-channel video installation, courtesy carlier | gebauer,
Berlin and The Project, New York

214–317    **Aernout Mik, *Mock Up*, 2007**
four-channel video installation, courtesy carlier | gebauer,
Berlin

**Foreword**

Every two years the international art world gathers for the Venice Biennale, where the latest state of affairs in the art world is presented. This year, the Dutch presentation in the Rietveld pavilion is embedded in the larger context of a three-part project. *Citizens and Subjects* explores the current condition in western society with regard to issues of major cultural, political and moral consequence: (illegal) immigration, violence and enforcement and practices of maintaining security through fear and anxiety. The project is grounded in a belief that art is part of the world, and as such it can respond to the urgencies of our time by engaging with questions that affect us all. It consists of a complex, multilayered video installation and architectural intervention in the Dutch Pavilion by artist Aernout Mik; this critical reader, with contributions by Netherlands-based artists and theorists from a variety of fields that analyse and elaborate upon the issues raised by Mik's work; and an 'extension' of the pavilion where an additional platform for debating these issues, as well as the Venice Biennale in general, is created. We are particularly pleased that this 'extension' gives the contribution a home in a number of cities in the Netherlands in autumn 2007 as the result of a collaboration between BAK, basis voor actuele kunst, Utrecht, Utrecht University, Van Abbemuseum, Eindhoven and Witte de With, Rotterdam.

We are very pleased that curator Maria Hlavajova has developed such a challenging project in collaboration with Aernout Mik and a number of important writers and theorists in response to the appointment from the Mondriaan Foundation. We are confident that this project will fuel the discussion about the place of art in society that we find so essential today.

Jos Werner
Chair, Mondriaan Foundation

# Introduction
## Citizens and Subjects

Maria Hlavajova

*Citizens and Subjects* is a three-part project developed as the Dutch contribution to the 52nd Venice Biennale. *Citizens and Subjects: Aernout Mik* is a complex installation by artist Aernout Mik in the Dutch Pavilion, consisting of three new video works embedded in an architectural intervention in the Pavilion. *Citizens and Subjects: The Netherlands, for example* – the critical reader you hold in your hands – is an ensemble of texts and conversations written for this occasion. It is envisioned as a discursive space where the themes around 'citizens and subjects', as Mik introduces them in this project, are debated by a number of scholars and artists based in the Netherlands. In autumn this year, we 'extend' the project from Venice back home with the aim of contributing an additional forum to discuss the *subjects* of fear, anxiety, violence and national security that this project evolves around, as well as a question that we feel is critical to pose time and time again: why do we find it important to reflect on these notions in art? This 'extension', titled *Citizens and Subjects: Practices and Debates*, is the result of a collaboration between BAK, basis voor actuele kunst in Utrecht, the Dutch Pavilion, Utrecht University, Van Abbemuseum in Eindhoven, Witte de With in Rotterdam and the German Pavilion at the Venice Biennale.

Informed by the notion of national representation on which the Venice Biennale is based, *Citizens and Subjects* reflects on the nation-state in the present day circumstances of the so-called West and asks how we can negotiate its prospects vis-à-vis the challenges posited by that which defines our contemporary condition: (illegal) immigration. The starting point of this project – the work by Aernout Mik realized for the Dutch Pavilion – addresses this issue, as well as the fact that so far we have been incapable of resolving this equivocal riddle of major political and moral consequence. Instead of engaging a political imaginary of another kind, as Mik's work suggests, we seem to have handed over responsibility and power to the police to regulate the conundrum, turning the question of immigration into a key issue of national security. The project proposes this predicament as the paradigm of our contemporaneity and prompts us to think further about other possible ways that a new kind of political community could emerge.

To put it simply, a *subject* is a person who is under the rule or authority of a sovereign, state or a governing power and who owes allegiance and obedience. *Citizens*, by contrast, are generally those with rights, entitled to the full privileges of belonging to a state or nation. In his complex multichannel video installation enveloped in an architectural intervention in the Pavilion, Aernout Mik brings such defining dichotomies of the privileged and disadvantaged into intricate interplay, exploring the mechanisms of power, fear and violence involved. The starting point for him is the question of how the police learn and make use of various methods of carrying out the law against refugees. Not only does Mik stage and film a 'training' situation (testing how stand-ins temporarily adopt the roles of policemen and refugees), he also employs documentary 'rushes' from actual police exercises or real situations in which violence is deployed against asylum seekers. It becomes clear that this is part of the larger context of how we train ourselves to respond to crises and threats to national security in general. On multiple levels, the work questions the simplified distinction between subjects and citizens today, asking, aren't we all actually subjected in the same way to this disquieting reality? Yet, Mik seems to suggest, it is from here that new possibilities can perhaps emerge. What if we interpret the scenes he stages before us not as training for the enforcement of law and the maintenance of power, but rather as a ritual through which to transgress the status quo consensus today? In this way, Mik's *Citizens and Subjects* represents an instance of cultural resistance that functions through the appropriation of existing modes of the politics of domination, reminding us of a field of ambiguity between subjection and possible liberation. The use of parody, the building of irrational excess, mimicry and re-enactment of situations can be read as a ceremony of inversion, overcoming the divide between subjects and citizens by questioning to what extent, and if at all, the traditional citizenry can offer a foundation from which to address the acute challenges of our day.

Contemporary art here is understood as a site where larger networks of cultural, political and social discourse intersect, thus creating new possibilities; a site where ideals that could potentially counterbalance troubling developments in the public sphere can be reimagined, where the moment of critique is offset by the creation of affirmative alternatives. The project *Citizens and Subjects* developed from the urgency to create a space within the traditional context of a large-scale perennial exhibition in which artists, writers, curators, scholars and the general public can engage in a critical discussion. In that respect, I feel encouraged given the prominence this project has already gained in the public debate in the Netherlands.

I would like to take this opportunity to thank artist Aernout Mik, who inspired this project, who has been a supportive companion in articulating all its facets and whose creative labour has defined the key parameters of our shared efforts. I owe my gratitude to philosopher Rosi Braidotti and curator and writer Charles Esche for joining me in editing this critical reader and turning their attention to critical thinking about the current processes of renegotiating the social contract in the Netherlands. Also on behalf of them, I wish to sincerely thank the contributors to this reader, whose texts and conversations will surely inspire public discussion and enliven the discourse. I also owe my gratitude to Jill Winder, associate editor of the reader, for her immense dedication and inspiring commitment to the entire project. For developing the forum through which the Dutch Pavilion comes 'back home' in autumn, I would like to thank my colleague Binna Choi at BAK, basis voor actuele kunst, Rosi Braidotti and Melanie Peters of Utrecht University, Charles Esche and Annie Fletcher of Van Abbemuseum in Eindhoven and the *Be(com)ing Dutch* project and Nicolaus Schafhausen and Sophie von Olfers of Witte de With in Rotterdam.

For the realization of this project I would like to extend my compliments and thanks to Arjan van Meeuwen, executive director of BAK, for his patience and serenity in accommodating ever growing financial and organizational demands. My gratitude also extends to Marente Bloemhuevel, who has been of great assistance to the project, as well as to Danila Cahen for her research work and support. For handling the matters of public relations and communication in an utmost professional way, thanks go to Beate Barner and Hanna Sohier. Similarly, I would like to thank Suzanne Tiemersma for her devotion to the project in all its conceivable facets and for helping me research and organize it all in a friendly and professional way, as well as Ankie Schellekens for her assistance in Venice. I would like to thank the entire organization of BAK for making sure this project is realized at the highest professional level, while equally dedicating themselves to our other programmes, as well as to BAK's board for support and advice.

I would also like to thank the board of the Mondriaan Foundation, commissioner of this project, and its director Gitta Luiten for their trust and enduring support of the choices I have made. I would like to thank the Municipality of Utrecht for kindly supporting the 'extension' of the Pavilion, as well as Vrede van Utrecht and a number of other financial partners named elsewhere in this book.

Last but not least, I would like to especially thank my husband Peter Baren and sons Samo and Luka, who were willing to make the sacrifices this work requires in one's private life, and who made me aware that both successes and failures in this profession are nothing more than a matter of the usual course of things.

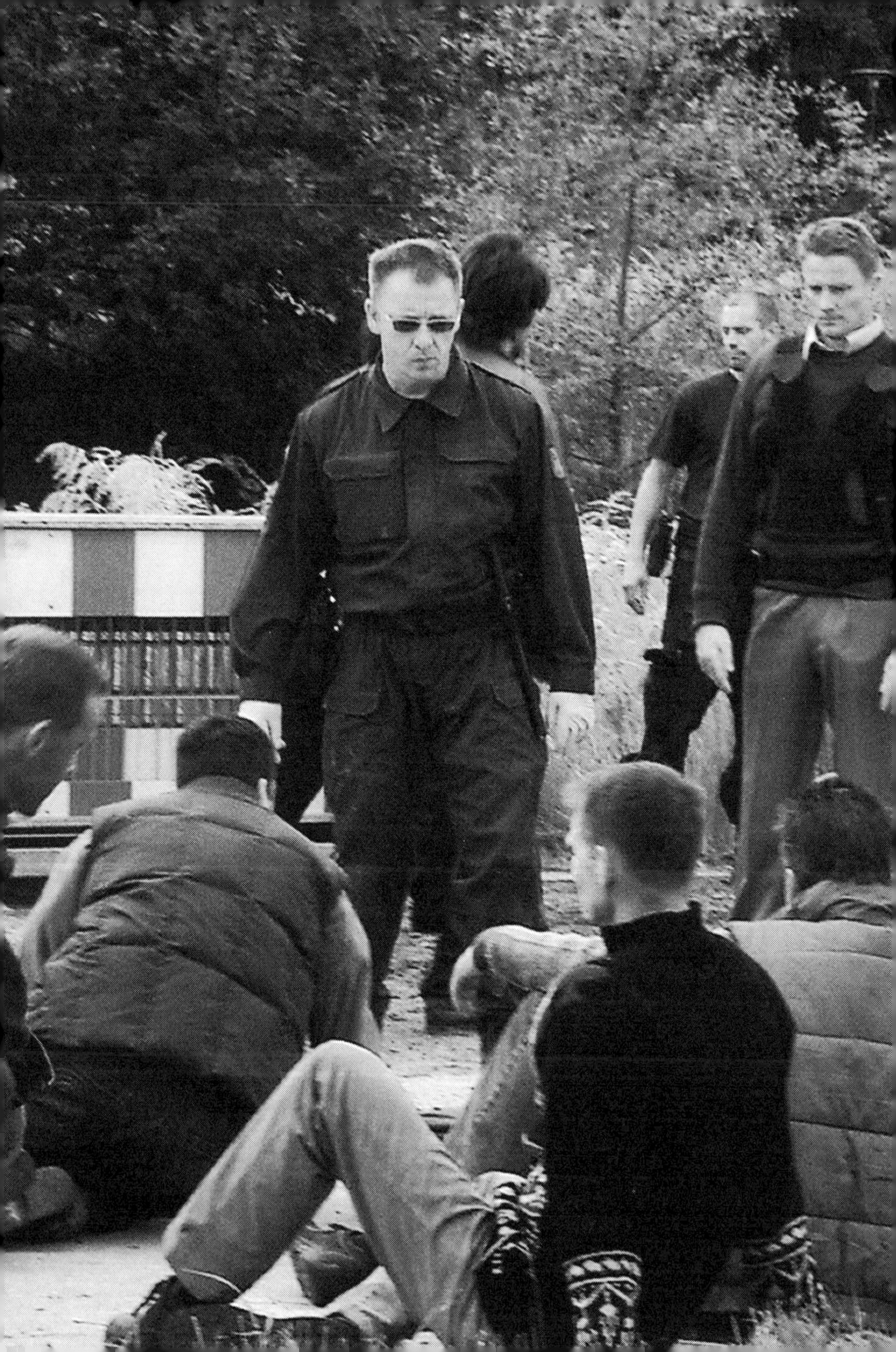

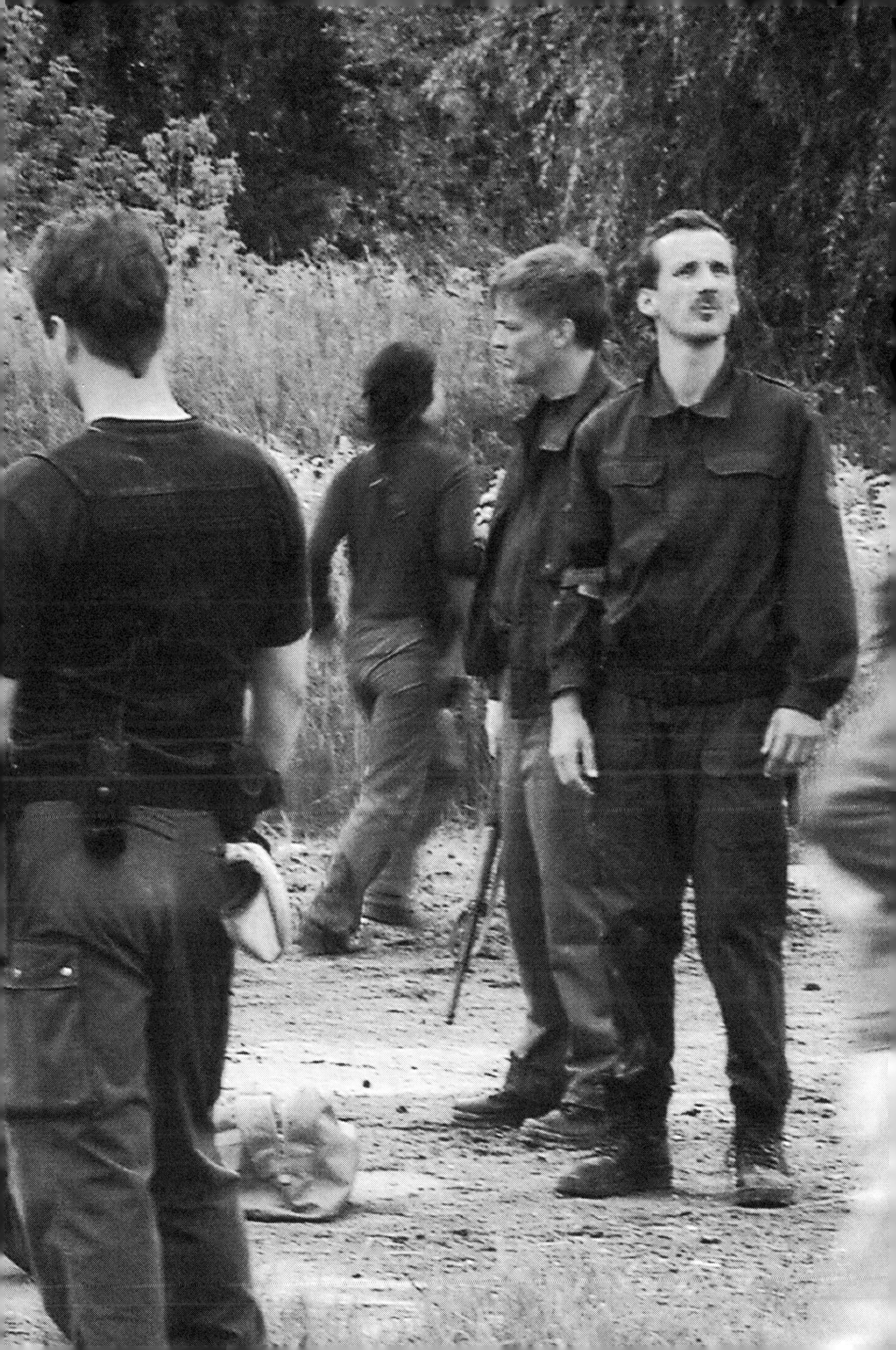

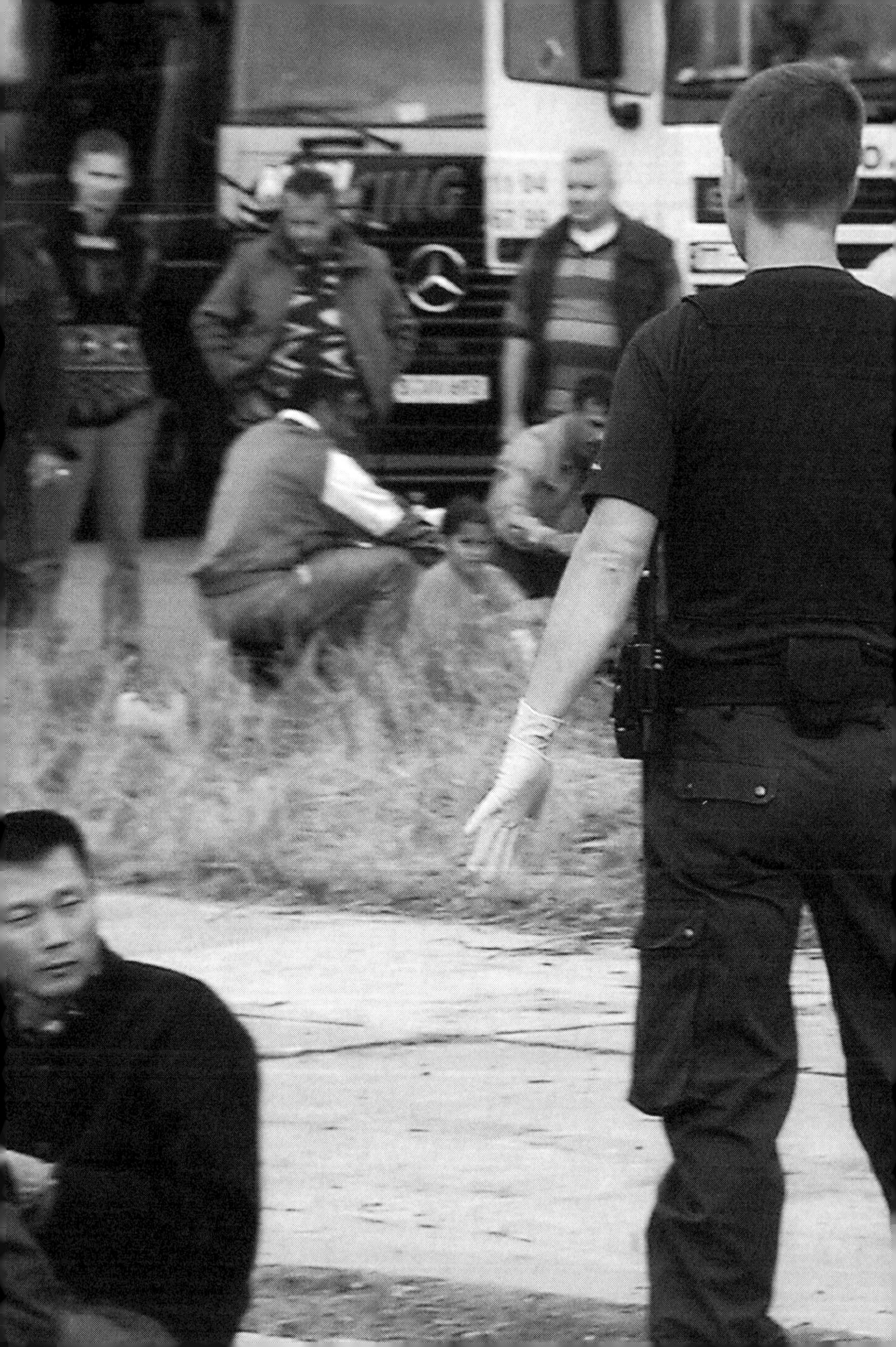

# The Netherlands, for example

Rosi Braidotti, Charles Esche, Maria Hlavajova

Let's take the Netherlands, for example. In a globalized and technologically mediated world, the protocol of national representation upon which the Venice Biennale historically and by convention insists offers the opportunity for renewed critical efforts. The project *Citizens and Subjects* reflects in different registers on the nation-state in its present-day circumstances. The reader that you have in your hands is one element of a three-part project also consisting of new work by Aernout Mik in the Dutch Pavilion and an 'extension' of the Pavilion through talks, discussions, reading groups and research residencies taking place in Utrecht, Eindhoven and Rotterdam later this year.

The nation-state that we have inherited from the nineteenth-century struggle for political representation still defines our best effort to bring about democratic accountability in the so-called West. In this context, it is worthwhile remembering that nationalism and social emancipation were once fellow travellers, with nationalism defining a progressive agenda in opposition to unelected autocracies. Still today, national citizenship encapsulates most of our democratic rights as citizens and subjects of our various territories. Despite the apparent waning of national influence, it is still national elections, the national press and media and the national heads of state that command the most attention in each country. While economists have long ago abandoned the nation-state for an analysis of larger trading blocks, almost every other form of social engagement is ruled by nation-states even when, with regard to such issues as climate change or pollution, the idea of borders is patently absurd.

It was not only the structure of the Venice Biennale that led us to the subject of this reader. The real existing condition of cultural politics and artistic production within this one nation-state – the Netherlands – is currently under review in a way not seen in decades. The old system of subsidies and state support is changing, though not being abandoned entirely. The international market alters almost everything at the level of expectation but almost nothing on the ground of general artistic survival. Institutions that once held themselves autonomous from governmental agendas and aloof from trade and industry now suffer from the shock of private caprice and public money tied to a mission. In many respects, the Netherlands is different from Belgium let alone Belize. It can neither claim universality nor a particular status that is unique to itself. Its peculiarities are tempered by generic Western-European and global conditions but they do not override them and, as such, the Netherlands is as valid a starting point as any other on the surface of the planet. It just happens to be our starting point and therefore our example.



**The Netherlands, for example**
Rosi Braidotti, Charles Esche, Maria Hlavajova

The status of the example is an interesting and idiosyncratic one that has a significant heritage. As Giorgio Agamben writes in *The Coming Community*: 'One concept that escapes the antimony of universal and particular has long been familiar to us: the example.... It is one singularity among others, which, however, stands for each of them and holds for all. On the one hand, every example is treated in effect as a real and particular case; but on the other, it remains understood that it cannot serve in its particularity. Neither particular nor universal, the example is a singular object that presents itself as such, that *shows* its singularity. Hence the proper place of the example is always beside itself [Ger: *beispiel*, Gk: *paradeigma*], in the empty space in which its undefinable and unforgettable life unfolds.'

Being 'beside' is as good a definition as we are likely to find for the time being. It addresses the relationship of this reader to both the artworks by Mik and the general ambition of the Venice Biennale. Modest as its starting point is, the reader is intended to make us reflect on the global context in which the Biennale is taking place through the specific conditions found in the Netherlands. The aim is to think together through the words of individuals. The texts that follow try to account for the tensions and contradictions of our era from the point of view of this nation-state outwards. It is, in this sense, parochial or 'situated' – as feminist theorist Donna Haraway put it – but doing this may, at least temporarily, offer a resistant alternative to the onset of global travellers' syndrome, where we are everywhere and nowhere at the same time, only secure in the waiting lounge of the 'utopia station'. This syndrome is one that, while often very seductive, can never avail itself of influence over the citizens and subjects who are the focus of this project, at least under present political conditions.

Yet, geopolitical power relations are global and transversal to a degree that not only defies national boundaries, but has prompted Michel Foucault to target the notion of 'life' as 'biopower', a central political concept. The regimes of modern government need to simultaneously include and control the intellectual and psychological resources, but also the biological, generative, living forces of the very people (*demos*) who constitute the social sphere (*polis*) of democratic regimes. According to Foucault, ever since modernity a political technology of disciplining the bodies of the population has come into being, which takes the individual as a stand-in for the perpetuation of the group, the collectivity and the species. Regimes of 'biopower' aim to include as fully controlled elements the very vital forces that, per definition, escape political control – including the collective social imaginary. The paradox of biopolitical regimes is therefore that they unfold onto the question of *Thanatos* or death in the sense of elimination, exclusion, and even worse, extermination or extinction. The politics of biopower affect those who are allowed to survive as well as those who are doomed to perish. It is a rather brutal regime of gradual, all pervasive selection, which takes the form of distributing and controlling the forms of entitlement to 'life', 'legality', 'visibility' and 'citizenship'. Agamben plays on different variations on the theme of subjection by referring to the human body's capacity to be reduced to sub-human, marginal and even non-human states by the intervention of sovereign power. 'Bare life' is that in which sovereign power can kill. It is the body as disposable matter in the hands of the despotic force of destructive power. In other words, to be a subject in an advanced liberal democracy means that one is simultaneously subjected to regimes of regulation and is also the active subject of self-implemented forms of affirmation. The gap between the negative and positive poles of power, however, and of the means to gain access to self-empowerment, is growing wider and deeper by the day, under the pervasive pressure of negative political passions, global warfare, structural injustices, gender inequalities, growing racism and a state of enforced fear and suspicion of others.

The further assumptions behind the project, in keeping with these theoretical insights, are relatively straightforward. Firstly, we take the Dutch situation as an example of what we perceive to be the failure of political imagination since 1989 to create concepts and invent practices that offer an adequate response to the challenges of our times. The political field fails the progressive forces in society at every turn, while many of the individuals who make up that society seek to gather round older centrifugal forces, most often those defined by the populist or racist right. This failure is tragic for our day and age and we believe it must be met by a response from a cultural field concerned with the furthering of emancipatory ambition. How it could or does do that is explored in these pages.

Secondly, we are concerned and distressed by the impoverishment of public debates about the intertwined yet conflictual relationship between citizenship and immigration, a state of anxiety that defines our contemporary condition. If fear and exclusion are simply part of national culture, it is surely one of the responsibilities of those who make and present that culture to take it up as a subject and context for their work. At a time when fear is at levels unprecedented since 1945, this becomes even more urgent. How to address this and to contribute to public debate, whether through the outspoken subject matter within artworks, or as spoken and written positions from artists, social scientists and philosophers, is explored here. The chance to exert some, however limited, sway over public opinion at the Biennale, back in the Netherlands and beyond is one all the writers and interviewees here found too valuable to resist.

Thirdly, we believe that we need to learn to think differently about ourselves, as Gilles Deleuze put it. In times of accelerating changes more conceptual creativity is necessary. Instead of falling back on the sedimented habits of thought, institutionalized by tradition, we propose a leap forward into the complexities and paradoxes of our times. The project of creating new concepts and practices of active subjectivity, in opposition to pervasive forms of subjection, inertia and nostalgia, is a serious ethical as well as intellectual challenge. It positions us between a future perspective that cannot be immediately guaranteed and the fast rate of progress that demands the development of new propositions. We do need to address this deficit in the scale of representation about ourselves and the deep-seated processes of transformation we are undergoing.

We feel we need to elaborate up-to-date, lucid and situated accounts of the kind of subjects and citizens we are in the process of becoming. Learning to think about processes, rather than essences, means that we need to confront diversity (rather than confirm sameness) on all levels: cultural, ethnic, religious, linguistic, aesthetic and otherwise. This entails as a necessary step that we abandon the self-replicating certainties that are bred from the repetition of over-familiar and taken-for-granted platitudes about our cultural identity. It is time to self-style alternative modes of identity – hybrid, multilayered, nomadic and complex – while keeping the notion of identity itself in play, elaborating new forms of flexible and transversal citizenship to match them. It is an urgent call to elaborate together new cultural, spiritual and ethical values – be it as myths, narratives or representations – that are adequate to today's world that we inhabit.

Last but not least we are passionate about our civil rights and freedom – and concerned about the fact that, in the absence of a political imaginary and leadership capable of meeting the present challenges, we seem to have handed over responsibility for regulation and enforcement to the police. If Mik's work depicts this in its complexity, this critical reader hopes to offer a way of thinking with and beside the current obsessions, to a moment where the broad field of art could open up emancipatory possibility again at the level of intimate exchanges between viewers, artworks, readers and speakers.

The choice to replace the traditional catalogue with a critical reader was made with all these considerations in mind. The main strength of this collection, in our view, is that it negotiates the complex tension between the multiplicity of political forces on the one hand and a sustained commitment to emancipatory politics on the other, without falling back on essential identities. While it is customary to argue for the primacy of the visual in art, our endeavour is grounded not only in the current urgency but also in the modern history of art as a propositional model and social experiment. This is a history that constantly returns at moments when it seems to be required, as we judge it is today. The contributors themselves explore many alternative cartographies of the Dutch situation and creative suggestions regarding how to go about addressing the current crisis. The voices vary from the analytical to the anecdotal, reflective, descriptive and provocative. In these different registers, we garner a picture of the potential for thinking about an exemplary location to generate broader resonances. The aim is thus to inform the global audience of the specificity and at times peculiarities of the Dutch situation, as well as to offer insights into the many resources and forms of resistant thinking that are at work in the Netherlands and that might determine the cultural development of this country in the future. The academics, artists and critical theorists who contribute to the reader also make a forceful case against racism and xenophobia and the extent to which both have intoxicated the public debate in the Netherlands. The stultifying effects of acquiescence, fear, verbal and political violence (the Netherlands have witnessed two political assassinations in the last five years) are analysed critically in a way that illuminates the complexities of the Dutch case.

Where the emphasis falls time and time again in the project, however, is on the need to work together towards renewing the grammar of our social interaction, the social imaginary about citizenship and cultural identity and the passions and emotions that go with them. The need to *reinvent* our social interaction clashes over and over again with the notion of a multiethnic society that seems only to evoke fear of invasion by alien 'others', whether out of true belief in the threat they pose or (and far worse) as an opportunist grab for power that eliminates nuanced discourse and provokes equally dumb and violent counteractions. The series of texts that follow combine criticism with affirmation to define, exploit and question this territory of *politica povera*. Terms that circulate and get reiterated in the public debate in the Netherlands today such as *klein* (small), *Nederland is vol* (The Netherlands is full), *angst* (fear), *kwetsbaarheid* (vulnerability), *poldermodel* (polder model), *intolerantie* (intolerance) and *allochtoon* (foreign-born) need to be scrutinized and


**The Netherlands, for example**
Rosi Braidotti, Charles Esche, Maria Hlavajova

reinvented in a way that might infuse hope and emancipation into the discourse. In a modest way, we hope this might strike a more appropriate balance or even generate excitement about the possibilities that citizens and subjects of this state – and by example this planet – might see in their future.

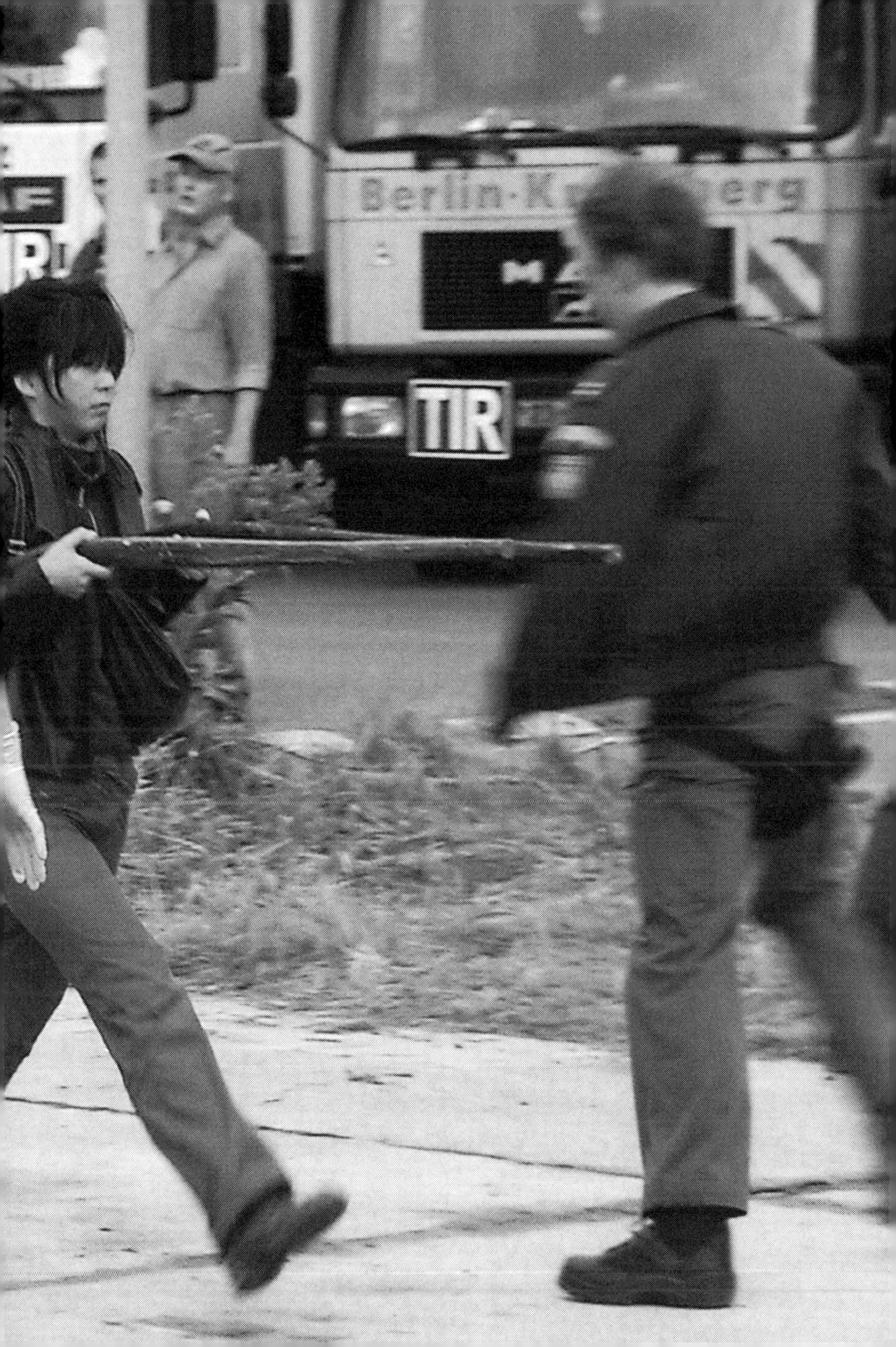

Berlin-Kr...erg
TIR

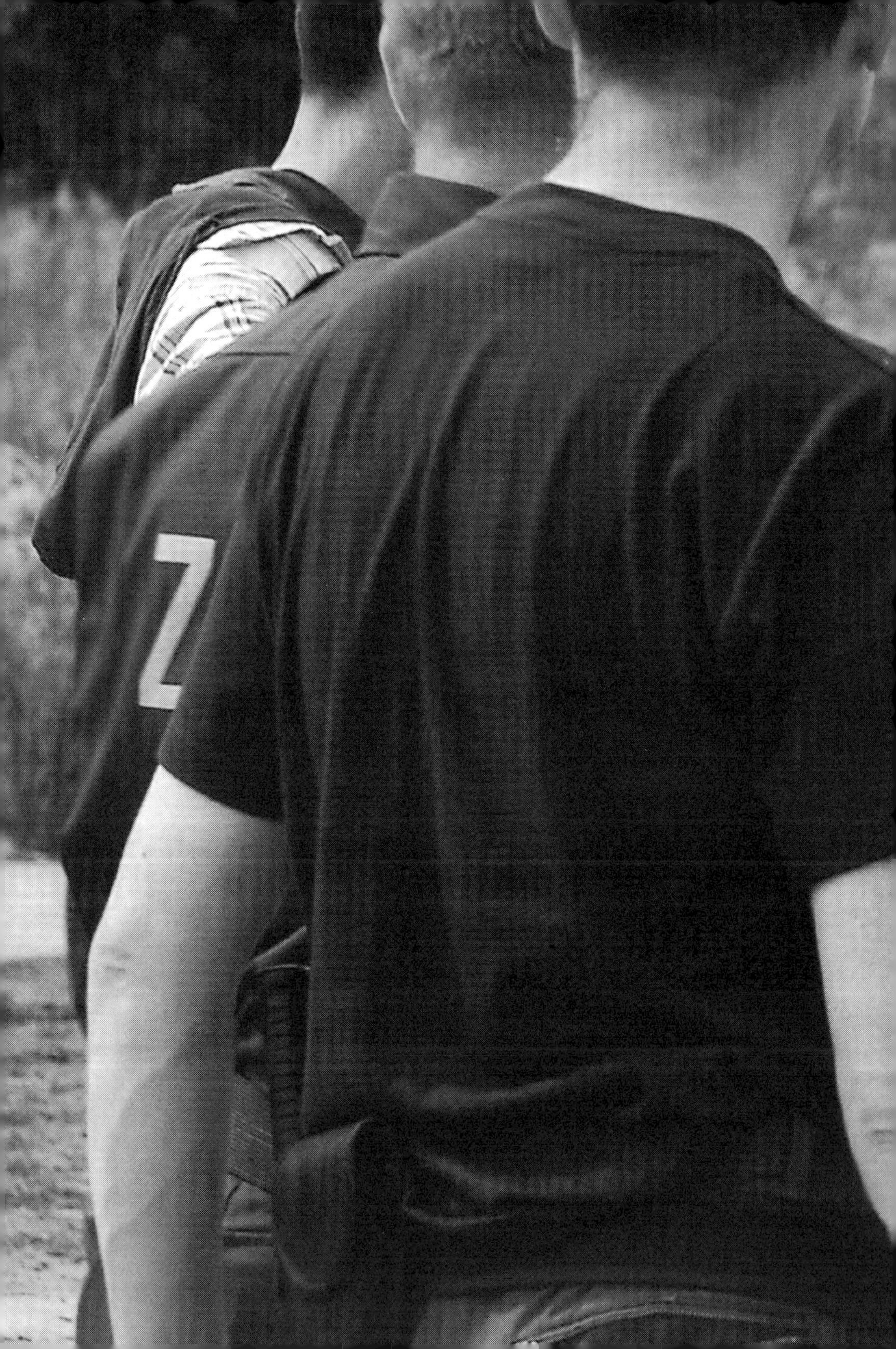

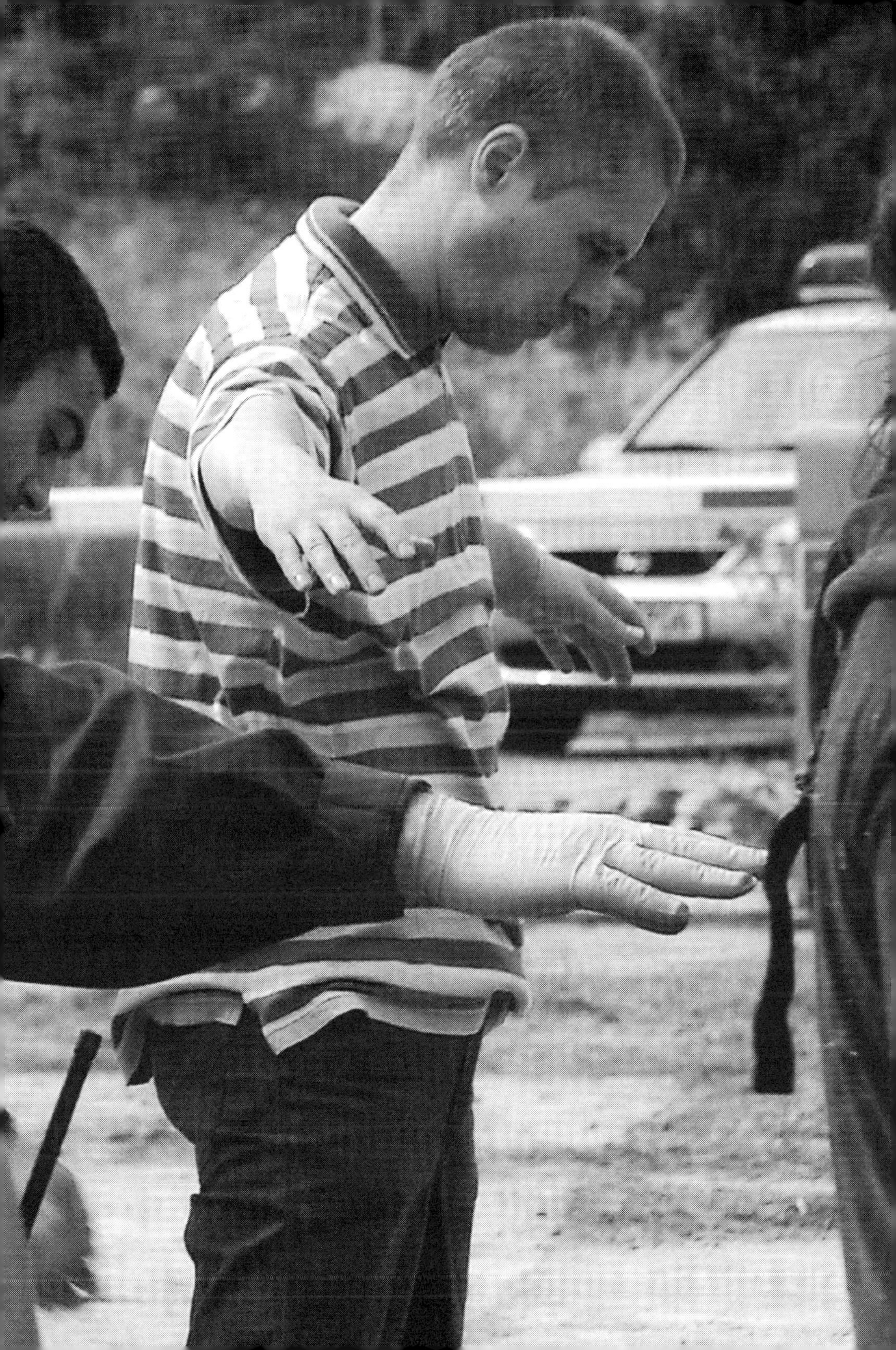

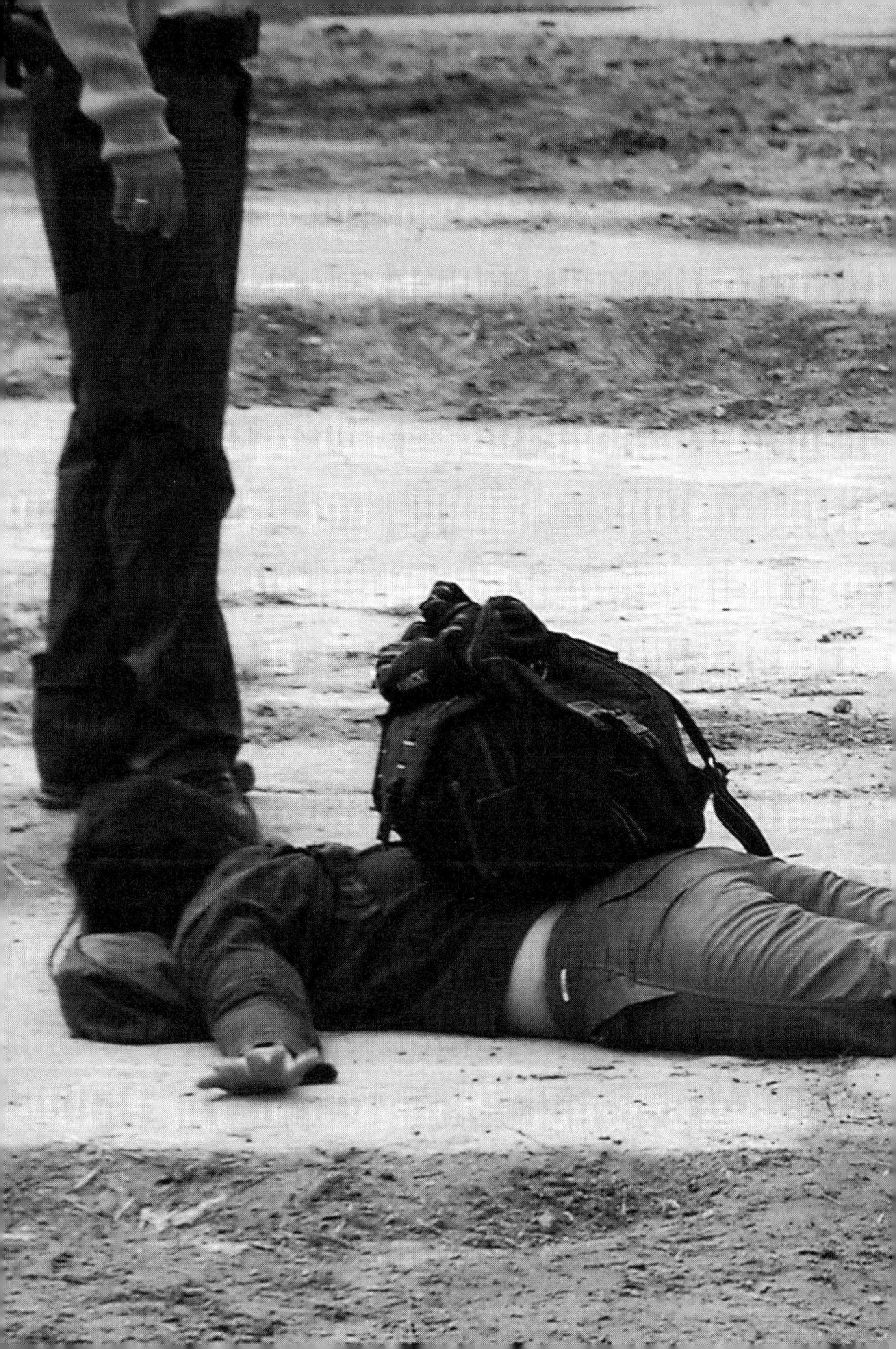

# Of Training, Imitation and Fiction
## A Conversation with Aernout Mik

**Maria Hlavajova** Amid the preparations for the Venice Biennale exhibition in the Dutch Pavilion I would like to see this conversation as a moment for us to pause to reflect on the project you have been engaged with. When I approached you with the invitation to think about a project for the 52nd International Art Exhibition in Venice, we both felt excited about its challenges. Sceptical as I am of the populist outline of the Venice Biennale in general – as a grand 'parade' of 'achievements' in contemporary art filtered through various national(ist) agendas, enveloped in the strategies of spectacle and feeding on the needs of the all encompassing market – I am at the same time convinced of the importance of large international perennial exhibitions. I did not want to ignore the complex network of contradictions exhibitions like the Venice Biennale involve. I thought it would be interesting to see if the Pavilion could be treated not as yet another, indifferent exhibition site, but as what it is: a *national* Pavilion. This loaded connotation should not, however, become the foundation for a project that would be just a simplistic outlet for a tired critique, but a modest attempt to say, in a way only art can, through both its poetics and politics, that there are ways to revive hope in the possibility of emancipating our-selves from the restrictions that the current re-embodiment of nationalist sentiments in the West posit before us.

Back then, in autumn 2006, you were immersed in realizing the work *Training Ground*. The work immediately felt like a starting point from which you could develop other pieces to show in the Pavilion.

**Aernout Mik** *Training Ground*, a two-channel video installation (2007) came out of a series of investigations into different constituents of our contemporary condition in the West. I realized the work soon after two pieces that explored the notion of civil war as one of such constituents – actually the works that we produced together, *Raw Footage* (2006) and *Scapegoats* (2006).[1] I was interested in questions such as, how do we imagine that the first responders – policemen in this case – and ourselves prepare to deal with illegal immigrants or refugees? What, as a result of this, happens to the physical domain of the refugee, and finally could this somehow be a metaphor for our own uncertain condition?

----------------------------------------

[1] … w *Footage/Scapegoats* (2006) is …-part project on the experience …epiction of war, and how …ality and extremity are inter-…n in wartime situations. In …*Footage*, a two-channel video …lation, Mik worked with …mentary footage for the first … The installation is made of raw, …ted images of the war in former …slavia, which the artist unearthed …searching for months in the …a archives of Reuters and …endent Television News (ITN). …rch of other layers of reality, …ocuses his attention on the war …mer Yugoslavia with the aim …overting the superficial, yet …oxically spectacular imagery of …e know from the mass media. …ideo installation *Scapegoats*, on …her hand, is a fiction staged by …rtist questioning the contempo-…ondition in which waging war is …astating yet ever present feature. …ideo seems to show a wartime …ct taking place in Western …e. Groups of soldiers, prisoners …rmed civilians are involved in a …nuous power struggle, in which …le of victim and oppressor …antly shifts.

**MH** I believe that immigration, and illegal immigration in particular, is one of the key aspects that defines our day and age, and as such it is an issue of major political and ethical consequence. However, there has been little political imaginary invested in dealing with this in the long term. It feels at times, and you point us in the same direction, as if this lack of vision translated into delegating the power to handle it. I recall that Giorgio Agamben argues similarly in one of his writings titled *We Refugees*, expanding on Hannah Arendt. He says that within the nation-states that are in decline and incapable of dealing with refugees themselves (especially in times when 'refugees no longer represent individual cases but rather a mass phenomenon (as happened between the two wars, and has happened again now)) . . . the question was transferred into the hands of the police and of humanitarian organizations.' He also suggests that the figure of refugee is 'the sole category in which it is possible today to perceive the forms and limits of a political community to come'.

> **AM** Yet, *Training Ground* speaks of the nation-state and immigration in a much more indirect way. It addresses these issues through 'depicting' an imaginary training of policemen, which could be anywhere 'in the West'. They are obviously learning how to deal with people who cross borders illegally or move about *sans papiers*. The work 'reconstructs' the fictive procedures of a training, in which participants are taught different strategies for handling the arrest of refugees and how to apply various techniques of law enforcement. The 'refugees' playing a role in the training are clearly stand-ins who are hired for the job. At the beginning, the atmosphere is rather fluid, with the hierarchies of power and specific roles clearly defined. At some point however, the pace of the training unfolding in front of us gains a different dynamic; the distinctions between 'policemen', 'refugees' and even the 'truck drivers' eating lunch near the scene become blurred as the roles they perform no longer correspond to the conventions we know: some refugees take over power temporarily; the policemen exercise arrest techniques on each other; and some of the drivers are captured.

**MH** At a certain point, some of the people on the set enter an inexplicable state of trance or delirium, while others continue to perform their roles. What is going on?

**AM** While I never provide actors on a set with a precise
scenario, nor do I rehearse any scenes – I am far more
interested in interactions and relations among people that
evolve amid action and in situations when actors or groups
react to each other – this time I instructed a few performers
to play out a sort of citation, or allusion rather, to a 1950s
ethnographic film by Jean Rouch, *Les Maitres fous* (*Mad
Masters*). In this film Rouch follows members of the Hauka cult
in Africa; they were usually rural migrants from Niger who
came to cities such as Accra in Ghana to work in the
lumberyards, at the docks or in the mines. Members of this
cult claimed to be possessed by 'colonial figures of power'.
Through their rituals and ceremonies they undergo a serious
conversion and become entranced by the spirits of the 'white
men', former western colonial authorities: they start drooling,
their bodies get cramped . . . The transformation of their
civilian appearance into one possessed by colonial power is
really dramatic. Hauka members, so Rouch seems to suggest,
undergo a cathartic experience that enables them to go on
with their lives despite the colonial trauma they endured.

**MH** The movement is known as one of the critical instances of
cultural resistance in colonial Africa and at the same time it is
an example that contains a strong critique of modern Europe.

**AM** Of course, these aspects interest me strongly. However,
there are other elements as well that have been important to
my work and that make me feel connected to Rouch's film and
I do not only mean the particular case of *Training Ground*. In
practically all my video works I have been investigating things
such as repetition, mimesis, re-enactment, ritual and irrational
excess, to name just a few. This is all acted out within an
isolated group, as is the case in Rouch's film, in order to
provide ways to master an internal or external threat.

**MH** All of these aspects in your work you have just named
seem in various ways to conceptually point to the idea of
'training' or 'exercise'. If you look up a basic definition, you
would be referred to the acquisition of knowledge, skills and
competencies to establish or improve performance in
particular areas. Although aimed at acquiring ability to
perform (and in military or police use, to survive), a training
situation is not for real, it is just 'as if'. In your work, it even

goes further; it is not only a training, it is *playing out* a training. In my view, this lends a very particular dimension to this work, which is the space for moral ambiguity[2] you offer the viewer. You provide the viewer with a space to take a position in place of insisting on accepting a particular one.

[2] With thanks to Paul Scheffer f
reminding me to be aware of how
important this space is.

**AM** It is of utmost importance to me that an art work deepens one's doubt about and within the situation under discussion – especially when entering the realm of the social or the political – and that it by no means offers a false pretence that it 'knows' where the problems reside, who is to blame for them or how to resolve them. What my work does suggest, however, is that solutions *do* exist. Even when some pieces seem to create just an 'over-intensification of the same', they do this to such an extreme that the ground is cleared for potential difference.

**MH** As we briefly touched upon earlier, in *Training Ground* the roles of those on the set seem crystal clear initially: there are police(wo)men, refugees and truck drivers. At a certain point, however, a strange and inexplicable process of swapping roles begins. Through this you destabilize the meaning of the narrative on the set and divorce the course of action from expectation or rational consideration. One even gets the feeling that there are different, disassociated frames of action superimposed on one another.

**AM** Exchanging the roles can further contribute to this space for ambiguity, I think. The idea of the work comes down to the imbalance of power between different groups of people and I find it helpful to speculate on what happens if you simply experience the given conditions from both – or multiple – perspectives. I try to create dialectical images in that sense, which host all these different perspectives in a very condensed way, at the same time and in the same spot.

**MH** To 'enter' the confrontation from both the positions of the privileged and the disadvantaged ...

**AM** Yes, and to overcome in a simple manner this artificial division between people which is acted out. In its naiveté and simplicity it is a liberating experience, which in the case of *Les Maitres fous* refers to something that has been, and in *Training*

*Ground* to what might be. One should not forget that the actors work without inside knowledge or instruction as to what such training really entails. They move about according to their (and my own) projections or assumptions about how the police might be instructed to handle the refugees and how refugees act in such circumstances. But as such, they are enacting a game, a non-existent situation. I have never done any research into how police are trained to enforce the law on illegal immigrants. I am more interested in what kind of collective images we carry within us about these issues, what can be deduced through the play from our thoughts and sentiments. And also how these images relate to the images provided to us by the media, because that is where they partly originated. And as a similar movement but in an opposite direction, I am also interested to look again at these media images themselves. And to see what more these images could contain, and what else they could produce, by going back to the raw material from the press agencies, the tapes that were in camera while shooting.

**MH** What do you mean?

**AM** In the second work in the Pavilion, *Convergencies* (2007), which is also a two-channel video installation, I work with existing documentary footage. The idea of 'training' reappears as an element in this work too, but within a much larger field of preparation for disasters or crises in general, and is combined with material from very different sources, such as the handling of refugees.

**MH** So you looked at material from (anti)terrorist or riot exercises.

**AM** Yes, for instance. The artificiality of those trainings interests me. We have this instant urge to be ready, to prepare for the future, to anticipate or know what it will be and how to react. And this imagination of what is awaiting us is largely informed by fear. Complex as it is, it also seems that in the very idea of training, of preparation, a desire is embedded for things to happen in order to be able to employ the skills acquired. Does it not make things more likely to happen?

**MH** I guess that contributes to processes of normalization within a social landscape that evolves around concepts of fear, standardization and control, as well as mechanisms of discipline required in the name of 'security' for society. But I have the feeling that you expose these mechanisms in such an excessive way that it comes close to ridicule, and that these grave social and political issues are almost made into a parody of the world we live in.

**AM** Actually you've touched on a key point. I do find the activity of ridiculing, as a by-product of all the mimetic aspects that are active in my work, interesting. In both the work that uses documentary material and in the staged pieces, I seek out moments with a potential to expose a kind of possibility in situations that seem hopeless, using irrational excess to transgress the status quo.

To name an example, I am intrigued by the figure of the fake victim within these exercises, as an embodiment of what I just mentioned. The stand-ins sometimes adopt this role very seriously, more than seems necessary for the exercise. But at other moments it is acted out as something that is just funny or comical. As if mocking it would avert all potential danger, and would put us indefinitely outside the realm of the real wounded and dead.

Also for this reason I decided to combine the found footage from exercises with documentary footage from real situations. This other material, showing for example how the police handle the refugees or how riot police wander without purpose through the streets, is edited and presented in a way that one is not completely sure whether it is authentic or enacted. Thus the fictional and the documentary do not form a contrasting experience; they rather create a continuum, a site of the current world's conundrum. You see that we actively shape our present and future through imagining things to come through the prism of fear, anxiety and violence. We are all both producers and the products of these circumstances. Perhaps that is also why, after reviewing hours and hours of film material about these issues, I felt a strong urge to seek out a space where there is a possibility of hope and emancipation, or at least a space to test whether a creative obstruction of the existing pattern is a possibility or not.

nex is an acronym for *Vierde
Ruimtelijke Ordening Extra*. The
is used by the Dutch Ministry for
ing, Spatial Scheduling and
onment management (Ministry
OM). Large outer city areas were
d for massive new housing
lopment under this programme,
h began in 1993.

**MH** You refer here to *Mock Up*, a new work yet to be filmed for the Biennale?

**AM** The work is yet to be made, so at this stage I can only speak about my intentions. Perhaps it is good to begin with describing a few starting points. Location is rather important for the work. I am going to film in Marnehuizen, an exercise village in north Holland, which is the biggest urban army exercise setting in Europe. You have to imagine a ghost-like village built for military troops to prepare for missions in urban environments. It contains over a hundred 'exercise objects', including the ruins of various buildings, a station, archetypal houses, a city council and even recycling bins and telephone booths. It feels a bit like an enlarged toy for children, or perhaps something between a village in Eastern Europe and a Dutch Vinex-location.[3] Nonetheless, some of the 'mock' houses look like they are under construction and not yet inhabited and at the same time they appear as leftovers of sorts: a strange moment in-between that which is yet to come and past experience.

Inside this area I will construct a 'detention centre' for illegal immigrants by means of putting together prefabricated container units. I know I would like to create a situation of an exercise, again, to figure out through repetition how to evacuate the building in the case of a fire alarm. This time, I am going to work with some seventy people on the set, nearly half of whom are young people in their early teens. In this constellation I envision complex overlaps and distinctions among them; in terms of clothing, one will recognize civilians, detainees, guards, fire brigade, medical team, police, but on other levels there will be divisions in term of skills, nationalities, generations, etc.

**MH** I wonder, why young people?

**AM** There is this tension I want to bring up between them as a group of the powerless in legal terms (as different rights apply to them in comparison to the adults) versus the powerful as the new energy that society insists on relying on for now and in the future. And if we spoke of mimicking, enacting, etc. – this is how children and young people enter the world; they imitate what their parents and other adults do, and they do

that only to overthrow these actions as outmoded. In this way,
they reinvent their own reality. There will be a number of
various narratives unfolding, which in some way synthesize
what I have been busy with recently. In the midst of the puzzle
of this emergency exercise, I hope to cross a certain line so
that something playful and connected appears. A sort of rising
above the rigidity and grim actions that we are embedded in
can lead to thinking of other possibilities.

**MH** How do these works relate to each other in the Pavilion?
And further, you intend to intervene into the architecture of the
1954 Rietveld Pavilion in a significant way.

**AM** As I said, although these three works are separate entities,
they revolve around similar issues on an abstract level,
although from various angles and with different formal and
aesthetic means. As such, and embedded in the spatial
installation, they together have a capacity to form a
continuous loop: a cyclical pattern of fear and violence
constantly feeding each other, but brought to a point where it
either exhausts itself or transgresses into other directions.

I am eager to see how the viewer can actually – through his or
her physical presence in the complex installation I have in
mind – recognize partaking in the world as discussed in the
work. I work with the prefabricated and furnished containers –
the same ones I use in *Mock Up* – to somehow destabilize the
borders of the type of architecture the Rietveld Pavilion
represents. Extending through the three entrances to the
Pavilion, these prefab units sort of spread inside and out of the
building. It is both something that penetrates the architecture
within in a firm way, as well as stresses an opening to the
outside world. In both a literal and metaphorical way, these
are foreign bodies that challenge the modernist clarity of the
Pavilion. As such, it is not built to reference anything that it
contains; now it is put into a dialogue with architecture of
seemingly another order. Yet both – the Pavilion and the
prefab unit – represent a non-place. It could be anywhere so
it becomes everywhere.

**MH** I recall once you talked about this idea of physicality that
is very pertinent in this new installation. In some way it is
parallel to what you said about the estranged types of dwelling

you bring into the Pavilion. You talked about how important it
was to stress the way people subjected to power or authority
were handled in a physical (often aggressive) way. Like for
example how they are moved around and are touched all the
time, while the hands of the 'toucher' remain covered with
latex gloves.

**AM** The strategies for how to dehumanize these situations of
confrontation between the powerful and the disadvantaged
are remarkably many. It is indeed visible in the constant tactile
approach to the illegal immigrant as can be seen in the work
made of raw documentary footage (*Convergencies*), but also,
on the other hand, in the protective aura of the sci-fi like suits
the rescue workers wear during anti-terrorist exercises. For us,
the 'public', it seems all done under the guise of some medical
or security requirements, which are often rather incomprehen-
sible from the outside. These are ways to strip you of your own
personality, or even your right to it. I am very aware of this; that
is why the clothing I provide my actors with defines the course
of action within the work to a great extent.

**MH** How do you relate to the viewer? What aesthetic means do
you have at your disposal to have him or her 'participate' in the
situation, as you mention above, or at least feel that we are all
to some extent part of this – notwithstanding our status as
individuals – be it nationality, culture, political or religious
orientation or wealth?

**AM** The works, enveloped in an architectural construction,
extend into one another to create one complex ensemble.
I believe in this way each work is to be considered mainly – or
perhaps even only – in relation to the whole. All three works
are structured as loops and as such offer the viewer a
possibility to 'just' glance at them to experience their
atmosphere or engage with their distinct narratives unfolding
over time. The two staged works are installed in such a way
that they touch the floor and as such mirror the position of
the viewer: this means that a visitor in the crowd already
populates the scene and 'enters' into a larger social body
under discussion. Only *Convergencies* is projected on two
walls and just off the ground, because the found footage
somehow requires different rhythm and concentration.
Although ... the images shown, despite their content, have

a certain quality of familiarity that I believe establishes a particular connection in and of itself. Perhaps this is because these are recognizably media images. I do not follow the regime of the spectacle we're so accustomed to, but seek a registration of what appears 'just before' or 'just after' the footage that might have had a news value for the agencies I researched at, or show images so long that the spectacle simply transforms into normality itself.

**MH** I would be interested in asking how you view the development of your own work. Although you have always engaged with everyday situations through a kind of absurd or surreal conversion, and dealt with physicality, touch, repetition and other aspects we have discussed here – your earlier works seem to be more about intimate or personal relations, while recently the focus seems to have shifted more towards the larger picture: to an individual in a crowd, within a social body and in the world.

> **AM** I think that description is quite accurate. It has to do with both the internal dynamics of my own development and with the changes around me. I even think that this shift in my work started gradually taking place in sync with the alterations of the political context in the Netherlands and abroad. On a private level – and I am aware this might sound over exaggerated, but I feel very strongly about it – this also has to do with becoming a father. This radically changed my perspective on the world. Everything becomes less about yourself and much more about others, to put it simply. I discovered a different urge to take responsibility for certain things in the world. I started to work more and more with larger groups of people that were, already somehow by their size, positioned in the public sphere. And that is what I can do, to describe and reflect the change that is going on around me, and inside me and suggest it is important to engage in discussing it.

**MH** You speak about responsibility in the public sphere, and thus implicitly about the political. Why then is 'the political' in art under suspicion in the Netherlands?

> **AM** It has to do with many things I think, although I could not claim I know the answer. For one, the discourse about the

    **Citizens and Subjects:** The Netherlands, for example

political in art is by and large lacking here, as well as vocabulary through which to address it. Most attempts end up in a confusion about the concept of 'politicality'. It is often misunderstood as a simple instrumentalization of art by a one-dimensional political agenda, instead of an open and dynamic concept that needs to be explored to gain its meaning, although I do not deny instrumentalization is a potential danger that we always need to be aware of. A part of the problem in the Netherlands has to do with education, because its institutions are not prepared for this question themselves. And then, with regard to the subsidy system for the arts, a kind of horizontality and security was built into the system that both allowed and prevented things from happening for a long time. In the Netherlands we do not really have a tradition of political conflict playing out through public debate. But now things are rapidly changing in society on all fronts. I am convinced this will stimulate an alternative kind of art practice, which will function more inside, or in relation to, the public arena.

**MH** What is it then that your work in the Dutch Pavilion at the Venice Biennale contributes?

**AM** You cannot reduce art to its idea. This work is not about immigration, it is not about fear, violence or national security, nor is it about staged fictional scenarios versus documentary footage from real situations. I specialize in none of these issues and if language allowed me I would rather say I 'generalize' in them. In this respect, if the work contains *all* these references – and they are there to be found – it is with the intention of over saturating it with unbearably weighty comments on how we conceive of the world. By the virtue of having this excess implode or transgress onto another level, it no longer coincides with the possibilities we know or can rationally account for. In this newly created field there is no other option left for us but to speculate about what else this all could become, and start again.

*This conversation is a compilation of numerous informal discussions that took place in autumn 2006 and spring 2007 in Amsterdam and Utrecht in preparation for the project Citizens and Subjects.*

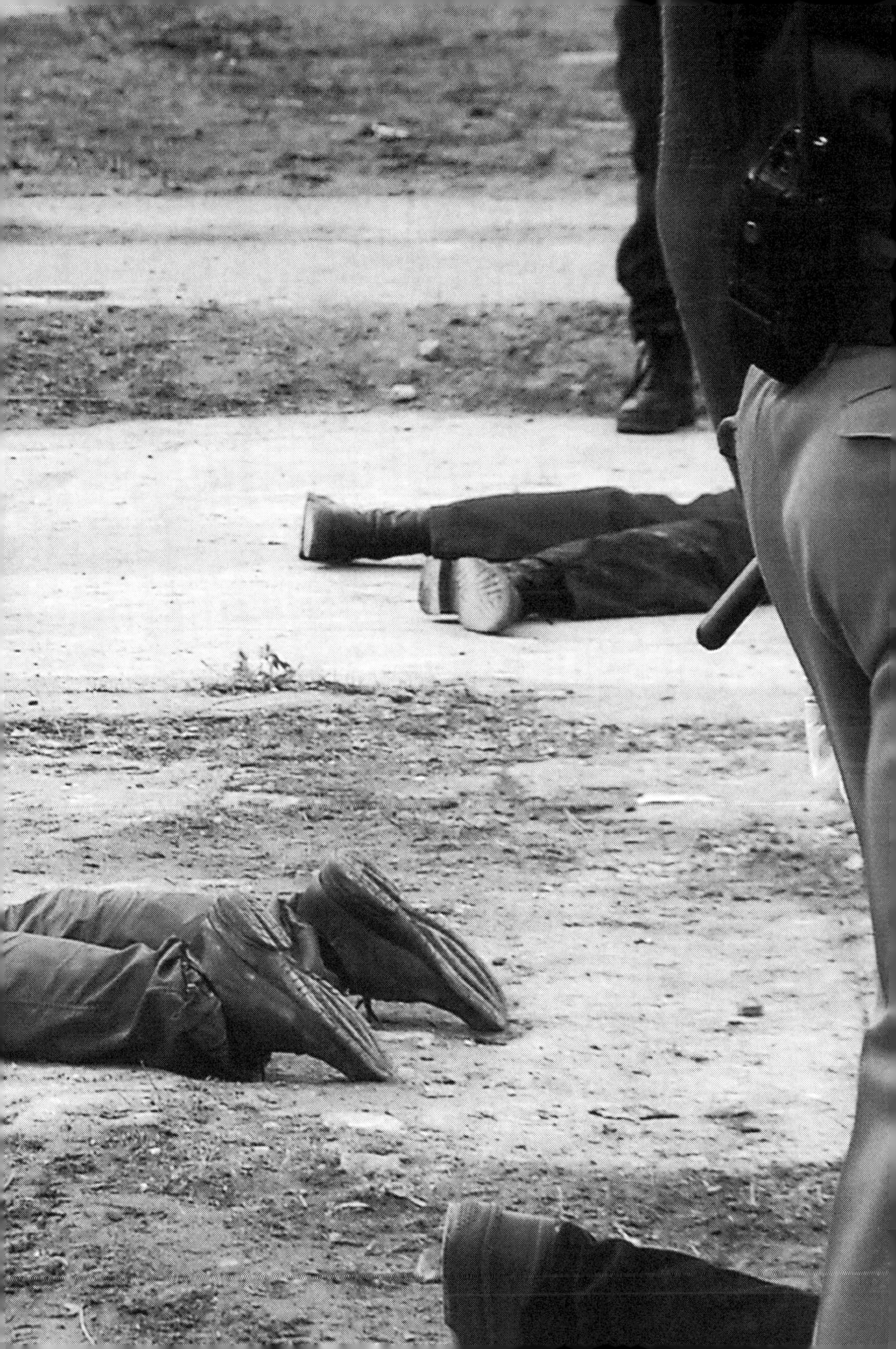

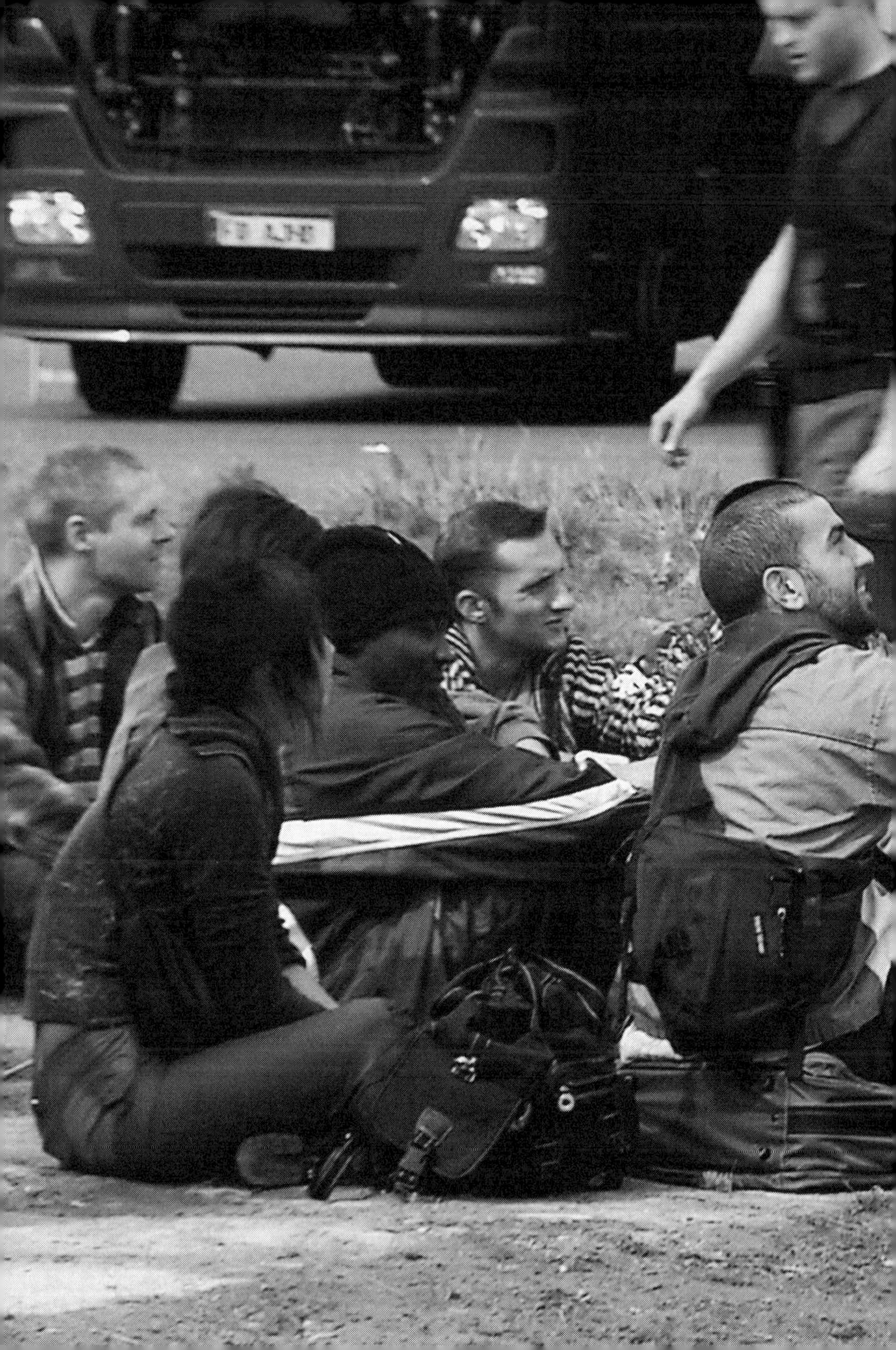

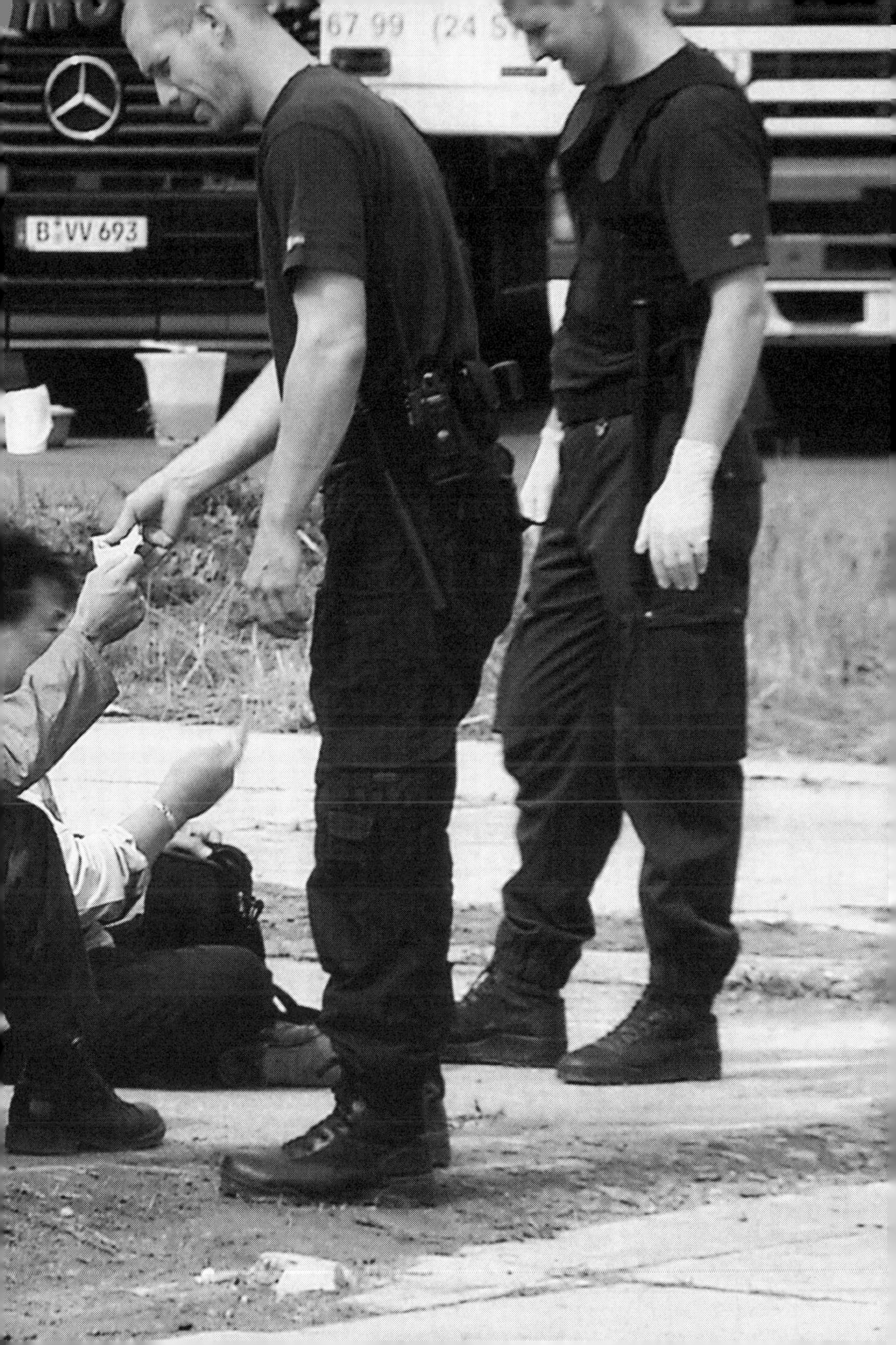
B·VV 693

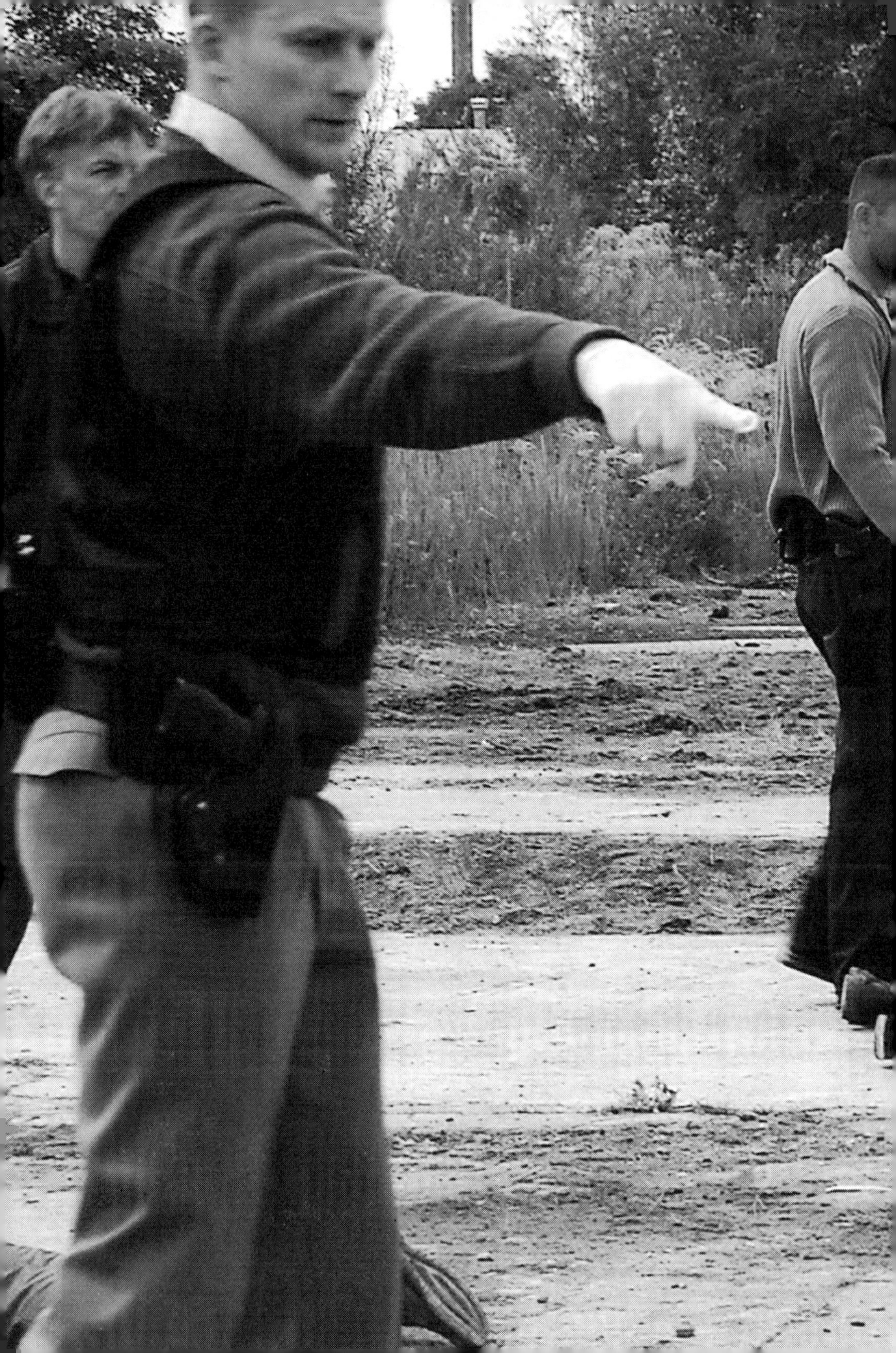

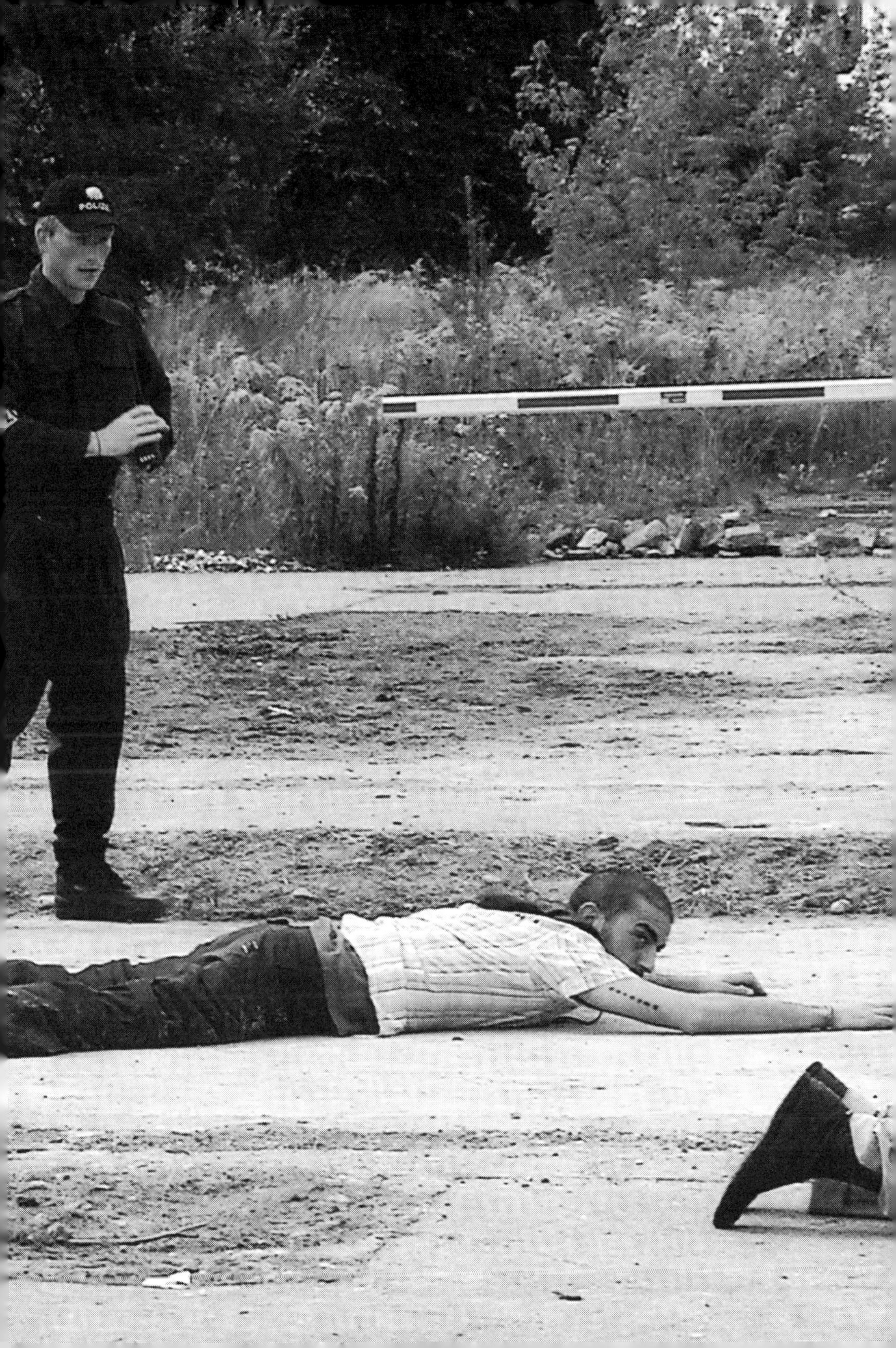

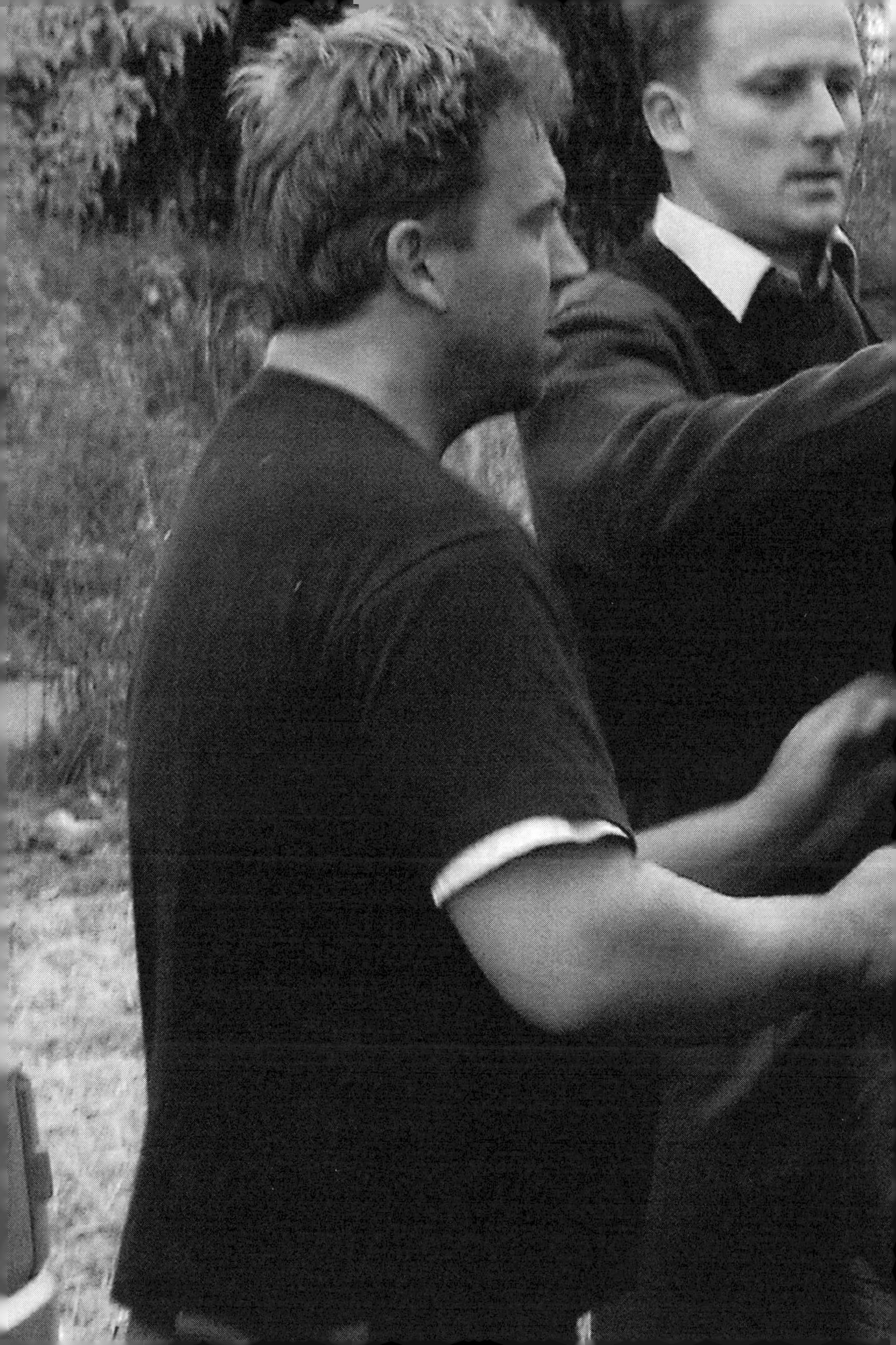

# Neoliberalism with Dutch Characteristics: The Big Fix-Up of the Netherlands and the Practice of Embedded Cultural Activism

----------------------------------------------------

BAVO (Gideon Boie & Matthias Pauwels)

----------------------------------------------------

## Processes of normalization in post-socialist Netherlands

Today, we live in the heyday of consensus. Perhaps the most powerful consensus still is Francis Fukuyama's notion of the end of history, the thesis that in the big clash between world systems the joint forces of market and democracy beat the competition – state socialism – fair and square. Even though fiercely criticized since its publication in 1989 (recently even by Fukuyama himself),[1] the degree to which this thesis still holds the political imagination in a firm grip cannot be underestimated. If philosophy, defined as one relentless battle with common sense, has any practical application, it might be apropos of this consensus of the end of history.[2]

To start with, what is often forgotten in this so-called 'friendly takeover' of the East by the West is that the losses were not merely on the side of the 'losers' – post-socialist societies that have had to endure the tough 'cure' of market reforms (referred to by a euphemistic reapplication of the term 'processes of normalization'). The alleged winners in the West *equally* lost something. To be more precise, the 'victory' of western liberal democracy struck a final blow against the tradition of social welfare democracy and, inversely, meant the final breakthrough of aggressive neoliberal and neoconservative political models.[3] In this sense, we can claim that since 1989, both the East and West have become post-socialist, suffering from a similar post-socialist condition.[4]

Symptomatic of this condition are the vicissitudes of social housing in the Netherlands.[5] With 40 percent of the housing stock owned and managed by publicly financed housing corporations, the Dutch housing market has long been regarded as *the* prototype of a social democratic housing market. However, with the 'regime change' of 1989, it didn't take long before attempts were made to 'tap' this enormous reservoir of 'dead capital' – both from the side of the government and the real estate market, but even from within the housing corporations themselves. Accordingly, since the beginning of the 1990s the Dutch housing market – especially in the big cities – has been subjected to one of the most intensive restructurings in recent history, also referred to as 'The Big Fix-Up',[6] changing the Dutch city as we know it.

What follows is a consideration of the logics, discourse, consequences and contradictions of this sweeping liberalization operation. Similar to the countries of the former Communist bloc, Dutch society is also being subjected to a 'process of normalization', the norm in this case being 'market' plus 'Dutch norms and values'. However this so-called normal-

----

[1] … e his recent *America at the … roads: Democracy, Power and … eoconservative Legacy* (New … n: Yale University Press, 2006).

----

[2] … rt of the difficulty of resisting … onsensus of the end of history is … ubt the intuitively convincing … r of Fukuyama's anthropology … last man. Indeed who would … t to the idea 'that we are all … n beings' striking a fragile … ce – a *modus vivendi* – between … ers of the body and the … ations of the mind, self- … rvation and altruism, individual … expression and co-belonging … o on? One of the contemporary … sophers who has attacked … yama's anthropology most … iously on this score is Alain … ou. In his philosophy 'man' is split … 'human animal', egotistically … ng for his preservation and small … ures and as such despicable, … he bearer of 'a truth', with no … e for the possibility of a 'peaceful … ment' between the two.

----

… he intermezzo of 'third way' … l democracy not withstanding, … n, apart from already being … d politically by now, is perhaps … timate Fukuyamian constellation … ts mix between modernity and … ion, the individual and society, … s and welfare, etc.

----

[4] … ee Immanuel Wallerstein, *After … alism*, part 1 (New York: New … , 1995), and his *Historical Capital … Capitalist Civilization* (London: … , 1995), 151.

----

[5] … ee also BAVO, *The Undivided City … ts Willing Executioners* (in Dutch).

----

[6] … his term was coined for the … ition and symposium 'The Big … p. Transformations in Post-war … ing' that took place in the … erlands Architecture Institute … in 2004. See also the … mpanying publication: … ueline Tellinga (ed.), *De grote … ouwing. Verandering van … rlogse woonwijken* (Rotterdam: … ublishers, 2004). The more literal … lation of the Dutch term '*De grote … ouwing*' would be 'The grand or … efurbishment'.

ization comes at a high social cost – a cost moreover that is unevenly distributed, paid for as it is by those groups in society that are least able to do so and are the least likely to profit from the operation. Through an evaluation of the interventions of artists, designers, architects, video artists, etc. with regard to the 'post-socialist' housing question in the Netherlands, we discuss the political role of cultural production in relation to today's consensus of the 'end of history'.

**Social housing in the age of self-solvency . . .**
One of the key documents that set the scene for the liberalization of the housing market in the Netherlands was the 'National Policy Document on Housing in the Nineties' issued in 1989 (sic).[7] Its main objectives were to make the housing corporations independent,[8] encourage the workings of the market with regard to housing and stimulate homeownership. It's not difficult to construct the ideological presuppositions behind this policy document. It is for instance seen as a natural development for renters to want to become homeowners, which is valued as unambiguously good because it would ensure that people take better care of their house and its environment (since, as proto-capitalists, they are now out to protect and enhance their investment). It also clearly promotes the idea that even social sectors should operate in conformity with market norms and criteria because it's the only way to make them perform better, be more efficient, more consumer-oriented, etc.[9]

Cut off from the state and abandoned to the market, housing corporations developed all kinds of hybrid schemes in order to be able to build housing for those who could not pay the full price, while still making enough profit to be solvent – or 'to keep one's own pants up' as it was phrased. Housing corporations entered into partnerships with project developers, sold large parts of their stock to the inhabitants in order to build up capital, demolished strategically well-located stock to sell the land and build houses for middle and higher incomes as a way to finance social apartments, etc. This led to some remarkable reversals. For instance, while social housing was traditionally seen as a way to create the right conditions to ensure the stability of capitalism, now the capitalist organization of housing was put forward as guarantor of the future of social housing. Also, the standard reasoning that the workings of the market are always beneficial to the customer – allowing him to have 'more for less money' – was reversed: inhabitants were expected to pay more money for a smaller apartment *precisely because it now conformed to market standards.*

This liberalization operation – which some refer to as a 'silent revolution' –

[7] In Dutch: 'Nota Volkshuisvesti 90'.

[8] Housing corporations had to operate without the so-called 'ob subsidies', a government subsidy compensating for the inevitable losses related to developing soci housing. This virtually meant the withdrawal of the state from the s housing sector. In its place came so-called rent subsidy (*huursubs* that is given to individual citizens low incomes and is meant to pay the difference between the rent tl can afford based on their income and the rent asked by the housing corporation or landlord. The prob with this rent subsidy is that the amount offered and the conditior for obtaining it are liable to chang according to the political flavour the day.

[9] In this sense the Dutch government was already implementing, *avant la lettre*, the neoliberal General Agreement on Trade and Service treaty (1995) th also pleaded for the liberalization public services such as housing.

led to the demolition of a huge chunk of the social housing stock, for the most part of good quality. This not only displaced a lot of socio-economically vulnerable people for the duration of the restructuring, depriving them from their much-needed local social networks. Since as a rule only 30 percent of what was rebuilt was social housing – which was often already less than what existed before – it became unaffordable for the majority of the residents to ever return to their neighbourhoods, leaving them to fend for themselves in a tight housing market. The result was somewhat predictable, yet nonetheless overlooked or downplayed by the ideological fervour of the restructuring's supporters. In the wake of the Big Fix-Up, a reserve army of what was appropriately called 'demolition nomads' was produced: displaced renters who, due to the invisible yet iron hand of the market, wound up in other corporation housing that was often next in line for restructuring. They were thus forced to move from one 'condemned' area to another.

So how could it come this far? The necessity, moral desirability even, of the liberalization was partially asserted by depicting the typical inhabitant of social housing as a middle class yuppie (single or couple) who is doing quite well for himself, but still opportunistically clings to his cheap, large apartment strategically located near the city centre or station. Needless to say, in the face of such a clear-cut case of a free rider, it was easy to generate a consensus on the necessity of a market-style restructuring of the social housing stock 'to trim the fat'. On the one hand such asocial parasitism was felt as a blow in the face of people in real need – the prototypical Turkish or Moroccan family with up to ten kids packed together in a small apartment. But also the middle and upper class felt cheated because good locations were artificially kept outside the market, leaving them no other choice than to move to the suburbs. The figure of the free rider – in itself an archetypical product of the neoliberal imagination – thus allowed the better-off to play victim of an allegedly corrupted and perverse social housing circuit. Could there be a better example of what social geographer Neil Smith calls 'the revanchist city': a city torn between different population groups targeting one another for obtaining all kinds of advantages?[10]

See Neil Smith, *The New Urban
*ier: Gentrification and the
*nchist City* (London: Routledge,
.

### If we don't act now ...

Today's elites rule by permanently maintaining a state of emergency that allows them to push through all kinds of measures that go against the interests of society as a whole – the US-led war on terrorism being the most obvious and most quoted example of this thesis. However, it is often more difficult to recognize the reality of this principle at home, in the Netherlands. This reinforces the relaxed attitude (even among critics) that such scandalous policies would never be tolerated here – inversely upholding the caricature of 'those wacky Americans'. Let's not fool ourselves. The liberalization of the housing market is a case in point of how a sense of emergency is produced – albeit not military but social and economic – to legitimize decisions that obviously serve the narrow interest of elite groups.

Every criticism of the quick, massive destruction of social housing met with the rejoinder that the Dutch housing market, due to its strong social democratic heritage, is exceptional for its high quantities of social housing and that in this regard, it is unique in Europe if not the world (the former communist countries not included). It was further argued that precisely due to this historical heritage of a 'distorted' housing market, with 'abnormally' large chunks outside of the reach of the market, Dutch cities lagged dramatically behind their competitors around the globe and were at risk of missing out on crucial investments from national and multinational real estate groups. Consequently, it was said that all means were justified to undo this historically developed yet, within today's world, aberrant, untenable and potentially lethal situation.[11]

This 'discourse of emergency' is meant to put public opinion into a mental state of panic: 'If we don't act now, then the downward spiral in which our cities are caught will be irreversible!' Usually one doesn't even specify exactly what it is that will happen. 'If we don't act now. . .', leaves it to the audience to fill in the three dots with all kinds of visions of the imminent doom and decay that will befall Dutch cities if no drastic measures are taken. This production of panic is used to blackmail people into endorsing a neoliberal, competitive approach to the city, in which the worst thing that could happen to Dutch cities would be to wind up in the lower reaches of what Ricardo Petrella calls the CR30 – the thirty most powerful city-regions in the world. Urban policy documents are full of references to studies revealing how Dutch cities sank several points on the charts of most popular investment locations for companies in recent years.

This economic-financial state of emergency, in which neoliberal kill-or-cure remedies have free reign, is further strengthened by the circulation of everyday metaphors like 'to be the weakest pupil in the class', 'the weakest brother' or 'the last rider in the peloton'. These expressions serve the purpose of triggering all kinds of fears about imminent marginalization and humiliation in the public.[12] The problem here is not only that such rhetorical devices are used to push through neoliberal

[11] It is obvious that the producti of such a generalized condition o self-righteousness and anxiety depicts the current state of affairs an emergency only to impose anc new state of emergency in which neoliberal and neoconservative measures are granted free reign.

[12] Perhaps the figure in Dutch politics who championed this atti was the former Minister of Financ Gerrit Zalm, for whom no sacrifice was too big to make the Netherlar the strongest pupil in the class wh it came to obeying the notoriously stringent financial disciplinary measures the EU imposes upon it member states. He even shameles pleaded for hard punishment of o less successful 'pupils'.

policies. On the level of *form*, and therefore more unconsciously, it makes people accustomed to the neoliberal attitude of always wanting to be the best, to stay ahead of the competition no matter what the cost. The recent proliferation of the word 'top' – top companies, top research centres, top universities, top medical facilities, top museums, top talents – is also exemplary in this regard. All these rhetorical-tactical devices are mobilized to normalize neoliberalist dogma and prevent people from asking the right political questions about their own best interests or from having the mental calm to consider alternative, non-market centred strategies for the city.

This fear of 'lagging behind' takes a particular national-chauvinist character in the Netherlands. We are told that the Netherlands has always been at the forefront of things, a leading or guiding country ('*gidsland*'), years ahead of other countries and that it cannot 'slacken off' now in the face of new global challenges. The spectre of the 'Golden Age' – when, according to historian Immanuel Wallerstein, the Netherlands arose as the first global Empire – always lurks in the background of these sort of statements. One only has to think of the recent plea by Dutch Prime Minister J.P. Balkenende in the House of Representatives to restore the 'good old' entrepreneurial attitude of the colonial Dutch East India Company to its former glory. This was hardly a slip of the tongue, as was obvious from Balkenende's rejoinder to the protests of some members of the House: 'Ain't it not so?'[13] Is there any better proof of how well established the consensus is on neoliberalism as *the* recipe for a prosperous and healthy future for the Netherlands?

### The rise of the problem neighbourhoods

The liberalization of the social housing market was reinforced with the advent of the discourse on so-called problem neighbourhoods, itself part of a more general policy offensive focused on the specific problematic of the large Dutch cities.[14] Again, a state of emergency was declared, now in the socio-cultural sphere. It was propagated that the Netherlands had been far too tolerant, 'lax' even, towards marginal population groups living in its cities – especially foreigners or people of foreign origin. This was said to have led to dangerously high concentrations of socio-urban pathologies in a few areas that, precisely because of their geographical concentration, had become self-reinforcing and thus necessitated a set of tough measures to reintegrate these 'potential ghettoes' into the city at large.[15] Since it was then quickly noted that these neighbourhoods usually contained a high percentage of social housing, this reinforced the consensus on the necessity of the Big Fix-Up and accelerated its implementation.

In Dutch: 'toch?' Another classic
ession is, 'And what is wrong with
?', which puts the opponent
ediately on the defensive, making
appear as a politically correct
alist who still uses rigid notions of
t and wrong' to schematize and
uate the world.

The 'Large City Policy'
(*testedenbeleid*) was a covenant
ween the Dutch state and the
en largest cities (later extended
venty-five) drawn up in 1995.
s later followed by the '56
bourhoods Approach' in which
cific neighbourhoods were
sen in the large and middle-sized
s in the Netherlands to which
cial attention and investments
ld be devoted.

This problem neighbourhood
ative was part of a broader
que of multiculturalism as too soft
naïve as well as too modest and
ative towards the Dutch norms
values or history, too much
ect leading to indifference, etc. In
post-multiculturalist age on the
er hand, it was not only again
sible but imperative to defend
s culture and not to be in self-
al or belie one's own roots.

The particular content of the notion of the problem neighbourhood in the Netherlands was seen as twofold. On the one hand, there were the prototypical foreigners, closed off in their own religio-ethnic network and often earning a living by renting out rooms in their overcrowded and badly maintained social apartments to yet more newcomers. On the other hand, successful 'ghetto members' who, through hard work and integration in Dutch society, did well economically but were hindered by the lack of housing options within their (problem) neighbourhood appropriate to higher social status – i.e. a more spacious, differentiated space that could above all be bought rather than rented. Again the revanchist undertones are obvious: the good, hard working, good-natured middle class subject held hostage by the bad immigrant.

To undo these 'unnatural' situations, which were said to prevent the neighbourhood from growing into a middle-class ideal, all kinds of exceptional measures were undertaken. People from higher socio-economic strata were mixed in so as to restore the proper balance and, most importantly, 'set a good example' – one of the key slogans was 'to see people being entrepreneurial is to make people entrepreneurial'.[16] 'Successful' inhabitants were rewarded by being allowed 'social promotion'. Multicultural shops with market potential were given special management training for branding their business more professionally. Less successful inhabitants (at least the ones who were not displaced) were subjected to zero-tolerance measures and 'integrated' through a forced treatment of Dutch 'norms and values'.[17]

We should connect this upsurge of what has been called neo-racism [18] – especially considering the specific targeting of citizens of Arabic origin – to the rise of neocolonial and neoliberal attitudes in the core of Dutch politics. It is for instance an often-heard claim – even within enlightened circles – that the immigration of cheap labour has introduced groups that have turned the clock back by some forty years. It is implied that they are the main reason that the Netherlands lost its pole position in the global arena. There is, in other words, an immediate relation to be made between the many frustrations and disappointments that result from a tougher, less fair and often obscure global economic battle and the search for scapegoats for that unwelcome state of affairs: a lazy, retarded 'other' who thwarts full exploitation of our competitive capabilities 'from within'.

Neoliberal and neoconservative politics thus come together in the case of the Big Fix-Up to enforce a consensus on the inevitability of the restructuring of social housing. These two constellations might on the

[16] In Dutch: 'zien ondernemen is doen ondernemen'.

[17] The latter is of course the seco fad of J.P. Balkenende (apart from his nostalgia for the Dutch East Ind Company): his continuing effort to restore the traditional Dutch 'norm and values'.

[18] Ètienne Balibar and Immanue Wallerstein, *Race, Nation, Class. Ambiguous Identities* (London: Ver 1992).

surface seem rather strange bedfellows, the first being a predominantly economic-financial doctrine related to the laissez-faire nineteenth-century free trade tradition, the second a neocolonialist programme, a 'civilization offensive' that imposes mainly western values on society through military force. Nevertheless, it is a much-noted fact that the two are very complementary, at least for the moment.[19] In Dutch politics, the discourse of J.P. Balkenende, with its dual emphasis on entrepreneurial dynamics and norms and values is proof of the complementarity of this 'winning combination'.

## Art within the Big Fix-Up: a case of interpassivity

The Netherlands would not be the Netherlands if in the wake of the demolition cranes and concrete mixers there would not have been a myriad of artistic interventions engaging with the radical makeover of the Dutch city. We can even say that over the last decade, a new artistic genre and repertoire has developed alongside the Big Fix-Up. In virtually all of the neighbourhoods up for restructuring, a heterogeneous bunch of cultural agents have organized projects varying from urban events, poster campaigns, neighbourhood safaris and parties, cooking workshops, do-it-yourself training programmes, farewell rituals, debates, expert meetings, mapping sessions, participatory websites, artists-in-residence programmes and so forth, all tackling issues related in one way or another to the on-going restructuring.[20] Although this willingness to engage with on-going social processes is definitely heartwarming, the majority of these initiatives seem to suffer from what Slavoj Žižek calls 'interpassivity': hyperactive behaviour that has to prevent what really matters from manifesting itself and therefore from being contested.[21]

Symptomatic of such art projects, and not the worst example in many ways, is the project *Dwaallicht* [22] by Jeanne van Heeswijk. She is a well-recognized figure in the artistic scene surrounding the Big Fix-Up and has developed a sophisticated set of strategies for addressing certain target groups and participants. The project was a response to the restructuring of Nieuw Crooswijk, a so-called problem neighbourhood in Rotterdam. This restructuring basically involved the socio-economic cleansing of the area, and rightly provoked mass protests from the existing population who were declared personae non gratae in their own neighbourhood. Against this heavily polarized background, the artist developed a participatory programme that was meant to 'bring consolation', as one newspaper put it, to the affected population by allowing them collectively to search for the soul of the neighbourhood.[23] They were asked to collect interesting stories reflecting the socio-cultural history of Nieuw Crooswijk as well as identify its vital energies. One of

See for example David Harvey, *ef History of Neoliberalism* (New Oxford University Press, 2005)

---

These initiatives were either ced directly by the government, et partners or housing orations as part of the ucturing, or through cultural res operating as commissioners/ iators, or partly through self-erated funding.

---

Slavoj Žižek, *Pleidooi voor erantie* (Amsterdam: Boom, 1998),

---

Translation: 'will-o'-the-wisp'. project was commissioned by the Arts Centre Rotterdam (Centrum dende Kunst Rotterdam), the ning and Housing Department the municipality of Rotterdam, took place in 2004 and 2005. www.dwaallicht.nl (accessed 14 ch 2007).

---

See Ron Meerhof, 'Slopen die e teringzooi, en een beetje snel!', *olkskrant*, 24 March 2005. The le also refers to the Rabobank nportaal where it is stated that, ct, Jeanne van Heeswijk guides nsels) the mourning process that nhabitants have to undergo.'

**Neoliberalism with Dutch Characteristics: The Big Fix-Up of the Netherlands and the Practice of Embedded Cultural Activism**
BAVO

the results was an interactive website where, on a map of the neighbourhood, one could drag a set of virtual moving dots representing an endangered asset of the area back into the neighbourhood and with a click of the mouse indicate what things one wanted to preserve.[24]

What are we to make of this? To begin with, the project does not problematize the fact that most of the current inhabitants won't be in the neighbourhood anymore to enjoy the preserved 'old' parts of the 'new' Nieuw Crooswijk. The website, for instance, doesn't contain any dots representing social housing, excluding that even as an option. Even worse, the entire idea of offering consolation by making an inventory of elements for preservation purposes already assumes that the demolition will take place and that the exodus of the majority of the existing population is inevitable. The maximum stake of the project is therefore to secure a 'new' Nieuw Crooswijk 'uploaded' with some socio-culturally valuable remnants of the 'old' Nieuw Crooswijk. As the description on the artist's website reads: 'Het Dwaallicht tried to capture the cultural history of Nieuw Crooswijk and its residents for the future to create a narrative monument to the community.'[25] When, thanks to the protests of inhabitants and action groups, the restructuring plans were temporarily put on hold, it became clear that the project was grounded in a far too pessimistic assessment of the possible outcomes of the conflict situation. From this alone, it is clear that the interactive website reflected a deeper, passive attitude towards the neighbourhood and resignation about the deportation of the majority of its inhabitants. Moreover, the consolatory manner, which the project took to be its role in relation to the 'victims', objectively performed interpassivity.[26]

### Embedded cultural activism

This 'interpassive' project is anything but an isolated case. If there is one common denominator of the eclectic mix of artistic interventions in the context of the Big Fix-Up, it is both its excess and lack of activism.[27] Or to be more precise, the enthusiasm and freshness of the majority of initiatives stands in opposite proportion to the political courage needed to tackle the highly questionable agenda behind the current makeover of the Dutch city and attack the broad consensus. This contradictory combination is what architecture critic Roemer van Toorn identifies in the field of architecture as 'Fresh Conservatism', which combines a seeming willingness to tackle hot issues in an unconventional way with a deep depoliticizing effect on these very issues themselves.[28] How else to evaluate cultural interventions that treat the marginalization and socio-economic cleansing of a neighbourhood as an inevitability and not as the result of a deeply neoliberal and neoconservative politics?!



[24] Apart from the website, a do[…] events were organized within the Dwaallicht project. The events we[…] basically live enactments in the neighbourhood of the stories tha[…] were chronicled there during the project. For instance, one piece w[…] composed based on the sound of Crooswijk and performed at vario[…] venues in the area. Further, there [was] an event by children in which the[y] expressed their vision of their stre[…] a guided audio tour of the local graveyard, a performance of youngsters about their bad reputa[…] and so on. Reports on all these ev[…] were distributed door-to-door through a newspaper. There will a[lso] be a novel written based on all the stories. See also www.jeannewor[…] net (accessed 14 March 2007).

[25] See www.jeanneworks.net (accessed 14 March 2007).

[26] Žižek also claims that by kee[p] the real issue undisturbed, one legitimizes or 'fuels' one's own act[…] ('I remain active thanks to the passivity of the other' (Pleidooi vo[…] intolerantie, 108) (my translation). Indeed, if the discontents of the affected population are never allo[wed] to manifest radically, artists are assured of plenty of feelings of frustration, misrecognition, etc. to[…] projects with.

[27] See BAVO, Too active to act. Cultural activism after the end of history, unpublished manuscript.

[28] Roemer van Toorn, 'Fresh Conservatism. Landscapes of Modernity' (1997), available online http://www.xs4all.nl/%7ervtoorn/ fresh.html (accessed 8 March 2007[…]

In searching for the causes behind this tendency, we should perhaps return to the discourse of emergency that is one of the most important tactical devices by which the Big Fix-Up is pushed through. Creating a general sense of urgency makes it easy for the key decision makers to neutralize any opposition. It allows them to put critics on the spot by demanding that, in the face of the 'crisis', they come up with a realistic alternative. If they fail to do so, which is not surprising considering the immensity of this demand, they can easily present opponents as 'irresponsible children' who shrug away from implementing radical, long overdue measures. Any voice of dissent is thus silenced by the Dutch motto '*doe gewoon, dan doe je al gek genoeg*' – which could be translated as something like: 'act normal and you're already acting crazy enough'. In the face of such threats, one should defend the right to 'mere criticism', to protest policies without being blackmailed by those responsible into solving the contradictions for them.

These tactics on the part of the ruling elite seem to be very effective. Also within cultural circles it has become commonplace not merely to 'shout from the sideline' or engage in deep criticism but, instead, to 'do', to 'get real and make oneself useful for a change' (as architecture historian and urban activist Wouter Vanstiphout once claimed apropos his engagement with problem neighbourhood Hoogvliet in Rotterdam).[29] The task is thus defined as one of invention, of micro-solutions to alleviate the many concrete, everyday needs, discomforts and grievances of those affected by the restructuring. The unspoken command is that in making oneself useful, one does not radically contest the bigger political decisions and presuppositions behind the social process. It doesn't take much to see how the latter is the precondition for being able to work 'constructively' towards feasible actions, in dialogue and cooperation with the main players in the restructuring process. Or to put it bluntly, the high cost of so-called post-critical cultural commitment is political pacification.

All this brings us to the claim that with the multitude of cultural actions within the Big Fix-Up we have the cultural counterpart of the infamous phenomenon of embedded journalism – in other words, an embedded cultural practice operating in the wake of the exodus of all undesirable elements out of the neighbourhood and obeying 'rules of engagement' that are partly imposed from above, and partly self-imposed. As a rule, the scope of cultural agency is limited to softening the 'collateral damage' caused by the restructuring and inventing humanitarian, compensatory measures or 'ways of dealing with it', as opposed to radically contesting the neoliberal and neoconservative measures *as such*.

See www.strangeharvest.com/
rchive/read_mes/qa_wouter_
tiphout.php (accessed 13 March
.



**Neoliberalism with Dutch Characteristics: The Big Fix-Up of
the Netherlands and the Practice of Embedded Cultural Activism**
BAVO

Needless to say, the self-limitation of this type of cultural activism merely serves the 'making' of a post-socialist Netherlands.[30] There is no doubt that the far-reaching co-option of oppositional forces by the ruling order accounts for the seductive power of Žižek's recent suggestion to progressive forces 'to do nothing'.[31]

### Conclusion: It's about the relationship between things, obviously!

Perhaps the ultimate, hidden reference behind the embedded cultural production in the Netherlands is the art theorist Nicolas Bourriaud, the godfather of 'relational aesthetics'.[32] Indeed, the art practices in the problem neighbourhoods appear as a sort of 'street version' of Bourriaud's relational art – a kind of 'Bourriaud in the polders' so to speak. It also concerns an art practice that no longer aims at producing 'objects' or 'provocations', but instead wants to generate new social bonds, organize encounters, encourage dialogue, etc.[33] The decisive question here concerns what it is one precisely understands by encounters. In Bourriaud's discourse these concepts clearly fit in a post-critical conceptual universe that stresses mutual respect, the creation of a *modus vivendi* and non-oppositional dialectics. With the Dutch case in mind, one has to seriously question the effectiveness of such a model in a context where the existing order mobilizes these very same values as a means to neutralize any deep resistance against its policies. Cultural agents in the Netherlands would therefore do better to endorse Jacques Rancière's theory of political art.[34] According to him, the social relevance of art is to produce what he calls 'dissensus', the radical political moment in which two social factions cannot simply 'agree to disagree' without a fundamental restructuring of the social order.[35]

Still, in another way we can understand the failure of cultural activists to generate a genuine political passion within the context of the Big Fix-Up through Bourriaud's framework of relational art. Within the latter, emphasis is on imagining new ways in which people can interact with each other – which is also one of the dominant aims of a lot of cultural interventions in the Big Fix-Up. What is downplayed, however, are the 'relationships between things', i.e. the economic and property relations upon which pro-free market governments and corporations who increasingly act like dogmatic neoliberals have a monopoly. However transgressive it might be to organize encounters between people from different socio-cultural backgrounds or competences through a relational artwork, this will never reach a critical mass if the very same participants are increasingly divided through neoliberal or neoconservative spatial policies. Artists could instead focus their creative imagination on

[30] The structural nature of this co-optation of cultural agents wi the Big Fix-Up makes it justified speak of a 'neoliberalism with Du characteristics' or 'neoliberalism (the 'plus' symbolizing the many cultural interventions working wi the population groups or areas affected by the neoliberal policie to supplement the harsh, repressive policies) to name the more enlightened, soft blend of neoliberalism of Dutch Big City P in particular and Dutch society in general.

[31] 'State of Emergency' sympos Stedelijk Museum CS, Amsterdar 23 September 2004.

[32] Nicolas Bourriaud, *Esthétiqu relationelle* (Dijon: Les presses du 1998).

[33] Think of the subtitle of the project *Dwaallicht* by Van Heeswi analysed earlier: 'Search for the bonds, connections and relations within the neighbourhood and its inhabitants.'

[34] See Jacques Rancière, *Le partage du sensible. Politique e Esthétique* (Paris: La Fabrique, 20 and *Malaise dans l'esthétique* (Pa Editions Galilée, 2004),

[35] See Jacques Rancière, *La Mésentente. Politique et Philosop* (Paris: Editions Galilée, 1995).

the relationships between things and not between people if they are to be more than palliative actors.

In considering some ten years of cultural interventions in the Netherlands, it is perhaps more telling to see what was *not* produced in the loaded context of the Big Fix-Up than what was. Where, for instance, is the documentary activist who, in Michael Moore style, took on the monster alliance between government, housing corporations, project developers, neighbourhood organizations and cultural experts? As we argued, there is plenty of material for such an intervention. How long do we have to wait for a 'wild gesture' of the same calibre as the one Thomas Hirschhorn made to raise awareness of the alarming right-wing infiltration of mainstream politics in his home country Switzerland? By occupying Switzerland's cultural centre in Paris, pimping it up with slogans and organizing video screenings and debates, Hirschhorn used all his symbolic leverage to politicize the current worrying developments. If one of Žižek's definitions of a true act is that of a crazy gesture performed by the subject regardless of the consequences within the symbolic order, then Hirschhorn's installation *Swiss-Swiss Democracy* (2004) definitely qualifies. His direct blow against the Swiss political class ultimately resulted in cutbacks to the subsidies of the art foundation Pro Helvetia, which sponsored the event.

In conclusion, we can identify another way in which Hirschhorn's act is political in Rancière's radical sense of the word. According to Rancière, democratic politics proper occurs when somebody makes a claim that he or she is seen as unauthorized or unqualified to do – in other words, when somebody is 'out of line'. It is such a radical political gesture that is lacking today in the Dutch art scene. In this sense the contemporary projects we talk about suffer from what Rancière calls the 'post-utopian condition' of art,[36] which can be seen as the manifestation of the post-socialist consensus within the artistic field. The time has come for artists here to break this post-utopian consensus through a crazy gesture striking at the core of the ongoing normalization processes in the Netherlands. They could thereby open up a space in which alternatives, or even the *desire for* alternatives, can come to the fore and take new cultural form.

Rancière, *Malaise dans*
*étique*, chapter 1. See also BAVO,
rt save democracy' available
e at: http://www.
umofconflict.eu/singletext.
id=32 (accessed 8 March 2007).

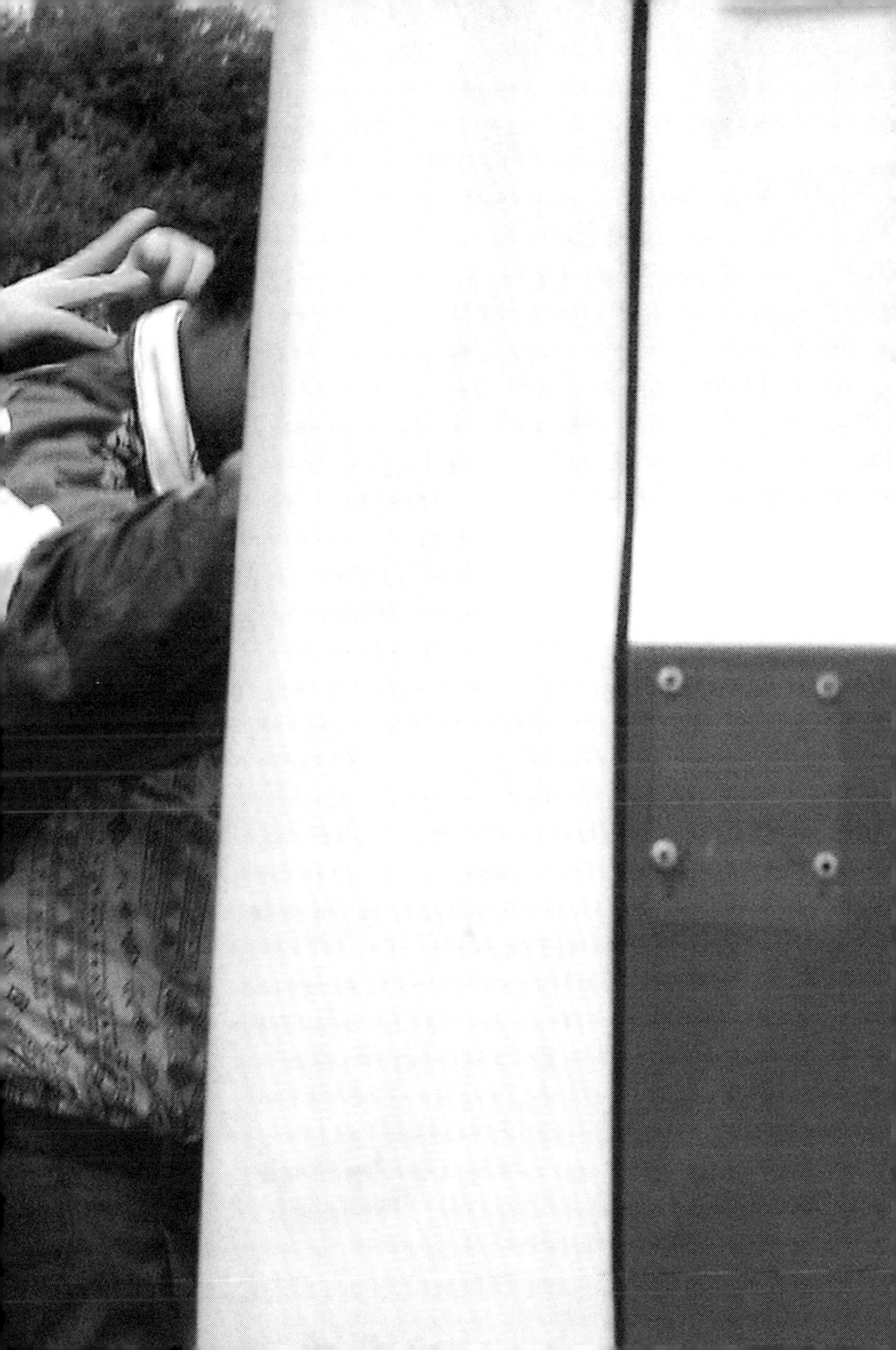

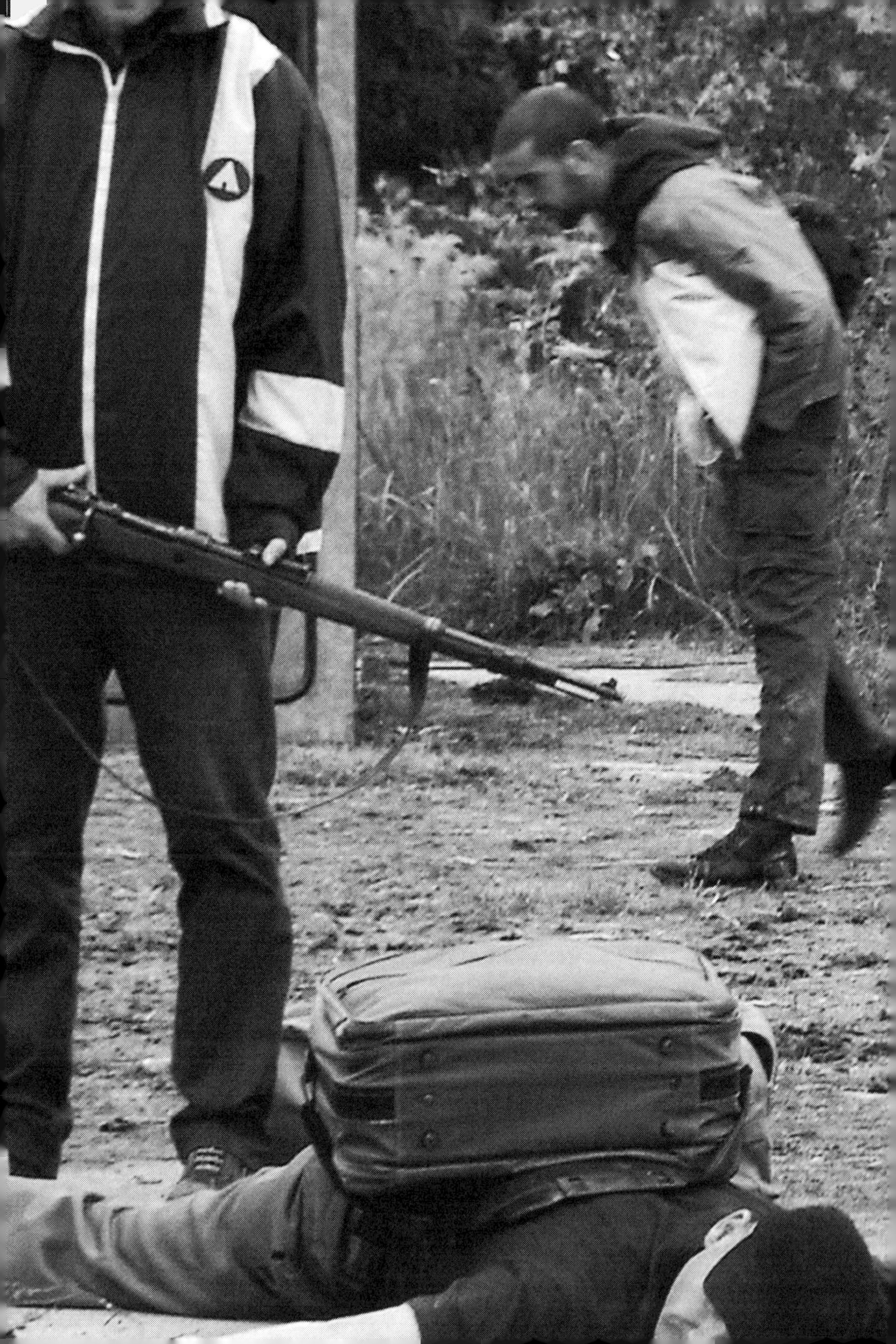

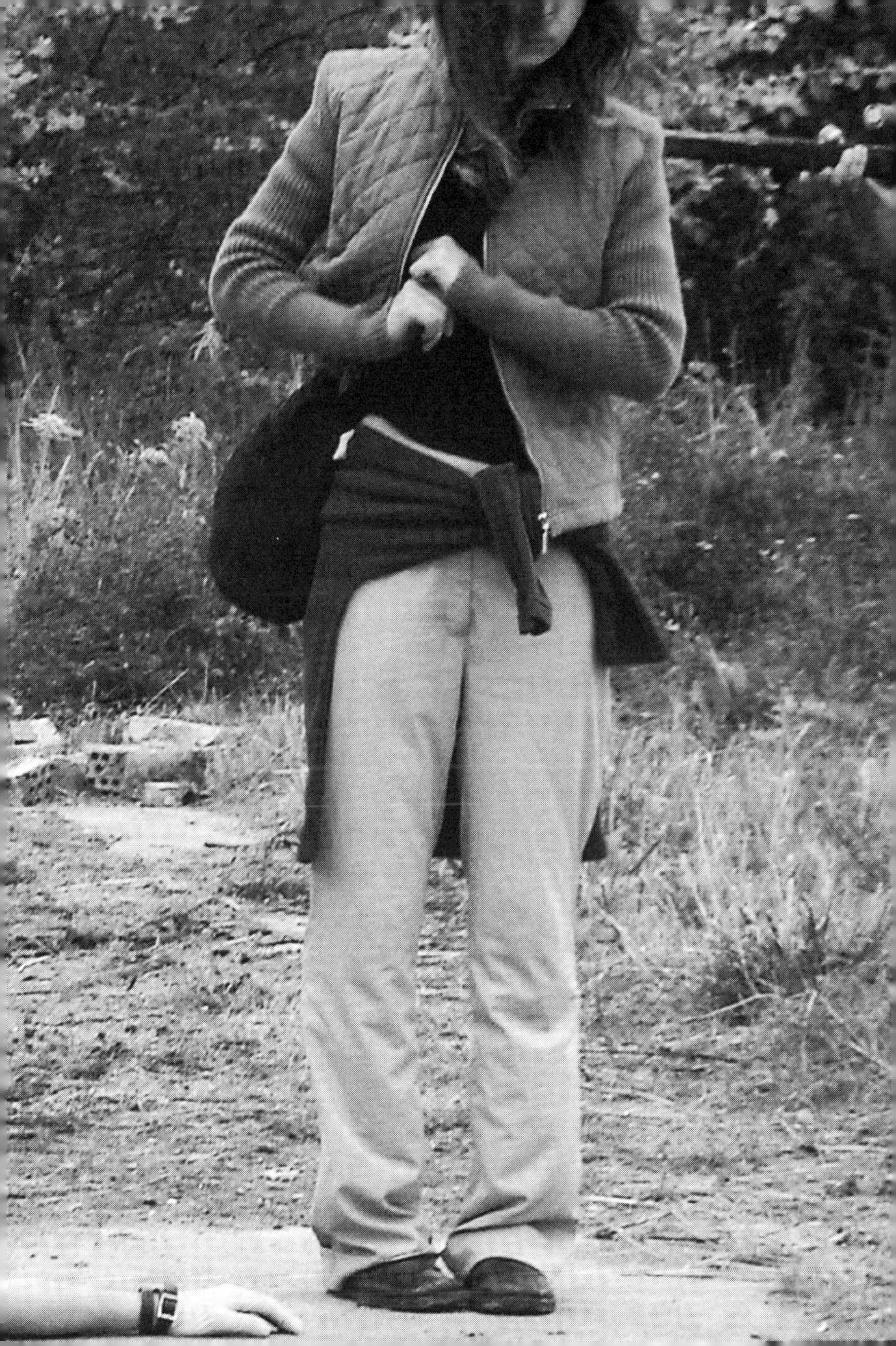

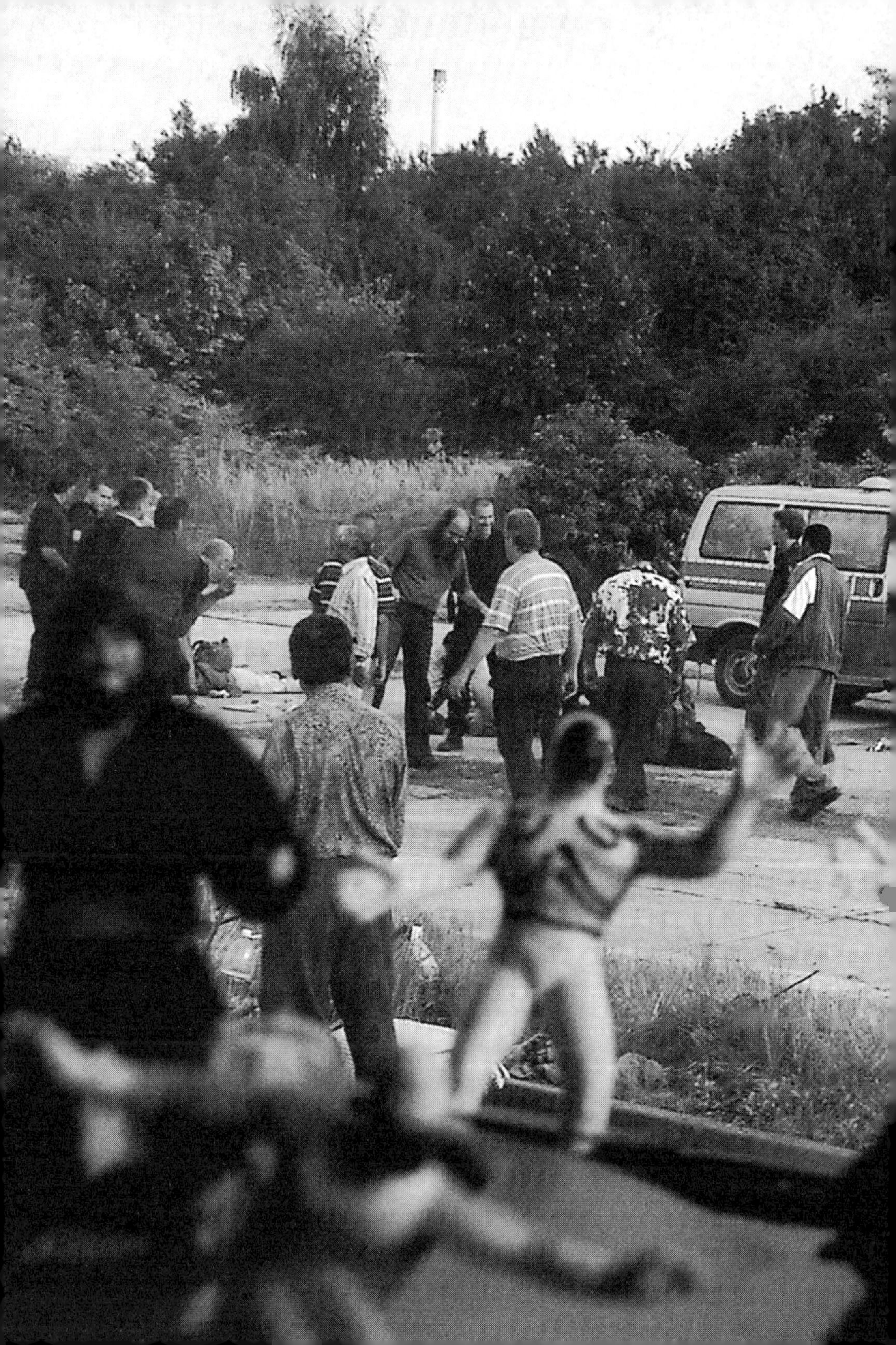

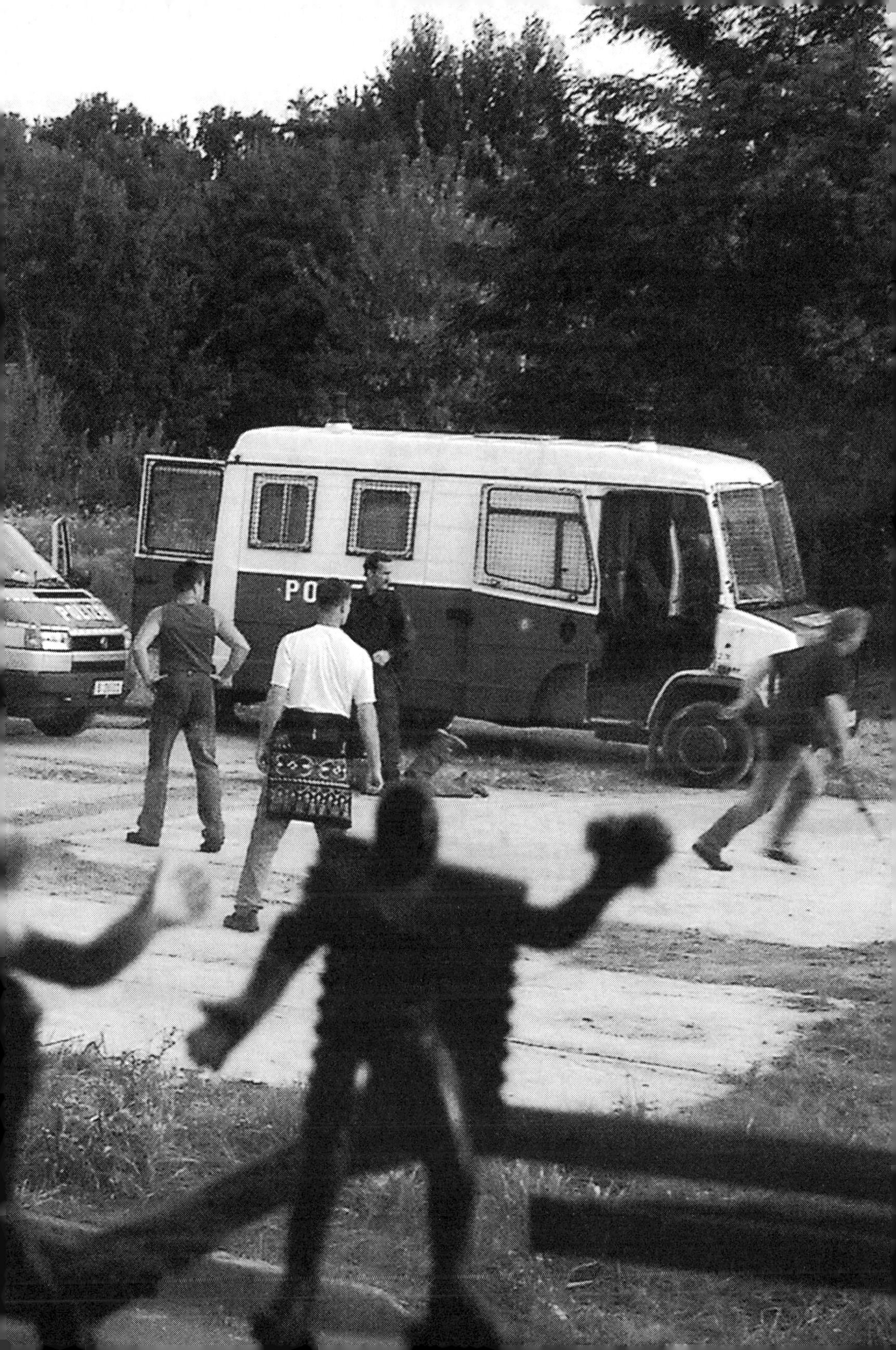

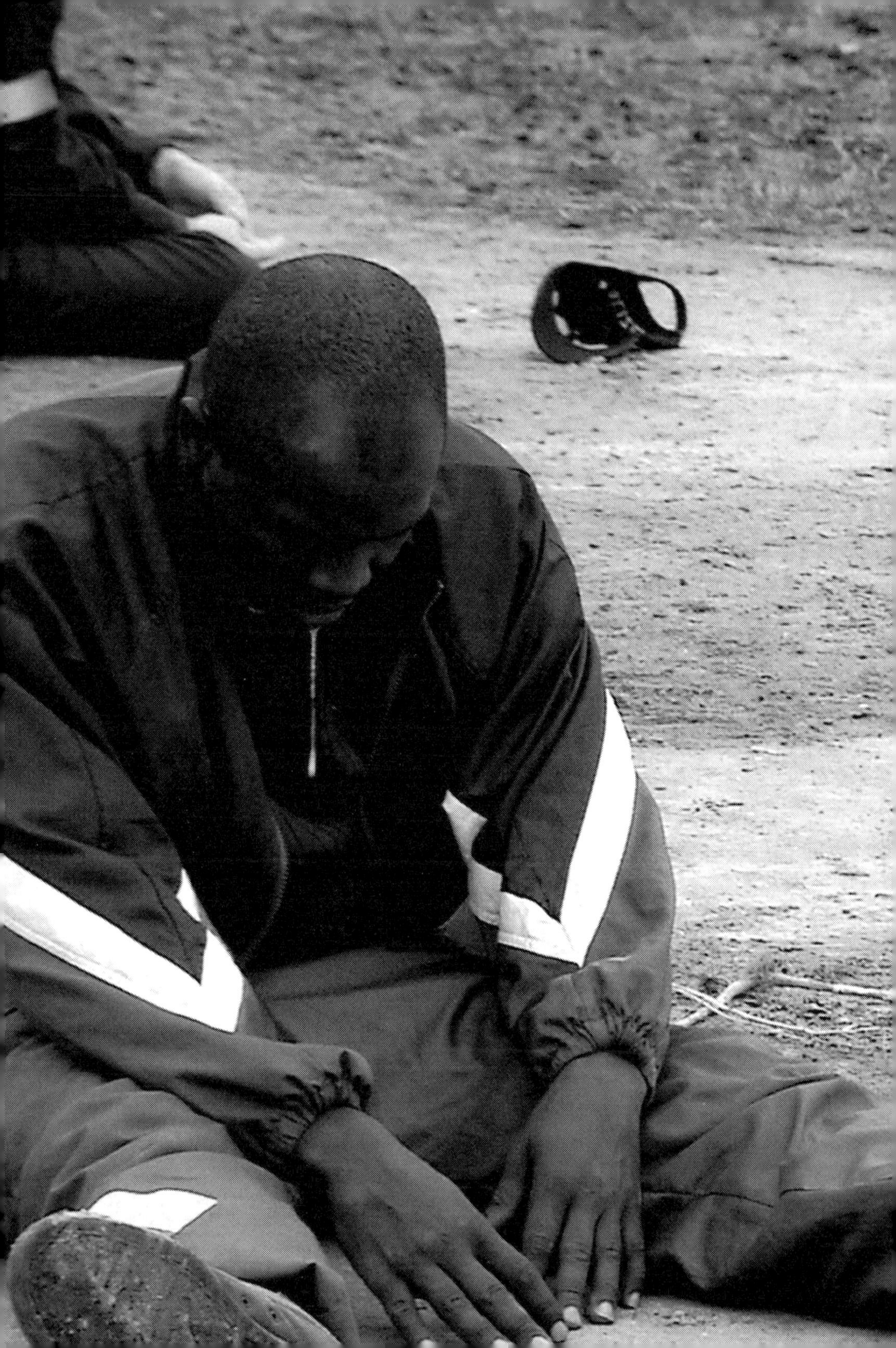

# Ex-Corporation.
# The Dutch Secular
# Contract in Transformation

Sarah Bracke

'What would I do without Dutch landscape paintings?' Their landscapes awaken dreams animated by sea breezes, drifting clouds and twilight colours. They reflect a melancholic universe of infinite spaces and palpable silences – a universe whose mystery is intensified by light. Yet this mystery remains alienated and far from God, E. M. Cioran avows in his book about saints, mysticism, music, passion and tears.[1] Because melancholy resists the absolute. This country is not pregnant with God, Cioran claims, not like Russia, and not like Spain, where even atheists are inspired by the Almighty. And for Cioran, whose fascination and repulsion for mysticism drives him to seek solace in the figure of the failed mystic, melancholy is far more inhabitable than the absolute.

The landscape Cioran recalls invokes a piety which has inhabited it for centuries: the piety of the strictly Orthodox or 'heavy' (*zware*) Protestants, concentrated in the Bible Belt stretching from the south-west to the north-east of the Netherlands, and known as *de kleine luyden*, the little folk.

'When we think of the "heavy" believers (*de zwaren*) often the image in which Smijtegelt captured them appears before our eyes: the silent of the Land (*de stillen in den Lande*). "[W]ho like to serve God in silence, who harm nobody, peaceful and faithful in Israel, forgotten citizens but not forgotten by God. Silent in their homes, silent in their profession, silent in conversations and social intercourse with other people, silent in the policy of the government, delivered by God. Silent under the cross that God has sent them, silent in their social intercourse with people in respect to public life".'[2]

Seldom do they own the language in which they are represented in the public sphere of the modern Dutch nation. The fragment above was written by Anne van der Meiden in the aftermath of the incidents in 1963 (Tholen) and 1966 (Elspeet) when, after an outbreak of polio, a minority of strictly Orthodox Protestant parents refused to have their children vaccinated, invoking the providence of God. In the national controversy that followed, images of modern science, medicine and parenting were juxtaposed with images of an old and sclerotic way of life, turned malicious as it harmed its own children. Public rhetoric fashioned the construction of a foreign body *within* modern society: a religious 'other' perceived to fall outside of modern life, which at the same time allowed the nation to define its modern character.[3] Van der Meiden's compassionate attempt to render the ways of the little folk intelligible for a modern audience is in fact not less othering than the mocking or dismissive comments from the new modern citizens. And his nostalgia for

M. Cioran, *Tears and Saints* [1939] [Chi]cago: University of Chicago Press, [1995].

Anne van der Meiden, *De zwarte-sen kerken. Portret van een [b]ekende bevolkingsgroep* (Utrecht: [B]oboeken, 1968), 168.

Susan Harding, *The Book of Jerry [Fal]well. Fundamentalist Language and [Poli]tics* (Princeton: Princeton [Uni]versity Press, 2000).



**Ex-Corporation. The Dutch Secular Contract in Transformation**
Sarah Bracke

a 'paradise lost' comes with a message to the 'heavy believers': their way of life is not sustainable, and the 'axe of secularisation' is ready to cut down their old world and old faith.

Yet we should not forget the extent to which the modern secular contract depends on its religious others. And secularisation in this country did not happen through cutting God and his churches down. Talal Asad qualifies secularism as an enactment by which a political medium (the representation of citizenship) redefines and transcends particular and differentiating practices of the self that are articulated through class, gender and religion. Secularism, in other words, is transcendent mediation, transcending these different identities and replacing conflicting perspectives by unifying experience.[4] In the Dutch case, this operation of transcendence did not do away with religious differences, but rather organized the social body along confessional or sectarian lines in a segmented polity – a process that became known as pillarisation (*verzuiling*). A pillar is an integrated complex of societal organizations and/or institutions on a confessional basis; a certain internal cohesion is mirrored in a separation from the rest of society, and the pillar can be recognized as a parallel network or social body.[5] Pillarisation is a politics of accommodation and pacification,[6] in which different faiths and ideologies are organized in a structurally similar way: Dutch nation formation began with a Protestant, a Catholic and a 'general' (Humanist) pillar; a Socialist pillar followed in the nineteenth century. The structure stabilized in 1917, with a 'trade-off' between the school battle (the Protestant and Catholic pillars insisting on public funding for confessional schools) and the battle for the extension of suffrage (vindicated by the Socialist pillar).[7] Thus the 'agree to disagree' principle was moored to the Constitution. Dutch pillarisation has been praised and ridiculed, defended and criticized, and analysed in terms of its functions: first, an emancipation strategy of structurally disadvantaged groups, second, the conservation and protection of identity, third, social control, or an instrument allowing elites to counter and channel claims for emancipation and finally, the continuity of a tradition of pluralism and politics aimed at compromise.[8]

Since the end of the 1960s, the 'depillarisation' (*ontzuiling*) of Dutch society is regularly announced, over and over again, only to be called into question once more. Even if religious adherence seemed to decline or shift into the private sphere, the architecture of the Dutch social body is revealed to be more persistent. If pillarisation was the Dutch way of modernization, the postmodern era inherited a more general (less confessionally differentiated) ideology of pluralism and tolerance,

[4] Talal Asad, *Formations of the Secular: Christianity, Islam, Moder* (Stanford: Stanford University Pres 2003).

[5] Marcel Hoogenboom, *Een miskende democratie. Een andere visie op verzuiling en politieke samenwerking in Nederland* (Politi Bestuurlijke Studiën 18) (Leiden: DSWO Press, 1996).

[6] Arend Lijphart, *Verzuiling, pacificatie en kentering in de Nederlandse politiek* (Amsterdam: De Bussy, 1968).

[7] Hoogenboom, op. cit.

[8] Ibid.

including, among other things, the idea of a redistribution of resources according to different religious and political lines. Thus the Dutch pacification model is still in place. 'The politics of accommodation did not undergo a complete metamorphosis into its very opposite. No revolution ever happened.'[9] Yet a break did become visible in the early 1990s. Politician Frits Bolkestein delivered his famous speech on the integration of minorities, in which he asserted that European civilization, and in particular the political tradition of liberalism, has generated a number of fundamental political principles (the separation of church and state, freedom of expression, toleration and non-discrimination), which have universal validity and value. Islam, he insisted, is in tension with these principles. He subsequently denounced the 'cultural relativism' of the 1980s minorities policies grounded in the principle of 'integration with the conservation of one's own identity'. Pillarisation is a thing of the past, Bolkestein declared, an idea and social formation that contemporary Dutch society has surpassed. This was a declaration that fused well with other epochal announcements of the decade: the 'end of ideology' and the beginning of the 'clash of civilizations'. As other public voices continued to elaborate on the theme (Pim Fortuyn, Ayaan Hirsi Ali, to name the most obvious two), we were informed that Dutch society had also moved beyond tolerance. Did this reflect a fundamental transformation of the Dutch model? Or a case of Enlightenment fundamentalism, as Halleh Ghorashi suggests?[10] If Cioran were alive today, would he consider that the Dutch landscape has lost its melancholy and moved closer to God?

The part of the transformations of the Dutch model that I want to highlight concentrates on what happened on the side of religion. If the secular contract was held in place by the silent presence of a religious 'other', what happens when the 'heavy' believers begin refusing to be the other? Dutch Orthodox Protestantism relies in a constitutive way on a separation between faith and the world, which profoundly shapes its worldview and identity.[11] In that sense, its world fits quasi-seamlessly with a secular model, give or take a national controversy (polio vaccinations, women's exclusion from membership of the theocratic political party SGP) or two. It is, one could say, secularisation looked at from the other side. Yet it is precisely the separation between faith and the world that has come under pressure as new generations of believers, in the last couple of decades, searched for ways to combine Bible-steady faith and engagement in contemporary society. The establishment of the Evangelical broadcasting corporation (EO) at the end of the 1960s couldn't have made the point more clearly; after all, in a strictly Orthodox world, television is 'of the devil'. An Evangelical impulse shaped an

rend Lijphart, 'From the Politics
:commodation to Adversarial
ics in the Netherlands – A
sessment', *West European
ics*, vol. 12, no. 1 (1989), 139–53.

Halleh Ghorashi, 'Ayaan Hirsi Ali:
per of dogmatisch?', *Tijdschrift
Genderstudies*, vol. 7, no. 1 (2004),
52.

Hijme Stoffels, 'Survival
tegies of Conservative Protestants
Dutch Society. The World as
eat and Challenge', in *The Search
Fundamentals, The Process of
Modernisation and the Quest for
ning*, eds. Lieteke van Vucht
sen, Jan Berting and Frank
nner (Dordrecht: Kluwer Academic
ications, 1995), 63–81.



**Ex-Corporation. The Dutch Secular Contract in Transformation**
Sarah Bracke

entire set of churches and organizations of its own, as well as revitalized existing ones. Both in the eyes of wider society as in those of the strictly Orthodox, the Evangelical drive passes as part of a (slower than expected, or dreaded) process of secularisation, and to some extent it might be precisely that. But something was at stake: younger generations of believers who had grown up in an Orthodox world insisted that its out-of-fashion traditions and imaginary, which fail to speak to current conditions, were precisely the source of secularisation and religious decline.

Harsh critiques of the Orthodox emphasis on separatism and exclusivity ran through a set of conversations I had (in 2001 and 2002) with young women from strictly Orthodox backgrounds who had been drawn to Evangelical communities, tendencies or churches.[12] They refuted the Orthodox emphasis on sinfulness and perhaps even more importantly the lack of joy. *God doesn't work like that. . .*They began situating the world of (strictly) Orthodox Protestantism, the world they came from, in terms of a specific tradition and culture, which, they insisted, was often not grounded in the Bible. *The foundation of the Church, I believe, is not the tradition, but the Bible. Not our own traditions and rules. Where is it for instance written in the Bible that you cannot bike on Sundays? If you, as parents, subsequently get into fights with your children because you do not let them bike on Sundays, then you shouldn't be surprised.* And above all, they were impatient with the churches' failure to be relevant for contemporary society. For Rianne there was little doubt on the question of accountability: *It is not the people who have dropped out of Church that have failed, but it is the Church that did not manage to keep these people that has failed. I think you really need to look at yourself and say: What did you do about this situation? What is your contribution to the future? For me, it is not about going to church every Sunday. Mind you, I do think once you stop going to church, and stop living according to your religion at home, and that it starts becoming weaker, you really need to go to Church. But the Church is not something you do only on Sunday and not the rest of the week.*

'Doing church' was about a faith reflected in and spoken through all instances of life, a piety that could not be confined or bounded in time and space to a religious service in a building designed for the purpose, or a set of activities one does or is supposed to do, or a small universe enclosed in itself and separated from society. It was about living faith, or believing 'with hands and feet', in the words of the Evangelical community where many of the young women lived. Yet their faith was Bible-steady, and resisted liberal notions of religious community and God.

[12] Sarah Bracke, *Women Resisting Secularisation in an Age of Globalization. Four case-studies within a European Context*, Utrecht University, Ph.D. dissertation (unpublished), 2004.

Among these notions was 'God is love and beautiful', Ruth explained, *cause then it's not really about God. . . . They [liberal Christians] consider the Bible as a very human book, and they turn religion into . . . well maybe I'm saying things now that aren't totally true, but this is my image of them. All what we say about God . . . God might not even exist, let's say that you could even leave Him out of the picture, it's more a kind of image or anchor upon which people put they notions of happiness or something like. God becomes more a concept, I feel. In their scheme, He doesn't really have to exist in fact.* Ruth was one of the few women in her circle who had ventured into liberal churches in search of a practice of social engagement, indispensable to her religious sense of being in the world, but lacking in the Orthodox Protestantism she knew. The more liberal church she began to attend was embedded in a neighbourhood with many homeless and unemployed people, through various social income-generating projects. *But it was really a pity that it wasn't very clear what they believed, and that it didn't matter. I found that a great pity, that they [the believing and social aspect] could not be combined. . . . [I want] the combination of both. I find holding on to the fundamentals . . . I am still convinced when I read the Bible, and I'll stay convinced, that it's not the aim to let go of a number of things, thinking, 'Oh well, they don't matter'. I simply cannot read that into the Bible. I do believe that is important to hold on to the Bible, it is the word of God. . . . But I do find that in many churches there is way too little concern with the world around us. While that is also very clearly written in the Bible. I cannot see how you cannot read that. And even if it wasn't written, I would still find it very important. But I am happy to see that God also finds it very important.*

The relatively recent presence of Islam in Dutch society, related to the labour migration (mainly from Morocco and Turkey) that began more than forty years ago, represents another crucial transformation in the Dutch religious landscape. The Islam of the new Dutch residents and citizens was at first often traditional or nominal in character, a predicament which subsequent generations criticized as they began to revitalize the Islam their parents transmitted to them. The conversations I had (in 2002) with young Muslim women connected to Milli Görüş, a movement of political Islam in the Turkish diaspora, resonated with the conversations with Evangelical women in a number of respects. The Islam of their parents, they insisted, was infused with traditions and culture, it was 'uneducated', it was often not in accordance with the Koran and, most importantly, they yearned for a faith and practice that was relevant to contemporary society.

 **Ex-Corporation. The Dutch Secular Contract in Transformation**
Sarah Bracke

But another concern marked their discourse, as they interpellated the Dutch secular contract on its promise of pluralism and toleration, and its apparent inability to integrate a new religious traditions into the model, i.e. to extend the organizing principles of the Dutch polity to Islam. The story of the law student Ayse Kabaktepe spoke of this concern. When Kabaktepe went through an application procedure to work as a substitute clerk in the court in Zwolle, she was told that her headscarf prevented her appointment for two reasons: it was in contradiction with the dress codes and with the principle of impartiality (a principle that in fact specifically pertains to the judge). In April 2001, with the support of one of her law professors and Milli Görüş, Kabaktepe took her case to the Commission for Equal Treatment (*Commissie Gelijke Behandeling*). When the Commission reached its verdict, after more than the regulatory eight weeks, it claimed that the court of Zwolle discriminated against Kabaktepe. The verdict was not well received in the public and political arena. While the case was mediatized for many weeks, with strong voices defending the impartiality principle that was considered to be under threat, as soon as the verdict was announced, media attention almost immediately withdrew – in fact many people remember the case, but not the verdict. The current affairs programme *Nova* had invited Kabaktepe to the broadcasting studio on the evening of the verdict, but as soon as the verdict was made public, they called her to cancel. *Simply because I won the case, and they were not prepared for that. They really had a programme in mind in which I would have lost the case. When that was not the case, I was not interesting any more.* Whether this explains *Nova's* cancellation or not, the fact is that Kabaktepe's victory sat uneasily within the dominant representational scripts, both of Muslim women and of the self-identity of Dutch society. The verdict was equally eroded on the side of political authorities. When she subsequently continued the procedure to effectively begin working in the court in Zwolle, Kabaktepe received a phone call from the Minister of Justice – himself a liberal – who informed her that he thought a headscarf was not appropriate in court. He proposed to continue the discussion, but never did.

During the public debate, while the Commission was considering the case, the question of impartiality was translated in terms of 'neutrality', which Kabaktepe problematized. *But how neutral can you be as a person? I mean, a white judge also embodies certain things. That was my argument. I might wear a headscarf, but I study Dutch law. I study what is allowed and what is forbidden by Dutch law. . . . And in Dutch society, Dutch law is in force, full stop. I think it's a process of getting used to it, people still find it scary. They mobilize examples like, imagine that you have a gay person in front of you, then he would not feel comfortable, he would feel prejudiced. Yes, okay, but then how does a woman feel in a rape case in front of only male judges? Or a black person in front of white judges? You weigh things, right . . . I understand, and the impartiality of the juridical power is very important, I agree, but on the other hand the juridical power should also be a reflection of society. And excluding a whole group from it [juridical power], how just is that? So it's about conflicting interests. What has more weight?*

Kabaktepe's argumentation stressed that nobody can *be* neutral. Neutrality is a not quality of embodiment, a characteristic of individuals. And the supposed neutrality of a hegemonic notion of juridical power reflected in the image of an old white male judge is radically interrupted from the perspective of a raped woman or black person. But the inevitable embodiment of the subjects involved in jurisdiction, she insisted, should be distinguished from a notion of impartiality, which resides in the *exercise* of Dutch law. As she was pursuing a degree that prepared her to practise Dutch law, Kabaktepe claimed the right to represent the impartiality inscribed in Dutch law, with and through a 'different' mode of embodiment – at odds with the modes of embodiment, which, most often unacknowledged, have informed Dutch political principles and thought. She did not seek to reject these principles, but to stretch the range of embodied subjects that can co-construct them.

What became known as the Dutch model has been crucially shaped by a history of religious difference and strife and a specific mode of secularisation that is pillarisation. Today that historic modern secular contract is challenged from different sides. A segment of its historic religious 'other', the strictly Orthodox, ceased to be silent and began to question the separatism that is constitutive of the secular. A new religious other, Islam, began to claim space within the existing secular arrangement and its pillarised structure and principle of freedom of religion. Believers in ideology's end and civilization's beginning have declared the era of pillarisation and tolerance to be definitively over. (Many of them, *comme par hasard*, have also been at the forefront of the economic wars of neoliberalism and the destruction of the tissues of social welfare.) As the Dutch social contract is questioned and transforming, Islam could well become the religious other against which a new Dutch social contract and self is established and consolidated. The heated arguments insisting on Islam's incompatibility with secularism dismiss or ignore the Dutch tradition of pillarisation; and while secularism's transcendent mediation stretches beyond the old religious differences that animated Dutch society, it draws firm boundaries at what it refuses to incorporate. Dutch secularism hasn't looked as Christian (in a plethora of religious, nominal, humanist and civilizational modes) as it does today for a long while.

*I wish to thank María Puigde la Bellacasa and Giulia Garofalo for careful readings and Sahar Sadjadi for fierce interpellations.*

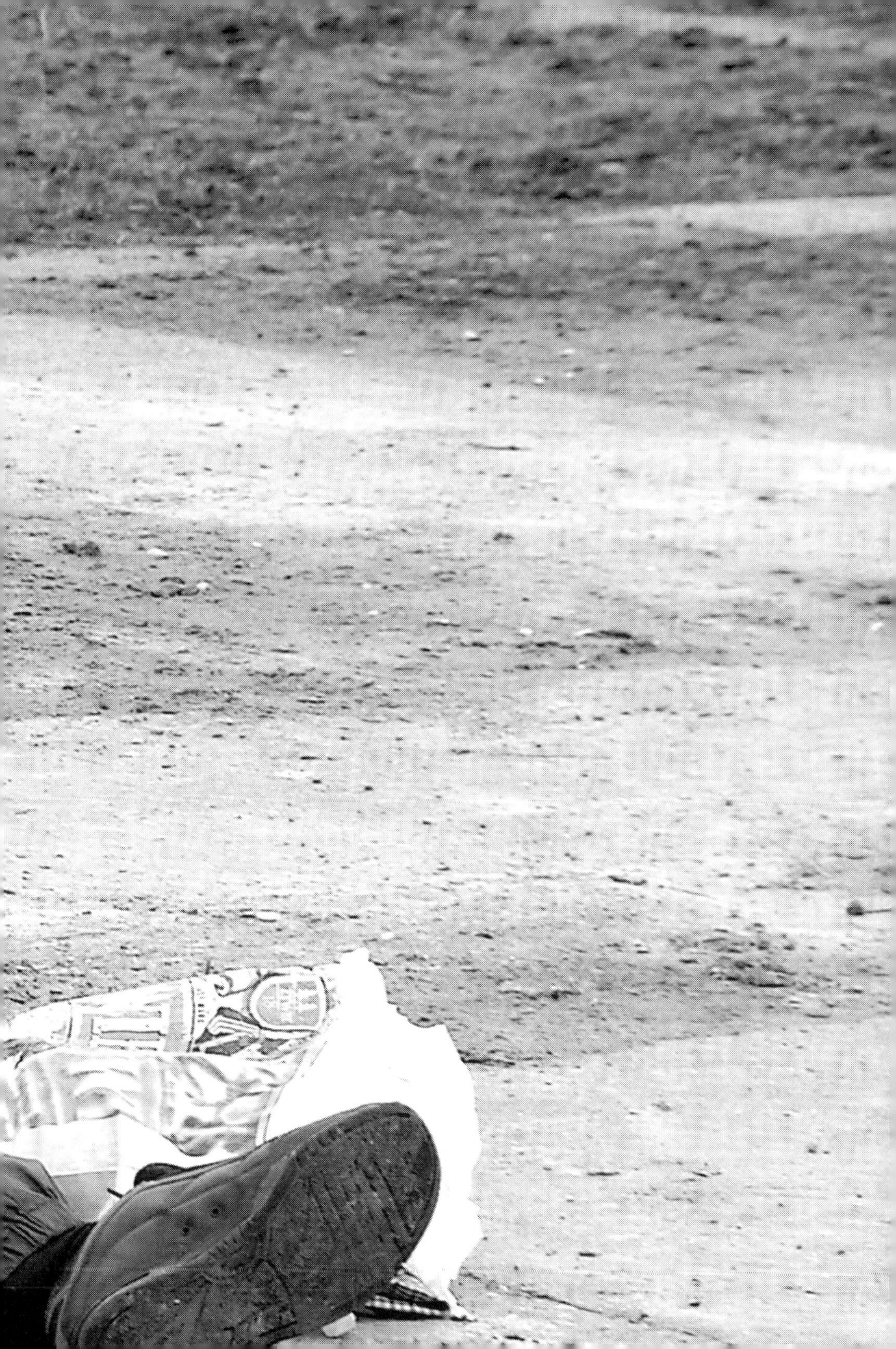

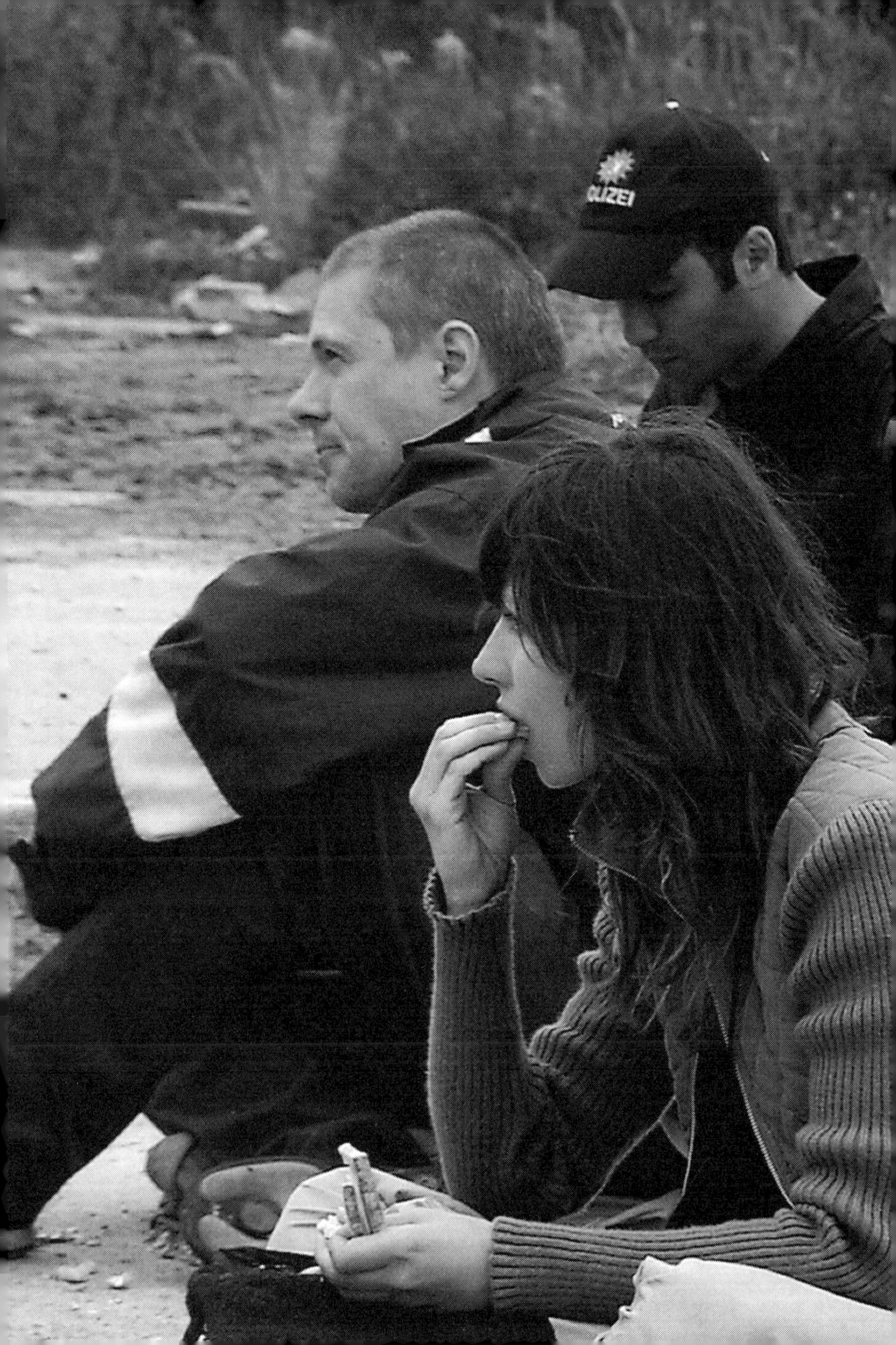

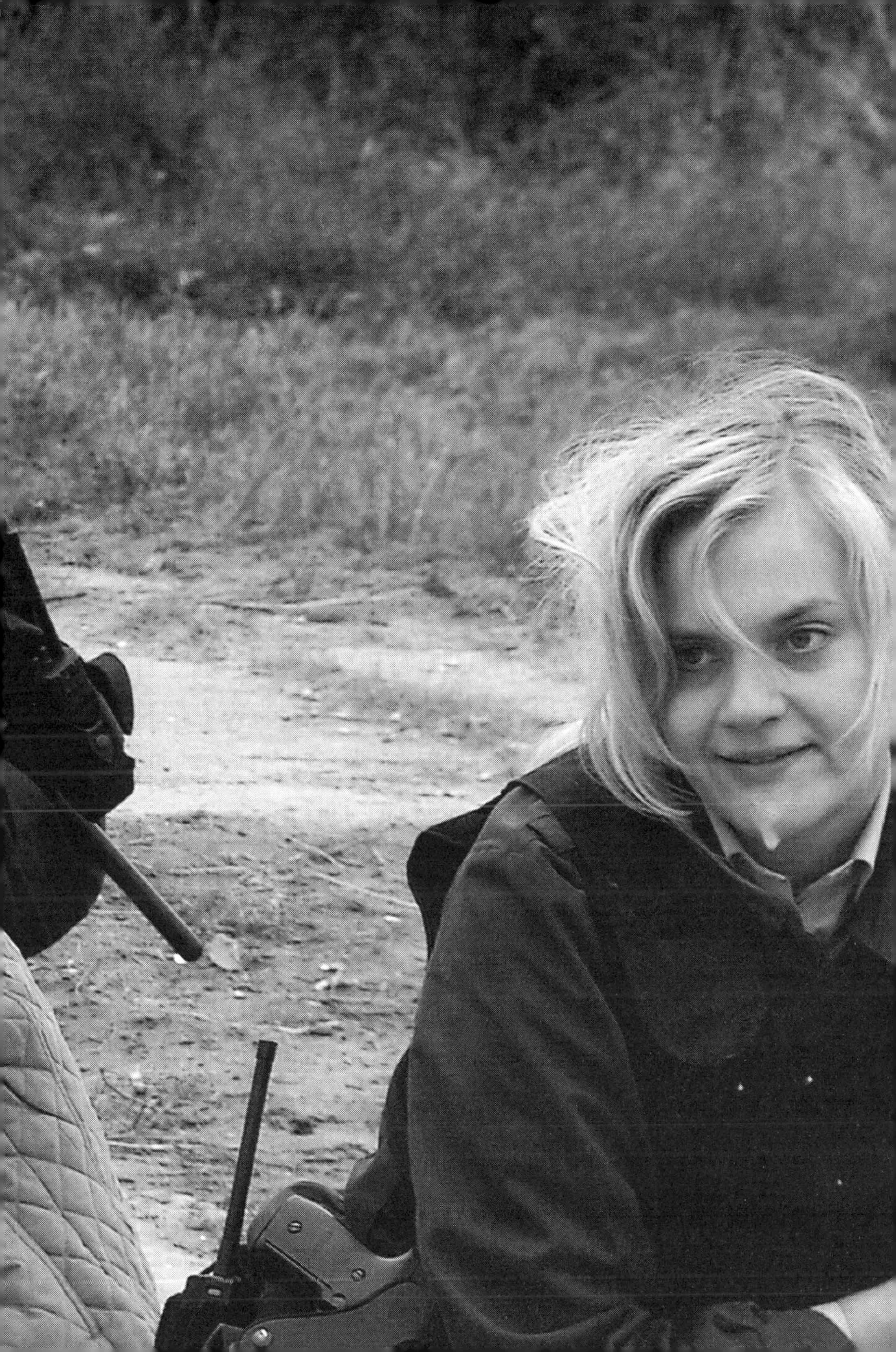

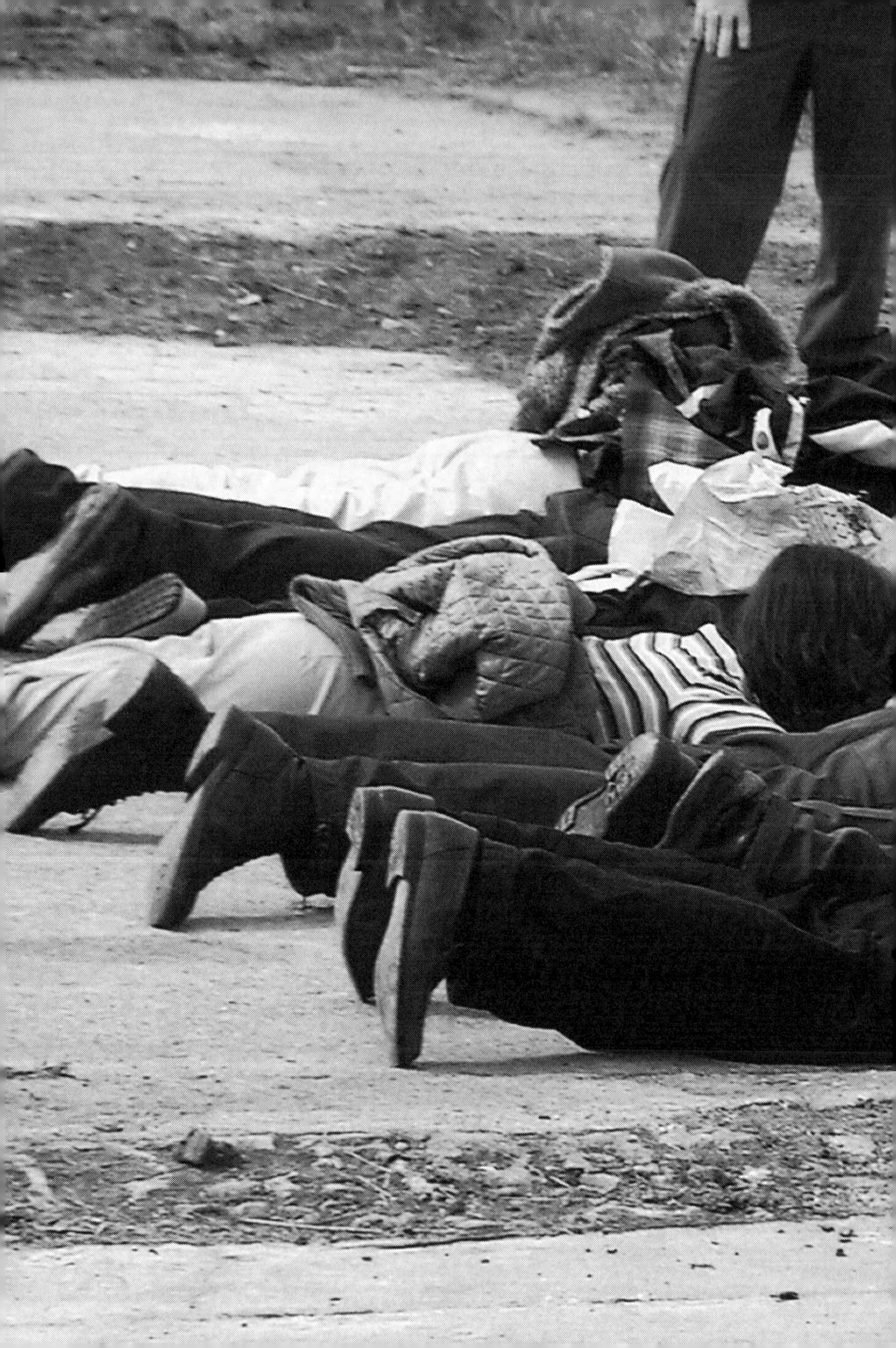

# A Passport Is a Piece of Paper, or the Enrichment of the Netherlands

Esther Captain &
Guno Jones

The first decade of the third millennium has been claimed by Dutch and international academics, journalists and other opinion-makers as a test case for Dutch identity. Though the discourse on national identity for centuries has centred on images of the Netherlands, boasting a history as a 'progressive', 'open', 'international oriented', 'aid-giving', 'tolerant' guide for other countries of the world, it has become the most introverted nation in Europe. After the 9/11 attacks in 2001 (with their impact on the Netherlands), and the murders of right wing populist party leader Pim Fortuyn in 2002 and writer and filmmaker Theo van Gogh in 2003, boundaries were drawn between 'we' and 'them', between the 'real Dutch' and 'others' within the nation-state of the Netherlands.

In the same period of time, however, this small country of the Low Lands also saw testimonies of a Dutch past, which exposed another side of its orientation to the world outside the Netherlands and Europe. Like other former imperialist nations, the Netherlands has heard strong critical voices raised against colonialism and colonial institutions. It's important to pay attention to these voices, not only for the authors of this article, both of whom are postcolonial Dutch citizens of mixed ethnic descent with family linkages to the East (Captain) and West (Jones) as well as to the Netherlands, but for a more balanced historiography of the impact of the Dutch colonial past on its contemporary society and citizens.

The year 2002 proved to be significant in this respect. Firstly, the 400th anniversary of the *Verenigde Oost-Indische Compagnie* (VOC) [Dutch East India Company] was commemorated by a special government-funded committee set up for this occasion, and by other official institutions. These activities were contested by various private initiatives, varying from symposia featuring highly critical appraisals of Dutch colonialism by speakers of Eurasian, Dutch, Indonesian and Moluccan descent to a committee called 'Celebration of 400 Years VOC? No!'. Secondly, a long-awaited monument commemorating the abolition of slavery in the West Indies was unveiled in Amsterdam by Queen Beatrix, in the presence of many distinguished Dutch and international guests, on 1 July 2002. This represented an important step in recognizing slavery as an integral part of Dutch history. Yet many visitors of the inaugural ceremony, mostly black visitors, were kept out of sight of the dignitaries and away from the monument itself by fences, treatment that provoked tension and fierce protests.

We would like to address the issues of the (supposed) current Dutch identity crisis from a historical and anthropological point of view, reflecting our belief that there is a continuing link in the way the Netherlands has manifested itself towards its subjects in the colonial past and its citizens in the post-colonial present. The difficult nature of a public discourse about the Dutch colonial experience is affecting the current debate on migration and the fear and hatred of 'other' people. It is therefore instructive to explore the experiences of Dutch colonial and postcolonial subjects to help us illuminate the present attitude towards Muslim subjects in the Netherlands of today.

The Netherlands is a small and very rich country. Until 1949, seen from a Dutch perspective, it was the centre of a vast colonial empire, which stretched from the East Indies (the Dutch East Indies, which in 1949 gained independence as Indonesia) to the West Indies (Suriname, formerly known as Dutch Guyana, which gained independence in 1975). Although not an imperial power anymore, the present Kingdom of the Netherlands includes the Caribbean islands of Bonaire, Curaçao and Sint Maarten with Saba, and Sint Eustacius as future Dutch municipalities, while Aruba is claiming its *status aparte* within the Kindom. The presence of the Dutch in the East and West Indies as colonizers accounts for exploration and exploitation at the same time. The colonies provided for the enrichment of the Netherlands in many ways: from the fortunes made by private persons and money earned for the national treasury to the birth of new population groups of mixed ethnic descent and thus an increased demographic diversity in the country. In order to be aware of this twofold heritage, considered by some to be controversial, one must focus on these two faces of the enrichment of the Netherlands.

### Threat

While the 1980s established a political consensus in the Netherlands on the acceptance of religious and cultural difference as a given, and was critical of manifest xenophobic rhetoric, the recent political consensus shows signs of accommodating Islamophobic discourses. To a certain extent, these discourses have become mainstream. The Dutch right-liberal governments Balkenende II (May 2003–June 2006) and Balkenende III (July–November 2006), notably with Rita Verdonk as Migration and Integration Minister, agreed to implement restrictive immigration laws, increasingly legitimized in a discourse in which migration and migrants were perceived as a threat to the 'Dutch community'. These two governments carried out legal rules concerning the expulsion of 'undesirable aliens', regardless of whether they were socially integrated in Dutch society or not.

In drawing the boundaries between the global and the national through restrictive migration policies, the Dutch government became a contender of the international law regime concerning migration, of which it once was a fierce proponent. Within the borders of the Dutch nation-state, the picture couldn't have been more different than in previous decades. Cultural and religious diversity, advocated and institutionalized as routes to integration into Dutch society in the 1980s, were now perceived as obstacles to integration and as a threat to the reified Dutch nation. In the new political consensus, under the motto that 'we should be proud of Dutch culture and history', Islamic minorities in particular were proclaimed enemies within the borders of the nation-state. Apart from restrictive migration policies, assimilation to an essentialized and mystified uniform 'Dutch culture' was thought to offer a remedy: so-called 'non-western newcomers' were subjected to integration programmes, even before entering the Netherlands.

We signal a continuing link in the way the Netherlands has manifested itself towards its subjects in the colonial past and the overheated political debates about the newly constructed others in the postcolonial present. The current crisis in Dutch national identity is partly grounded in an insufficient public discourse on the history of Dutch colonial past and on postcolonial citizens. While Dutch postcolonial citizens from Indonesia, Suriname and the Antilles nowadays (first, second and third generation) make up about one million individuals, they are virtually unheard and unrepresented in political discourses.

What does this mean when evaluating the Dutch identity crisis? What can we learn from the Dutch colonial past and political discourses on postcolonial citizens who came to the Netherlands after the Second World War? Do these experiences offer a way out of the crisis? In this increasingly globalized world, we believe that hybrid and multiple identities (as opposed to homogeneity and pureness) can offer an answer to the Dutch identity crisis. We even would like to question the supposed crisis, especially when looking at artists and art production in the Netherlands. We want to ask the rhetorical question of whether it is accurate to characterize the Netherlands by signalling growing cultural, ethnic or religious differences between its inhabitants.

In our view, notably intellectual as well as artistic expressions provide the space for quietness of mind, (self)reflection, imagination and enrichment of the body, mind and soul. Instead of proposing the cultural patrimony of a static Dutch nation, the hybrid and multiple identities of postcolonial and other migrants, 'rooted' in a trans-national genealogy, can (continue to) nurture us as a source of inspiration for the production of art. The arts in return can serve both as a vital representation and critical companion of an everchanging, never finished, Dutch society.

### Kinship

While the colonial empire of the Netherlands was still intact, both colonies in the so-called 'East' and 'West' were cherished. The Dutch East Indies were referred to as 'The Emerald Belt', while Dutch Guyana as well as the Moluccan region (in the Indies archipelago) were called 'The Twelfth Province' of the Netherlands. Both the East and West Indies were also known as 'Tropical Holland'. When the Empire was stable and far away, its inhabitants and their indigenous cultures were appreciated.

This attitude is visible, for example, in the way the Netherlands proudly 'displayed' people from the East and West Indies in a series of world exhibitions in the late nineteenth and early twentieth centuries (Amsterdam 1883, Paris 1889, Amsterdam 1898, Paris 1900, Brussels 1910 and Paris 1931). The colonized others were depicted as belonging to an attractive and exotic people. Persons belonging to the aristocratic Javanese and Balinese courts with their music and dance, for instance, were highly appreciated. But even when considered very refined and civilized in their cultural and artistic expressions, mentally and intellectually most of the Indonesians were regarded by Dutch colonizers as belonging to a primitive species. Therefore, they were merely treated as children that had to be educated. Guided by the Dutch, they could be raised towards intellectual maturity. In daily colonial life in the Indies, Indonesians were 'close, but yet so far away'. Because of this familiarity, it was necessary to create a clear division between 'modern' Dutch persons, possessing superior knowledge on the one hand, and 'traditional' indigenous people in the colonies on the other hand. This in fact is the very nature of exhibiting people colonial-style: it is about having the power of representation in creating a separation between 'us' and 'them'.

When the Dutch colonial empire started to fall apart, its place of action shifted from the periphery towards the centre. The arrival of colonial and postcolonial migrants in the Netherlands changed the inclusive rhetoric of Dutch colonial empire. When people from the (former) colonies gave expression to their kinship by migrating to their Dutch fatherland, the reaction of the receiving country was politically defensive and symbolically excluding. Persons from the (former) colonies who claimed their Dutch citizenship experienced that the relationship between them and the Netherlands was not so evident to a lot of Dutchmen. The empire with its colonial subjects 'over there' was seen as natural, while the Dutch citizenship of postcolonial citizens who migrated to the Netherlands was not.

Dutch politicians also constructed the empire as inherent to Dutch national identity. Hegemony was, besides earlier practices of exposing colonial subjects, also a matter of control over territory. The Netherlands then went to great lengths to hold on to its 'Emerald Belt', as the Indonesian archipelago was called. When, after the Second World War, the Dutch government and Indonesian nationalists were unable to agree on the content of post-war agreements that would give the country greater autonomy, armed warfare broke out. The two decolonization wars that took place in July 1947 and December 1948 were euphemistically referred to in the Netherlands as 'police actions', while in Indonesian historiography they are called Dutch military aggression. The Netherlands eventually handed over sovereignty to Indonesia on 27 December 1949, but only after lengthy debates in the Dutch Parliament. Historian Arend Lijphart spoke of 'the trauma of decolonization', a trauma that – judging from political rhetorics in the Dutch Parliament – certainly had a poetic dimension. Pieter Gerbrandy, a member of Parliament, expressed the general feeling as follows: 'We are shockingly abandoning the magnificent country of Insulinde [the East Indies] which winds along the equator like an Emerald Belt, since we can do nothing more there now to restore law and order.'

### One-way traffic

After Indonesian independence, the Netherlands invested heavily in relations with its former colonies in 'the West', symbolically as well as politically. After 1949 Suriname and the Dutch Antilles became new 'anchorage places' for the Kingdom of the Netherlands. This was only meant as one-way traffic, however. Dutch politicians considered the relation between the Dutch East Indies and, after 1949, Suriname and the Dutch Antilles as a natural phenomenon. The Dutch Empire with Dutch people travelling, working and living in its overseas territories was self-evident. But the arrival of persons from the colonies, wanting to travel from the so-called periphery to the centre, was not obvious at all.

The political discourses on migration and integration of postcolonial citizens from the former Dutch colonies underline the fact that colonized inhabitants of the Dutch empire were meant to be colonial subjects of the Dutch empire, not members and citizens of the Dutch nation-state. The difficulties faced by Eurasians – persons with a double ethnic (Dutch and Indonesian) background – who wanted to enter the Netherlands in the 1950s offer a painful case in this respect. Despite the exclusion of Eurasians by the post-war Indonesian society, the Dutch government implemented policies to discourage Eurasian migrants from settling in the Netherlands. Instead, Dutch officials encouraged Eurasians to integrate in Indonesian society and looked for new 'tropical homelands' for them. This goal was legitimized by essentialized identity narratives, which held that Eurasians were 'mentally, physically, culturally and socially maladapted to Dutch society'. Secretary of Social Affairs Frans-Joseph van Thiel argued then, 'migration to the Netherlands often results in irresolvable uprootedness'.

Until the mid-1950s, Eurasians seldom received requested loans for the costs of transportation to the Netherlands. Journalist and distinguished writer Jan Boon, better known by his pseudonyms Tjalie Robinson and Vincent Mahieu, is one of the many Eurasians who faced major difficulties in securing a loan for passage to the Netherlands. Notably, he had been born in the Dutch city of Nijmegen when his parents were on leave in the Netherlands. It took Robinson more than four years of writing requests and pleading with politicians before he and his family could leave Indonesia. In 1955, a year after his arrival in the Netherlands, Robinson wrote assertively: 'I am a Dutch citizen because my father was one. If my father had been an Indonesian citizen, I would have been one too. But I have remained myself. The passport doesn't determine me as a person, but (sadly) determines some kind of power of control over me. But the state doesn't possess me.' The overwhelming majority of Eurasians gave voice to their kinship with the Netherlands by sticking to Dutch nationality. At the risk of being left in-between, they very well understood the symbolic and real-life consequences of the piece of paper that a passport is.

### Welcome

Similar to the treatment of postcolonial citizens from the Dutch East Indies/Indonesia, inclusion of citizens from Suriname and the Dutch Antilles in the Kingdom of the Netherlands was conditional. Dutch politicians, after the traumatic loss of Indonesia, invested symbolically as well as politically in relations with the remaining overseas parts of the Kingdom. They accentuated a single Dutch nationality for all the inhabitants of the Kingdom. Initially, as part of the reconstruction of the Kingdom of the Netherlands, these postcolonial citizens met a cordial welcome by Dutch politicians, regardless of social background. The idea was that, after a certain period of time, they would return to Suriname and the Dutch Antilles.

After 1969, anti-imperialist and anti-colonial discourses became part of the mainstream political discourses. In light of continued process of worldwide decolonization, the 'police actions' against Indonesian nationalists were redefined as 'deep dark pages' of Dutch history. Relations with remaining parts of the Kingdom of the Netherlands, Suriname and the Dutch Antilles, were constructed as a 'neocolonial anachronism'.

With the numbers of migrants (especially from Suriname) on the rise, decolonization became a means of drawing the boundaries of the Dutch nation. Politicians increasingly constructed the Dutch nationality of inhabitants of Suriname and the Dutch Antilles as 'unnatural' and perceived them as 'victims of Dutch nationality', while the Netherlands was presented as an 'unfit' social-cultural habitat for Dutch nationals from overseas.

According to Dutch politicians, in conjunction with a small but influential nationalist movement in Suriname, Surinamese were 'in need' of independence. Before independence the plea to restrict migration from the overseas parts of the Kingdom to the Netherlands was frequently heard. The Dutch government condemned proposals like these as unconstitutional. However, the quick independence of Suriname in 1975, widely advocated by the Dutch government as well as Dutch Parliament, resulted in the end of free migration. Thus the legal boundaries of the Dutch nation-state were drawn.

Today, postcolonial citizens are *grosso modo* considered to pose no threat to Dutch community at all. The Eurasian Dutch and Surinamese Dutch play no significant role in current political debates concerning the so-called crisis of Dutch national identity. The Eurasian Dutch were declared 'assimilated' in Dutch society in the 1960s and the Surinamese Dutch were considered to be (more or less) integrated in the 1990s. The memory of the Second World War in the Dutch East Indies and the remembrance of the history of slavery, which constitute an important part of respectively Eurasian and Dutch Surinamese identity, have been included as histories of a particular subgroup in the Dutch collective memory. However, the recognition of these two vernacular histories and the political acceptance of postcolonial citizens has happened in parallel with the exclusion of migrants who arrived after the (post)colonial migrants from the East and West Indies. Labour migrants from Morocco and Turkey and refugees from Iran, Iraq and Somalia are pinpointed as the new others. The big difference now is that religion (read: Islam) is regarded as the defining factor: the boundary between 'us' and 'them'.

### Embracing

The present discussion in the Netherlands is again focusing on the supposedly enormous differences between Dutch citizens and the newcomers, who are depicted as persons who are unlikely and/or unwilling to assimilate or integrate. This debate is made possible by forgetting the experiences of and with postcolonial migrants. Or, in other words: we are dealing with a very selective historical memory. The absence of postcolonial migrants in this discussion obscures the fact that the history of migration shows that boundaries and identities to mark the other, once depicted as strict and stable, have proven to be relative and flexible.

This fact perhaps paradoxically gives us hope and inspiration for the future. Migrants from the former colonies had previously been stereotyped as being unable to assimilate and integrate. Nowadays, these individuals (especially the second and third generation) present themselves as proud Dutch citizens, often conscious of their mixed ethnic and cultural heritage. It turns out that this long-term message is difficult to communicate, as the mass media and policy makers sometimes tend to focus too much on short-term problems and solutions. An active and institutionalized remembrance of the diverse genealogies of the Dutch nation seems of crucial importance to overcome the current 'crisis of Dutch identity'.

To conclude, we would like to signal the development from the nineteenth and twentieth-century exhibitions that depict the other, to the present self-representation of Dutch identity in a globalized world at the Venice Biennale. It is our wish and expectation that the old colonial representations will give way to critical and self-conscious self-representation. Especially in the realm of daily life as well as art, we believe the embracing of qualities and characteristics that are perceived to be contradictory is already happening – for a long time. Yes, we are black and Dutch; yes, we wear headscarves and are feminists; yes, we are out, proud and legally married with children; yes, we are white and Muslim. This is our life. Perhaps you can call that art too.

     **Citizens and Subjects:** The Netherlands, for example

**Bibliography**

Bloembergen, Marieke. *De koloniale vertoning. Nederland en Indië op de wereldtentoonstellingen (1880–1931)*. Amsterdam; Wereldbibliotheek, 2002.

Captain, Esther and Guno Jones. 'The Netherlands: A Small Country with Imperial Ambitions'. In *Overseas Empires in the Early Modern and Modern World,* ed. Robert Aldrige. London: Thames and Hudson (forthcoming).

Captain, Esther. 'The Lady and the Gentleman. Constructions of European-ness in the Diaries of Civilian Internees in the Dutch East Indies'. In *Recalling the Indies. Colonial Culture and Postcolonial Identities,* eds. Joost Coté and Loes Westerbeek. Amsterdam: Aksant, 2005, 205–226.

—————. '"Geen spoortje Indisch, geen bamboe, geen prikkeldraad." Het tweesporenbeleid van Indische zelforganisaties (1946–2000)'. In *Binnenskamers. Besluitvorming over terugkeer en opvang na de Tweede Wereldoorlog,* ed. Conny Kristel. Amsterdam: Bert Bakker, 2002, 325–355.

Grever, Maria and Berteke Waaldijk. *Feministische Openbaarheid. De Nationale Tentoonstelling van Vrouwenarbeid in 1898.* Amsterdam: IISG/IIAV, 1998.

Grever, Maria and Fia Dieteren. *A Fatherland for Women. The 1898 'Nationale Tentoonstelling van Vrouwenarbeid' in retrospect.* Amsterdam: IISG/VVG, 2000.

Jones, Guno. '"Het belang van een gedenkteken." De discussie over het Nationaal monument Nederlands slavernijverleden'. In *Kleio. Tijdschrift van de vereniging van docenten in geschiedenis en staatsinrichting in Nederland,* vol. 42, no. 5 (2001), 9–13.

**A Passport Is a Piece of Paper, or the Enrichment of the Netherlands**

 Esther Captain & Guno Jones

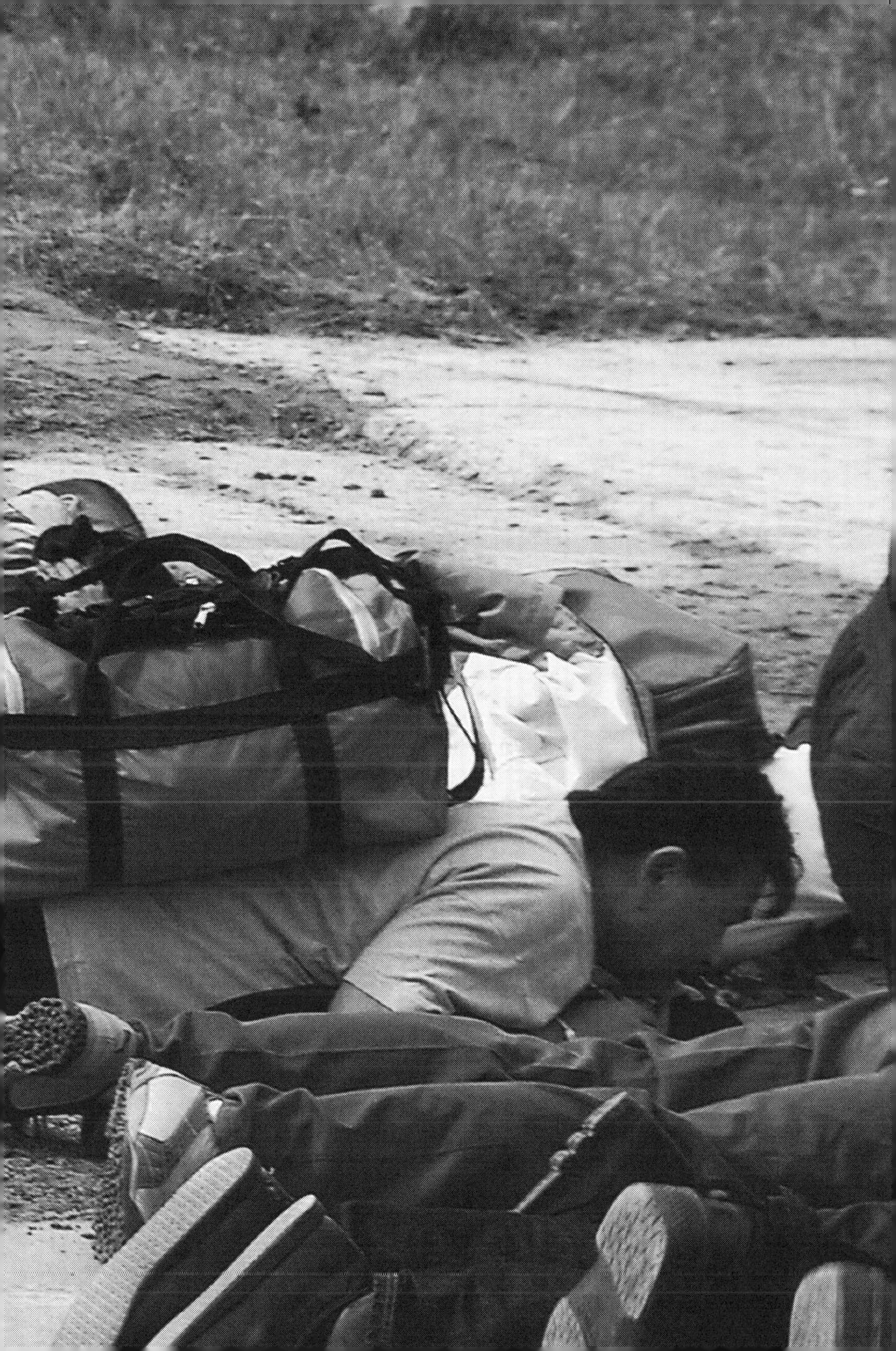

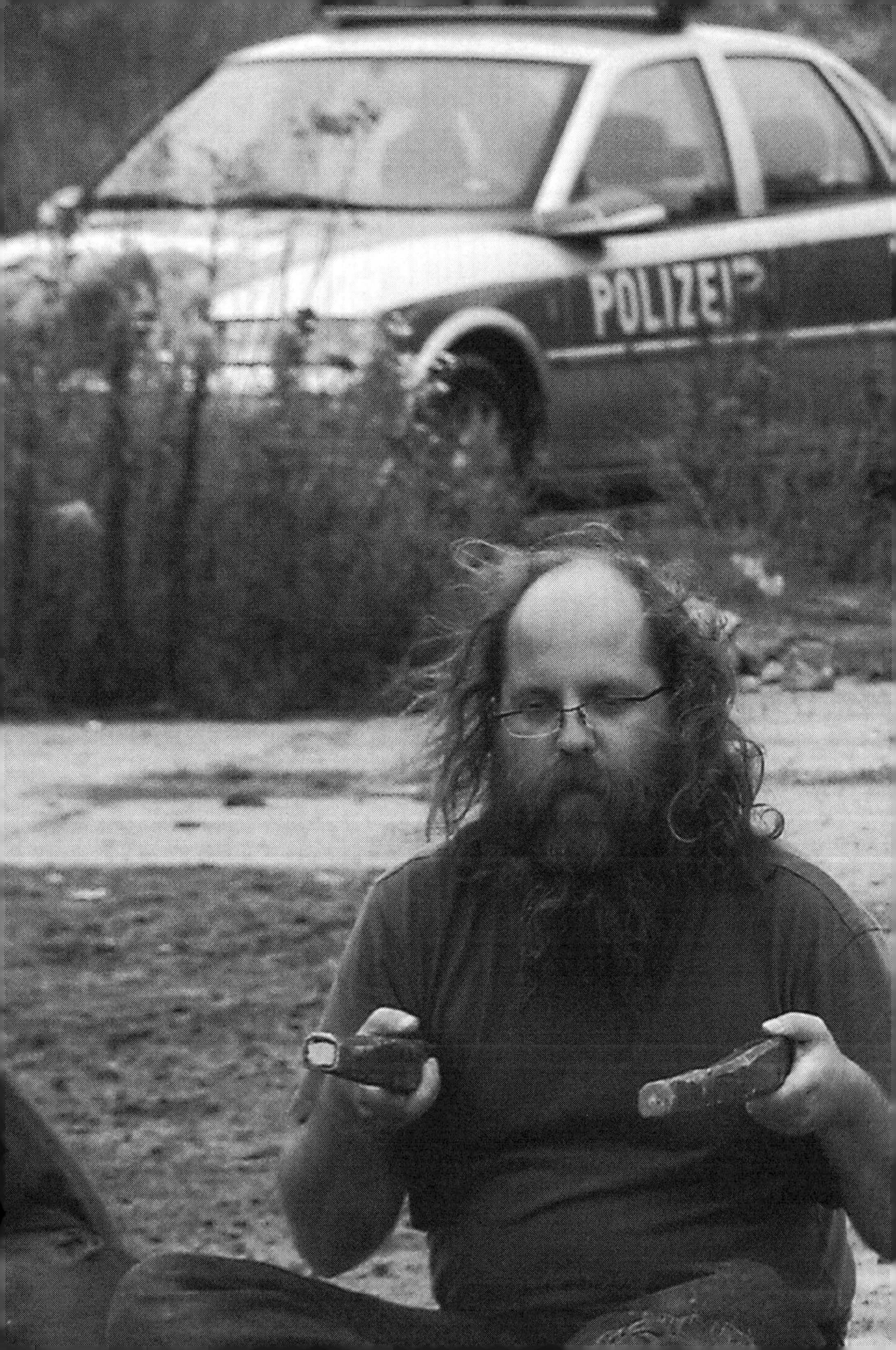
POLIZEI

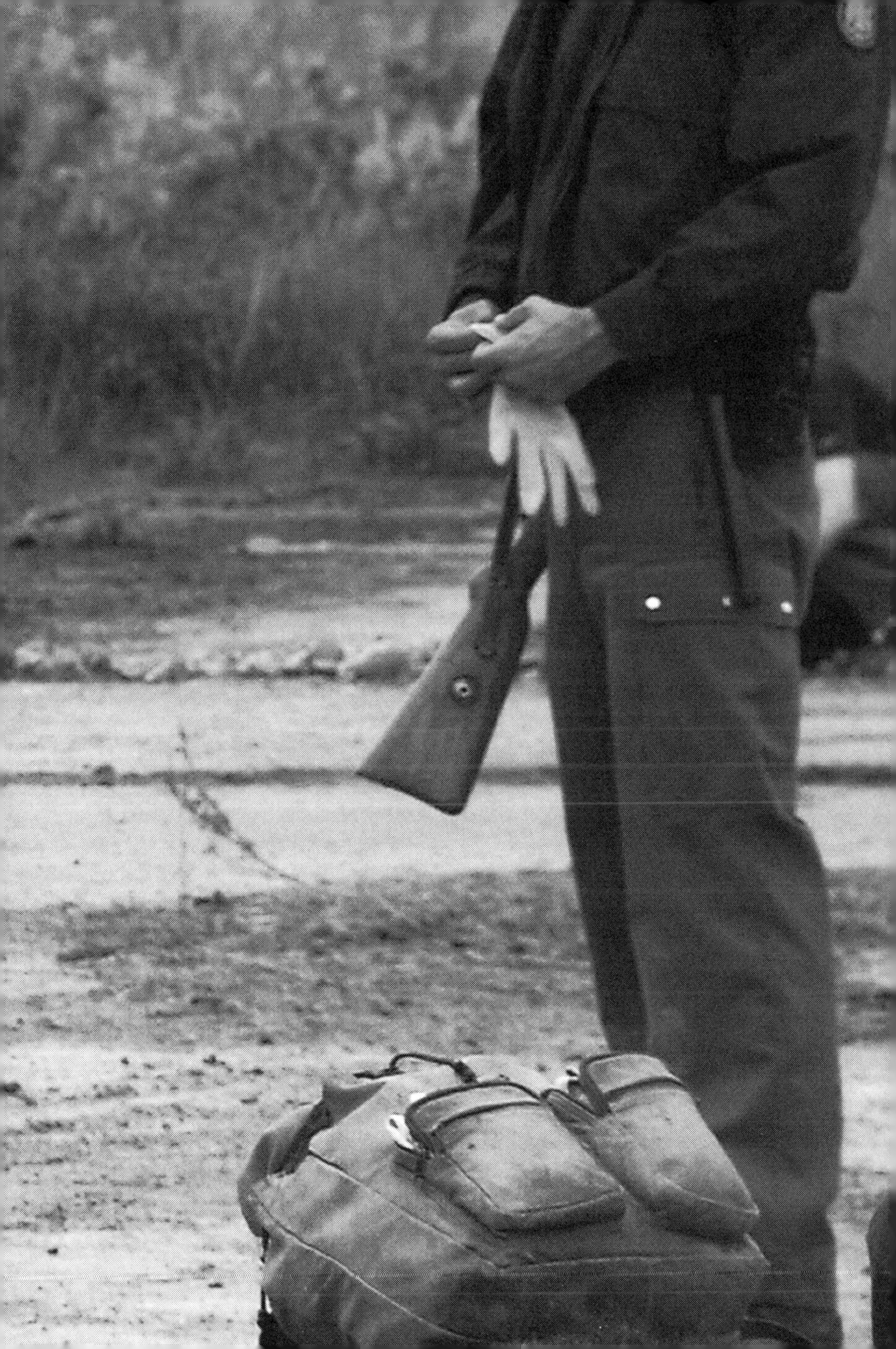

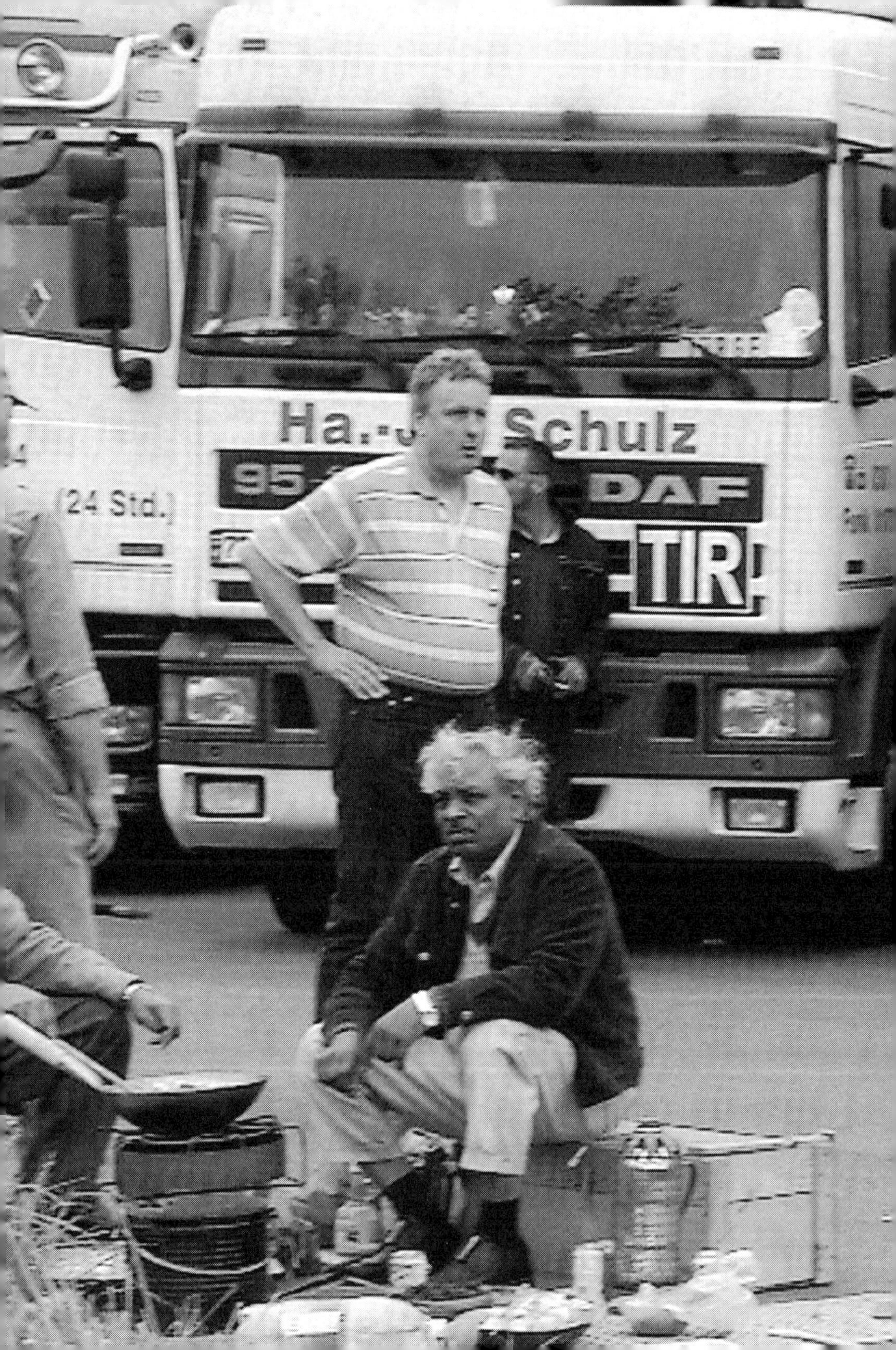

Ha..-Schulz
95
(24 Std.)
DAF
TIR

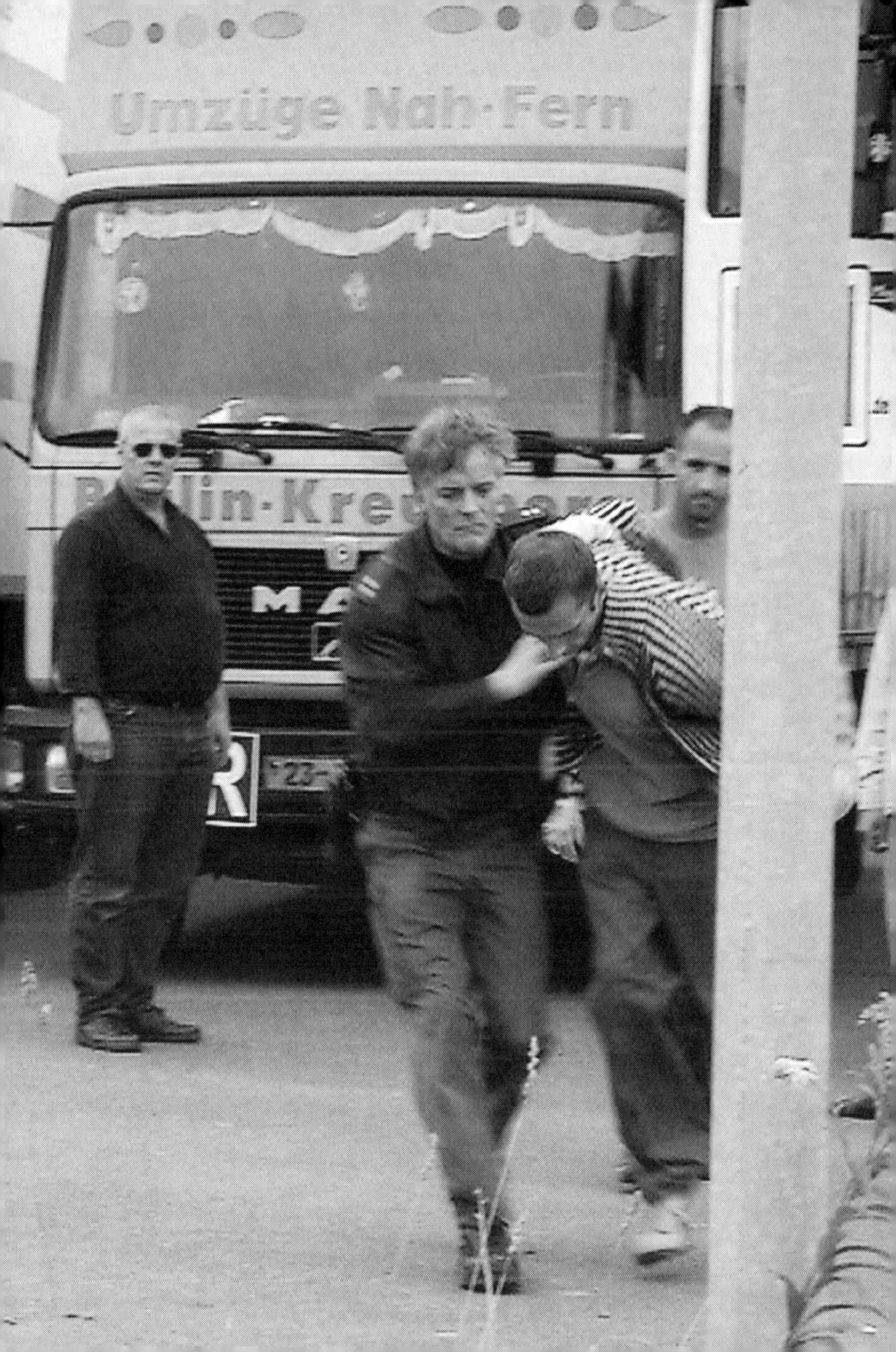
Umzüge Nah·Fern
Berlin-Kreuzberg
MAN

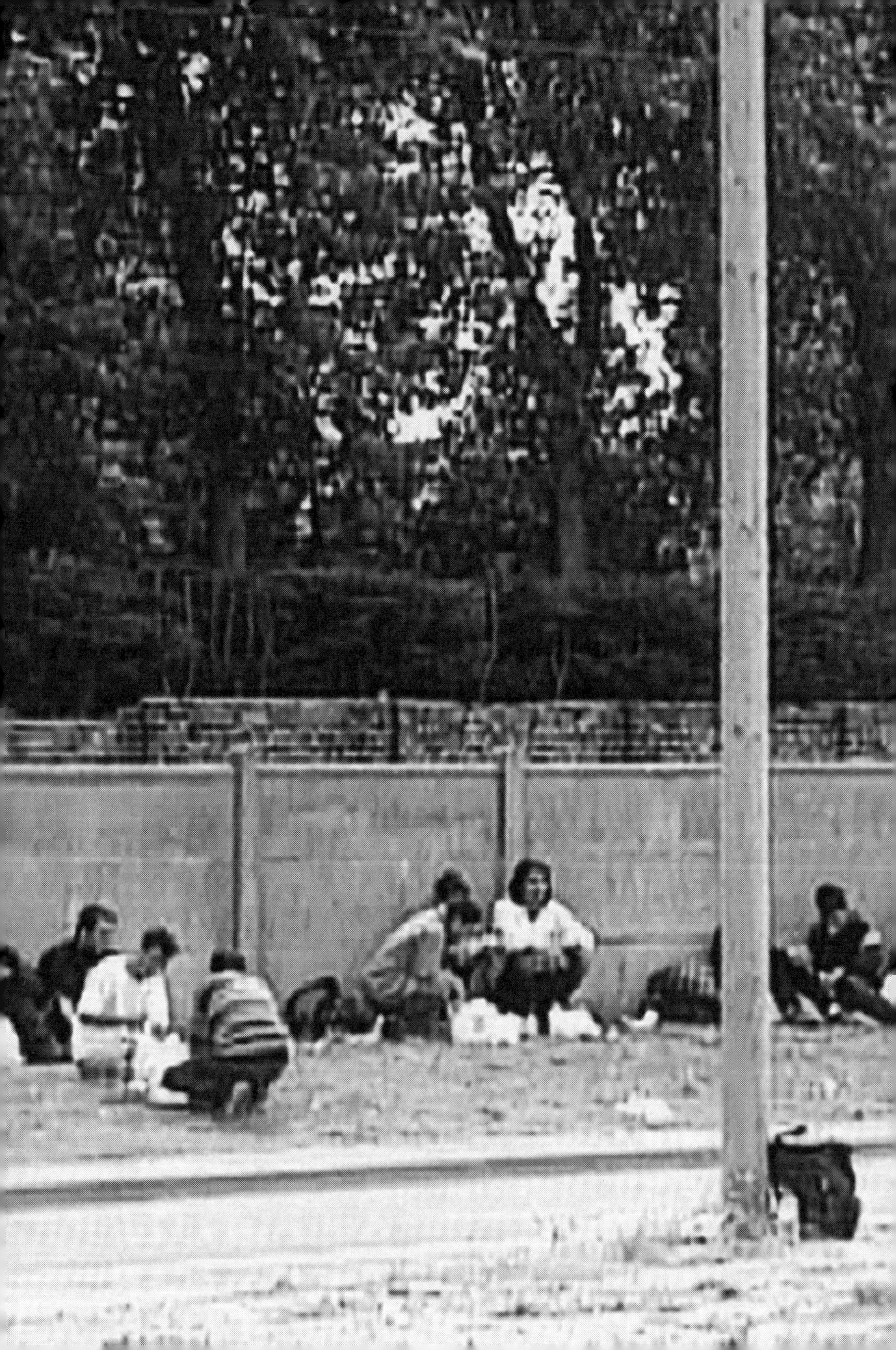

# '*Ik is een allochtoon*'
# A Conversation with Marlene Dumas

**Maria Hlavajova** I would very much like to discuss the recent series of paintings that you exhibited in 2006 under the title *Man Kind*. The series of portraits depicts young men who might be recognized by the viewer as terrorists or suicide bombers, but could equally 'just' be the (immigrant) neighbours from around the block (*Young Men* (2002–2005), *The Believer* (2005), *Look-alike* (2005) and *The Neighbour* (2005)). Would it be correct to say, in your opinion, that the portraits navigate through the condition of fear we experience currently in the so-called West? Could you tell us what prompted you to engage with this subject?

> **Marlene Dumas** In *Man Kind* I painted a series of male subjects with a Mediterranean appearance, dark hair and often a beard. In the current context, these images are not innocent. They are charged with suspicion, although a Belgian politician, a Dutch comedian and even a friend of my daughter – a Dutch boy of Moroccan ancestry – are among those portrayed. Encouraged by the media we almost 'wish' to see these images as images of terrorists. The painting series thus speaks about us rather than about 'them'.
>
> I am immersed in current affairs and politics as a sort of source material for what I then end up painting. I used to look only at the images, but nowadays I have become more and more aware of where the source comes from, who controls and who transmits the 'source'. But I also have to stress that I have never looked at any image as innocent. As I wrote in the catalogue *Suspect* (2003):
>
> Looking at images does not lead us to the truth.
> It leads us into temptation.
>
> It's not that a medium dies.
> It's that all media have become suspect.
> It's not the artist's subject matter that's under fire,
> but their motivation that's on trial.
> Now that we know that images can mean whatever,
> who ever wants them to mean, we don't trust anybody
> anymore, especially ourselves.

**MH** You refer directly to imagery from the mass media; you choose to paint and draw from photographs that you either

gather from newspapers and magazines, or which you have
taken yourself. The starting point of your relationship with the
viewer thus can be imagined as one of familiarity. Yet, you put
this familiarity to the test when giving your works titles that
undermine the possibility of reducing the interpretation to the
known or even to the cliché. In this way you infuse the work, in
my opinion, with great ambiguity. This, in turn, creates a much
more dynamic relationship with the work. Is this also a way to,
'neutralize and even compensate for the image that we have
formed by way of the media' (Paul Andriesse)?

> **MD** No, not neutralize. I think I add to the image bank the
> viewers already have in their heads. All the images your
> conscious mind might have forgotten are stored among your
> other memories and get mixed up with your personal history.
> I'm talking about all the confusing collages that keep you
> awake at night. I cannot see how one can deal with represen-
> tations and reproductions in our times and not deal with
> ambiguity. But as you know, if you have ever laughed at
> something, it can never bear the same authority again. So
> maybe my work can unsettle some prejudices and make
> someone at least admit that they don't know what they see.
>
> Most people still assume that photography displays the 'truth'.
> My paintings cannot prove that something actually happened
> and do not pretend to. Even though everyone who under-
> stands the nature of images knows you can manipulate
> photography, one still uses photographs as some sort of
> authentication of experience or identification of persons. It is
> absurd – just think about it – that we believe photography still
> equates to truth. I call into question this notion of identity
> photographs in the *Man Kind* project. But this is not at all new
> in my work. I have always been especially interested in how
> different cultures deal with portraiture. How does one
> recognize someone? For me a good portrait conveys a point
> where attraction and alienation meet.

**Rosi Braidotti** Your South-African background seems to have
given you an immediate, almost 'epidermic' sensitivity to
political violence. Is that a sort of heritage you work with?

> **MD** I have never suffered from physical violence, but coming
> from South Africa made me more sensitive to how changes in

[1] [Ed]itorial note: *allochtoon* is a [a] demographic term that literally [mean]s 'originating from another [count]ry'. It is the opposite of [autoc]*htoon*, which refers to someone [born] in the Netherlands.

language affect the relationships between people. The political use of language during apartheid framed individuals as groups. That's why I object to the word *allochtoon*;[1] it affects people in the same way. You know, when I came to study in the Netherlands in the 1970s, I was really surprised about my generation, because they just had no sensitivity to political issues. It was perhaps because they had not experienced war or political crises of that kind; they 'just' missed the Second World War. They seemed to have no notion of guilt. Art was a quite normal thing to practice. I felt I had a duty towards politics but the politics seemed to mean, 'be part of a group' and art seemed to say, 'stay separate, independent'. I could not manage to bring the two together either! Politics demanded that one identify oneself as part of a specific culture with a common language, but in South Africa I saw the horror that results when a certain group tries to preserve a certain way of life and they do it in my name, to protect a static identity. Identity – I can't stand that word. When you hear it everywhere you know that a scared nation is scaring its own people. Look at the United States. Contrary to their rhetoric on peace and liberty, they have been at war – although not on their own territory – for many decades. This casts a whole new light on the event of 9/11 in my view. I feel great compassion for the victims of the attack and their families; however, there are different angles and political perspectives you can take when analysing the event. When I look back into this recent history through my archive of images, which I collected unsystematically and for different reasons, I still see a pattern emerging. I see a picture of a dead terrorist, hijacker or kamikaze. And if you see how long these things have been going on, you wonder why we still treat these events as exceptions; surely, they are an integral part of how international politics has been shaping up since the 1950s. The 'other' is also a mirror image of ourselves! Look in the mirror and talk to Al-Qaeda.

**RB** There is something that makes the Dutch memory very 'short term'. They don't seem to remember a lot; it is always about 'here and now'. They forget many things about their own history, particularly when it comes to violence. They talk as if terrorism had just been born yesterday, and elsewhere. I come from a very violent country, Italy, which gave the world many things, including fascism. But there is a public discussion

about it in Italy – also because of the terrorism of the 1970s.
So it's like in South Africa; people don't pretend that it is not
a problem or that it never happened before.

**MD** Dutch culture is open about the violence it has suffered –
like the bombing of Rotterdam by Nazi Germany, but it seems
that they don't feel as if they've ever committed any violence
or, as someone once said: they always left it behind, in far
away places, like in some of the colonies overseas. Colonialism matters a lot in this respect.

**RB** How do you think this plays out in the current Dutch
situation?

**MD** Let's take an idea that is important for me: 'hybridity'.
Hybridity has been around in the art world for a while as a
serious concept to work with. But in Dutch politics I haven't
heard it at all. I remember when I came here to study; it was in
the 1970s as I said, and South Africa was really at its political
worst. The public mobilization and protest against apartheid
in Holland seemed huge, though simultaneously, it provided
an opportunity for gatherings and even picnicking together!
As a South African I felt very uncomfortable indeed because
back home you could get killed and here, of course, there was
not that threat. Anyway, my point is that at least there was
mass protest then, but now?

**MH** How does an artist respond to the urgencies of this kind?
Could you tell us how you see that art actually can – or should –
relate to concrete political issues?

**MD** An artist can also respond as a person. One cannot
compete on all levels and I am not prepared to speak the way
politicians do. But I am interested in a public discourse about
important issues of our times. One can do it through writing,
for example, like Donald Judd. When the Gulf War started he
changed his text in an exhibition catalogue into a manifesto
against the war. I was so impressed.

**MH** You are a very good writer yourself – and that reminds
me of a question I wanted to ask. In one of your recent poems
(*Pretty Boys*, 2005) you wrote the following:

Once upon a time, you didn't exist
When I came here, to Holland (thirty years ago)
You didn't yet exist here then
(your fathers did, but they were different)
You didn't exist yet
As The Moroccan
As a specific group
As a concept
As a subject, as a picture
For every newspaper, TV, and magazine column
(I was not an 'allochtoon' yet
And so neither were you)
But when you came
So did the attraction and the fear.

I wanted you to expand a bit on the personal biography you
refer to in the poem. When and how does an artist like you,
born in South Africa as we discussed, living and working in
the Netherlands, become an *allochtoon*?

    **MD** Back when I first came to the Netherlands I was really
impressed by the hospitality extended to foreigners. There
were many things that did not impress me, like the weather
or the food, but this hospitality was really special.

**MH** How did that change and when?

    **MD** Those were strange times. I was very unhappy for personal
reasons, mainly because I could not understand the culture.
Besides, the Dutch looked extremely pale to me, not white but
very pale. I remember in those days meeting a black person on
the street was extremely rare. In Holland, in my generation of
students, they all said there were no Surinamese people in
their school . . . For me, the more 'colourful' the country was
becoming, the happier and more at home I felt. Only the Dutch
grew more anxious, so it seems. You have to understand my
point of view: the Dutch back in South Africa have a rather
terrible history of racism. So this was a complex legacy for me.
I spoke Afrikaans and in that sense the relationship to Holland

remained sort of unresolved. We were, because of the
language, Dutch but not quite Dutch. We were not *allochtoon*
for the same reason, until we became it.

The term was introduced in 1971 to replace the term 'immigrant',
but it was not actually used that much. Later the meaning
started shifting and changing till it became pejorative. Now it
is mostly applied to a 'non-western' person, which means
black or Muslim. It just polarized the society more and more.
It was not so much that I was treated as an *allochtoon*, as I am
white, but I was not Dutch either. That is why, and out of
solidarity, I once made a T-shirt for myself, which read: '*Ik is
een allochtoon*' – 'I is an *allochtoon*'. I remember my daughter
being embarrassed about how I wrote it! Yet she was the one
who brought me in closer contact to some of the *allochtoon*
families in Amsterdam. When she became a teenager, she
specifically fell in love with boys classified as such. Therefore
my poem continues:

You the Mediterranean type
The physiognomy of the Latin lover
The Arab on the white scooter
The lover boy, the rapper, the Palestinian brother.
And the Dutch daughters fell I love
And their fathers grew confused
And called all Turks Moroccans
(All Moroccans are named Mohammed, Rashid or Ali
and all Dutch boys are named Piet or Jan)
Her new Turkish boyfriend said;
Your father and I have at least
One thing in common:
Neither of us likes
Moroccans

**RB** Dutch politicians are not pushing the cause of mixed
cultural identities and multiple belongings. They talk about
multiculturalism as if it is now officially dead. They don't want
a multicultural society and they talk about this otherness with
a touch of disrespect. There's a lot of cheap populism going
around. I do think however that there are other forces in Dutch
society that would like to work towards a transversal idea of
citizenship, based on participation and involvement, not on
cultural sameness.

One of the explanations we give in social theory for the recent
swing to populism is that the poor, dispossessed whites in
Holland but also in Flanders have switched from being
progressive and leftwing to being racist. Actually we have to
look at the behaviour of whites and at the category of
'whiteness', which is proto-fascist and objectionable, but also
invisible and all the more powerful because it is taken for
granted as the norm.

> **MD** Yes, I can understand that. I know that the poorer classes
> tend to always be the most openly racist, because they have
> the most to lose. In South Africa, my brother was a minister in
> the church. He was in a church in an area populated by white
> miners in Johannesburg and they liked him a lot. But when he
> said that the church had to be opened to all races, they kicked
> him out. But what was very interesting was this switch. He had
> so many white, religious working-class members and they
> really loved him, but when he said, 'If you're Christian, as you
> say you are, you cannot believe that all people are not equal
> in the eyes of God.' And then they turned against him.
> Sometimes a job is worth more than a belief.

**RB** But the Dutch situation is complicated by a few extra
factors. In Holland the switch happened with Pim Fortuyn, in
fact on issues of civil rights. Fortuyn used gay rights against
Muslims. I have a lot of students living in working-class
neighbourhoods and when they went into the neighbourhood,
they knocked on the door and literally said, 'We're a lesbian
couple, and do you mind if we move here?' And the people
said, 'No, because you're one of us.' So when did lesbians and
gays become part of the Dutch working class? That class, to
which I also belong by background, is notoriously homophobic.
This combination of factors makes it difficult to explain the
current Dutch crisis to the outside world.

> **MD** That was the progressive aspect of Fortuyn – his position
> on gay rights. I did enjoy some of his interviews. I didn't totally
> dislike him because he made me laugh.

**MH** I recall you saying, 'South Africa is my content and
Holland is my form.' Do you ever think of yourself as a Dutch
artist?

**MD** South Africa taught me that everything is worth loving and Holland taught me that not everything is worth painting. I have travelled to all sorts of places for my shows but I have only actually worked in two places in my life: South Africa, where I grew up, and Holland, where I live and have my studio. In fact, if I were to choose a nationality for myself it would be that of an Amsterdamer – this city is my place. And my studio is my home. This makes me think of a line from a love song: 'Home is where the heart is and my heart is anywhere you are.'

This brings me to the issue of dual citizenship, a theme currently discussed in the Dutch Parliament. Ideally I would like us to care about everybody, ideally I would like us to have a universal mankind, but one cannot, it's like having too many lovers or something . . . Unfortunately, there are limits to how cosmopolitan one can be. Loving your neighbour is already impossible. But that is nothing to be proud of. Everyone should love at least two countries. That one physically cannot be in two places at the same time is one of the saddest truths of life. But that one's spirit can be in more than one place at a time, that makes for imagination. If you ask me if I am Dutch, and I think about all the things that I don't like about the Dutch, then I'll say no, I am not Dutch. But when I go to South Africa, then they say I've become quite Dutch.

**MH** I would like to quote your earlier writing one more time: 'Art is not a mirror. Art is a translation of that which you do not know, but of which you want to convince others or rather, that which no one knows . . . ' Could this be, on an abstract level, a place for art in the process you suggest we all need to engage with, a place in which to articulate a new grammar of how to coexist in diversity at times like this? It sounds to me like a good point from which to depart.

    **MD** Yes. But I would like to add . . .

**The Fog of War**

Here is to the dead, those killed, for us, and by us.
To those who are dying now.
To the 'incidents' that happen.
The occupations that continue.
The mindless glorification of military solutions.
The terminology that grows softer,
as attitudes harden and hatred increases.
Inventions not to lighten the load,
but to erase the road.

Operation Rainbow, Operation Enduring Freedom
Operation Summerrain . . . it sounds as sweet and coy,
as calling the bomb on Hiroshima – Little Boy.

There must be other ways, to deal with the pain.
To not side-step the blame or to mask our shame.
Diplomats specialize in refraining from it,
while the civilians die for it.

It's a war against terror, one is sold,
but one cannot fight a 'noun',  I was told.
One cannot colonize a land if you call it empty,
but when you do a body count, you'll find plenty.

I've always been afraid of dying
in a foreign land
and to not feel at home in that sand.
Where would death find me and by what hand?

Then I heard that someone said:
'We shall die in these bodies.
This is one thing certain of your place of death;
you are there now,
you sit within your corpses; look no further:
there where you are
you will die.'


Amsterdam, September 2006


 *'Ik is een allochtoon'*
A Conversation with Marlene Dumas

**MAN KIND**
*(or here's to those who inspired me)*

This is not the times
for The Family of Man's smiles.
We travel in disguise,
so how would you know
friend from foe?

The devil is back, as two-faced
and as polarizing as ever.
Who's side you are on
depends on where you're from.

But for those of us like Edward Said
the tension between
the first names and last
determines what comes to pass.

Here is to the popular culture
of image suppliers,
the embedded journalists, the media managers,
the hotel warriors and the airport artists.

Here's to portraiture, more or less,
used by polititians, martyrs, murderers,
the military . . . be my guest

Here's to the skull of Charlotte Corday
who assasinated Marat, quite calmly they say
and faced the guillotine without rage
at 24 years of age.

Here's to the posters that Ad van Denderen
photographed in the region of the West Bank.
Here's to the Israeli soldiers who refuse to fight
in the occupied territiories.

Here's to Amos Oz who spoke about the fact
that the Jews and the Arabs are both
former victims of the same oppressor.
This makes their conflict harder not easier.
They have both been humiliated,

discriminated and persecuted by
European Civilization.

Here's to the guys that took a trip from Birmingham
to Pakistan, and then to Afghanistan, but met the USA,
and ended up in Guantanamo bay.

Here's to the actors of Shouf Shouf Habibi.
Here's to the boys in the streets of Amsterdam.
Here's to the difference between forgetting and forgiving.
Here's to the distinctions between, freedom, fate
and destiny.

Here's to where we start and where we go from there.
Here's to the fact that life is round
and what comes around
stays around
and for better or worse
we  are part of the same kind.

Amsterdam, September 2006


*This conversation took place on 6 March 2007 in Amsterdam.*


***'Ik is een allochtoon'***
A Conversation with Marlene Dumas

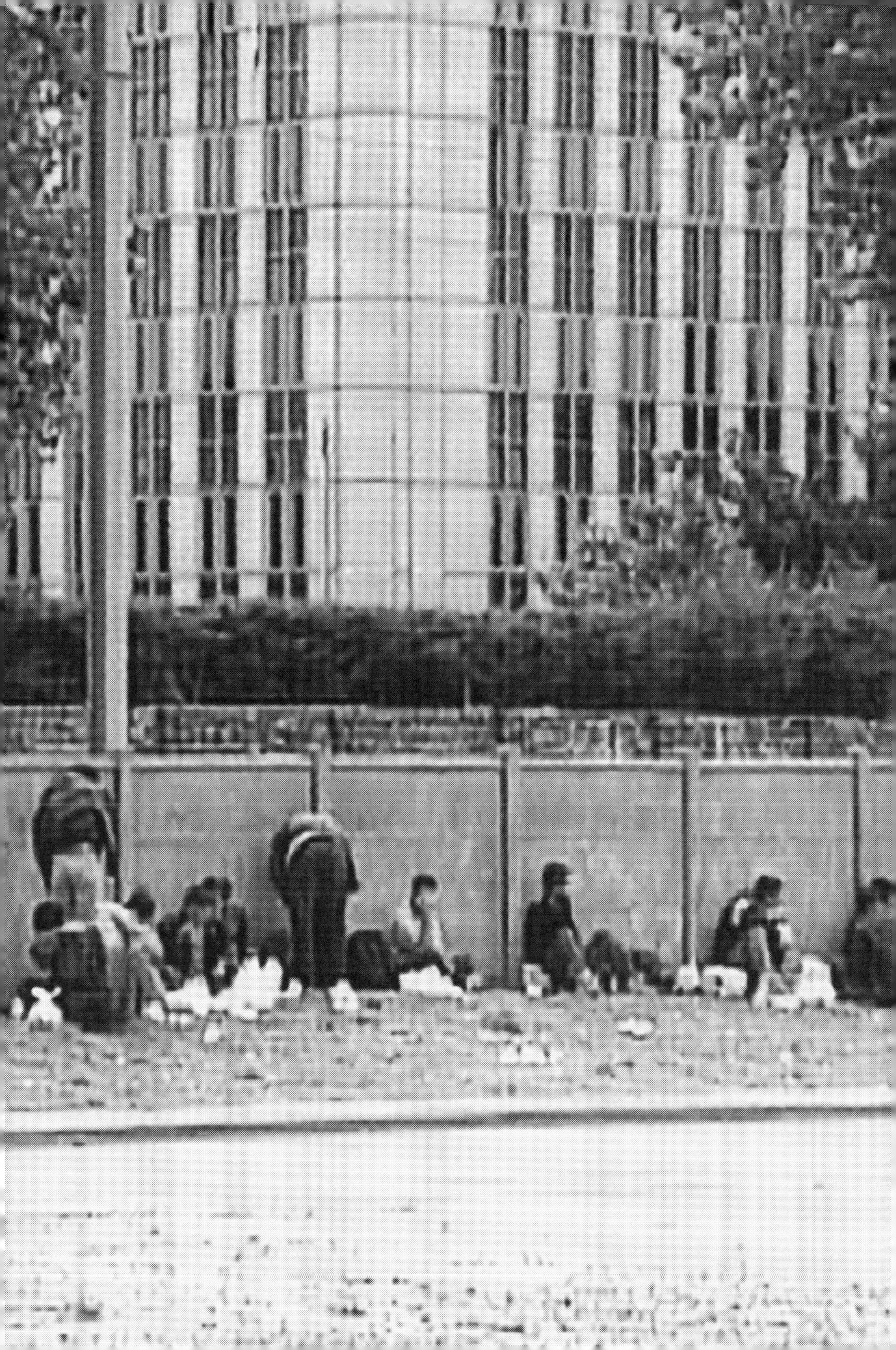

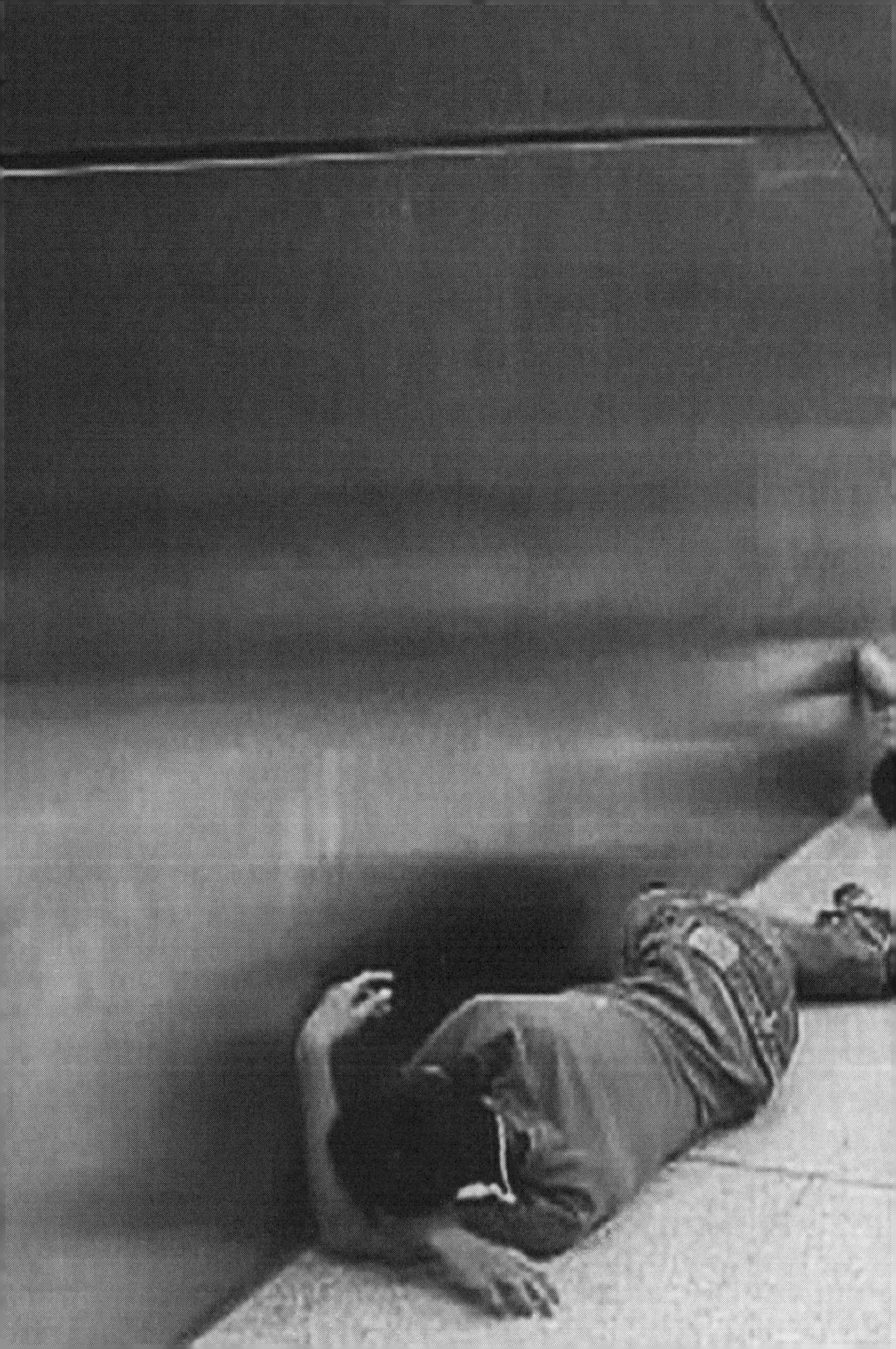

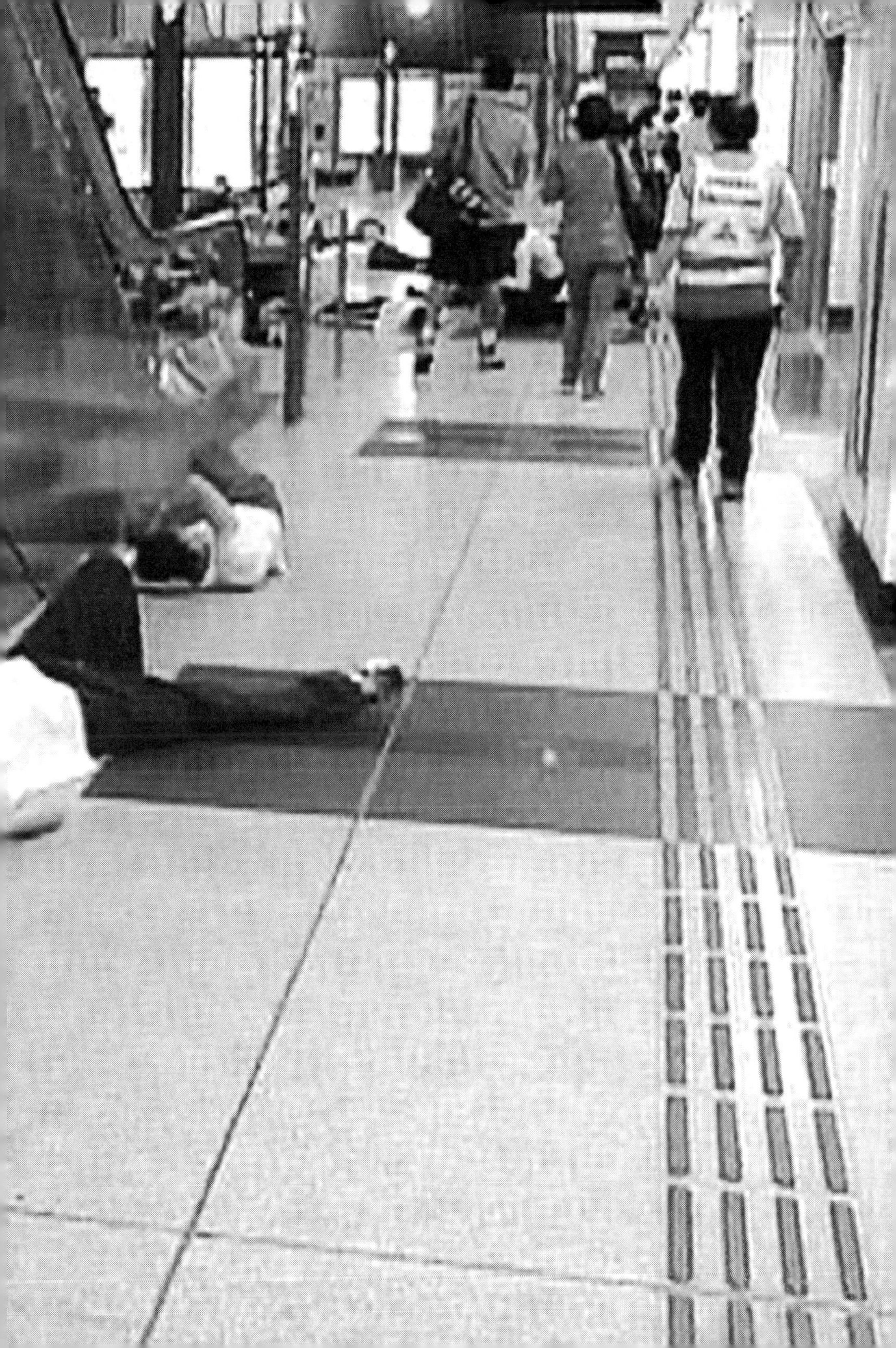

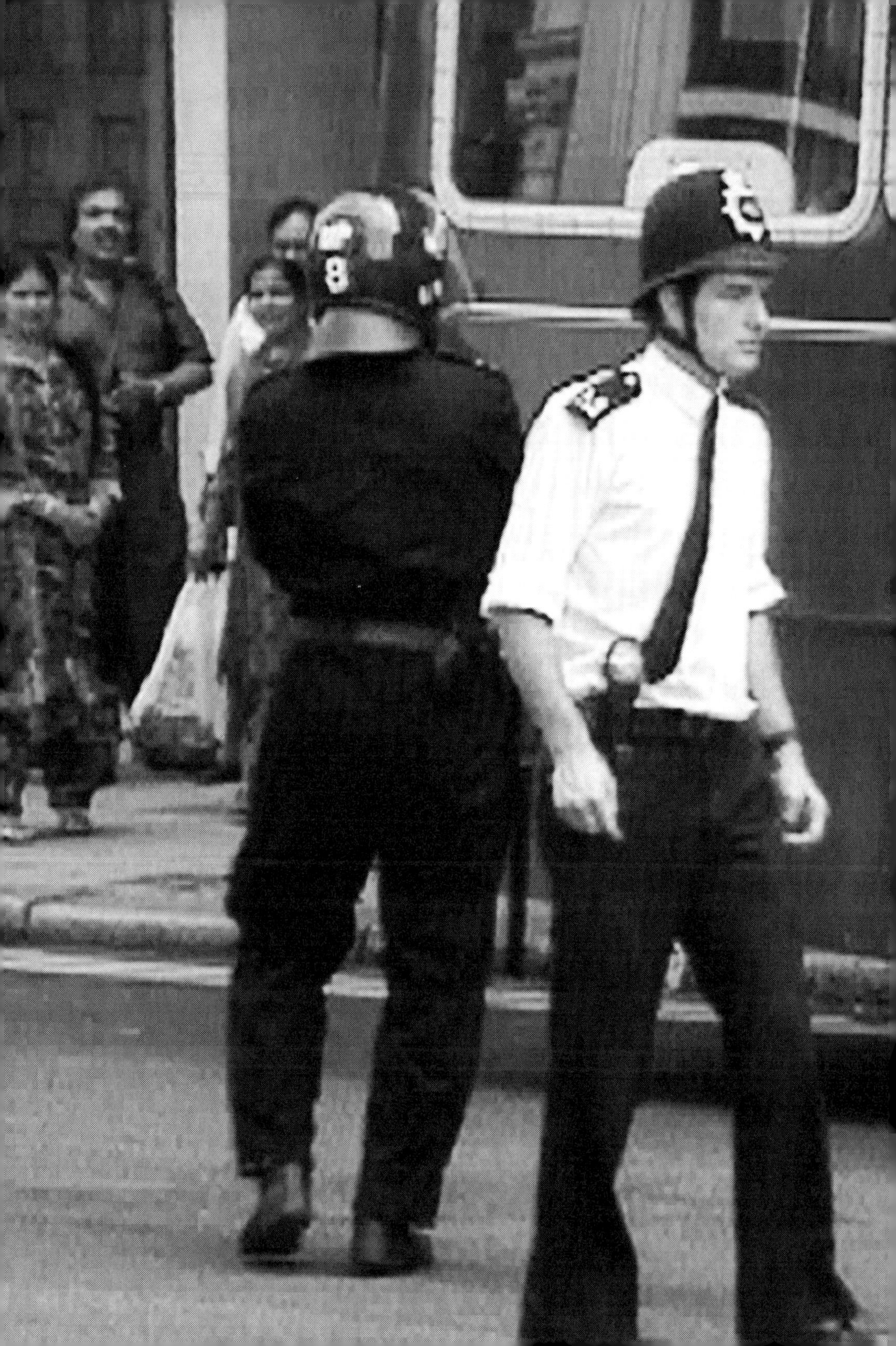

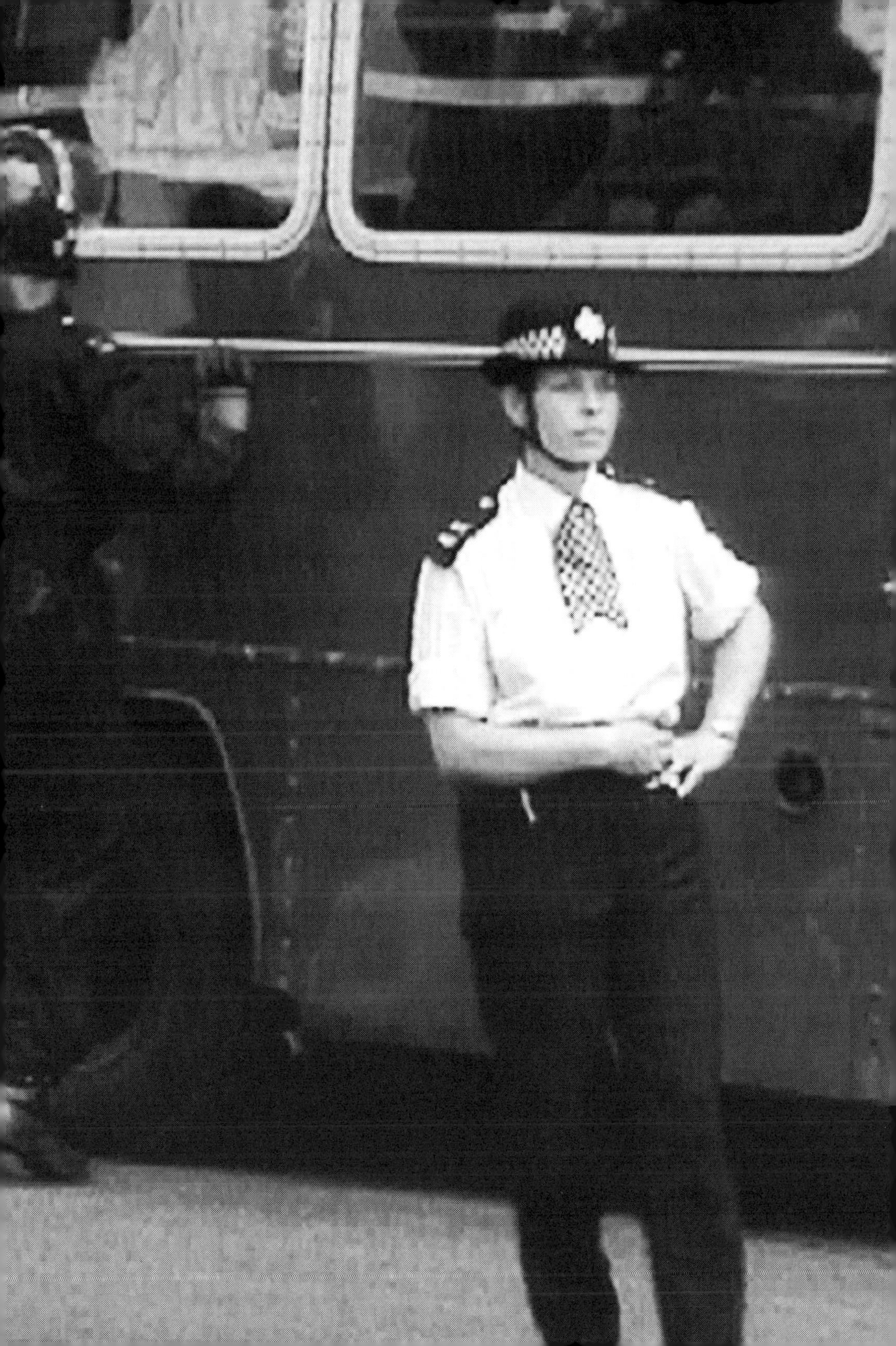

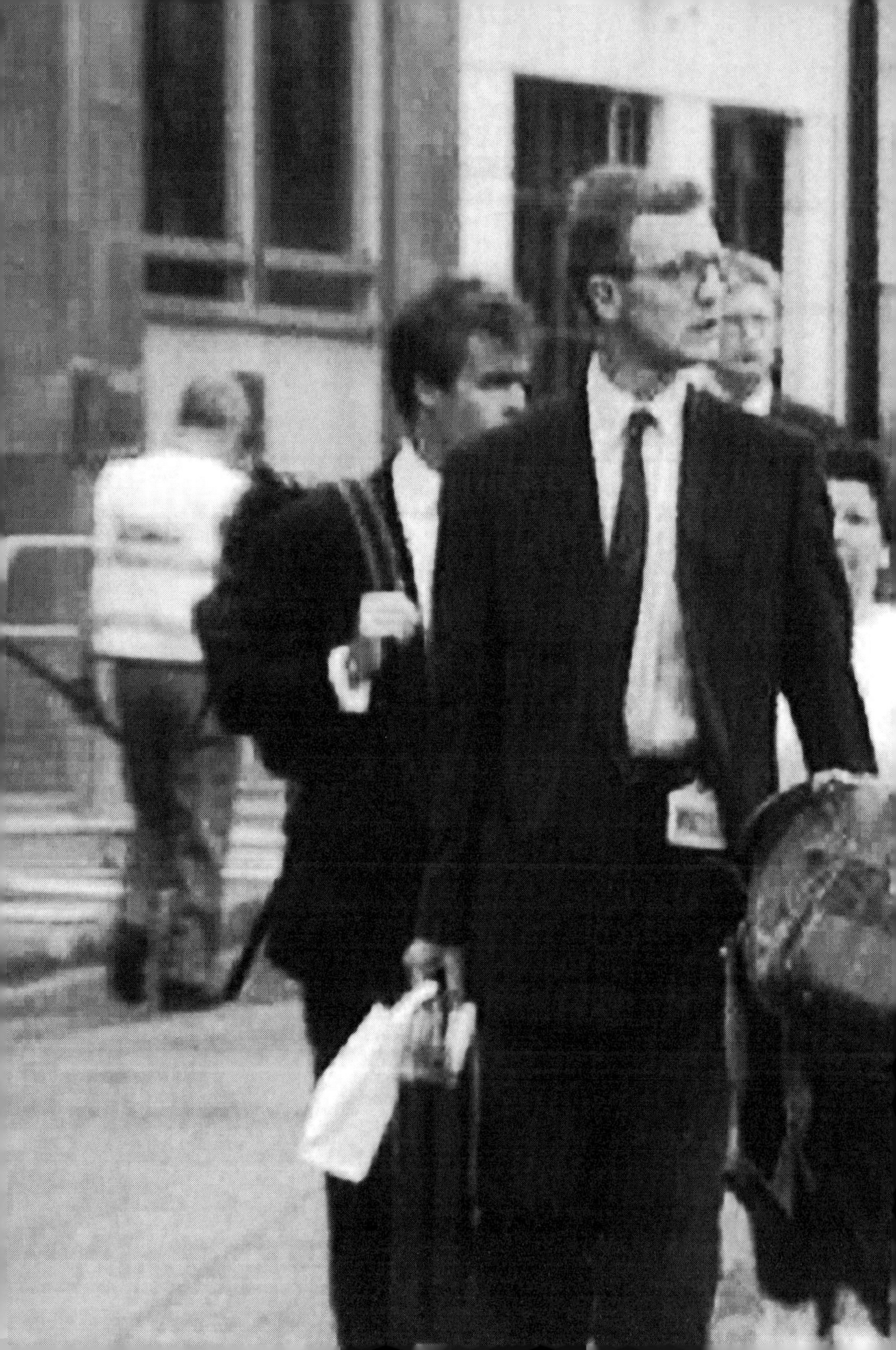

# Who Dares to Experiment with Culture?

Halleh Ghorashi

## The background of culturalist thinking

The dominant Dutch discourse regarding new migrants from Islamic countries has always been culturalist, in that it restricted individual identities to a set of assumed cultural norms based on birthplace or up-bringing. Right from the start, the culture of these migrants was considered to deviate from Dutch norms.[1] This attitude is founded on a static and essentialist approach to culture. Such an approach leaves little space for individual or communal interpretations, simultaneously emphasizes culture over social and economic factors and freezes cultural practices as unalterable.

The dominant discourse – as expressed in policies, political debate and public discussion – has shifted several times in recent decades. In the 1970s, it focused on the preservation of migrants' cultures as separate elements tolerated within Dutch society. The idea was that the so-called 'guest labour' migrants would eventually return to their homelands, so there was no need for them to integrate into Dutch society. Later, when it became clear that they would remain permanently, policies shifted towards integration into Dutch society while simultaneously preserving the migrants' own cultures. This meant much more attention to policies for developing language skills and encouraging the equal participation of migrants in society. At present, the central idea is that attacking so-called 'culture-based crime' and making civic integration mandatory is conducive to the same form of integration. The prevailing position is that in order to become 'Dutch' one needs to distance oneself from one's own cultural background. The main argument for this new shift is that the integration polices of the 1980s were not effective enough because migrants were never forced to integrate. The claim of 'indifference' regarding the policies of those years was related to a 'politically correct' attitude, which supposedly made it impossible to expect anything from migrants. It would seem, therefore, as if the discourse has had a complete makeover in terms of content. It is widely believed that the much-criticized approach of 'indifference' has been abandoned and that a shift has taken place towards the 'real' integration of the migrants – that the years of 'soft policies' are over. However, despite all the shifts within the discourse relating to migrant issues, its aim has hardly changed at all. This is because categorical thinking, in particular a culturalist approach, has remained a crucial feature of thinking about migrant issues in the Netherlands.

In order to be able to understand the dominant culturalist discourse in Dutch society, it needs to be situated within the context of pillarisation. The construction of pillars – 'own worlds' – along lines of religious

e Ghorashi 2006 and Rath 1991,
g others.



**Who Dares to Experiment with Culture?**
Halleh Ghorashi

denomination and political ideology after the Second World War has been the dominant framework for thinking about differences in the Netherlands. Pillars were social organizations based on religious and ideological affiliations. In the period of pillarisation, children were raised exclusively within the boundaries of their own somewhat 'closed' communities. The membership in a pillar determined the choice of schools, playgrounds and social contacts. During that period, pillars functioned as an intermediary between individuals and the state, particularly in areas of health care and education, which were either self-financed or based on state subsidies. Before the existence of a strong welfare state developed in the Netherlands in the 1960s, pillars served as safety nets and as such were believed by some to be emancipatory for their members. Eventually the increasing role of the state in social affairs led to secularisation and individualization of society and made the existence of pillars unnecessary and also unwanted. The contemporary spirit of depillarisation strongly dislikes the religion-based group formations of the pillarisation period.

Nevertheless, some aspects of the pillarisation model are still present. For example, tolerance was the main concept of the period, in which different pillars joined together, tolerating the other, to create a peaceful state based on consensus. Yet, tolerance was primarily understood as letting others be. Here boundaries and distance play an essential role. Not much space exists for interaction between different ideas, but rather a respect for boundaries reigns. 'The other' should be tolerated: 'leave them as they are.' In this way tolerance becomes a sign of indifference that excludes interaction between groups. The lack of interaction has led to a fear of the unknown, demonstrated by recent statements in favour of assimilation. This limited form of tolerance has not been able to change the negative approach towards migration and difference. It made the dichotomy between us and them even stronger, because the emphasis on tolerance is about distance and not respect for difference.

This dichotomy, with its emphasis on group boundaries, has latently shaped the ways in which new migrants have been approached. The consequences of this history of pillarisation for migrants have been especially evident for those from Islamic countries in the 1970s and 1980s: they were mentally fit into a new kind of Islamic pillar. This has caused new migrants from Islamic countries to find themselves in a confusing area of tension. The historical habit of thinking in terms of pillars was translated into the migrants' condition and left – and even created – space for these migrants to preserve their cultures. Paradoxically, that happened historically just as the pillarisation model was beginning to shift, in what many believed was a depillarised Netherlands in which individual autonomy prevailed and was protected. Thinking in terms of pillars has had a much wider effect than on Islamic migrants alone. To a certain extent, it has demarcated thinking about cultural differences and ethnic boundaries in general. This has led to the creation of cultural contrasts that make it virtually impossible to consider the individual migrant as separate from his or her cultural or ethnic category.

In the era that is now commonly called the post-Fortuyn period, that is in the last five to eight years, we have seen new modes of categorical thinking arise. The emphasis on the negative consequences of cultural contrasts or culturalization has gained much greater prominence and is now in evidenced in the 'Islamization' of discourse. Even though much influenced by the habitus of pillarisation, this new discourse of cultural contrasts breaks with the spirit of that time in its attack on the tolerance of difference and its claim of assimilation. From the 1970s, the discussion about migrants in the Netherlands has been alert to the possible threat cultural differences might pose to society. And yet, the most conspicuous feature of this period was its emphasis on socio-economic disadvantage and the optimistic view that the integration of Muslim migrants would eventually succeed. What has changed considerably however, since 2000, is a shift in tone, demanding that 'we must be allowed to say what we think', something which Baukje Prins has termed the era of 'new realism'.[2] I argue that this new realism in the Netherlands would never have acquired such a following if the basic assumptions of culturally essentialist categorical thinking had not already been present in the dominant discourse on migrants for many years. This means that – despite the tough language on the integration efforts of the past – in its substance, the new realism is entirely in line with the categorical thinking of recent decades. Both are rooted in thinking in terms of cultural contrasts and in the conviction that migrants are at a disadvantage and need to be rid of this disadvantage. There have been shifts in tone (from soft to harsh), in focus (from socio-economic to socio-cultural) and in outlook (from optimistic to pessimistic), but these are merely differences of degree.

## New realism and the emancipation project

In spite of the existence of culturalist thinking in the past, the position of migrant women has been invisible until recently, when this invisibility changed into extreme visibility. Now migrant women are seen as suppressed and in need of help in their path to emancipation. Many attribute this visibility to Ayaan Hirsi Ali and the ways that she has been able to introduce this issue to the political and public agenda. As a result,

r a further discussion of
'ealism', see Prins's text is this
1e.

current emancipation policies focus expressly on the emancipation of women of non-Dutch origin and, within this group, mainly on Islamic women. In late 2005, the conclusions of a European study on the emancipation of women in several European countries were presented.[3] One finding was that, in contrast to other European countries, emancipation in the Netherlands tends to be culturalized, meaning that emancipation issues are often linked to cultural/ethnic groups. Within this framework, we can observe that issues such as honour killing, forced marriages and female circumcision are commonly discussed in the public arena and have gained political priority. The most prominent aspect of the debates in the public sphere has been the images of migrant men as aggressors and of migrant women as passive victims. In addition, violence is often described exclusively through culture. This means that the social and economic aspects of the question are downplayed, if not ignored completely.

As a result of these developments within the new realist framework, we see that Dutch society is becoming harsh: it has become quite common to disrespect migrants' culture and religion in public, to call them backward and inherently undemocratic. An example of these developments – tightening of the rules, regulations and attitudes towards migrants – affected Hirsi Ali as well when it came to the dispute over her Dutch citizenship. Both the national and international media covered this issue extensively. The case of Hirsi Ali shows that the 'rightist', 'new realist' turn within the discourse on integration and migration did not even safeguard the position of one of the most integrated, if not assimilated, non-native Dutch people in the country, not to mention that Hirsi Ali herself was one of the key contributors to this culturalist discourse on migrants. These examples show that the culturalist discourse has gone so far that it has mainly contributed to growing fear, insecurity and absurdity instead of working towards new insights on diversity and migration for the future. Having said that, the question remains whether the intention of the new realist movement is to work towards new insights regarding the challenges of the new Netherlands, let alone to improve the position of the migrants in the society. Recent developments express a growing political opportunism in which the existing fears and insecurities in society are used and exaggerated to empower rightist, anti-immigrant goals.

### The way forward

My central criticism of the culturalist approach is that cultural categories are being made into absolute contrasts. In the social sciences, this type of conception of culture has been criticized since the 1960s, when the

[3] See http://www.mageeq.net (accessed 13 March 2007).

anthropologist Fredrik Barth (1969) argued that ethnic boundaries are not created and preserved by cultural content, but that these boundaries are constructed in order to pursue goals. Cultural characteristics are thrown into sharp relief precisely when they can be used to mark a difference between us and them. This means that ethnic boundaries between groups should chiefly be considered constructions that are situational, contextual and changeable, rather than entities that are inherent in the essence of different cultures. Thus, instead of emphasizing the essence of the Dutch or the migrant culture, we need to focus on the ways that defining these differences include or exclude people from becoming part of an 'imagined' nation. The increasing focus on Dutch culture as being 'Judaic-Christian-Humanist' and the growing interest in a Dutch historical canon are both examples of an essentialist approach, with its lack of focus on the ways that these constructions contribute to the exclusion of migrants (especially with an Islamic background) from the notion of 'Dutchness'.

A non-essentialist approach to identity leaves greater scope for analysing individual action with regard to the individual's own culture. The ways in which individuals perceive their culture and give meaning to it are diverse and variable. People are capable of criticizing their cultural habitus and opening themselves up to innovation and supplementation with new cultural elements. This often leads to diverse forms of connections. What is needed, however, for such reflection and innovation to be admitted is a feeling of security. The general precondition for reflection, therefore, is a safe space. When people feel excluded, threatened and coerced, they generally respond reactively. This considerably narrows people's space for making connections because it causes them to cut themselves off rather than open themselves up to potential new contacts and combinations. For people to open themselves up, they need to feel recognized in who they are: social recognition is of paramount importance for human development.

### Shaping a democratic culture

The necessity of social recognition of one's cultural background or cultural recognition is that it is part and parcel of a democratic culture. Democracy goes beyond the liberty to go to the polls. In contrast to what is often maintained, democracy is not just about the majority, but it is particularly about space for the minority. This is exactly what constitutes the difference between a constitutional democracy and a populist democracy: in the latter, the voice of the majority is given a relatively free reign but the voice of the minority is not secured. Democracy without opposition is not a democracy. A democratic outlook implies that you accept from the very start that another person may be different. A democratic structure does not amount to much without a democratic culture, and a democratic culture is only feasible if it takes not *the I* but *the other* as its starting point.

This basic precondition for a democratic way of life requires tolerance as an important democratic virtue. Tolerance served as the basis for maintaining unity in diversity when the Netherlands was a pillarised society. Experiences in the 1980s, however, demonstrated that tolerance conceived as *allowing space* – which may involve indifference – has not been enough to enable migrants to make an emotional commitment to Dutch society. For the new Netherlands, therefore, we need to take an additional step: not only allowing space but also *making space*.[4] This is about the will to meet the other, which requires the ability to make space or to step aside. This step to the side is an important and inevitable move in creating a common interspace in the new Netherlands, in which we can admit, meet and connect with the other and invite him or her into the common space of Dutch nationals.

### Making space for a new kind of Dutchness

The idea of the migrant as a guest has long lost its currency in the Netherlands, but the idea that migrants' most 'natural' link is the one they have with their country of origin is persistently dominant. You may be familiar with the oft-told joke by Ulrich Beck. A black man in Germany is asked: 'Where are you from?' He answers: 'From Munich.' Q: 'And your parents?' A: 'Also from Munich.' Q: 'And where were they born?' A: 'My mother in Munich.' Q: 'And your father?' A: 'In Ghana . . .' Q: 'Ah, so you're from Ghana.' Not so much a punch line as a stereotype, the joke reinforces the idea that the real, unbreakable tie a migrant has is to his or her 'country of origin', (which points to the event of the migration in the person's family), even if the person was born in his home country. This is evidently an either/or mode of thought: in order to become one, you must renounce the other. The recent debate on double nationality is a clear example of such thinking, in which a set of basic assumptions leaves little space for newly created identities that hold out possibilities for new combinations and new ways of being a Dutch national.

The dominance of the either/or scenario in the Netherlands is related to the construction of Dutch national identity. In my earlier work, I have shown that Dutch national identity is too 'thick'.[5] This renders it not comprehensive enough to be able to embrace the diversity of cultures present in the Netherlands. Until recently, Dutch national identity was hardly explicit, though there were implicit and unspoken notions about codes of

[4] In the way I elaborate the implications of this term, I was m inspired by the work of Janssens Steyaert (2001).

[5] See Ghorashi 2003. In makin distinction between 'thin' and 'thi constructions of national identitie I was inspired by Rawls's (1971, 198 distinction between thin universa and thick particularism in relatior pluralism. In addition, Stratton an Ang's (1998) work also helped me get a handle on the relation betw cultural diversity and national ide

conduct and appearance that established who was and who was not 'really' Dutch. The Dutch citizen has a body, which is white, and a religious background, which is Judeo-Christian. In line with categorical thinking, it has become self-evident that migrants, with their 'deviating' cultures, do indeed live in the Netherlands but can never be 'truly' Dutch. At the very most, they can hope to be assimilated into the community of 'solid citizens' that the Netherlands will tolerate. This unspoken, but all the same 'thick' notion of Dutch national identity has become more explicit over the past few years. These developments might mainly serve to further the assimilation of difference rather than help to open up a space for creating the kind of unity in diversity that does justice to a democratic culture.

In order to create a new unity in the Netherlands, it is essential for the Dutch national identity to be constructed as 'thinly' as possible, which would allow for differences to be included. This requires a redefinition of the Dutch national identity in which identity can function as a web that ties differences together instead of excluding them. The main condition for establishing such a common basis in the Netherlands is to take steps to create *interspaces* and, subsequently, to redefine what it means to be a Dutch national. These attempts at stepping aside and making connections would have to come from various sides. The new Dutch nationals will need to partly recognize the cultural patterns of their new country and make them their own; the 'indigenous' Dutch will need to make space for a new definition of Dutch national identity that will encompass the cultural diversity existing in the Netherlands. This is the only option for shaping a diverse society within a democratic and unequivocally constitutional state.

### Emancipation from the culturalist discourse
In my view, protecting the right to cultural difference and the claim to producing one's own culture are two essential ways to tackle the dominance of the culturalist discourse. In both, it seems that making space is essential. As the 2004 UNDP report shows, when individuals have the space and the right to their cultural identity, they feel safe enough to change and reshape their culture. In other words the space for cultural recognition seems to be an essential precondition for individuals to feel secure enough to experiment with their culture and to initiate new connections with the diversity of cultures in them or with other cultures. In addition to the right to cultural difference, it is essential to create space for producing cultural identity in the margins as a precondition of emancipation from the dominant discourse. Within this created safe space, self-narratives and self-appreciation seem to be crucial to resist the negative images produced by the dominant discourse.

The new culturalist approach, combined with a new attitude that allows 'everything to be said, never mind the consequences', has reached a point where it is beginning to erode the most valuable foundations of Dutch society. Many have already jettisoned one of the most important Dutch virtues, tolerance. The paradox, then, is that, at a time when an attempt to construct an essentialist Dutch identity with canonization and morals and values at its core, important historical Dutch virtues, such as openness and tolerance, are being violated. The breaking of taboos has tipped to such a point that Dutch communities find themselves pitted against each other. If culturally sensitive behaviour is our goal, we must first of all create an interspace for people to meet, recognize and acknowledge their similarities and differences. In a proper balance between being similar and being different, dialogue, encounter and innovation may arise. In the awareness that culture is only one aspect of our being together, working together and living together, ethnicity-transcending connections can be made. In the process, the role of art and literature could be crucial in creating interspaces and experimenting with cultural differences.

**Bibliography**

Barth, Fredrik. *Ethnic Groups and Boundaries: The Social Organization of Cultural Difference.* Boston: Little Brown, 1969.

Ghorashi, Halleh. 'Paradoxen van culturele erkenning: Management van diversiteit in nieuw Nederland'. Lecture presented at Vrije Universiteit, Amsterdam, 13 October 2006.

————. *Ways to Survive, Battles to Win: Iranian Women Exiles in the Netherlands and the United States.* New York: Nova Science Publishers, 2003.

Giddens, Anthony. *The Third Way: The Renewal of Social Democracy.* London: Polity Press, 1999.

IJsseling, Samuel. *Macht en onmacht.* Amsterdam: Boom, 1999.

Janssens, Maddy and Chris Steyaert. *Meerstemmigheid: Organiseren met verschil.* Leuven: Universitaire Pers Leuven, 2001.

Rath, Jan. *Minorisering: de sociale constructie van 'etnische minderheden'.* Amsterdam: Sua, 1991.

Rawls, John. *A Theory of Justice.* Cambridge: Harvard University Press/Belknap, 1971.

————. 'Kantian Constructivism in Moral Theory'. *The Journal of Philosophy* no. 9 (1977), 515–77.

Stratton, Jon and Ien Ang. 'Multicultural Imagined Communities: Cultural Difference and National Identity in the USA and Australia'. In *Multicultural States: Rethinking Difference and Identity*, ed. David Bennett. London/New York: Routledge, 1988, 135–163.

Taylor, Charles. *Multiculturalisme.* Amsterdam: Boom. 1995.

United Nations Development Programme (UNDP). *Human Development Report 2004: Cultural Liberty in Today's Diverse World.* New York: United Nations Development Programme, 2004.

 **Who Dares to Experiment with Culture?** Halleh Ghorashi

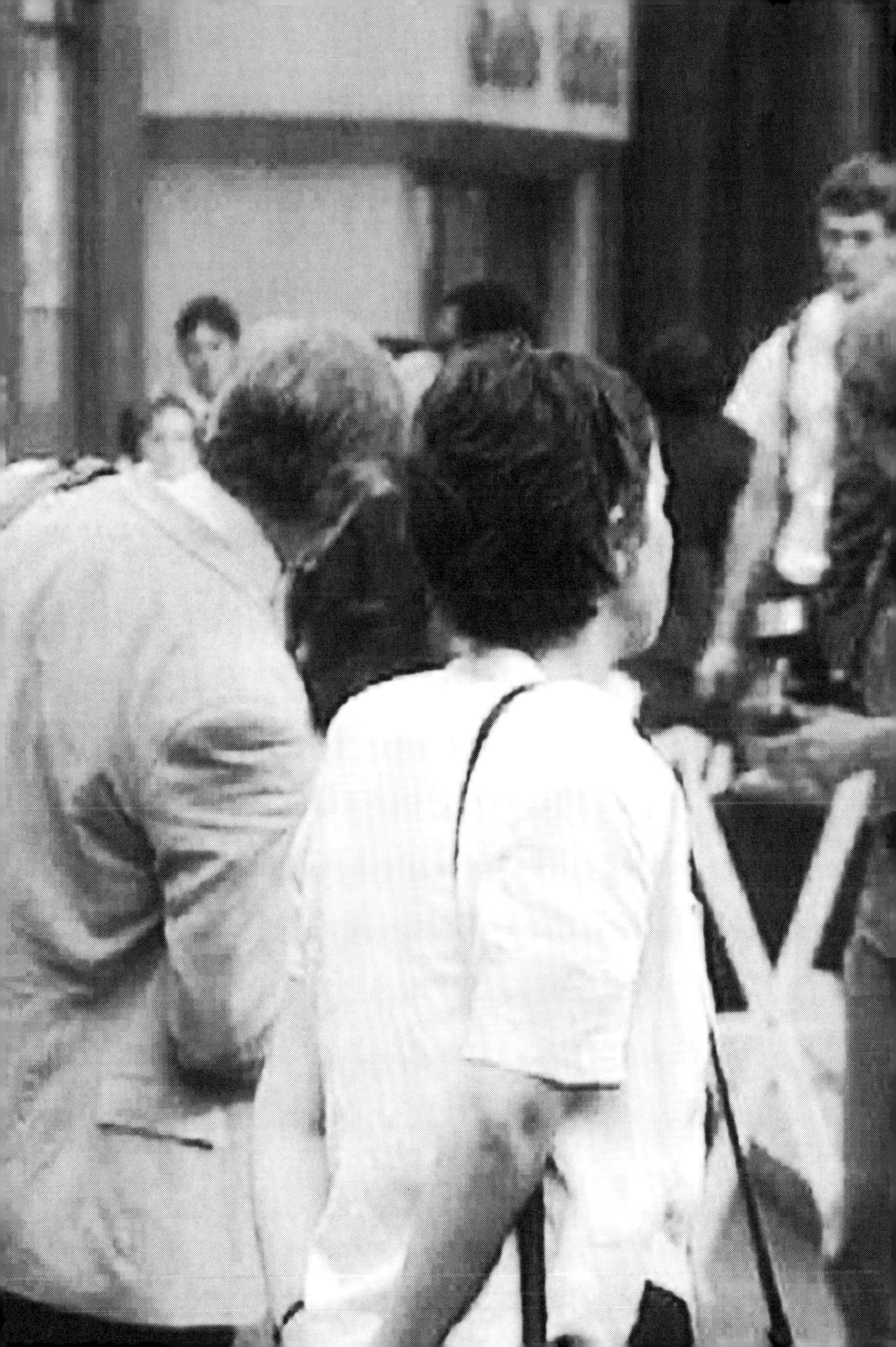

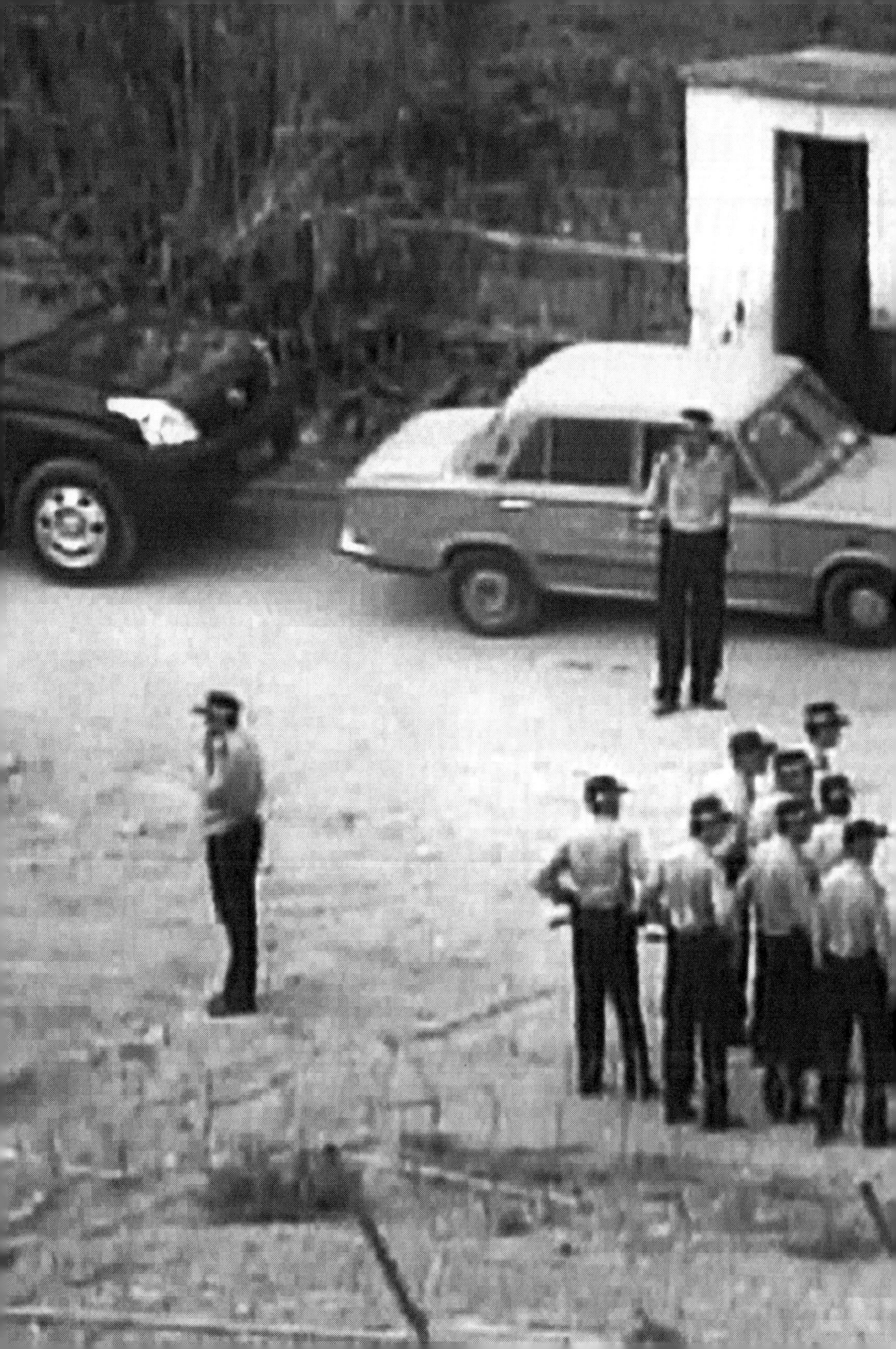

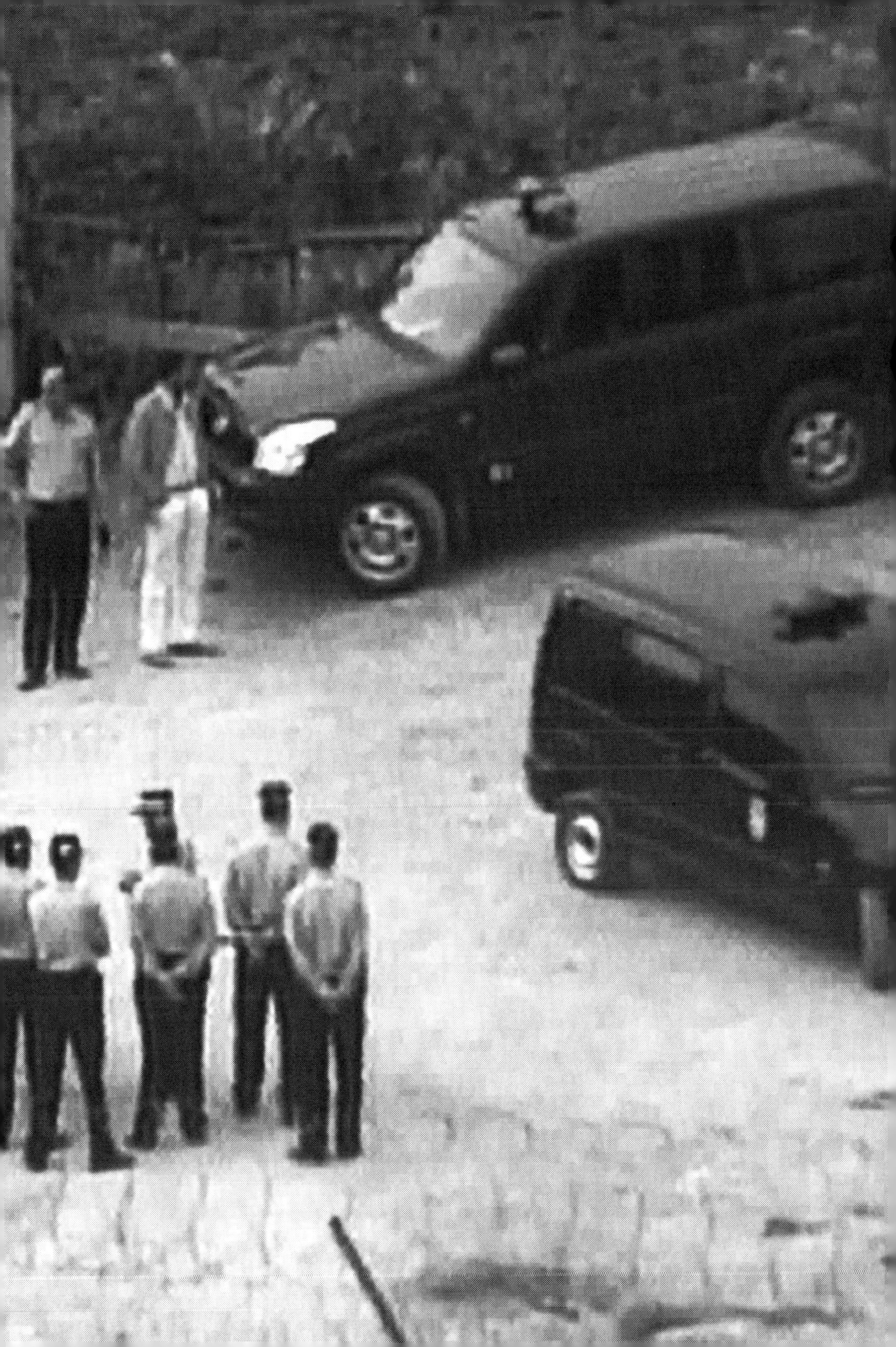

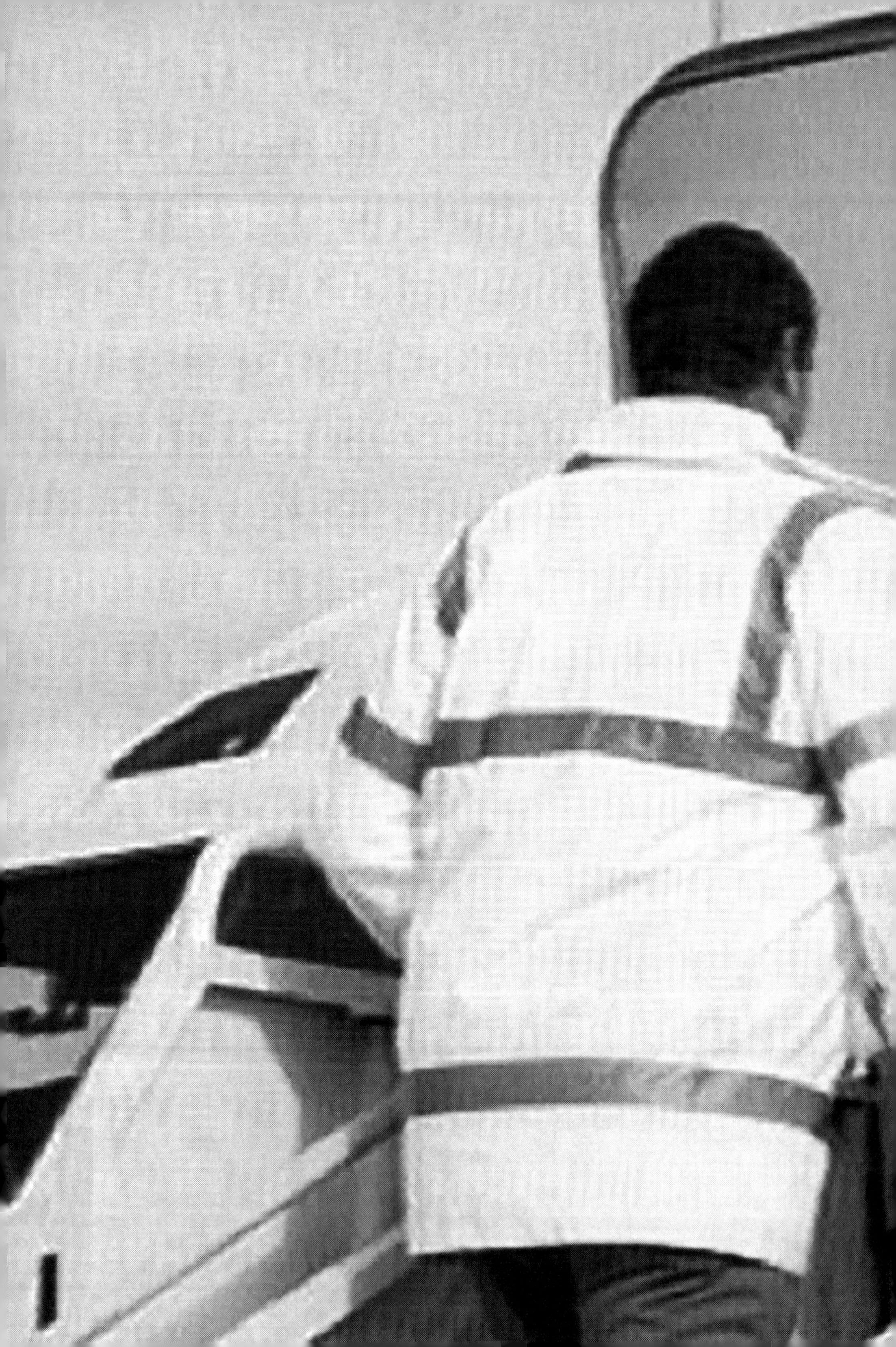

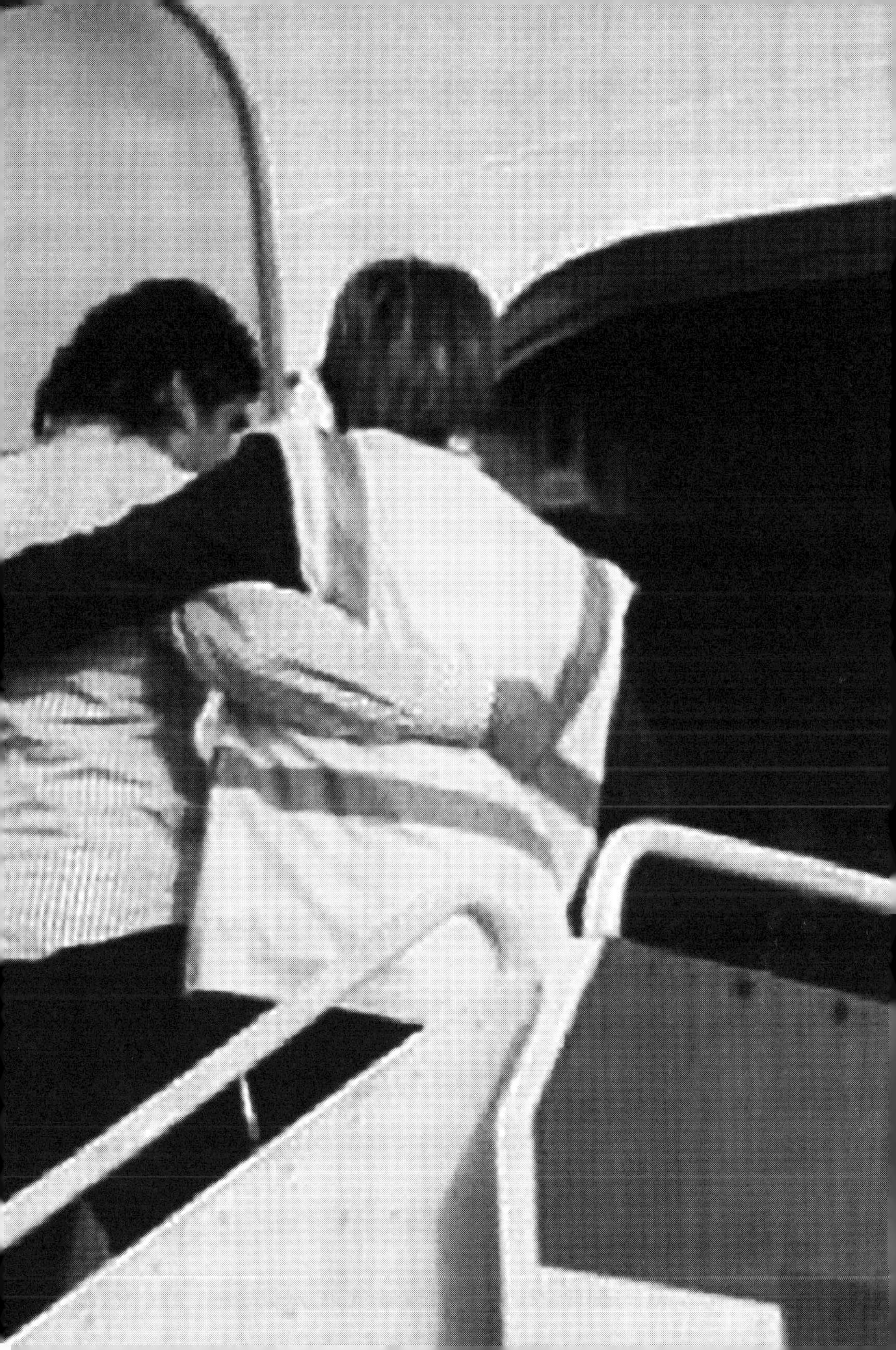

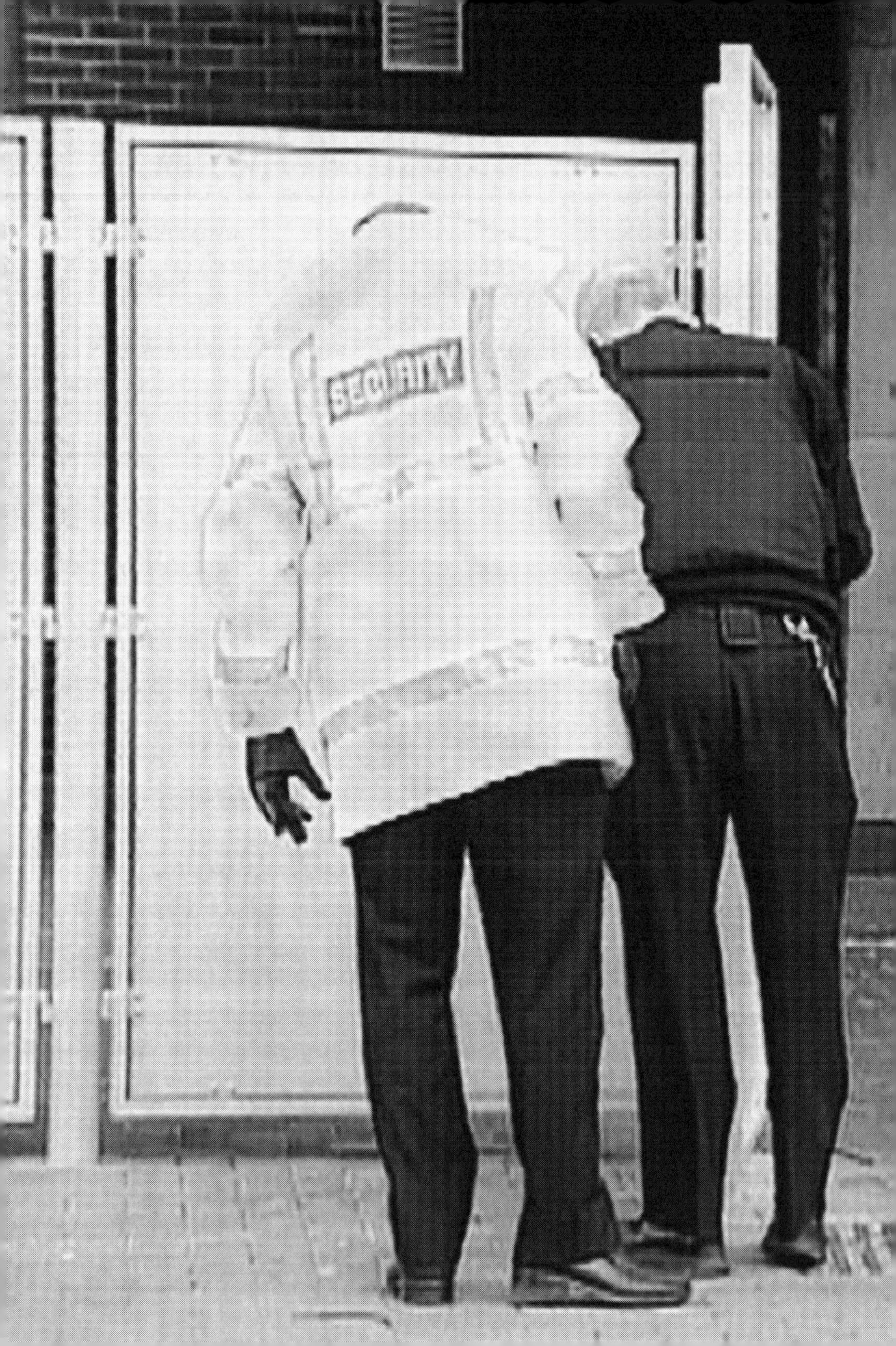
SECURITY

---------------------------------------------------------

# A Moment to Listen to Those Who Are Quiet
## A Conversation with Suchan Kinoshita

---------------------------------------------------------

---------------------------------------------------------

**Maria Hlavajova** The first time I saw an image of your work was back in the beginning of the 1990s. You stood next to a busy highway playing the violin (*Highway Image I*, 1991). It was an act that simultaneously drew attention to and obliterated your performance. I remember this as a statement about the impossibility of an artist gaining a voice in public. Yet later you engaged in a work where the artist would be given a different position, that of an 'in-betweener' or a mediator. Could you say more about this shift? What voice does an artist have in a public sphere in your opinion?

**Suchan Kinoshita** I am currently working on a project that is based on the game 'Chinese Whispers', also known as '*Stille Post*' (Silent Post) in German or '*Téléfone Arabe*' in French and, as I found out only recently, '*Telephon Maqtoa*' in Arabic, meaning 'disconnected telephone'. I am interested in the person as the translator of a message: the misformer or in-betweener. This whole 'in-betweening' subject interests me a lot, because it is exactly at that point that you move the meaning in another direction. It's a term used in animation. When you draw two different key-frames, the in-betweener has to draw all the frames in-between to illustrate the movement. This is a terrible job of course, but if you use the in-betweening as a way to follow your own logic and not to illustrate a given one, it can become interesting. The potential in Chinese Whispers is misunderstanding and misinterpreting, which becomes a new origin for the next act. There is no real 'original' but only different ways of (mis)understanding.

Yet I don't see myself having shifted in the way I engage in work as you describe. Rather, I would say that the shift itself, the very idea of the shift, is what interests me and is a material I work with. In the performance on the highway, I could describe myself as an in-betweener as well, in-between the way to and the way from spot X. I never intended to position myself as someone who was not heard, but tried to look at myself from the perspective of a driver passing by, who has no other choice than to let go of the image, grasping only a second of it, either forgetting about it the next moment or keeping it in mind as a kind of after image. The impossibility is a potential I work with.

**MH** What exactly do you mean with this notion of 'impossibility'?

**SK** It's where you meet the limits of your own understanding and that of others and use it as a potential to work with. If you invent something to solve a problem you create new ones at the same time.

There is an example of some Japanese politicians, who, in order to prevent really speaking about some content, introduce a speaking technique that stretches the vowels of some of the words in such a way that you start losing the beginning of the sentence and you only follow it as if listening to a 'singing' performance. My father really got angry when politicians started using this technique as an excuse for not really saying anything. I was fascinated by the extent that they could exaggerate this technique in order to solve their dilemma of speech, while creating a new one at the same time.

If you want a very literal example, there is one of my works called *Etüde*, which is a video that shows an exercise where four people try to imitate a movement and a sound being demonstrated in front of them by a fifth person (not visible in the video) as precisely as possible. All four players/imitators do this at the same time but each one does it in his or her own way, of course. It is *impossible* to exactly imitate the movement and the sound, so you get a quartet of translations that are dissonant and asynchronous and together create a new composition.

**MH** So how does this relate to my initial question, about the artist's role in society?

**SK** Let's not give artists a role that they have to fulfil. The only role that seems to make sense is the unpredictable one.

**MH** I think we agree about this; I'm not making a plea for art that could be foretold. But alright, I'll reformulate: what *voice* do you strive to have within society? Your work is all about voice and communication and the misunderstanding that comes with it as a constructive option. So if you do not want to speak about a role, can we speak about a voice in public instead? As you said in regard to your 'highway' piece, you never intended to position yourself as someone who was not heard ...

**SK** I would like to think of the voice as an instrument to play with. So it is actually not one voice but many different voices in different settings, the voice that tries out different ways of pronouncing. A voice that interrupts itself and the other, one that speaks and listens at the same time. And a silent voice is an option too.

**Charles Esche** Based on what you've said, I would be interested in hearing how this idea of the voice as an instrument in your view relates to the context in which we live and work. I wonder, for example, what your feelings are on Dutch pragmatism and its attractions and problems for art and cultural difference ...

**SK** I'm quite sceptical of the notion of pragmatism and the pressure to formulate everything in terms of practicability – the notion that art *has* to be understood by the people. That art *has* to be communicated to the youth clearly and directly, for instance, and how it pretends to be able to do that without any real evidence. We forget that people themselves have the ability to misunderstand, maybe completely, but in a way that is inspiring. I prefer the idea of not controlling viewers, as a sort of gift to them. How far do we go to interfere with people's reception of an artwork? In Dutch there is a perfect word for it: '*bemoeizucht*'.

**CE** I think this instrumentalization, which in a way is what you're talking about, is an instrumentalization of art for purposes of social cohesion or economic development or even just to make people feel a bit better about themselves. For sure this is a real danger in the Netherlands today as well as in other Western-European cultures. If unchecked, it will result in art that is pretty similar to vulgar forms of socialist realism. The really interesting question is: can we clearly recognize and declare it as such while it is happening? Do we have that courage and vision? And, once declared, how do we then react? What I often find here is a rather conservative reaction that tries to resist change by retaining the idea of autonomy, the autonomous artist or institution. For me this position seems nostalgic, not only because of the urgency of the political situation – with the rise of intolerance – but also because it perfectly fits to the commodification of art. Autonomy then becomes a plea for a sort of irrelevance and exclusion of political and economic discourses in which we really should be engaged. I don't want to choose between instrumentalization or isolation; both deny art its possibility.

**SK** The current instrumentalizing reaction is dangerous. But I think we also lack a proper vocabulary to speak with each other about these issues in a constructive way. These sorts of terms are contested because they simply try to define a territory for something, to describe where something has to happen, whatever that is – art, discourse or discussion. The thing is, in my experience at least, whenever you try to direct things completely then you miss the point. Because they are not to be directed and if you can, you're on the wrong track. This is the terrible trap one always falls into, probably you cannot even prevent yourself from falling, but being aware of it creates other perspectives. When it comes to the notion of autonomy for example, I am not entirely ready to write it off as useless, although I would not want to advocate its conservative meanings either. You can think of autonomy in the sense of keeping distance and not immediately interfering with a sphere you don't know. To realize that you don't know something – that can be quite fruitful. You take your time to look at it and allow for a productive misunderstanding. This could help us to exist somewhat besides the logic that requires an immediate involvement in solving problems and interfering in the public sphere without actually creating new possibilities. In Japanese they call it 'ma', the space in-between that is not touched but kept actually to activate the mind. And I think that if you fill in all the space in-between two different positions, you lose a lot of creative response and exchange.

**CE** That's a good example of precisely what we're missing here. What I find in the Netherlands is that there's an instantaneous leap from trying to identify the problems to demanding solutions. We had our *Be(com)ing Dutch*[1] symposium a couple of weeks ago at the Van Abbemuseum. We were trying to identify problems but what a lot of the audience did, particularly the ethnic Dutch audience, was to want to know what the solutions were. They seemed to think the responsibility of an art institution was not to identify the problems alone, but to provide the solutions. It's the problem of saying: I have identified what's wrong and in the moment of

[1] *Be(com)ing Dutch* is a two yea
project developed both inside an
outside the Van Abbemuseum, w
consists of debates, reading grou
artist's projects, exhibitions,
residencies and forms of collectiv
participation and production. The
project seeks to put our ideas of
cultural identity under pressure a
examine the processes of inclusi
and exclusion in the Netherlands
today, and asks whether art migh
offer alternative examples of thin
about how we might live togethe

identifying, it's already solved. We don't give ourselves space
to think problems through over time. We demand solutions
and the easiest solutions are those of the populists: lock
things down, stop integration, stop cultural change, stop
globalization, judge everyone according to their economic
contribution. But if we can't be unrealistic – and demanding –
in art, then where can we?

**MH** Suchan, I think you're interested precisely in non-
knowledge, not-knowing or the knowledge that is left out.

> **SK** I have a friend who tried to earn money in Japan by
> giving English lessons and the first sentence she wrote on
> the board was: MAKE AS MANY MISTAKES AS POSSIBLE.
> In my performance *Loudspeaker*, which I have performed in
> different settings since 1993, I have to listen to two people
> each whispering in one of my ears and me trying to repeat
> out loud what I hear. The challenge is not to focus on
> understanding but on listening to both sides equally. This is
> somehow impossible to realize, but while doing it you can
> exercise the impossible and get better and better in it.

**MH** This example makes me think of another work of yours:
*It must have been an early Tuesday morning* (2002). It consists
of three rooms made of polystyrene foam and wood, light and
text, but mainly a complicated tangle of voices that seem to be
making an attempt at communicating with each other, but
never quite connect. Those rooms, however, appeared to me
like interrogation cells, devices for absolute control and
domination.

> **SK** That was the dramaturgy of how I made the installation.
> I was interested in repeating the structure of the room so the
> spectator had to repeatedly enter and exit the different spaces
> in order to catch fragments of the piece. One voice is telling
> five different versions of the same situation happening in
> a hotel somewhere. The text is edited in such a way that
> the different perspectives intermingle and you lose your
> orientation about which of the stories you are actually
> following. The light changes create different views caused by
> perforated walls separating the rooms. The spectator does
> become the observer of the situation in another room or
> becomes an object of observation him/herself. Other parts

within the text resemble an interview situation, but listening carefully one realizes that the questions and answers do not logically follow each other but function on their own, although in the end you cannot help but relate them to each other. The attempt to reconstruct what happened creates a new understanding of it, a new reality.

**MH** Yet why did you choose the trope of interrogation or observation cells?

**SK** The size of those rooms creates a kind of intimate situation, yet at the same time the structure creates a distance from the situation. This setting intensifies how one listens and brings the spectator into the role of observing the others and him/herself within this set. On one hand you find yourself in the role of detective wanting to follow what has actually happened, and at the same time you become the object of observation for others. It's a kind of dilemma: dilemma coming from *dialemma* originating in Greek meaning 'the space in-between'.

**CE** How about the dilemma of the funding structure for arts in the Netherlands, which is undergoing reform nowadays? The system as such allowed you – and even now that it is changing still does to some extent – to ignore market demands or the demands of institutions and still survive. Up until recently, as an artist you could get a kind of salary provided by the state. That allowed artists to be quite individualist, perhaps even disengaged from the world.

**SK** I don't think so. It's difficult to generalize here, but the support of individual artists has a strong tradition in Dutch art policy, which has created immense production of art, whether you think it important or not. This support is valued by artists as they are provided with the space in which to say: ok, I *can* find my way also outside of the commercial system, temporarily. Because these supports are only for a few years and it gives a wrong image if you compare it to a 'job' situation.

**CE** But what has the system given us? Should there be an effect after so long, after two generations maybe, as we're talking about fifty, sixty years of public investment? It's a unique level of financial support that's been available here and I am genuinely curious about what it has created or made possible. What do we lose if we dismantle it in its present form, as is actually already partially happening?

> **SK** It has given people awareness of art and artists time and space. It is an amazingly generous offering, which does not even require a return on the state's investment in the traditional sense. It is about *belief* in art. Yet it would be challenging if the individual support system for artists could be made more and more risky. Not to throw the system away, but to transform it so that it is more adventurous and less dictated by consensus. The question is how to support people who are eager to work – on whatever projects, at whatever venues, in whatever situations – but be it experimental!

**CE** I still would like to talk about the unique Dutch exceptionalism when it comes to art and culture. One thing is that the artist is very much part of the official discourse here, both in politics and the press, in ways that it's not elsewhere. The websites of two major newspapers, *De Volkskrant* and *NRC*, list 'art' as a headline subject, alongside 'national news', 'foreign news' and 'business'. And we have this extraordinary discussion about museums and museum policy at the moment. I don't know any other country that would be interested in museum policy to this extent. And that's where you think – this is wonderful, art is important. But by being built so firmly into the system, it also seems to lose a certain amount of sexiness or 'underground' cultural credibility. It's normalized in a sense, made an official part of what being Dutch is about.

> **SK** Well, when you talk about how this discussion shows that 'art' is simply present in public discourse, and risks losing a critical stance due to that precise reason, it sounds like a dangerous generalization to me. This dilemma you're talking about is not something you can avoid. Anyway, I think the 'underground' is a romantic idea. Holland is a small country so if you go underground the borders are close by and your presence slips out of the national picture. Besides, the sexiness that you refer to is something like a game, and we know that game, right? The star system, the celebrity . . . we don't have to replay that game in Holland.

**MH** I am not sure I recognize this entirely. We might have built
'art' into the system as Charles suggests, but that does not
provide a guarantee that artists can – or do – voice their
opinions in the public sphere. The museum discussion that
has been going on in the press for a while now is just an
exception in my view. That is very unfortunate. It was caused
by the hidden, long-standing conflicts in the museum world
between different visions of art and institutions today that
imploded. A complex network of contradictions came to the
surface, destroying the idyllic picture of the Dutch museum:
autonomy versus engagement, entertainment versus content,
gender, generations … among many other issues at stake.
The case did receive quite some attention in the media, yet,
the artists – sad but true – have been absent in this public
debate to my knowledge.

**CE** But artists have opinions, it is just that the press has not
consulted them. Anyway, the museum debate should have
been covered more on the basis of content. It focused too
much on personalities rather than visions of the future of the
museum – something in which I believe there is the potential
for real ideological antagonism in the Netherlands. This is
something that artists have a position on for sure, because it
is the context in which a lot of their production will be
encountered over the long term.

**MH** I sense throughout the conversation that Suchan simply
does not believe that artists should speak the way the scholars
or the politicians do. Perhaps we need to create a space for
recognizing such a voice in a different way?

    **SK** A moment to listen to those who are quiet; I wonder
    whether that's possible.

This conversation took place on 23 February 2007 in Eindhoven.

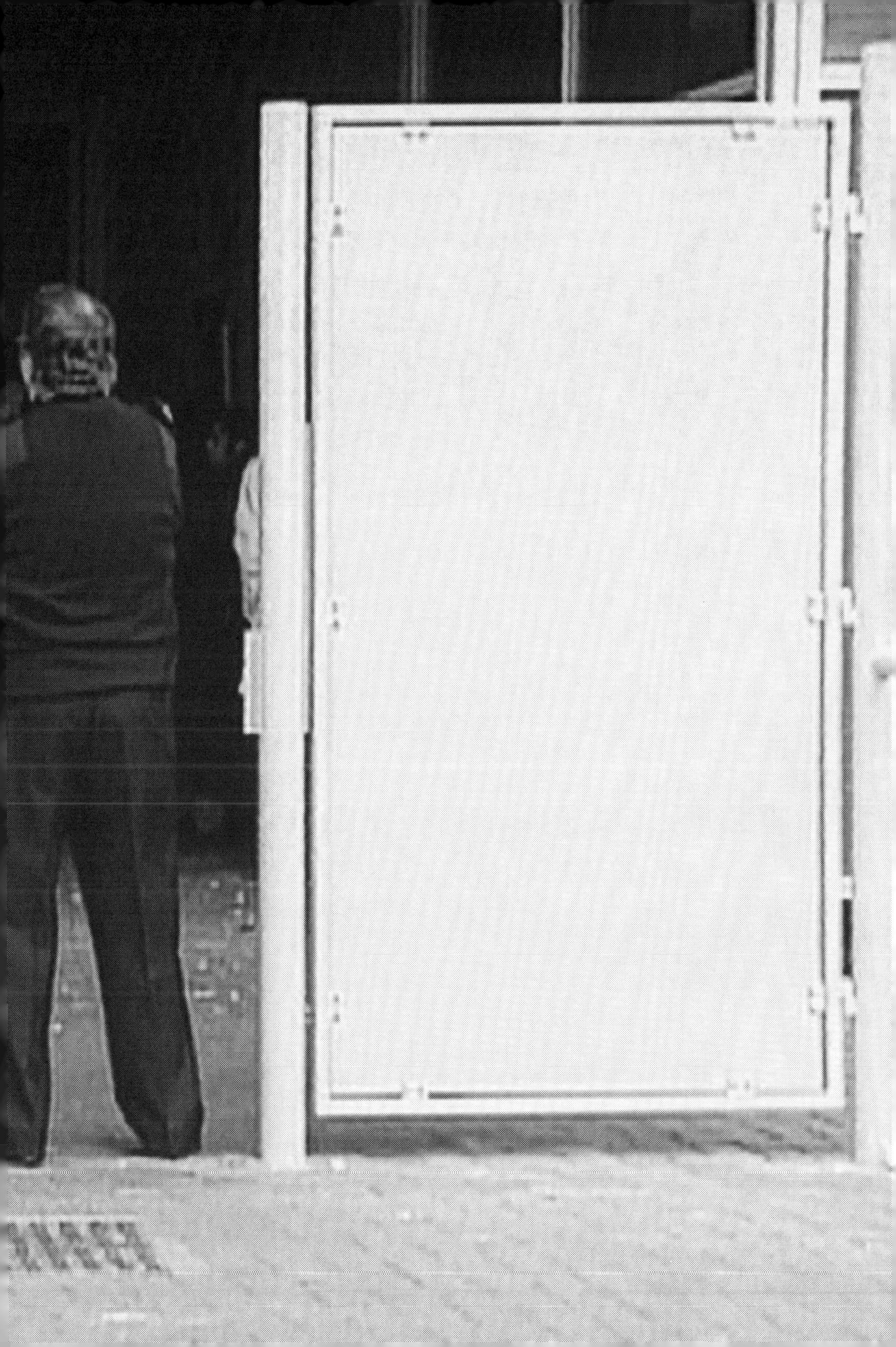

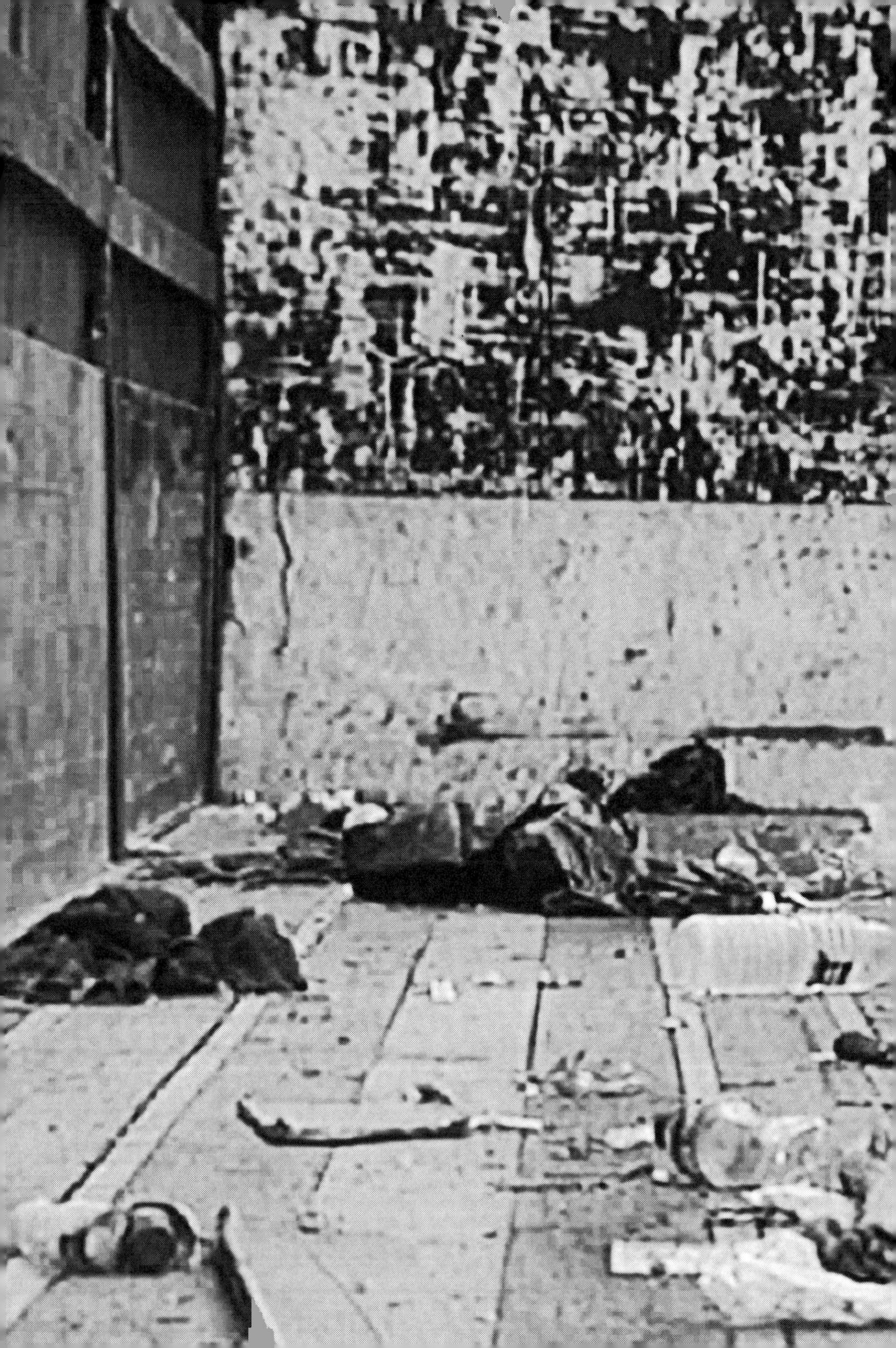

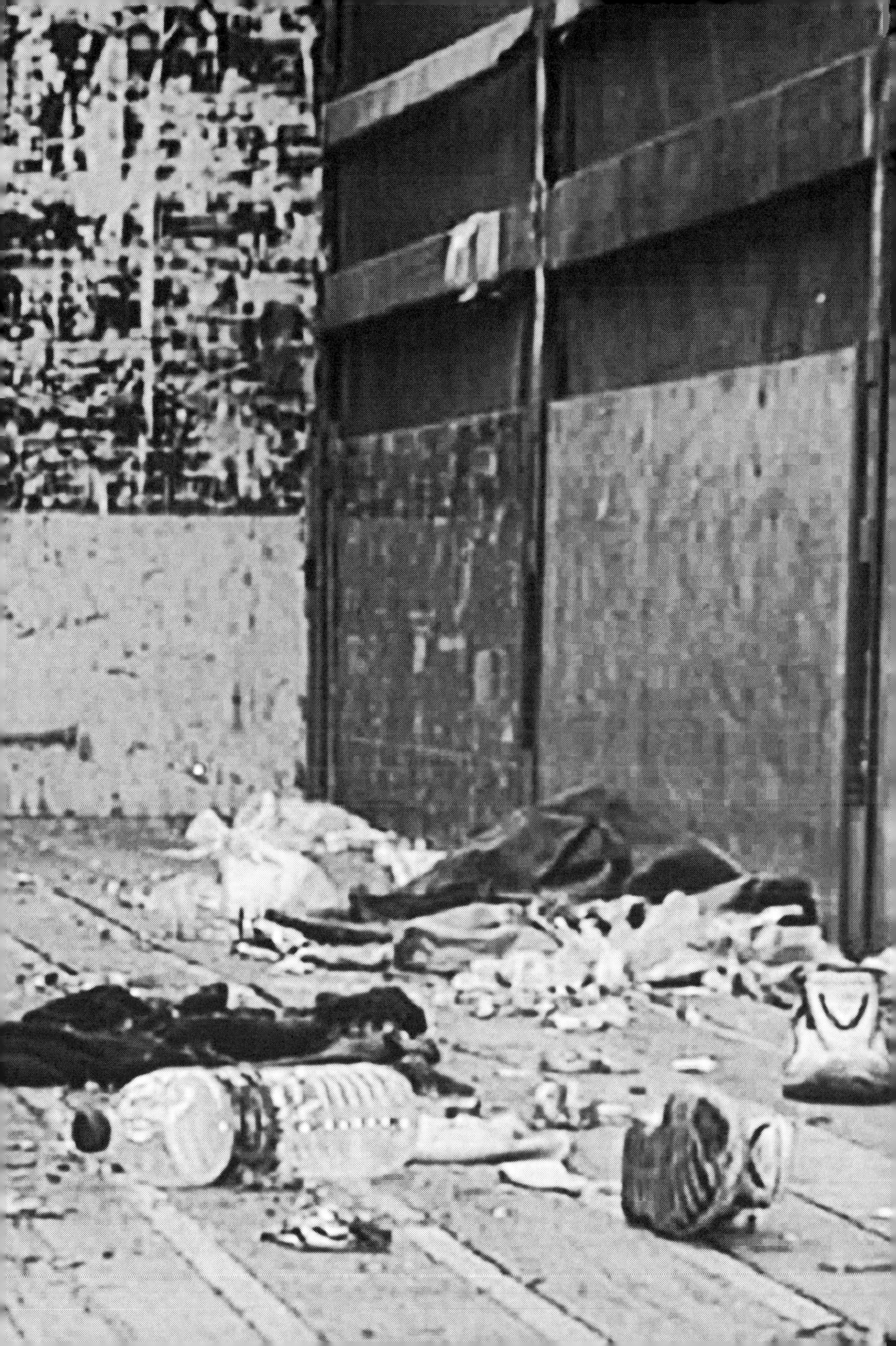

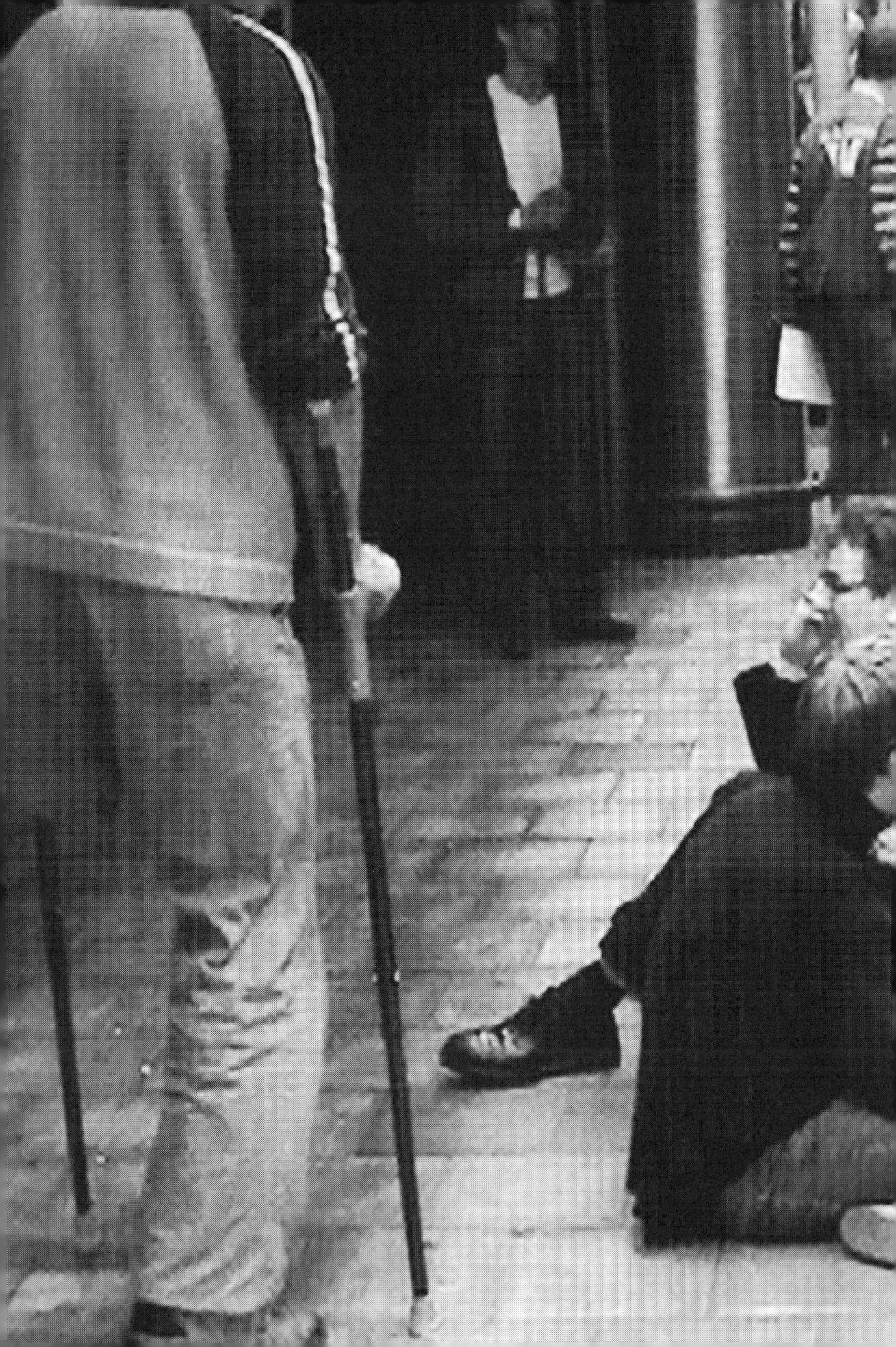

-------------------------------------------------------

# Art and the
# New Image Wars

-------------------------------------------------------

## Sven Lütticken

-------------------------------------------------------

For a considerable time, art has claimed the privilege (indeed, the duty) to criticize the images produced by the culture industry. Now, however, these media images and works of art are increasingly under attack for religious reasons – a tendency represented most clearly by Islamist fundamentalism, which effectively conspires with western media and their Enlightenment rhetoric to create a culture war that prolongs itself from one event to the next. These events (and pseudo-events) range from the dramatic murder of Dutch filmmaker Theo van Gogh to the Danish cartoon riots, Jack Straw's remarks on veils and the decision of the Deutsche Oper in Berlin to cancel a planned staging of Mozart's *Idomeneo* – in which the severed heads of Jesus, Mohammed and Buddha were to be shown alongside that of Poseidon. Sometimes there need be no event at all: media stories that some British banks no longer handed out piggy banks to children so as not to offend Muslim customers turned out to be just as unfounded as the end-of-year hysteria over the alleged banning of Christmas by overzealous politically correct bureaucrats and managers.[1] So far, the art world has shown little inclination – at least on the institutional level – to respond to such real or perceived challenges to the spectacular regime of visibility it is so keen on exposing itself. Nonetheless, individual artistic practices offer compelling reflections on the renewed vigour of monotheistic attacks on images and on the visual regime of the capitalist West as such; I focus here on Dutch examples, but within the broader context of the global religious contestation of the spectacle.[2]

### The body (un)veiled

Many of the most prominent incidents in the current image wars involve the veiling or unveiling of the female body, or depictions of it. In 2003, an Amsterdam tenement was decorated with a monumental mural of a nude woman, inspired by a poem by Jacob van Lennep, *Ode aan een roosje,* which is splashed across the façade and across the body of the woman; a clothed man, presumably the author, floats over the text and the woman's legs. Although the inhabitants of the neighbouring buildings, many of them Muslims, were polled prior to the work's execution (apparently with largely positive results), once completed the mural was attacked both verbally and physically, with black paint. In the end, a compromise was reached: the woman's pubic area was pixellated, turning it into an abstract grid. The ideological opposite of such revealing public art can be found in the town of Susa, Iran, in the form of a mural showing the upper part of a woman in Islamic dress, her face visible but her body concealed, her eyes modestly averted. An accompanying text proclaims: 'A woman modestly dressed is as a pearl in it's shell' [sic].[3]

the alleged piggy bank
al, see http://www.abc.net.au/
watch/transcripts/s1494636.htm
ssed 4 March 2007).

is text is from of a series of
s on the concept of idolatry in
mporary culture.

now the Susa mural though a
taken by Frank Denys.

Over the past few years, the increasing appearance of women who adhere to a strict definition of hijab dress (the modest and decorous clothing proscribed by Islam) in European cities has provoked controversy. Especially controversial is the veiling of the face, which leaves only a slit for the eyes – or even less, as in the Afghan burqa, which covers the eyes with an embroidered grille. After a group of Muslims who allegedly plotted to kidnap and kill a British Muslim soldier on leave from Iraq were arrested in early 2007, British newspapers showed a photo of three veiled women in Birmingham, one of them making a V-sign. Although this is an extreme case, images of veiled women have become a minor genre in European newspapers – one indication that the veil has come to function as a screen on which cultural anxieties and desires are projected, and not just from one side. This is not the place to explore the cultural history of the veil, which reaches back before the beginnings of Islam or Christianity, and often has social rather than religious connotations; nor is it the place to engage in the debate concerning the question of whether the veil is actually proscribed by Islam, or just a cultural habit; nor that over the veil as a means for oppressing women versus the veil as a choice made by strong and emancipated women.[4] The fact is that the polysemic veil has become a logotype of the dangerous Muslim 'other'; it has become a prop in today's image wars. Islamists use it as a highly visible statement against western society, while western liberals also perceive it as such, often focusing on the question of women's rights – in this respect they follow in the footsteps of the far from liberal Lord Croner, the British consul general in Egypt in the late nineteenth century, who already ideologized the veil as a sign of the oppression of women.[5] Such a reading is open to appropriation by Muslim women: A Dutch news photograph taken in late 2006 shows the full-body veil being used by Muslim women in a protest against their deportation to Afghanistan, where they would be forced to wear such burqas – they have not only wrapped themselves in burqas, but also a picture of the then immigration minister Rita Verdonk, or 'iron Rita'.

The status of the veil as a media myth that would have given Roland Barthes a field day (the veil as sign for oriental mystery, danger, hiding an inaccessible exotic feminine body) has been countered by (mainly female) artists including Shirin Neshat and Zineb Sedira.[6] The Dutch artist Fransje Killaars, who in the early 1990s switched from painting to making installations with textiles, has recently taken to draping some of her bedspreads, with their brightly coloured grids, on tailor's dummies. These abstract and impractical full-body veils draw attention to their materiality and sensuality – to their own surface and texture rather than their status as obstructions of the gaze, as a hindrance to seeing what

[4] On these aspects of the veil, various contributions in the exhi catalogue *Veil: Veiling, Represen and Contemporary Art* (London/ Cambridge: inIVA /MIT Press, 20

[5] Reza Aslan, *No god but God: Origins, Evolution, and Future of* (New York: Random House, 2005 72–73.

[6] The concept of the Veil exhib (see note 4) was Zineb Sedira's.

lies beneath. Titled *Figures* and posed in groups, they form a constellation that invites comparison and contrast. Usually, Killaars also shows one or two dummies that are not covered in the manner of a burqa, but around which a bedspread is draped from the neck down in the manner of a cape. In contrast to the 'burqa' *Figures*, the 'cape' *Figures* use dummies whose heads have been removed; the cape is crowned by nothing. By 'exposing' the veiled face as a void, these *acéphales* join the other works in privileging the cover over the covered, the veil over the veiled. If the media represent the veil as a blot that obscures the essence, the woman beneath – a woman supposedly in need of unveiling to make her free – Killaars's *Figures* make the veil visible as something integral rather than exterior to the figure.

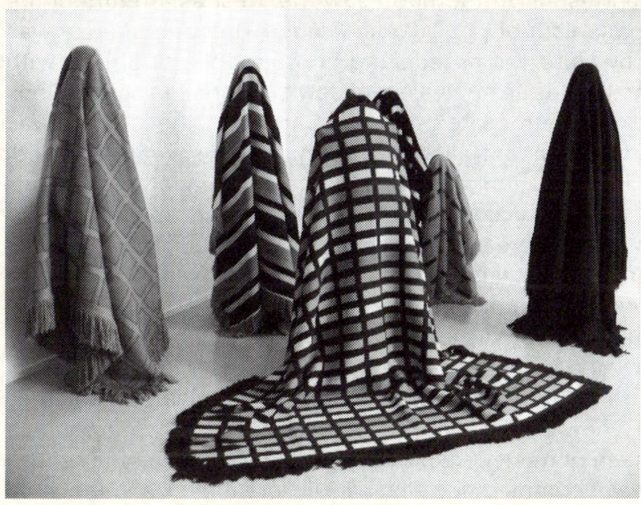



As important as work such as Killaars's is, there is no denying that it remains marginal in a culture in which the veil has been hijacked by right-wing mouthpieces who routinely invoke the Enlightenment in way that reduces critique to a neatly packaged dogma for the age of the sound bite. One such Enlightenment fundamentalist is Somali-born Ayaan Hirsi Ali, who during her years in Holland – she has since moved on to the US, to work at the neoconservative American Enterprise Institute – wrote the script for a short film on the role of women in Islam. Programmatically titled *Submission* (Part 1), the 2004 film was directed by Theo van Gogh, the filmmaker who famously described Muslims as backward 'goat-fuckers'; he paid with his life for *Submission* when he was stabbed to death on an Amsterdam street in broad daylight by a young fundamentalist now famous as Mohammed B.[7] *Submission*

shows a woman wearing a dark but transparent veil that reveals parts of her body, upon which Koranic verses on woman's submissive role have been written in ornate calligraphy. The film's voice-over monologue contains harrowing stories of various forms of abuse, and depicts the veil as a prison, the innermost circle of an extremely restricted world. In many cases this is no doubt all too true, yet Hirsi Ali and Van Gogh participate in the reduction of the veil's ambiguity and contradictions in favour of a cartoon image, thus turning women wearing hijab into the faceless face of otherness – and refusing to address the questions raised by the rise of the veil in Europe.

Mid-twentieth century pioneers of radical Islamism such as Sayyid Qutb of the Egyptian Muslim Brotherhood saw the West as a return of the *jahiliyya*, the paganism of pre-Islamic Arabia. This pagan state was characterized by *shirk*, the associating of other gods or beings with Allah; *shirk* functions as an equivalent of Jewish-Christian conceptions of idolatry.[8] Like idolatrous Rome for the Christians, the *jahiliyya* was also associated with uncontrolled and promiscuous sexuality; indeed, the early Jewish conception of idolatry frequently compared it to adultery.[9] Ever since Qutb, the comparative sexual freedom and the sexualization of the public sphere have been regarded as crucial symptoms of the new western idolatry. It is not only that thought itself is turned into an idol by the western rationalists, as Qutb stated with horror; sinking even lower than that, the Westerners also idolize the body.[10] But then, perhaps this is just a front for the true idolatry: as the Iranian thinker Ali Shariati stated, in an idiom that may seem oddly familiar, sexual freedom is 'part of a new exploitation, a type of limitless deception, which the impure system of western capitalism produces'. Behind the seductive appearance of commodified sexuality lie 'great idols and the three faces of the contemporary religious trinity: exploitation, colonialization and despotism'.[11]

By blending Islamic jargon with that of Marxist political theory, of which he is critical even while using it against capitalism, Shariati reappropriated and resacralized a discourse that itself appropriated and transformed Jewish and Christian elements. Today's European and American Enlightenment fundamentalists, who are masters at using the criticism of Islam and of Muslim societies to deflect attention from the West's destructive political, military and economic operations, attempt to disavow any link between religion and the 'western values' they claim to represent. However, the Enlightenment is scarcely thinkable without the monotheistic critique of idolatry, nor is modern and contemporary critical theory or artistic practice. The symbolic gesture of 'unveiling the

[8] On the early Muslim concepti shirk, see G.R. Hawthing, *The Ide Idolatry and the Emergence of Isl From Polemic to History* (Cambric Cambridge University Press, 1999

[9] Moshe Halbertal and Avishai Margalit, *Idolatry*, trans. Naomi Goldblum (Cambridge/London: Harvard University Press, 1992), 1

[10] On Qutb and the idolization thought, see Ian Buruma and Avi Margalit, *Occidentalism: The Wes the Eyes of Its Enemies* (New York Penguin, 2004), 117.

[11] Ali Shariati, Fatima is Fatima, http://www.iranchamber.com/ personalities/ashariati/works/fat is_fatima2.php (accessed 4 Marc 2007).

truth', which has been so popular since the Enlightenment, is indebted to this heritage – and the use of the veil in contemporary Islamism, as paradoxical as it may seem, can itself be seen as following rather than breaking the logic of unveiling.[12] Is the veil not effectively being used to unmask, to lay bare the limits of western liberalism – to reveal it as sham, as an ideology in the service of capitalism and its stooges?

As theorists and historians of iconoclasm gleefully point out, iconoclasm also creates new images; contemporary iconoclasts like the Taliban are media savvy enough to be fully aware of this dialectic of iconoclasm, and exploit it.[13] As used by Islamists, the veil is iconoclastic, an attack on the idolatrous adoration of the human body in the West; the veil is used in the fight against what is perceived as idolatry. When artist Lidwien van de Ven engaged with the ubiquitous iconography of the veil in her work, two forms of iconoclasm met. In an exhibition in Paris in 2006, Van de Ven showed a photo she had taken outside the French embassy in London, showing veiled women protesting against an anti-veil ruling concerning French schools. This and a few other images were pasted directly onto the wall; in the second stage of the exhibition, they were painted over with a thin coat of white paint that allowed the images to shine through. Both obscuring the photographed veils and giving them a new visibility, Van de Ven gave the media myth an ambiguously physical and at the same time unreal and ethereal status.

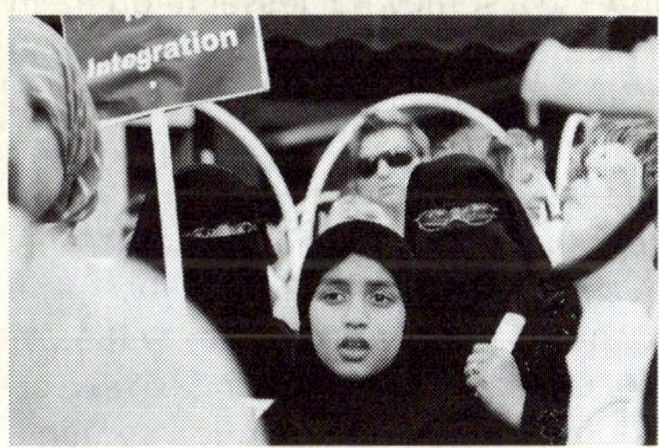


Van de Ven's gentle artistic iconoclasm makes the underlying image visible again – visible as representing not stubborn and dumb back-wardness, but an iconoclastic act in its own right, an act whose religious as well as political nature needs to be addressed, rather than sociolo-gized or pathologized.

### From one spectacle to another
The riots and protests occasioned by the Danish cartoons of the prophet Mohammed reflected not only anger (however manipulated) at the fact

)n the Enlightenment
·graphy of unveiling Isis
erious nature), see Jan
·ann, *Moses der Ägypter.
·fferung einer Gedächtnisspur
·kfurt am Main: Fischer, 2000),
·96.

or a routinely and somewhat
·mely provocative take on
·ist terrorists as iconophiles who
·orce rather than attack the belief
·ages, see Boris Groys, 'The Fate
·: in the Age of Terror', in exhib.
·*Making Things Public:
·spheres of Democracy*, eds.
·o Latour and Peter Weibel
·sruhe: ZKM, 2005), 970–975.


·vien van de Ven] *London, 4
·ember 2004* (International Hijab
·arity Day), 2004, photograph,
·esy Galerie Paul Andriesse,
·erdam

that Mohammed was caricatured, but at the fact that he was depicted at all. After all, this is a breach of the ban on depicting the prophet, which is derived from a certain interpretation of the Mosaic ban on idolatry. The current image wars represent a new wave of the monotheistic idolatry critique enshrined in the Second Commandment in Exodus 20:4, forbidding graven images 'or any likeness of any thing that is in heaven above, or that is in the earth beneath, or that is in the water under the earth'. This is elaborated upon in Deuteronomy 4:15–19, where the Israelites are reminded that they 'saw no manner of similitude on the day that the LORD spake unto you in Horeb out of the midst of the fire', and that representations of people and animals should be avoided because they might lead to 'corruption', to worshipping of these images (a similar danger existing in the case of the sun, moon and stars).[14] These are, in effect, two prohibitions: God must not be represented, and living creatures (and the planets) must not be represented so as to avoid idolatry. But the first error, or sin, is idolatry as well. Idolatry is not only the worship of false gods but also the worship of Jehovah in an image; the image itself becomes a false god.[15] At first, worshipping other gods was a real temptation; later, when this was no longer a danger, idolatrous tendencies within Jewish monotheism were seen as a risk.

In practice, the degree to which images were made and the way in which they were used over the centuries varied widely in the Jewish religion, as well as in Christianity and – to a somewhat lesser degree – in Islam. The Christian doctrine of the incarnation mitigated the ban on the depiction of God and his creation; God had become man, the word had become flesh, and therefore open to depiction. Of course, Byzantine iconoclasts and Protestants argued that such images could still be put to idolatrous use, sometimes adding that images of Christ could only represent one of his two natures, the physical one, not his divinity.[16] The Muslim fear of a relapse into *shirk*, the 'associating' of other deities or powers with God, manifests itself in a rather extreme ban on *tasweer*, on images that might stimulate such idolatry. However, although contemporary western as well as Islamist ideologues are intent on making Islam appear monolithic, the ban on depicting Mohammed was also subject to successive waves of radicalization and relaxation and is not as universal as some contemporary ideologists suggest, as quite a number of old miniatures show.[17] The repression of such unwelcome historical complexities allows fundamentalists to create a Manichean dichotomy between Islam and the idolatrous West – the new *jahiliyya*. This discourse can be seen as a more radical form of the Christian critique of western culture.

[14] Different religions count the Commandments in differing way: In Judaism and most Protestant churches, the ban on idolatry is p of the Second Commandment; in Catholicism, it is subsumed unde First Commandment.

[15] Edwyn Bevan, *Holy Images: An Inquiry into Idolatry and Image Worship in Ancient Paganism and Christianity* (London: George Alle Unwin Ltd, 1940), 39.

[16] Marc De Kesel has analysed consequences of the incarnation doctrine with particular cogency; for instance Marc De Kesel, 'Male als Verbrechen', *De Witte Raaf*, no (March/April 2002), 23–26. On the Reformation and its consequence with a focus on Lutheran doctrine practice, see Werner Hofmann (e exhib. cat. *Luther und die Folgen die Kunst* (Hamburg: Hamburger Kunsthalle, 1983).

[17] See the 'Mohammed Image Archive', compiled by a website t seems to see itself as a defender American liberty against evil lefti and Muslims: http://www.zombie com/mohammed_image_archive (accessed 4 March 2007).

For Christians, the Roman Empire remained the paradigm of an idolatrous society. Roman games in particular had been attacked by Tertullian in his *De Spectaculis* as prime examples of *eidolatreia,* and the fascination for Roman spectacle and decadence in late-nineteenth-century and early-twentieth-century culture, from the paintings of Gérôme and Alma-Tadema to later film productions, suggested that modern society might be a Rome returned – the triumph of idolatry disguised by Christian rhetoric. However, the Christian criticism of capitalist modernity was increasingly supplanted by a secularised discourse hailing from the Enlightenment and shaped by, yet also transforming and transcending, its monotheistic roots. In *Du Culte des dieux fétiches* (1760), a text that encapsulates the Enlightenment's transformation of monotheistic topoi into instruments of secular critique, Charles de Brosses claimed to unveil the most primitive form of religion, the embryonic first stirrings of idolatry: fetishism, or the worship of random objects rather than statues or other man-made images. Although the Enlightenment submitted religious dogma to an open-ended critique, this opposition of dogma and critique should not obscure the fact that the gesture of 'revealing' gods to be idols or long-held truths to be superstitions is fundamentally the same, and that monotheistic discourse on pagan religion constituted a nascent form of critique – an idolatry critique transformed by modern critique of religions and society.[18] Religious dogmatism already contained the seeds of critique, just as critique may still be crucially dependant on dogma.

In a letter written shortly after Theodor W. Adorno's death, in which he attempted to explain why his friend had not been buried according to Jewish rites, Max Horkheimer claimed that critical theory was based on the Second Commandment – the ban on representations of God, or, in more fundamentalist interpretations, of representation of all living beings.[19] Modern critical theory, in other words, analysed and opposed fascism and the culture industry as latter-day idolatry. Although Horkheimer's remark was obviously made during highly emotional circumstances, it is true that the modern critique of representation is in many ways a transformation of the monotheistic discourse on idolatry: the divine commandment fostered a suspicious and critical mentality that was finally turned against dogma itself. From De Brosses to Marx and beyond, the concept of the fetish as a primitive precursor of the idol still derives from monotheistic idolatry critique; Marx, of course, turned De Brosses's African proto-idol into a capitalist commodity fetish, just as irrational and mystifying.[20] However, in contrast to 'idols' according to monotheism, such fetishes are seen as a betrayal of what true humanity might be rather than as transgressions if divine law. The difference

Margalit and Halbertal posit
[fo]llowing 'chain of criticism of
[religi]on': the criticism of idolatry
[by m]onotheism, the criticism
[of mock religion] by the religious
[Enlig]htenment, the criticism of
[religi]on in general by the secular
[Enlig]htenment and finally the
[critic]ism of ideology. Margalit and
[Halb]ertal, 112.

Max Horkheimer, letter to Otto
[O.H. He]rz, 1 September 1969, in
[Gesa]mmelte Schriften vol. 18:
[Brief]wechsel 1949–1973 (Frankfurt am
[Main]: Fischer, 1996), 743.

See Karl-Heinz Kohl, Die Macht
[der D]inge. Geschichte und Theorie
[kulturel]ler Objekte (Munich: Beck, 2003),

between an early Christian diatribe such as Tertullian's *De Spectaculis* and Guy Debord's Marxian treatise on *The Society of the Spectacle* is immense, even if the latter is indebted – however indirectly – to the former.

Jeroen de Rijke and Willem de Rooij's film *Of Three Men* (1998) constitutes a montage – a possible dialogue – between the two forms of idolatry critique, religious and secular. The film shows the interior of an Amsterdam mosque that was formerly a Catholic church, built in the 1920s in a rather bulky and sober modernist-historicist style.

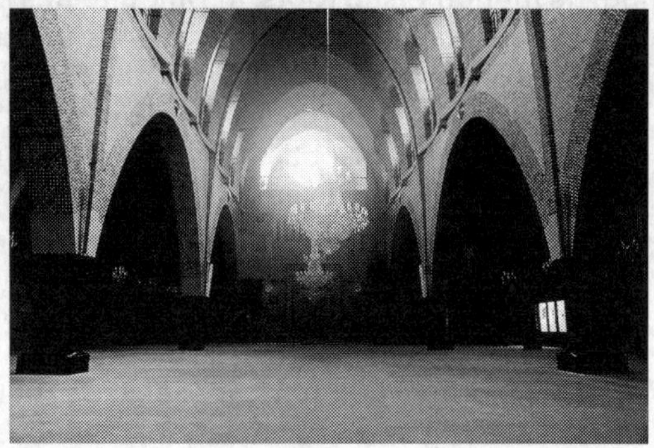

[Jeroen de Rijke and Willem de Rooij] Fatih Mosque, Amsterdam, November 1998, courtesy Galerie Daniel Buchholz, Cologne

The interior has been stripped of its Catholic paraphernalia; chandeliers and an empty floor complete the visual transformation. The film mostly focuses on the changing effects of the light coming through the windows; this light is largely artificial and changes quickly. There is an obvious connection with seventeenth-century paintings, by Saenredam and others depicting the whitewashed interiors of Protestant churches that were once Catholic. Whereas representations of such purified spaces are effortlessly contemplated for their aesthetic qualities, the image of a mosque sabotages such contemplation. In today's Europe, after all, mosques are often regarded with a wary eye. By treating the space in *Of Three Men* in a formal way, as a receptacle for a light show, De Rijke and De Rooij suggest that a mosque too is a potential place of enlightenment – or Enlightenment – and reflection, just like those former Dutch churches that now function as cultural centres or spaces of debate.

In addition to overlaying a church and a mosque with their diverging connotations, *Of Three Men* also juxtaposes seventeenth-century pictorial representations of spaces created by iconoclastic fury with the black screen's re-enactment of modern artistic iconoclasm. Before the mosque is shown, in the beginning of the film, the image is black; then it appears that the camera's view has been blocked by some men in dark cloaks. While this recalls a convention for disguising cuts by having black clothing or some dark object momentarily block the view sometimes used in Hollywood films, its length and position in the beginning of the film also recall modern artistic iconoclasm – for example Debord's first film, *Hurlements en faveur de Sade* (1952), which consisted mostly of a black screen. One need not accept Clement Greenberg's story of the Kantian origins and smooth progression of modernism to acknowledge modern art's self-critical bent – which also enables it to reflect on its own iconoclastic elements, and iconoclasm in general.[21] A 2006 installation by Krijn de Koning and Gert Jan Kocken combined three of Kocken's photographs of traces of iconoclastic rage in Dutch churches, showing mutilated stone reliefs, with a De Koning mural surrounding those pictures. Consisting of an irregular, meandering blue-and-white geometric pattern, the mural spreads out over the walls and ceiling like a bulky modernist ornament.

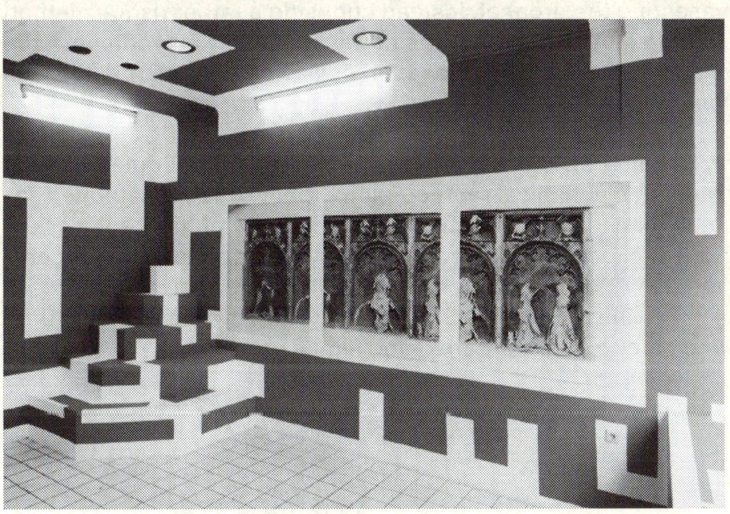

Clement Greenberg, 'Modernist
ing' (1960), in *The Collected
s and Criticism 4: Modernism
a Vengeance*, ed. John O'Brian
ago/London: University of
ago Press, 1993), 85–93.

n de Koning and Gert Jan
ken] Installation at CAPRI, Berlin,
ember/October 2006

Once more a montage of iconoclasms and critiques is effected, setting the stage for a possible debate against which the powers that be conspire with all their might.

### Idolatry in the age of mechanical reproduction
Although the Christian doctrine of the incarnation legitimized the creation of a rich visual culture, the growing autonomy of this culture from religion and its integration into the emerging capitalist culture industry

of the nineteenth century fuelled the fear of a relapse into idolatry. Lew Wallace, the author of *Ben-Hur,* the story of a Jewish prince whose life intersects at various points with that of Jesus, decided against the direct portrayal of Jesus in dramatic versions of his novel. Thus in the 1925 film version, we see a Last Supper scene directly inspired by Renaissance paintings, Da Vinci's *Last Supper* mural in particular, except for the fact that the sight of the centrally seated Christ is blocked by a lone Apostle sitting in the front, before Christ. All the viewer sees of Jesus is a halo and some hands. Possibly the figure in the front is Judas, who was often set apart from the others in Medieval and Renaissance paintings – but who was not, of course, placed in front of Christ. What made representations of Christ particularly sensitive in the context of *Ben-Hur* stagings was their character as commercial – even if devout – spectacles, complete with chariot races. It is no surprise that Islamic film directors took an even more radical stance on the issue of depicting Mohammed: In a 1976 film version of the life of Mohammed and the rise of Islam, *The Message*, director Moustapha Akkad scrupulously adhered to the ban on representing the prophet, instead choosing a rather risqué method of integrating Mohammed into the narrative – at certain moments, the use of subjective camera makes the viewer see things *through Mohammed's eyes.*

Not only Muslims, but strict Protestants too have long struggled with the rise of modern mechanical reproduction – today's media-saturated society amounting to a 'dictatorship of visibility' that multiplies the risk of idolatry.[22] The radical Calvinist opposition to this dictatorship is commemorated in a 2003 video by Arnoud Holleman, which shows girls in the Dutch Calvinist enclave of Staphorst ducking away and hiding their faces when they realize they are being filmed.

[22] Jorinde Seijdel, 'Staphorst Revisited', http://www.smba.nl/en/ newsletters/n-76-being-there/ (accessed 4 March 2007).

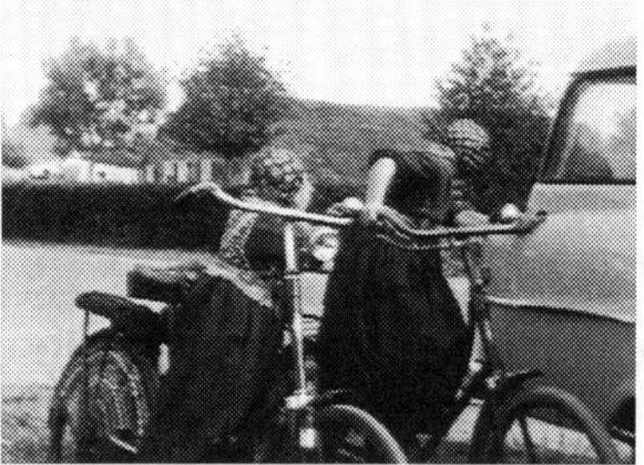

[**Arnoud Holleman**] *Untitled (Staphorst)*, 2003, video still

In this appropriation and editing of 1950s film footage, Holleman elegantly recalls that a radical rejection of being portrayed, of being subjected to the dictatorship of visibility, is not some strange and exotic recent import from the East. And of course, there are Islamic voices that reject the fundamentalist rejection of photography, film and video as such, although even moderate fatwas on this issue reflect the history of anguish over this question: 'Photography as a medium of communication or for the simple, innocent retention of memories without the taint of reverence/*shirk* does not fall under the category of forbidden *Tasweer*. One finds a number of traditions from the Prophet, peace and blessings be upon him, condemning people who make *Tasweer*, which denotes painting or carving images or statues. It was closely associated with paganism or *shirk*. . . . In other words, *Tasweer* was forbidden precisely for the reason that it was a means leading to *shirk*. The function of photography today does not fall under the above category. Even some of the scholars who had been once vehemently opposed to photography under the pretext that it was a form of forbidden *Tasweer* have later changed their position on it – as they allow even for their own pictures to be taken and published in newspapers, for videotaping lectures and for presentations; whereas in the past, they would only allow it in exceptional cases such as passports, drivers' licenses, etc. The change in their view of photography is based on their assessment of the role of photography.'[23]

However, photography can certainly be abused: 'To take pictures of leaders and heroes and hang them on the walls may not belong to the same category of permission. This may give rise to a feeling of reverence and hero worship, which was precisely the main thrust of the prohibition of *Tasweer*.'[24] In fact, the cult of 'martyrs' (suicide bombers) whose images are being widely disseminated and held up as models indicates that contemporary Islamist terrorists fully participate in the spectacle, eagerly producing images of destruction and embracing the dialectic of iconoclasm, in which destruction begets new – but unsettling – images. The media- and iconophobic Taliban took care to document the destruction of the giant Bamiyan Buddha sculptures; De Rijke and De Rooij have shown this image, surrounded by white, on the pages that had been allotted to them in the catalogue of a group show. However, artist Sean Snyder has made the intriguing suggestion that the image production by radical Islamists may still be deliberately iconoclastic; the bad technical quality of videos produced by Al-Qaeda may be intentional; far from primitive, these videos would be actively primitivist, opposing 'poor' images to the glitzy western spectacle.[25]

In 2002, Arnoud Holleman was one of the editors of an issue of *Re-magazine* that masqueraded as the Spring 2007 issue. In a series of entries dating from the distant past through the 1980s and 1990s to the

Fatwa on photography by Sheikh
ad Kutty, http://www.islamonline.
ervlet/Satellite?pagename=Islam
e-English-Ask_Scholar/FatwaE/
aE&cid=1119503545144 (accessed
rch 2007).

bid. For a fundamentalist
ion, see http://www.islam-qa.
index.php?QR=365&ln=eng
essed 4 March 2007).

Sean Snyder, 'Some Byproducts:
ghts on the Visual Rhetoric of
P', in *Concerning War: A Critical
er*, eds. Maria Hlavajova and Jill
er (Utrecht/Frankfurt am Main:
Revolver, 2006), 185.

future (from a 2002 perspective), a 'we' reflected on various public and private events, culminating in the decision to avoid image; a decision dated, tellingly, to the year 2001, the year of 9/11 and the beginning of the end of the iconophobic Taliban regime. 'We couldn't cope with the absence of pictures. It created irrational fears. We couldn't see what was happening in Afghanistan. We *needed* images.' While this still reflects the general western attitude, the 'we' soon make an iconoclastic turn of their own: 'Everything was image and nobody asked himself or herself why the ban was being violated. As an experiment, we covered or removed all images from our home. It cleared our heads. We asked friends to do the same.' In the end, this apparent iconophobia may be at the service of an intensified perception of images: 'We need the absence of images to appreciate the quality of an image when we see one.'[26] This iconoclasm, which is an 'internalized form of the second commandment' that is not explicitly religious, searches for 'an alternative for the maelstrom of the visual culture'.[27]

According to the Marxian analysis of Debord, the spectacle is not a matter of images or of media technology per se, but of the capitalist mode of production leading to the fetishistic projection of a social life onto commodities, lived reality becoming a reified representation. As if to prove that he was no iconophobe, Debord turned the second volume of his autobiographical book *Panégyrique* into a collection of pictures, noting that he appreciated images which have not been 'artificially separated from their meaning'. Although his stated intention of using pictures as 'iconographic proof' to illustrate a 'true discourse' betrays a secularised Christian desire to prevent images from becoming too autonomous from the word, the pictures in *Panéqyrique,* all relating to Debord's life and work, nonetheless develop a pull of their own.[28] Minimizing the number of images in the '2007' issue of *Re-Magazine,* which only contains a few photo sequences among the text pages, Holleman and his collaborators question precisely the production of images separated from their meaning – images that veil rather than reveal, or veil by revealing.

Recently, Bruno Latour and others have zoomed in on the relationship between monotheistic idolatry critique and modern secular critique in order to discredit both: if, on the one hand, monotheistic idolatry critique leads to iconoclastic violence while, on the other hand, secular critique has undergone inflation and degenerated into a habit, should not critique as such be treated with suspicion? Is not the whole rhetoric of unveiling the truth and destroying idols, fetishes and myths dubious and dangerous?[29] While it is undeniable that 'criticality' is prone to



[26] Preceding quotations in this paragraph are all from *Re-Magaz* #23, Spring 2007 (2002), unpagina[…]

[27] Arnoud Holleman, 'The Seco[nd] Commandment', text distributed [at] the Stedelijk Museum as part of Holleman's contribution to the gr[oup] show *Just in Time*, 2006.

[28] Guy Debord, *Panégirique. To[me] Second* (Paris: Artheme Fayard, 19[…]) unpaginated.

[29] Bruno Latour, 'Why Has Critic[…] Run out of Steam? From Matters o[f] Fact to Matters of Concern', *Critica[l] Inquiry*, vol 30, no. 2 (2003–2004), http://criticalinquiry.uchicago.ed[u] issues/v30/30n2.Latour.html (accessed 4 March 2007). See also Bruno Latour, 'What is Iconoclash Or Is There a World Beyond the Im[age] Wars?', in exhib. cat. *Iconoclash: Beyond the Image Wars in Science[,] Religion, and Art*, eds. Bruno Latou[r] and Peter Weibel (Karlsrhue: ZKM[,] 2002), 14–37.

becoming its own simulation, it would be the pinnacle of bad timing to abandon critique at a moment when both Islamist (and Christian) fundamentalists and the self-proclaimed defenders of the Enlightenment use their respective versions of idolatry critique to deflect attention from their incapability to solve today's pressing social, economical and ecological issues. Works like De Rijke and De Rooij's *Of Three Men,* Killaars's *Figures*, Van de Ven's overpainted photos, Holleman's magazine and De Koning and Kocken's installation strongly suggest the need to effect a montage of various forms of critique, religious and secular as well as 'western' and 'Muslim', in order to prevent them from becoming slogans in the culture war staged by both religious and secular reactionaries.

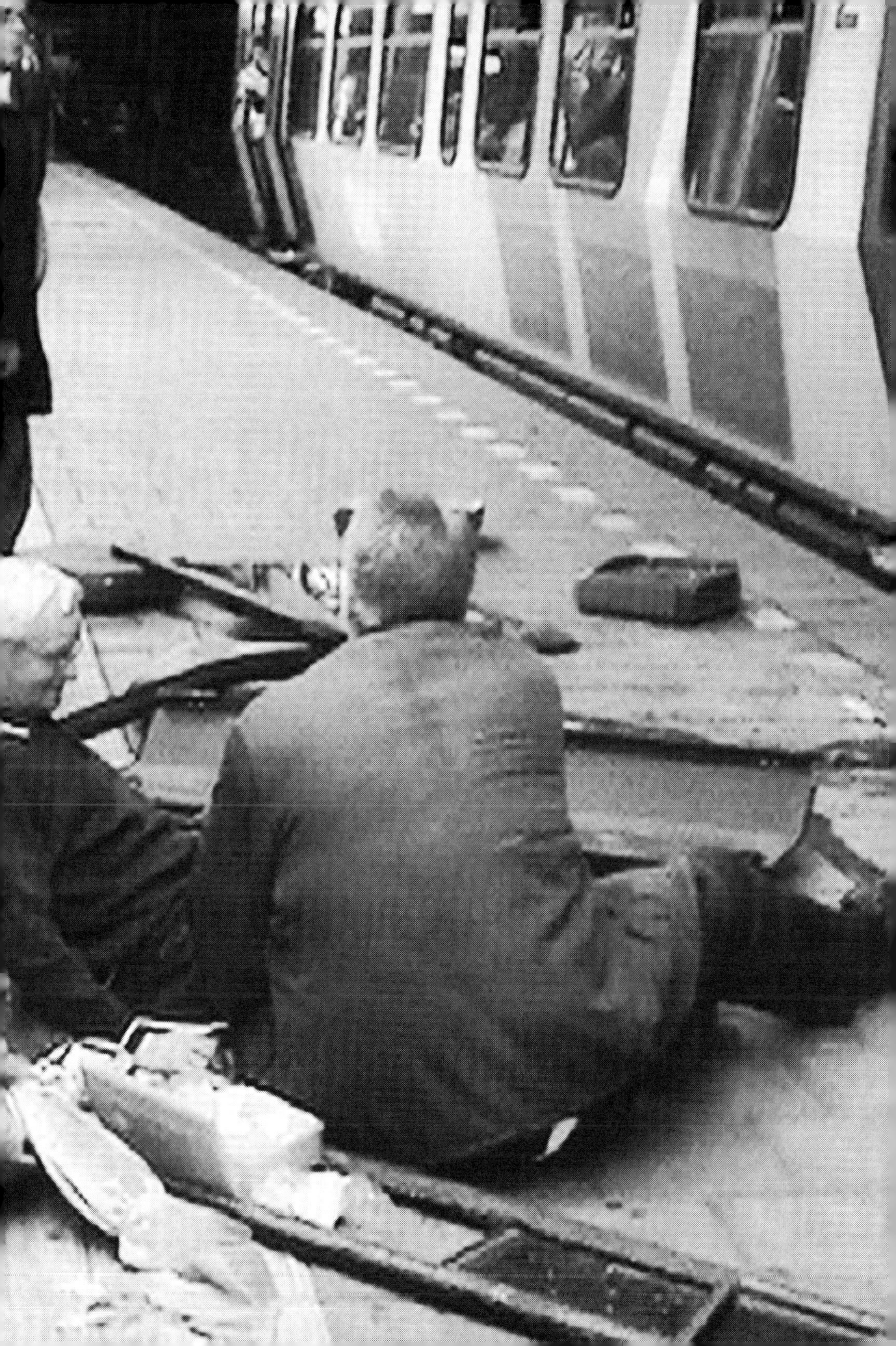

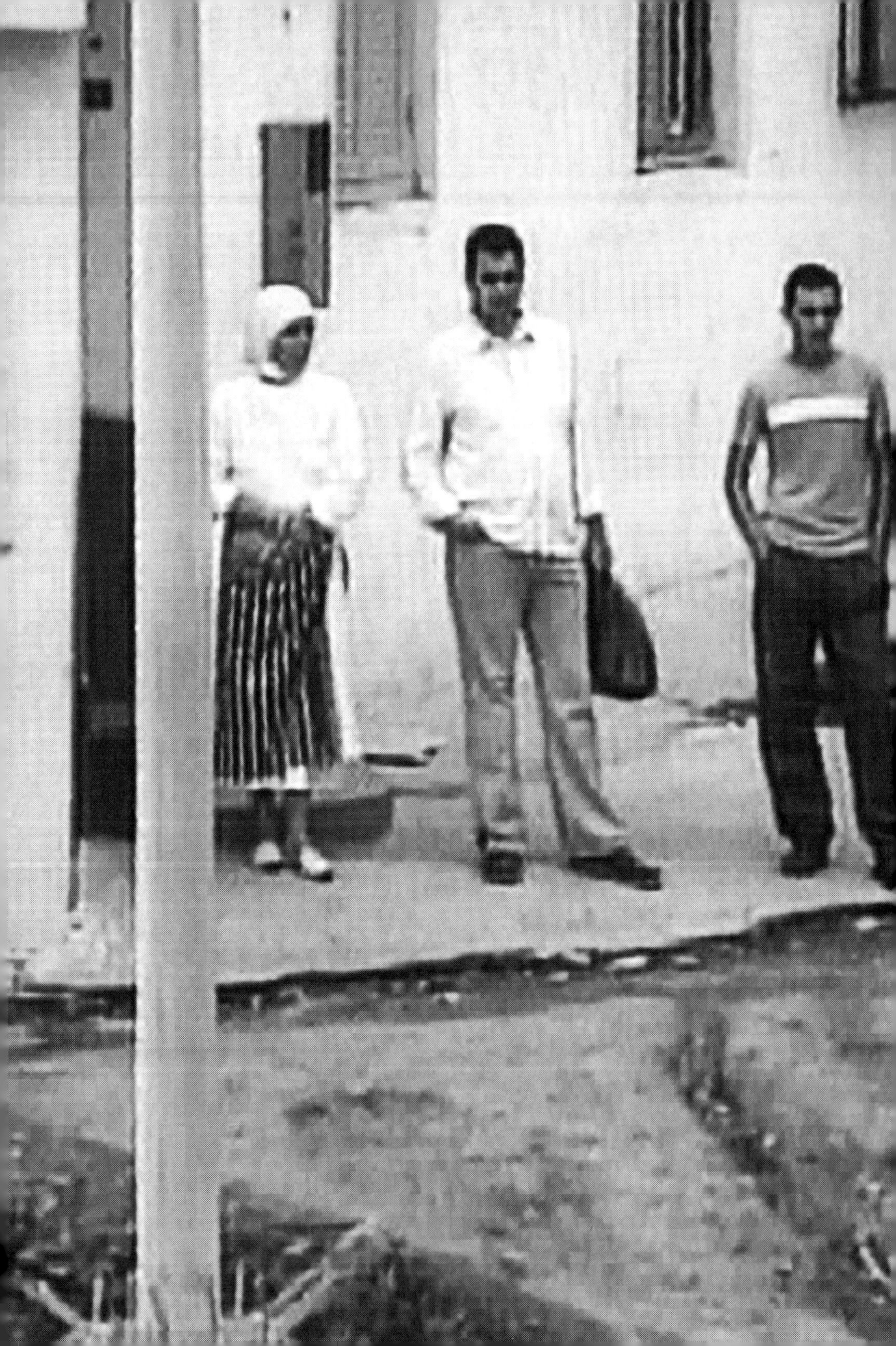

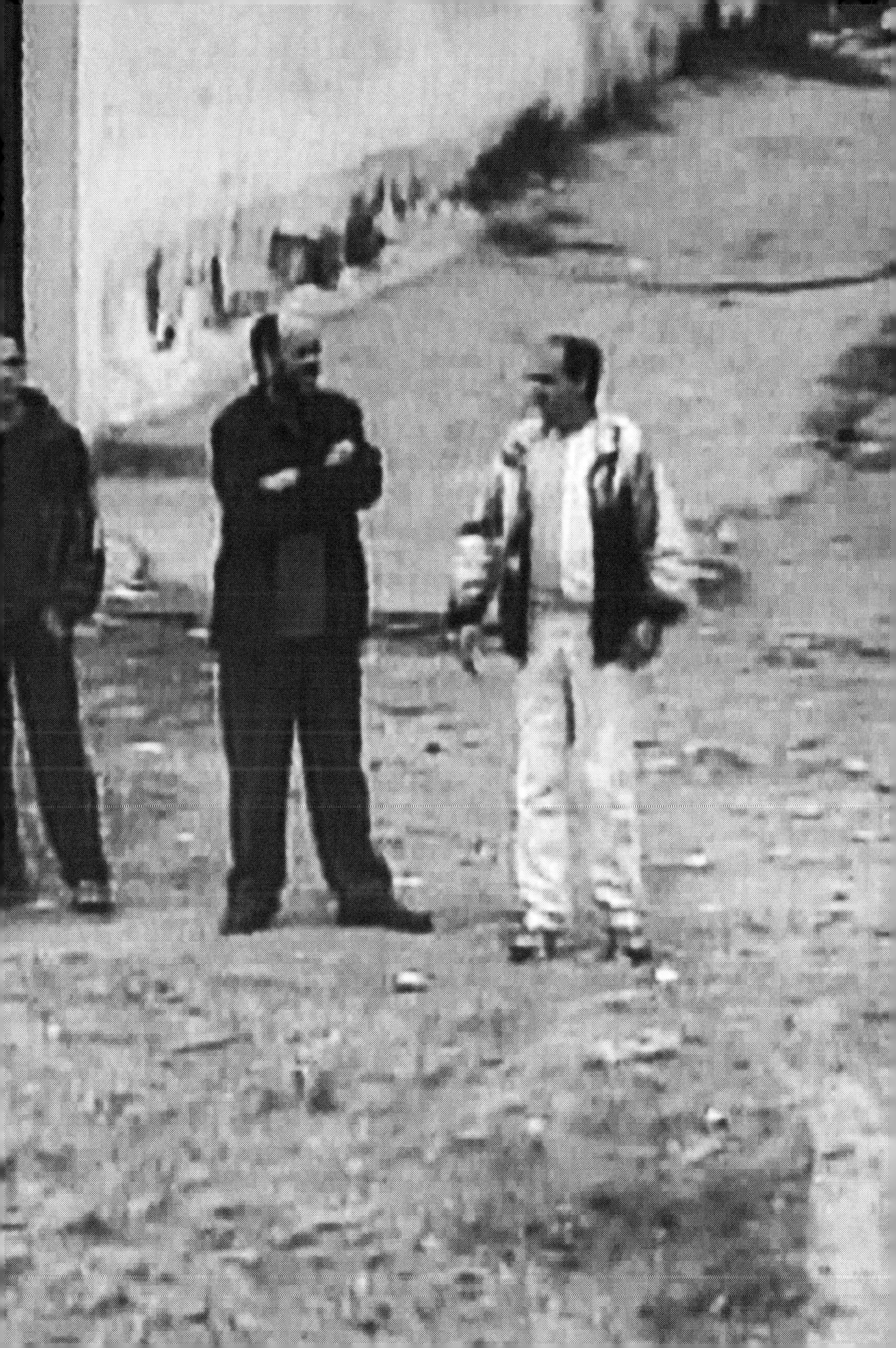

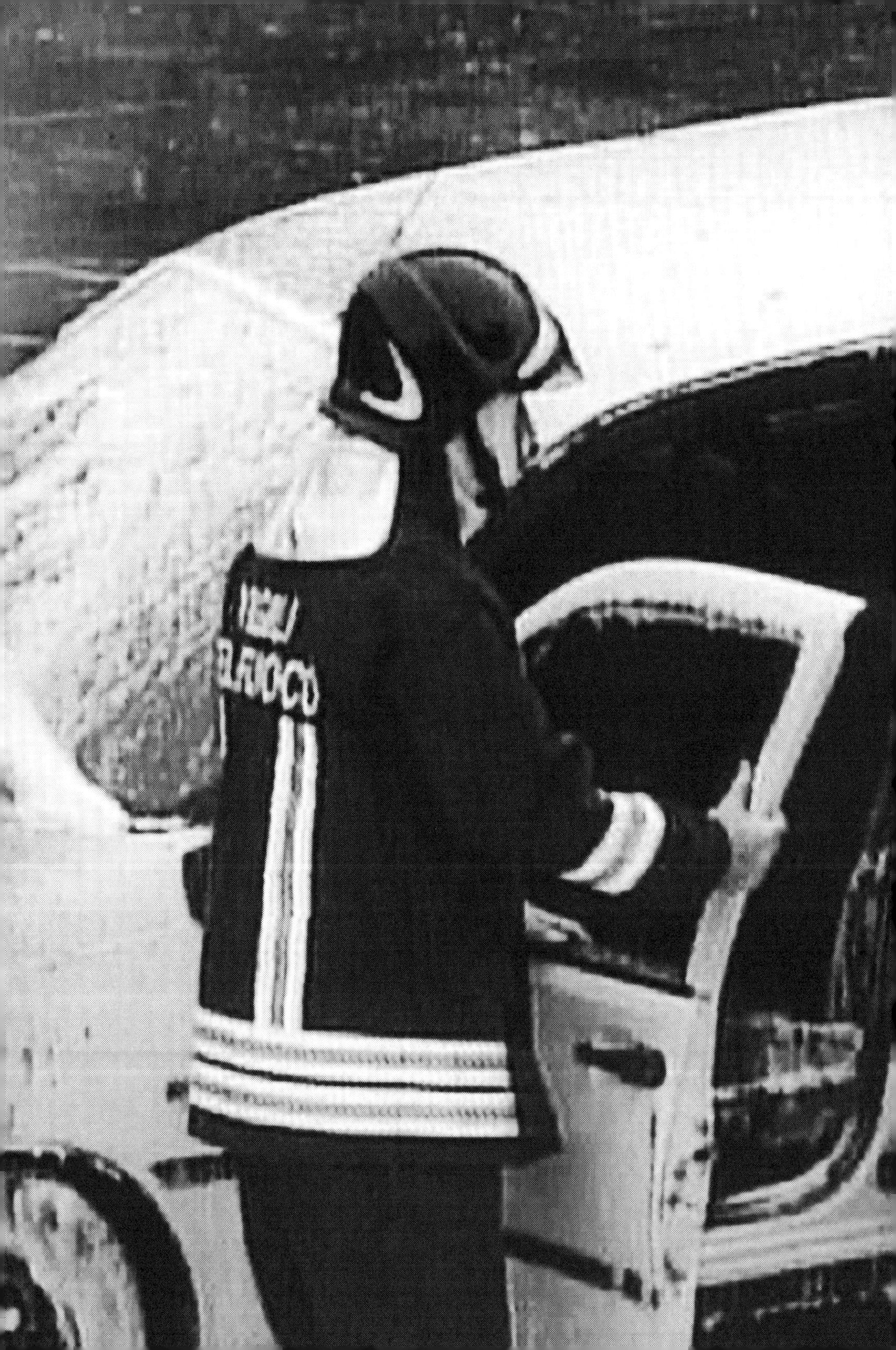
NEW
MEXICO

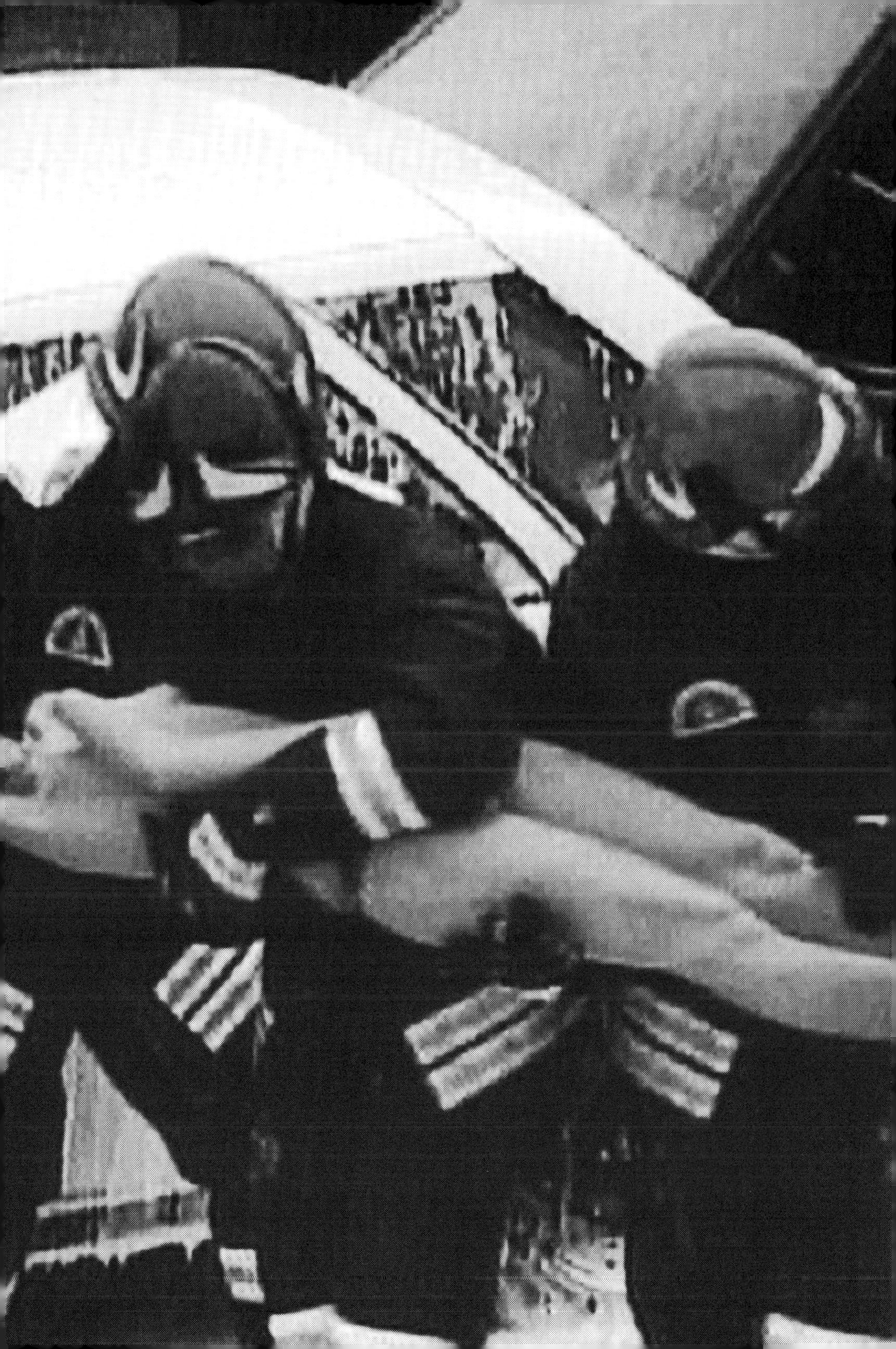

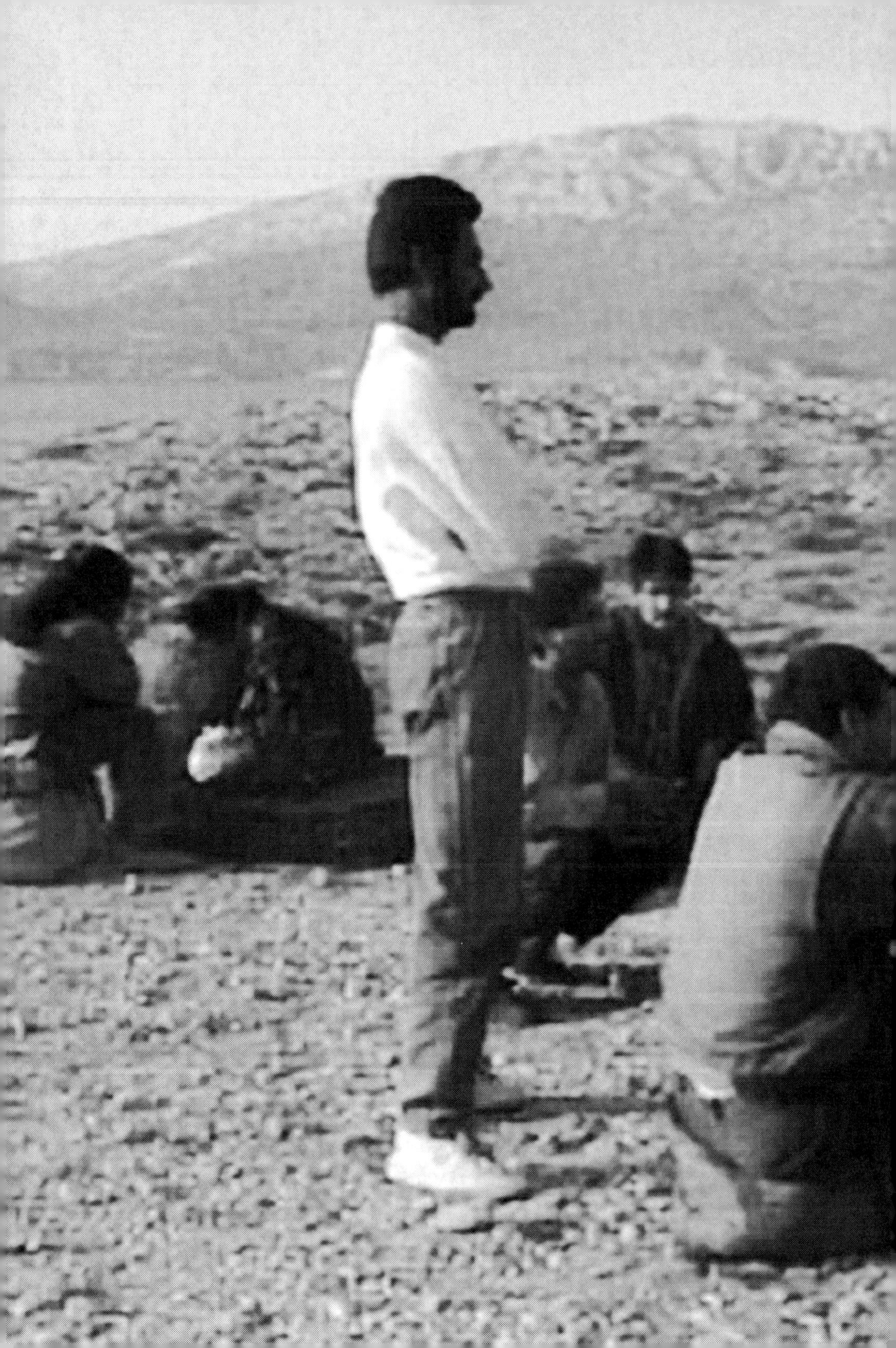

---

# **Proposals for the Future**
## A Conversation with Melvin Moti

---

---

itorial note: The title of this work
halen uit Suriname. According to
tist, Stories from Surinam is a
ation of the original title. While
ountry is sometimes referred to
rinam' in English publications,
ding to official government
ments and the Surinamese
nment, the correct spelling of
ountry is 'Suriname'. With the
ation of the title of Moti's work,
e 'Suriname' throughout the
r.

**Maria Hlavajova** I would like to begin with your work *Stories from Surinam* (2002).[1] It is a thirty-minute video in which you address the Dutch colonial past, which is still unresolved to a large extent. You highlight the period between 1873 and 1916, when at least 34,000 workers came from India to Suriname to work on Dutch plantations. Despite how long ago these events took place, you were able to locate a few of the labourers. Given your personal biography – you were born in the Netherlands to Surinamese immigrants – was this project a way of tracing your own past in a sense?

> **Melvin Moti** I think it's good to begin here, as *Stories from Surinam* is the start and foundation of my work. The film is partly an attempt at tracing my past and personal history within the Indian Diaspora, since it highlights the period of Indian immigration to Suriname, but there are other immigration waves that aren't discussed in the work (i.e. African and Indonesian). For that reason it cannot be considered a work on the history of Suriname.

**MH** You mentioned on another occasion that the only way your parents could live in the Netherlands was to divorce themselves radically from their past. Yet, if one could generalize about a few key conceptual aspects of your work, creating a dynamic relationship with history would certainly belong to the list.

> **MM** I think this dissociation was very important on an emotional level for my parents – to deal with feelings of 'longing' or 'desire' for the old country, and still be able to look ahead to a new life. I would prefer not to connect the dynamic relation to history that I indeed investigate in my films to this emotional approach of my parents. Most of the subjects I research are discovered 'in the night of forgotten historical memories', fished out, salvaged, brought to light and used for contemporary purposes.[2] But *Stories from Surinam* is definitely my most 'historical' work; in more recent works I see these black holes in history as a proposal for the future. *Stories from Surinam* resides in the past; it is now a memory of a memory.

**MH** *Stories from Surinam* is structured as an account of oral history, based upon the personal anecdotes and personal

chel Foucault and Sylvere
ger, *Foucault Live: Interviews,
1984* (New York: Semiotext(e),
139.

observations of the contract workers, at times juxtaposed with archival material. What relationship do you see in this work between these personal histories and the official historiography on this period?

**MM** Well, this question was one of the main reasons to produce the work. Of course there has been an exhaustive examination of this period of immigration by historians. Yet, because of the time span and the complex nature of the circumstances, publications are often written on the meta-level, focusing on the big picture and the larger economic and social consequences of this migration. I can understand this, but also understood that if the micro-level could be of any importance to this history, it was essential to try and grasp it now, since the personal anecdotes would probably not be handed down to another generation. Unlike with Creole oral history, the Indian stories aren't readily written down; there is no literature that developed around it. The tradition of storytelling was thus purely oral, but also something typically Indian. I didn't recognize this with my grandparents, for example, because they are from a more defensive and reserved second generation of immigrants. So because of this change in the community and the lack of a literary tradition, folk tales and small, everyday stories became vulnerable. Since the last generation of Indian contract workers was almost gone, this was really the last chance for me to focus on oral history. The people interviewed in Suriname were between 88 and 102 years old (at the time of my visit), and were children of the contract workers, most of whom were born in India. From the start I knew I was not going to censor them, or attempt to verify their recollections with 'official' historiography. I was interested in their pace of thinking first and foremost, and what it produces; memories which slowly and organically take form, with all the subjective changes and additions shaped by the time between the actual event and now – and the time spent thinking about them in-between. I asked them the most irrelevant questions, such as: 'Do you remember the names of the dogs?' 'What did you think before you went to sleep?' 'What shoes did you wear?' 'What were you doing all day, when you didn't go to school and didn't have to work?' I was looking for hyper-personal anecdotes, and was hoping for secrets that would emerge from a slip of the tongue (I did get some!). So I was mostly interested in their personalities and how these could fill a gap in the official history, and in stories on the level of gossip, rumour or things that were so extremely subjective that they would never be taken into account in any serious historical study. And unbelievably, while editing, I found I could sketch quite an accurate narrative, compared with the official historiography, with all this material based on memory and assertion, and even add a little love story in-between.

**MH** What kinds of observations did the plantation workers make about the Netherlands as a colonial power?

**MM** The Indian plantation workers were tricked into coming to Suriname with promises of lucrative work, but it's important to understand that they were British citizens at the time. After slavery was abolished in 1863, the Dutch were looking for another source of cheap labour for plantation work. Apparently Indians had a good name in Asia as cheap labourers, but they were also moved to British and French Guyana, both neighbours of Suriname (also known as Dutch Guyana). That's where the Dutch got the idea of cooperating with the British to transport some of their citizens, which then started in 1873. The Dutch never made an attempt to assimilate the first generation Indians and therefore they were left speaking their native language, practising their own religion and were not provided with any education in Suriname. They were also supposed to return to their native land after five years, something that didn't happen according to plan, as many of them stayed. The Indian plantation workers were offered a deal: they could go back and receive some extra money, or they were granted a piece of land for subsistence agriculture, in return for this same amount of money. So many of them stayed, and were able to build a life of their own through this modest farming.

So the Dutch weren't the only 'colonial power' active during the Indian immigration, as the Indians had to answer to the Dutch, but the Dutch had to answer to the British. The British made agreements with the Dutch to protect Indian workers, and were very strict in applying these protective laws – which dealt with wages, the length of the work agreements, duration of the workday, etc. During the contract period some Indian revolts arose, sparked either by poor working conditions or cultural clashes – one Dutch plantation owner was killed after trying to touch an Indian woman. So there were obviously tensions, but in general I found out that these first-generation Indians were somewhat left alone by the Dutch. After 1916, when this wave of immigration stopped, most plantation workers who stayed in Suriname became self-employed and their outlook on the Dutch was influenced more by economic than political arguments. In regard to power, one could say that the Dutch government indeed was a colonial power, but one that also stimulated independent and individual production, a form of stimulating self-determination. At least this was the point of view of most Indian immigrants whom I spoke to during my trip. They were fond of the efficiency, resourcefulness and commercial talents of the Dutch, all economic arguments.

As for the present day: there are more pictures of the Dutch queen in Surinamese houses than anywhere in the Netherlands. I think that says a lot about the complexity of the issue. There is a love-hate relationship, especially among older Surinamese. I think from the Dutch side there is traditionally not much reflection on the country's role as a colonizer. From the Surinamese side this role is discussed in very different terms. About half of the political rulers wanted independence to happen sooner rather then later, but the other half actually wanted to stay under Dutch rule for a while, to stabilize the country before gaining independence, which finally happened in 1975. Considering the inclusion of the Surinamese language into the Dutch language union in 2003 – which affords protection, conservation and examination of the language – there is an ongoing partnership between the two nations, not only on economic and political issues, but also culturally.

**MH** Although you were born in the Netherlands I recall you saying that being a son of immigrant parents created a sort of a distance to the country. What kind of a distance did you have in mind? Do you have an experience of being an '*allochtoon*' artist in the Netherlands?

**MM** I was afraid the question of the '*allochtoon*' artist would be asked. I believe there is no such thing as a 'Dutch artist', nor is there anything like an '*allochtoon* artist'. Of course there are the official definitions of the word, like non-western immigrants, or immigrants and second-generation immigrants, but let's face it: the question is always asked when the person – or artist – is non-white. To me, merely having 'a colour' doesn't assume a position, not as a person, nor as an artist. I always found it interesting how the infamous 'one-drop rule' formed the notion of blackness in the US. Whites invented the rule, which claimed that 'one drop' of African blood made you a black person, no matter how remote the connection with your African ancestry. As with so many things, this doctrine was eventually used as a source of pride for African Americans; so what was meant as a stain of impurity became a badge of identity. This far-reaching change in identity, and social and historic positions, came to life with nothing but a change in thought. The definition of the 'one-drop rule' is still the same, but the whole issue is turned upside down. We shape the world and ourselves by our thoughts, and I would like to suggest that in this, there are no limitations. I don't think that the notion of colour or identity is central in my work; I'm more interested in this shift of thought. It's possible to mentally and linguistically reinvent or recreate ourselves by reassessing the definitions.

**MH** How do you feel when confronted by the 'new realism' – an attitude aimed at breaking taboos and shifting the boundaries of what is politically acceptable when speaking of the migrant communities in the Netherlands?

**MM** To me it's a big relief! Finally things are out in the open. It's gone with the charade and time for some ugliness. For decades the Netherlands maintained the image of being a 'tolerant' nation – whereas it was obvious that the discussion regarding migration had always been ignored. I think it's important for us to keep in mind that the whole discourse developed in the last thirty years around issues like postcolonialism, migration and the notion of the 'other' has been completely circumvented in the Netherlands. Since a few years now, this new realism has had a firm grasp on the national debate in the Netherlands, moving from an outcast position to the mainstream, but it is in no way proposing a new situation. It's actually 'recreating' an antique-folkloric version of Holland, which never existed in the first place: it's this fantasy that they're selling! It seems to me much more favour-able to use the courses this discussion has left us – the work of

Edward Said, Stuart Hall, Homi Bhabha, V. S. Naipaul, Ngugi wa Thiong'o and all the others – and to stop asking questions like 'What does it mean to be Dutch?' or 'What does it mean to be non-Dutch?' in the Netherlands. These questions are basically being imposed on us by the integration discussion – one of the inventions of this new realist thinking – which is completely irrelevant in the highly globalized world we're living in right now. So it's good that the silence has broken, and surely it's better to stop whispering and start shouting,[3] but the shouting occurring now is offensive and hostile. I imagine a more constructive shouting, like through a megaphone at a 'block party' – loud, enhancing and empowering; this kind of shouting is supposed to create a movement and not fear.

**MH** So what's the place of art in all this? Could we discuss this through the example of *No Show* (2004), a 16 mm film transferred to video? Here you bring the viewer to the Hermitage museum during the Second World War. You found out that the exhibition rooms of the Hermitage were empty from 1941 to 1944. Valuable artworks were removed in order to avoid damage during the war, and the Russian Army assisted in bringing the works to safety. Only the frames were left on the walls, and, occasionally, guided tours were given, in which the pieces that originally hung there would be described from memory. You reconstructed part of one such walk-through in the museum given to a group of soldiers. I would like to hear more about the background and meaning of this work.

**MM** Pavel Gubchevsky was a member of the scientific staff of the Hermitage before the Second World War. At the time of the war, he was conscripted into military service, but due to a heart condition he didn't pass the medical exam, so he had to continue working in the museum. He was the only young man in his thirties among elderly women and men. Because of the occupation, the army assisted in heavy labour, like repairing parts of the building after bomb blasts or relocating parts of the collection that had been left in the museum. At the end of such a working day, the soldiers usually received a general introduction to the museum about the building, history and collection. However, Gubchevsky, being the most popular pre-war tour guide, conducted several tours in which he spoke about the content of the paintings, as if they were still

[3] Radiohead, 'Stop Whispering' Pablo Honey (Capitol Records, 199

hanging, while all there was left to see were empty frames.
I spoke about this with Lyudmila Voronikhina, his widow, who
ironically is currently in charge of training all tour guides of the
museum. This account, together with three sentences in a
book by Daniil Granin, is the only confirmation of this event.

Based on this information, the film I made is about many
things. For one, it's an indication of the unique environment
within the museum during the war. There were about 2000
people permanently living in the museum, and amazingly
beautiful watercolours were made of daily life in the
Hermitage by Vera Miliutina, many of which have never seen
light outside of the archive. There were exhibitions and
seminars held in the shelters of the museum. So there was a
continuous academic and creative force, confined within the
museum walls, while Leningrad was under siege. The most
interesting thing to me was the idea that Gubchevsky's guided
tour was a conceptual performance, occurring before
conceptual art was contextualized in the 1960s, and in a
location which positions itself as stridently anti-conceptual –
there is one Malevich on display, on the top floor, in a corner . . .
as if it's a disease. The display and most of the content of the
Hermitage collection hasn't changed since the 1930s; it's a
classic and very static museum. I think the air in there is at
least half a century old and most employees can be
considered living sculptures with perfume and fluent foreign
language skills. I think it's astonishing that in the 1940s such
a pure conceptual work was produced in such a context and
under such conditions. But considering the daily life in the
Hermitage during the war, it's another radical gesture, another
radical artistic approach, and not so strange after all. Both this
radicalism and pure conceptualism is what got me started on
this project.

**MH** You also published a book as a part of the project, as you
thought it important to provide another platform for the
precious information you found during your research. Could
you elaborate on this?

**MM** It took me about seven months of lobbying to get permission to visit the archives and libraries of the Hermitage!
The only reason I got in was because of my obsessive
behaviour – normally it's impossible to get permission.

When I was there, I saw one man leaning over a drawing with
magnifying glasses . . . I thought he was dead; he was so old
and pale. I realized I was probably going to be the only young
person and contemporary artist rummaging through those
documents for a long time. So I decided then, that if I made
it out alive, I would treat whatever findings I retrieved as
precious information. Of course, I contextualize most
information I get in the framework of contemporary art, which
is just the way I think of being an artist. I thought it would be
good to point out this attitude, connected to the impenetrable
archive in that publication.

While working on the film, which is based on all the research
I did in the Hermitage, I decided to continue the pure conceptual approach of the event, and make the film as minimal as
possible. The result is a twenty-four minute static shot of an
empty museum hall, which gradually gets darker, a result of
the setting sun outside of the hall. I also decided to include
as little extra historical information as possible in the sound,
so I only recreated part of one tour and left out all this fairly
interesting information. I wrote down my research in this
publication in a very dry way, without much historical or art-
historical pretence, thus minimizing the information in the
film itself. Apart from that, I just had to describe the surreal
experiences I had with the staff members and in the archive
to believe it really did happen.

**MH** In my opinion you created a homage to the power of art
with this work – a statement that is both poetic and political –
about art's capacity to deal with and react to hardship and
crises. How do you view the place of art vis-à-vis major social
and political challenges such as war, colonial history, or
immigration, for example? What kind of propositions for the
future does the current situation in the West call for, to follow
the conceptual premise of your film work?

**MM** You're right that *No Show* is a film about art in times of
crisis. It's a radical proposal to conserve and deal with art. This
event – the original guided tour – was made for the future, but
we're simply not there yet. To me, it's also a lesson in abstract
thinking in reference to art. What the event puts forward is the
idea, the abstract idea, that we don't need any pictures to
remind us of the power of art. Even in the worst case, if the

precious collection of the Hermitage would one day burn to the ground in flames, there is a way to preserve it: by creating a mental archive. Also the event is about observation: Do you remember what you saw? Can you recall it? No? So you forgot to look at it. All these layers are about an essence of art, which can be considered a 'survival' or 'guerrilla' mode, and which comes to the surface in times of scarcity – scarcity being a metaphor. It's all about a way to stretch the borders of our imagination, which is obviously called upon during crises.

This very radical approach is what interests me most in art nowadays, as a mechanism that creates the impossible. It's a mechanism for inventing – and thus influencing – the future, a mechanism to create new models. The belief in the impossible and in the imagination is a weapon. Let's forget about the present for a while. I see the place of art, in circumstances you refer to, definitely not as a way to discuss or describe problems, but to surpass them, look ahead and propose radical models for a different future. The future is formed by our imagination and discoveries, so we're on the good side of the story, since we're busy with imagination and discovery. In that sense, we are the future!

*This conversation took place via e-mail in spring 2007.*

 **Proposals for the Future**
A Conversation with Melvin Motl

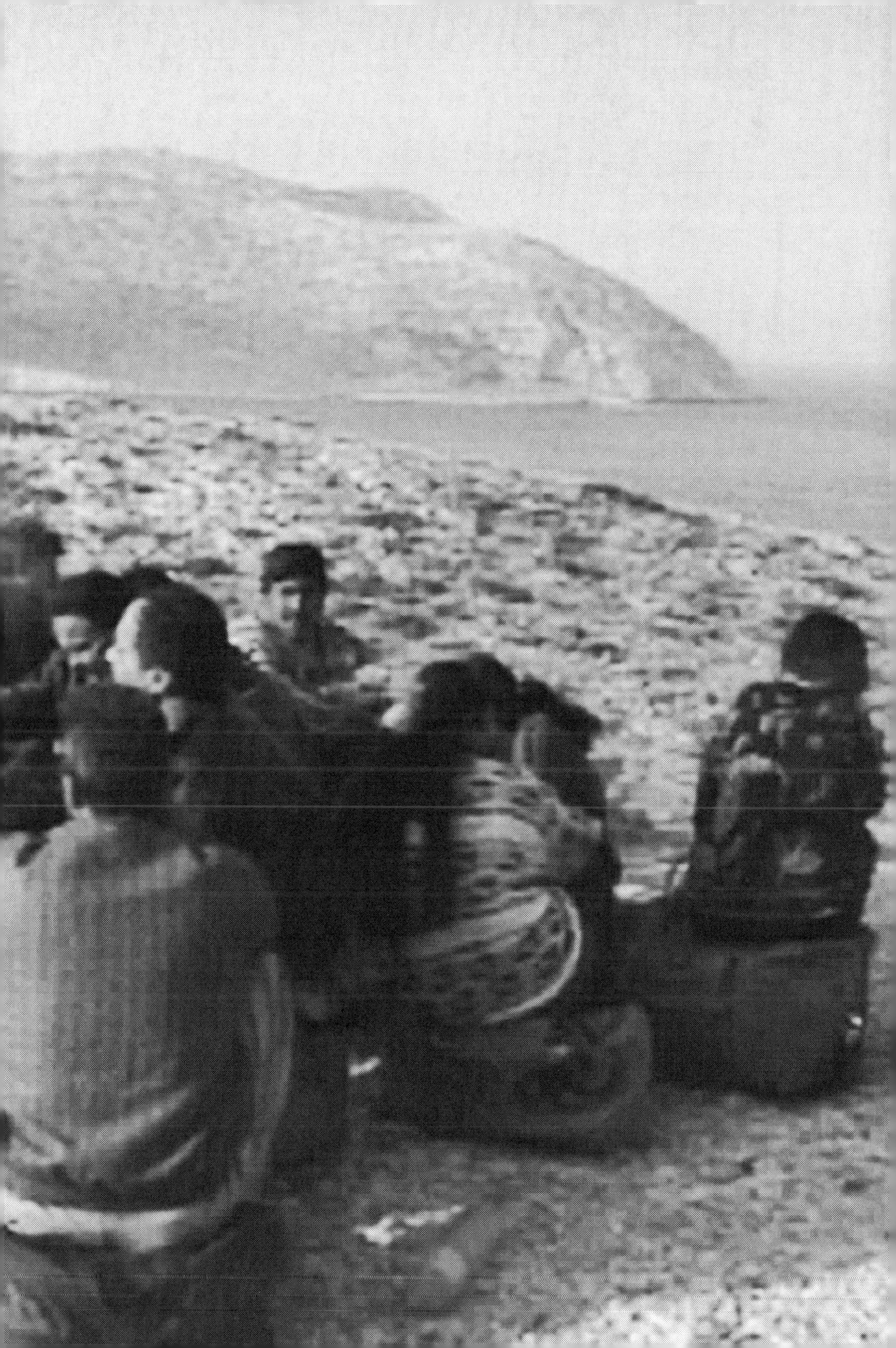

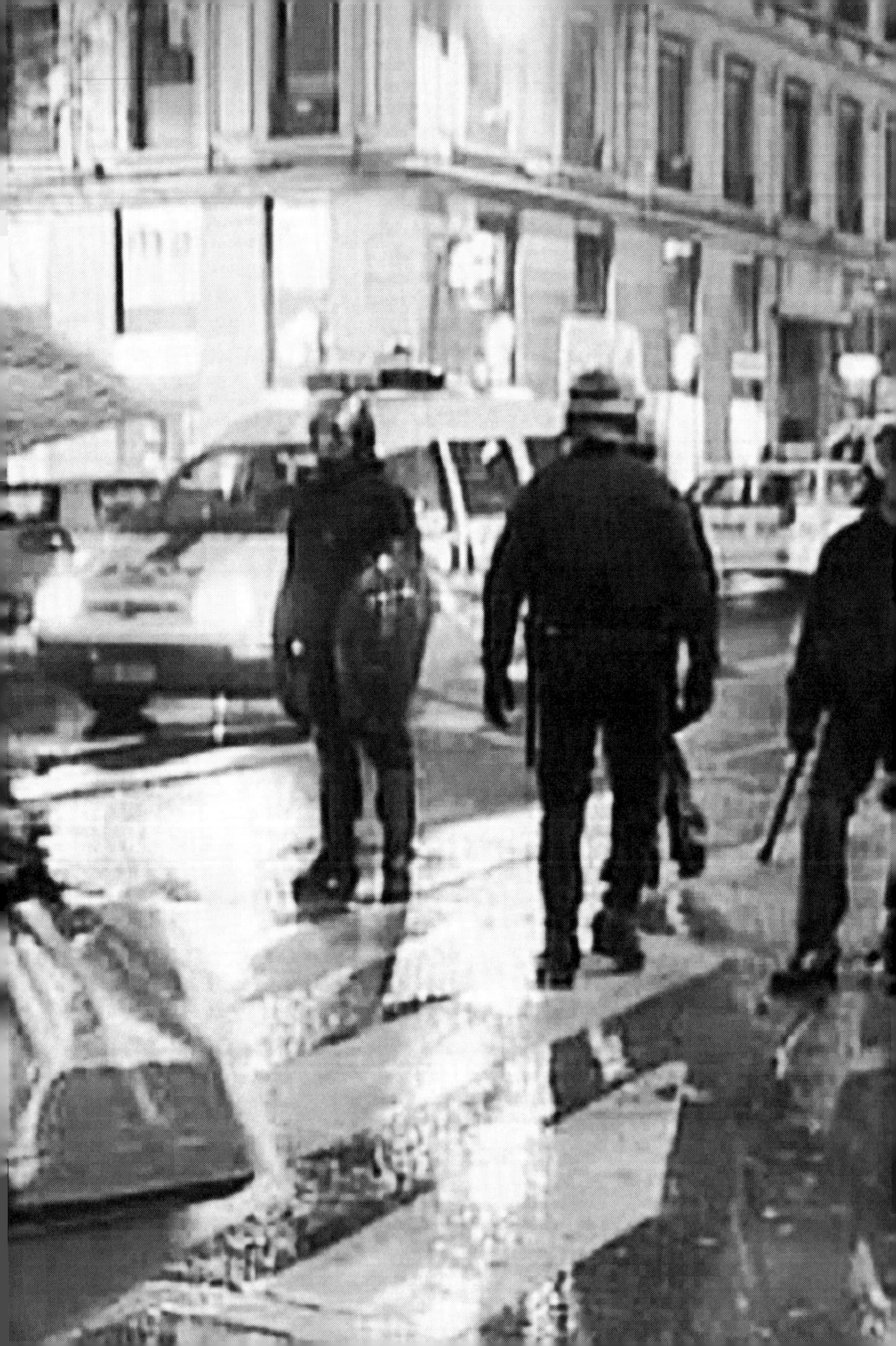

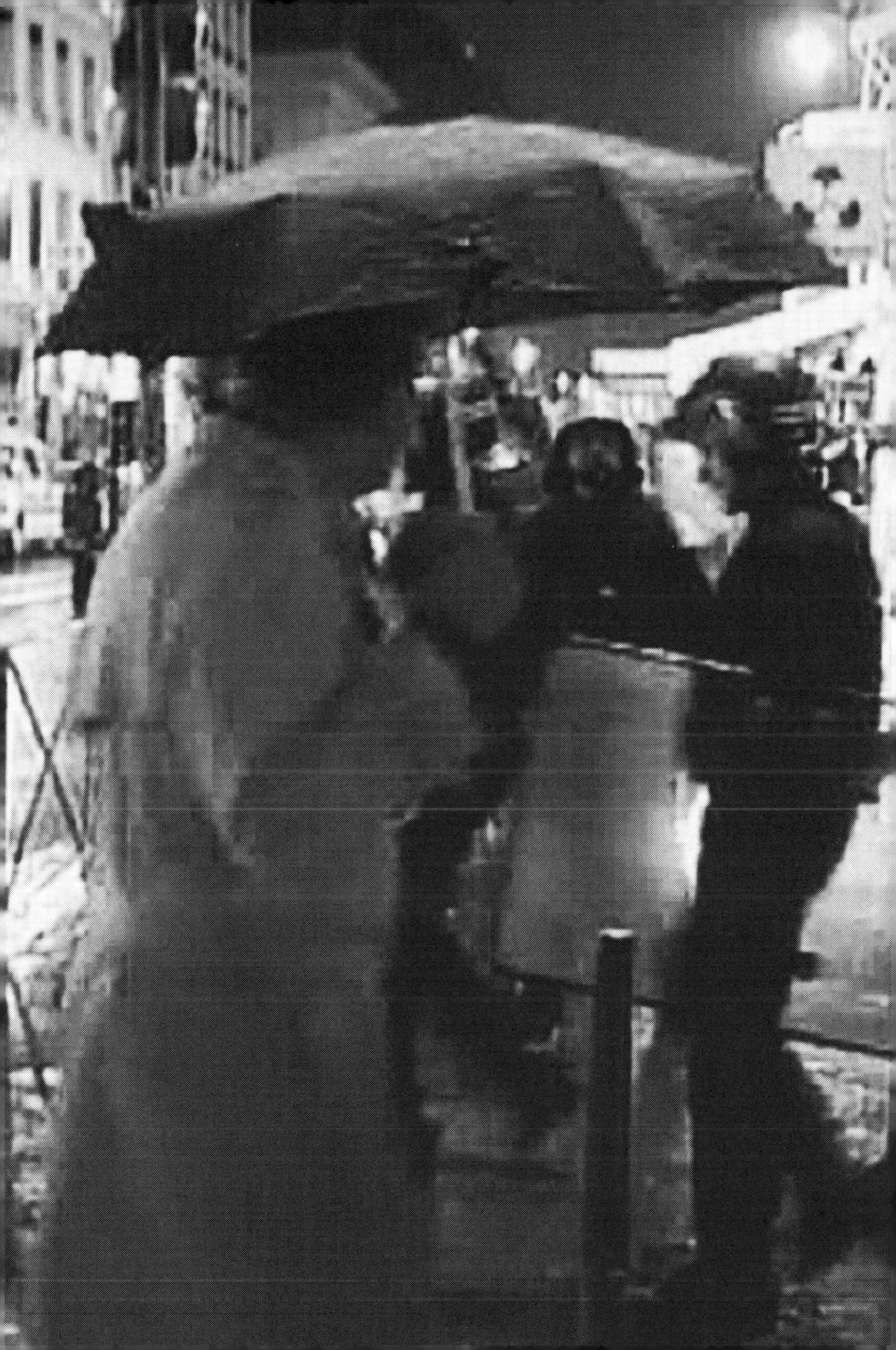

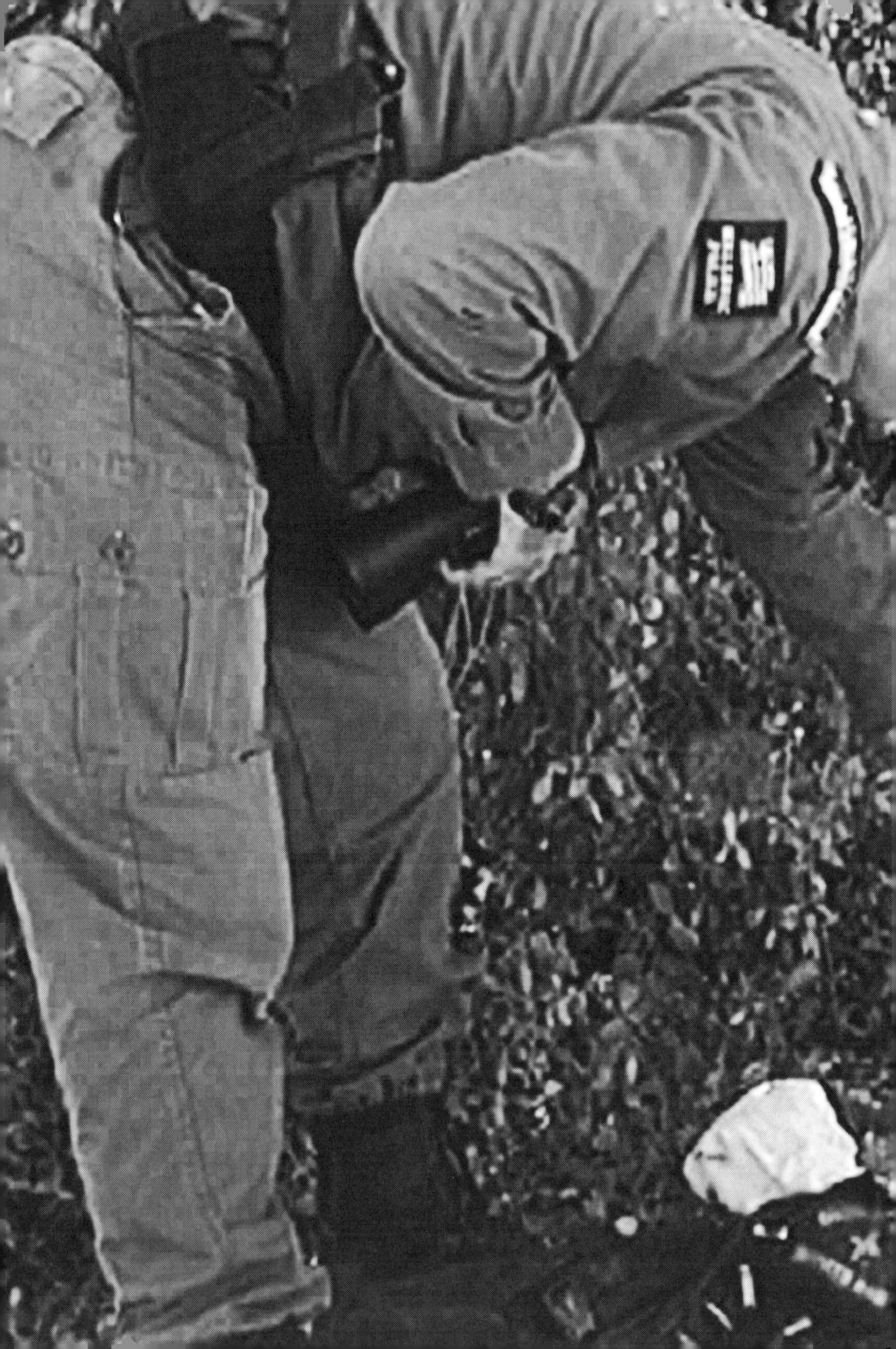

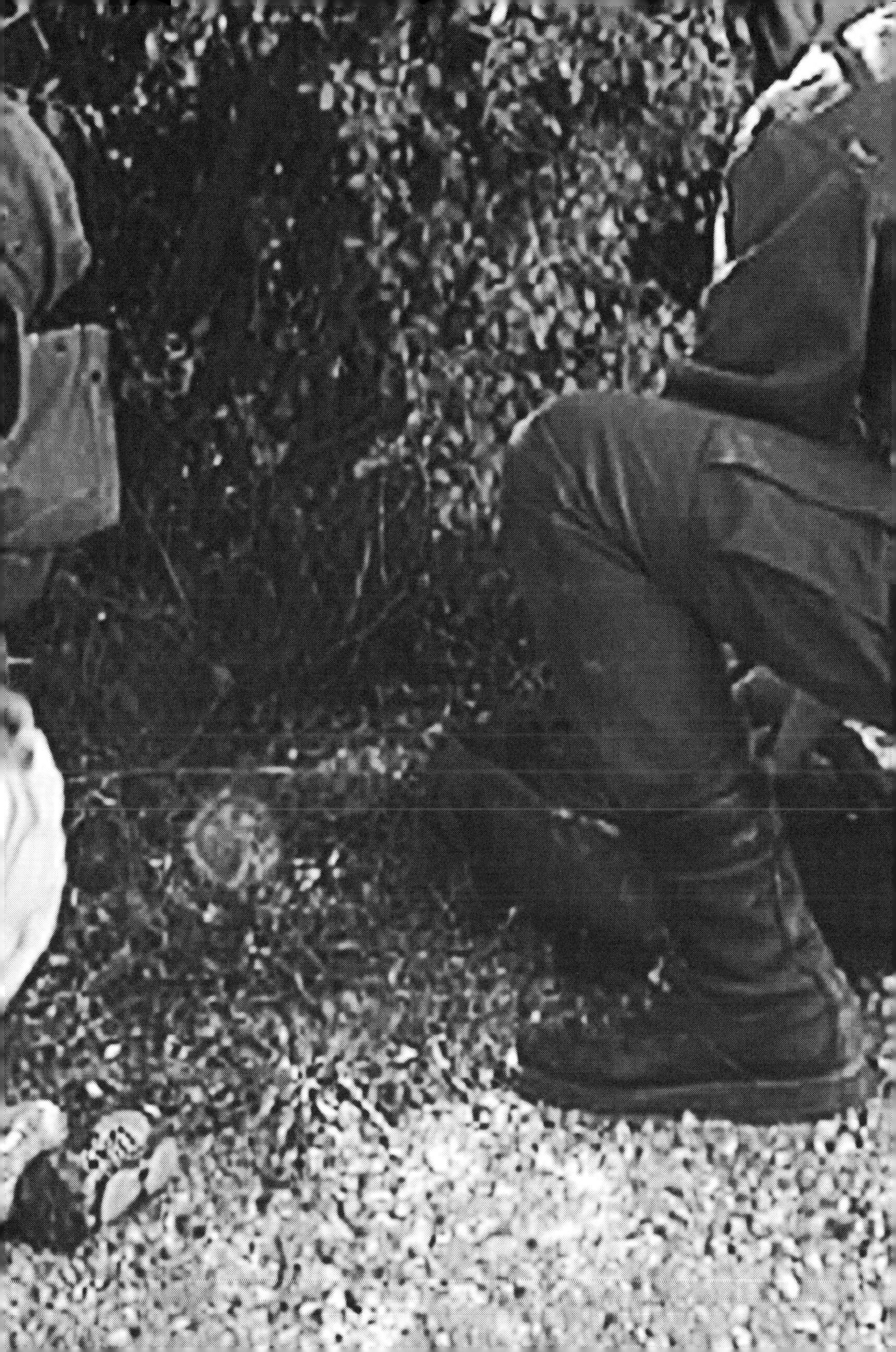

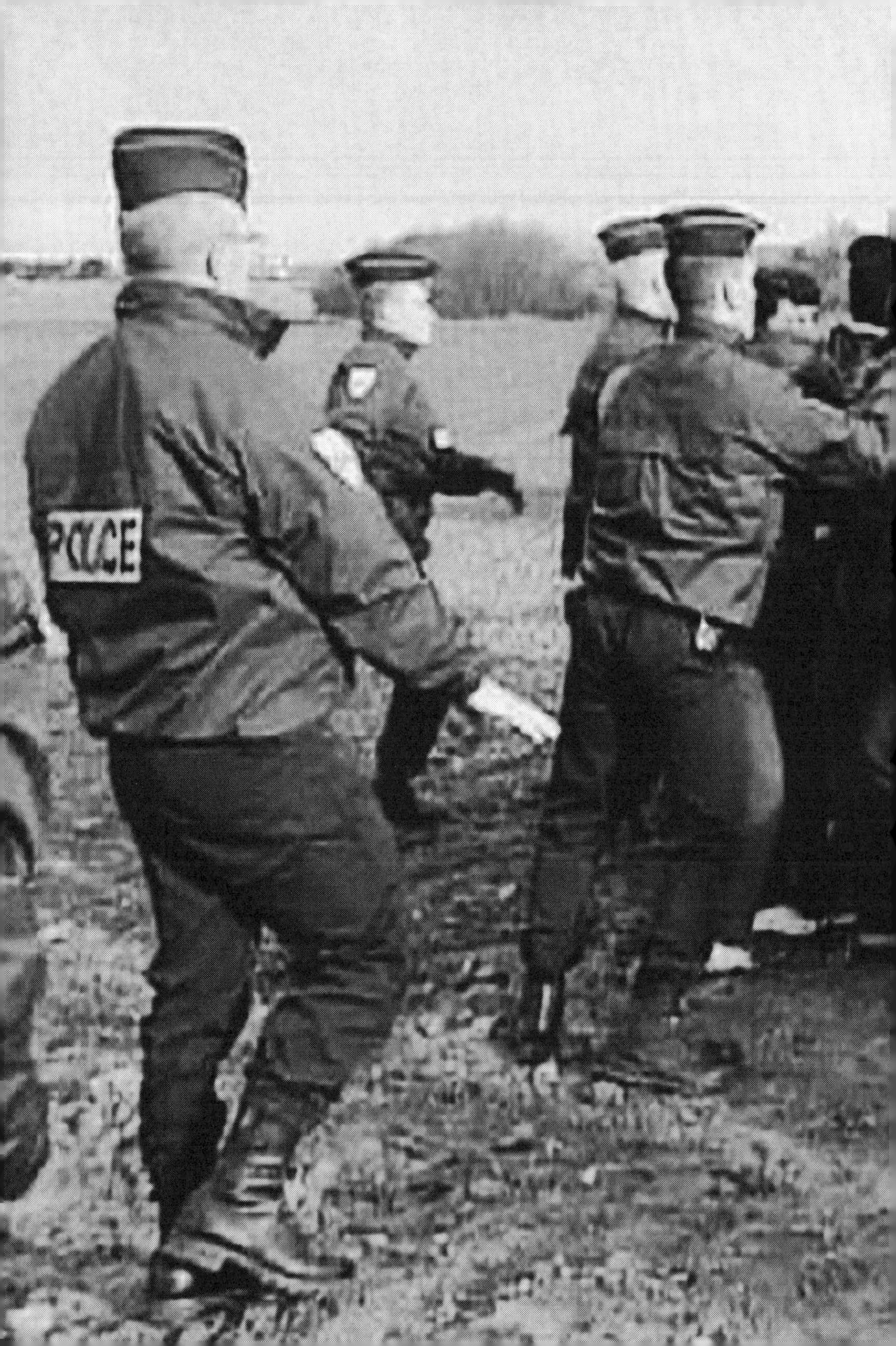

# New Cultural Citizens are Not Born but Created

Sohelia Najand

## Between individual and collective

In times of confusion and uneasiness it is good to get back to basics and pose a number of fundamental questions: What kind of world do we want to live in? Which responsibilities do we wish to have? Which rights and duties are involved, and which values? These questions, formulated well over 200 years ago by Immanuel Kant, are more valid than ever, but how do we answer them today? First of all, we need to examine the complex world in which we live. It is a world in constant flux due to far-reaching processes such as globalization, global migration, postmodern individualism and the digitization of information and communication; nothing is certain. Only accepting the fact that we live in a constantly changing world can offer any support. But how – within this context – do we arrive at a society where everyone feels safe and committed? What holds things together as they shift and fall apart?

In the Netherlands and particularly in its cities, countless cultures – as evinced by the huge diversity in religions, habits, music, cuisines, etc. – live packed together. However, this multiculturalism doesn't enrich everyone's lives. In fact, the diversity can be seen to undermine social cohesion and increase feelings of insecurity and uneasiness. There is little evidence today of that once famous Dutch toleration for migrants and cultural change. Instead, the call for traditional standards and values illustrates an increasing sense of panic. Often against their better judgement, public officials and policy makers use tools and make decisions unsuitable for this day and age, while old standards and values no longer suffice to answer Kant's original questions. Terms such as *identity*, *democracy* and even *freedom of expression* need to be redefined within this changing context if we are to find a way forward.

How can this sense of panic be converted into a positive attitude towards the future? The debates about multiculturalism often define cultural diversity as the problem and integration as the solution. But is cultural diversity really the problem and has the lack of efficacy of contemporary integration methods been amply proven? I am convinced that the key lies neither in a multiplicity of cultures ignoring each other while living side by side nor in integration. The feeling of uneasiness and lack of social cohesion should be seen much more in the light of postmodern individualism. Unity is no longer possible within this form of individualism, because reality is determined by what an individual can cope with. Differences between individuals and groups are emphasized more than ever if everyone is allowed to vent their opinion without fear of reprisal. At the same time there is something implicit in the call for integration that requires the relinquishing of your own identity in a way that postmodern humans cannot accept. The postmodern human refuses to have his/her freedom of choice taken away. That is why, for me, the challenge is to find equilibrium between individual freedom and social cohesion, to strike a balance between 'I think, therefore I am', Descartes's adage that constitutes the basis of western thought and 'we are, therefore I am', which is the precept of many non-western cultures. Only when we are able to achieve such equilibrium can a new form of community come into existence that does not obstruct individual identity development. The implications of this new approach, in which the individual is no longer central, can be both liberating and threatening. Threatening because solidarity is often confused with totalitarianism and is unjustifiably linked to terrorism and fundamentalism. Liberating because understanding that freedom is not an individual matter, but a social concept that can lead to a reformulation of etiquette and the development of social contacts in spite of and thanks to the many differences. It is therefore important to work on the quality of future citizenship and on new forms of social cohesion.

### New cultural citizenship

The foundation that I founded in the Netherlands, InterArt started exploring the term *new cultural citizenship* three years ago in order to stimulate the development of new forms of citizenship. New cultural citizenship is a study into the way in which individuals and groups can shape social changes and cultural innovation in times of globalization and cultural multiplicity, and into the way postmodern individualism can be united with collective responsibility and cultural diversity. New cultural citizenship should be taken to mean neither the assimilation of immigrants nor a shared cultural identity. In fact, new cultural citizenship bases itself on diversity. The uncertainty brought on by continuous change inspires the creation of other societal forms that provide room for groups and individuals to entertain different opinions. The objective is the actualization of the individual's autonomy in relation to others, i.e. within a social context. Lack of knowledge about the other and uncertainty about recognition by the other leads to fear and hampers the individual's development. The strength of autonomy is that it has both a passive and active side. It provides passive access to culture and democratic processes and an active right to their production and ultimately to the co-design of one's own living environment. An autonomous citizen is therefore not only a consumer, but also a producer. In new cultural citizenship everyone contributes innovation in culture and society in their own way. However, this is always related to a collective responsibility beyond the boundaries of liberal individualism. After all, if individuals feel responsible for their role in a process, their commitment to their own environment and their will to solve problems will increase. Shared citizenship entails a sense of a shared fate with regard to the future.

A new cultural citizen develops his or her (cultural) identity inside a pluriform, internationally oriented society. New cultural citizens will have to determine their own position within an unlimited quantity of ideas, opinions and stances and will have to be open to others and communicate with them. This demands a new, creative approach to the term citizenship, because cohesion between people is no longer natural – we are no longer automatically part of a group, a village, a town or a country. Heritage, family, the immediate living environment or nationality do not provide the same certainties they used to. We are all global citizens. Satellite television and the Internet keep us in constant contact with the whole world, but we don't even know our own neighbours. Sadly, as a result of far-reaching individualism, many people are alone. That is why it is important to redefine our current values, to go in search of hidden values and register the skills or competences people need to have now and in the future, in order to be able to understand and appreciate one another.

### Passions and talents

What are the competences a new cultural citizen requires to be able to function and be happy in today's complex society? To start with, he or she needs autonomy, flexibility and openness, competences that, ironically, the business sector has been demanding for years. However, from an economic perspective, autonomy is merely seen as independence with no social frame of reference. I therefore redefine the term on the basis of independence, authenticity and commitment, in the context of social responsibility and permanent consciousness raising. Flexibility harbours a risk as it can turn people into modern-day slaves. I define flexibility on the basis of personal curiosity, openness and the willingness to change. I define openness as internal discipline, perseverance and individual passion. It is important to note that these competences can fill the void created by the disappearance of child-rearing methods based on religion or humanist convictions. It is now up to individuals themselves to independently create a control factor such as time consciousness.

Another important competence is the stimulation and coaching of passions, as these create inspired, motivated and committed people. Working or studying without putting your heart into it makes you bored or worse still, frustrated and vindictive. It is in everyone's best interest that society consists of citizens who achieve maximum performance on the basis of their own curiosity and passion. Another important characteristic is the capacity to communicate well and to use this to empathize and reflect. Time consciousness, finally, is a competence with close ties to the rise and rapid development of modern technology. Digital technology is a complex new element in our society with which the older generations have little or no experience. Because the elements that provide a clear consciousness of time have disappeared, among other things due to a decrease in inter-human relations, extreme amounts of time are spent on the Internet, playing computer games, talking on mobile phones, etc. Adults, children and young people in particular require additional attention to develop time consciousness as a competence when becoming acquainted with digital technology.

Various institutions are eminently suitable for teaching citizens these competences. After all, a new cultural citizen is not born, but created, and there are institutions that need to take responsibility for such creativity. Citizens should be raised in the broadest sense of the word. Politicians are becoming increasingly enamoured with this idea and the debate on the social and child-rearing tasks of teachers, student counsellors, neighbourhood social workers, imams and the government are not new. In the past, citizenship was primarily promoted through education with – in most countries – enforced language unity. However, in my opinion, it is essential for the government to promote and facilitate actively the concept of citizenship much more than previously, doing so in education, but also in the cultural and media sectors themselves.

New cultural citizenship should be an important theme in education precisely because it concerns children and young people. Unfortunately, study programmes are almost exclusively focused on the demands of trade and industry, which limits education to merely preparing people for the labour market. Personal development and the actualization of an individual's autonomy have been entirely marginalized. Talents and passions that do not fit the demands of trade and industry are hardly recognized and stimulated. Neglecting to encourage and support passions can lead to indifferent, bored citizens. If we do not believe in young people, how are they supposed to believe in themselves? We turn them into uninspired people and then subsequently complain about their lack of motivation. In cooperation with young people, we should seek suitable means with which to make them conscious, autonomous citizens who feel recognized by society and can and want to put their all into their communities. Showing young people how to navigate the endless flow of information by teaching them how to use Google does not suffice. The question as to what all this information leads to and what we should do with it remains unexamined, even though it is precisely this competence which is crucial in order to question the media, that inundate and manipulate us with a flow of information, impeding the development of our own views on matters through its sheer unmanageable quantity.

### Art and culture create new citizens

But if education does not fulfil its duty, how are new cultural citizens to be trained, inspired and facilitated? It should be clear that art and culture can play an important role in this. Art offers inspiration, development and welfare for the individual. In my opinion, in a culturally diverse world, art also has major collective importance. After all, the arts respond to social, cultural, political and economic aspects of global development. Art provides an almost limitless framework for the interpretation of experiences and social commitment. The values expressed by art are – for a change – not (entirely) dominated by functionality and economic yield. For example, art can act as society's conscience and appeals for contemplation and reflection in the viewer.

I am of the opinion that art facilitates autonomy. Alongside offering context and knowledge, art also gives people room to discover things, to think for themselves, to give meaning and to produce things in parallel with their reflections on the artworks they see or hear. Art allows people to discover the talents and passions essential to actualizing autonomy. I am therefore convinced that exercising the imagination by looking at art, and by making it yourself, contributes to the improved understanding of the world and stimulates the realization of the individual's autonomy. Art and culture offer inspiration and an introduction to others and the other. We need art, or to use Oscar Wilde's words: 'Art wouldn't have been born if mankind understood itself and the world.' This is truer now than ever before. Art is a free domain that excludes no one out of hand. It operates akin to a public space in which people interact: rapprochement can develop, but also debate and confrontation. Art, by definition, deals with the relationships between people and their world and other people. Art clarifies and elucidates differences on a cultural, social and societal level. In a world in which many truths and opinions coexist, art is an important tool for finding individual truths and developing identities, just as it is for imagining new possibilities.

Such imaginations get people talking, provoke curiosity, generate questions and debate, force standpoints to be taken and encourage self-reflection. Artists' inquisitive attitudes can make people think about their own position and that of others in society. It can make people interact, and learn to understand and respect one another, so that they once again slowly become part of a single communal society. In the past, religion and ideology were the binding factors in the public sphere, but this has long since ceased to be the case. Now commerce and politics claim public spaces, but they do not add any real meaning. We will only begin to understand ourselves and the world around us again if we invest and embed ourselves in the social context.

Currently, the moods or atmospheres that mobilize and unite us are usually determined by political interventions. At present, these leave us feeling unsatisfied, even used by manipulative power players. At this historic point in time, art and culture can play a crucial role in promoting the process of consciousness raising, identity creation and cultural education so that our commitment is not abused and our link to society is not damaged. The art and culture sector should be positioned in the heart of society. Alongside becoming acquainted with various cultures and cultural expressions, it is primarily important to shape our own individual and collective identity within a social context. Art and culture can prevent conflict by organizing confrontations. They can allow a mutual history and collective memory to develop by establishing new rituals. Art and culture are therefore indispensable.

### Social aesthetics

If art and culture are to play such a crucial role in society they will require a new infrastructure to support them. Top artists, and in a country such as the Netherlands there are never many of those, should be given plenty of room. They should be fully autonomous, but not without obligations. Every society needs its own elite consisting of the avant-garde who push society forward and simultaneously give it cause to reflect. They are capable of adopting an extremely critical attitude and waking the rest of us up so that – through their work – we can understand the spirit of the times and learn how to look at the world differently. It is of great importance that serious investment in this group takes place to allow them to play a historic role. Alongside this small group of top artists, there is a large group of people whose inquisitive attitudes and capacity to develop creative processes enable society to shape an individual and collective identity. Basically, these people are the cultural producers and sometimes their efforts also result in art. This group can also play a historic role. However, our traditional tendency to make value judgements about art and its social positioning is hampering this development. The current tradition surrounding art prevents us from seeing the role of art and culture as essential. Because art with a capital 'A' is valued more, everyone who is incapable of producing 'quality' art tries to gain recognition nevertheless. That is why now is the time to relinquish these value judgements and to give art and culture the space they require to play an historic role. This development will lead to a redefinition of the existing infrastructure. The relationship between the art and culture sector and education will change and all sectors will have to relate more actively to the media. Art education will – as part of such a process – train entirely different students and artists.

Within the new infrastructure, socially committed projects or social aesthetics, formerly often known as 'community art' but now released from its limitations and palliative expectations, will become increasingly important. In principle, social aesthetics includes all forms of artistic endeavour developed in and undertaken by the community as led by an artist who conceptually sets up this process and is able to inspire, facilitate and direct this process and increase the reflexive quality of the end product which is aimed at publicly expressing the issues at stake in that community with artistic quality. The cooperation that characterizes this art form contributes to the mutual integration of the participants and stimulates their commitment to their own living environment and democratic processes. Projects often involve participants in finding creative solutions to (problematic) situations and encourage contact among those involved. Communication and cooperation, which fills the surroundings with stories and references, allow for the development of communality or cohesion so that citizens/inhabitants feel tied to a place, to each other and to time, and can develop into new cultural citizens.

As one example, here in Arnhem and elsewhere in the Netherlands, we have been developing social aesthetics projects that plot a course for new cultural citizenship. These projects look to art and culture for the generation of both a new grammar for communication and new forms of social cohesion. In other words, here art and culture have a twofold function: art as an objective and art as a means to an end. Art which further develops the discipline itself is the objective, and art which shapes culture is the means to an end. In some cases, culture also achieves art's objectives. In other words the end product of the process has the same quality as art. InterArt invites artists as autonomous artists. There are artists who translate their autonomy into social aesthetics and who view themselves and their audience as the raw material for the process, thereby retaining their own conceptual and directorial role and some function as researchers, observers who respond on the basis of their individual attitudes. InterArt approaches both types as equals, who lend their own shape and content to autonomy – inseparable contributors to the development of art.

There is no time to be noncommittal. Together we have to go in search of a redefinition of the contemporary and perhaps of the hidden values that unite us. Because no one knows the answer to all the questions this changing society poses, the government would do well to facilitate the arts and to turn education and society into a massive laboratory where questions can be asked and thought processes can be activated. This can create an historic moment in which art and culture play a crucial and central role in shaping a new society.

*Translated from the Dutch by Titus Verheijen*

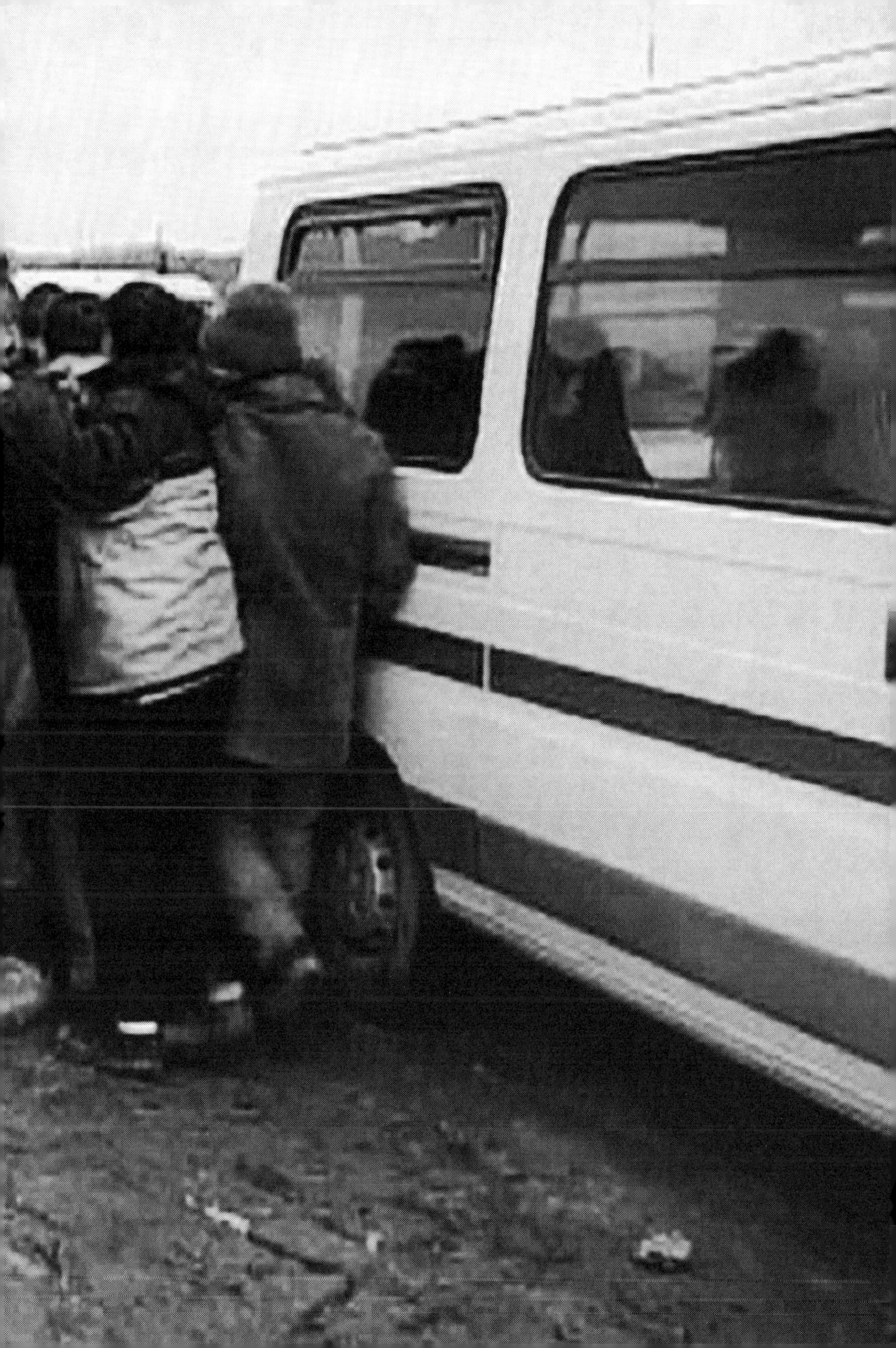

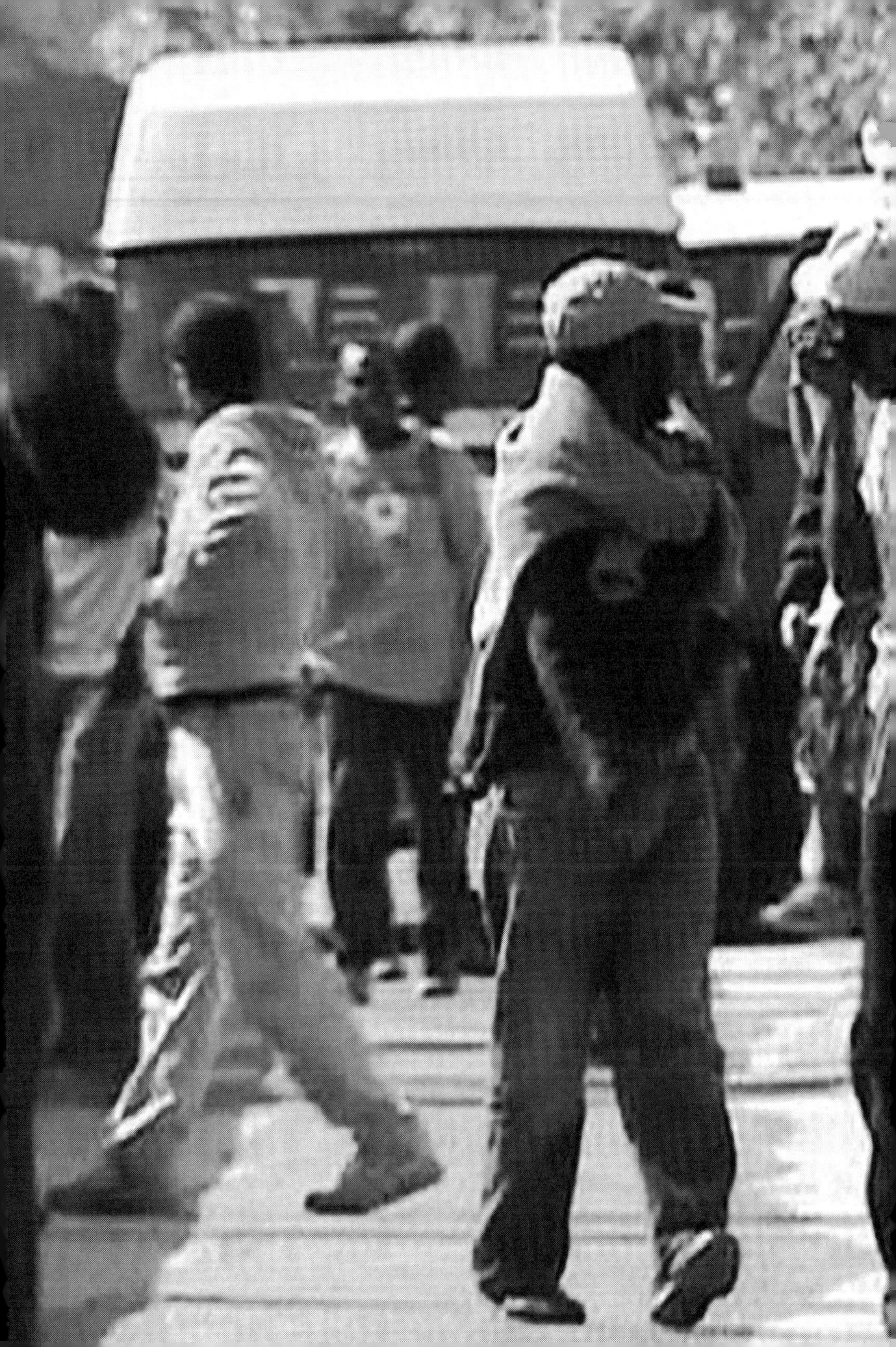

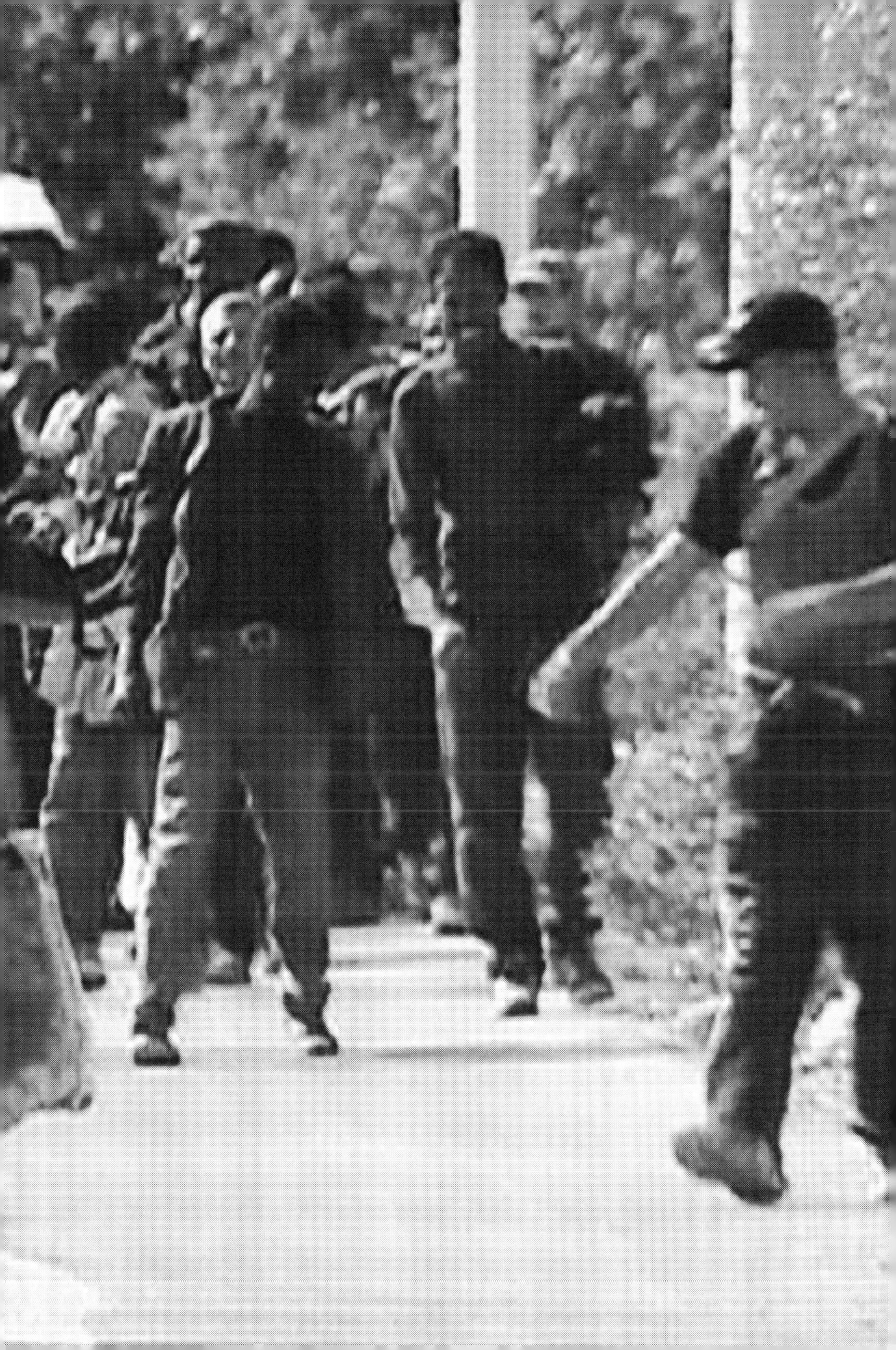

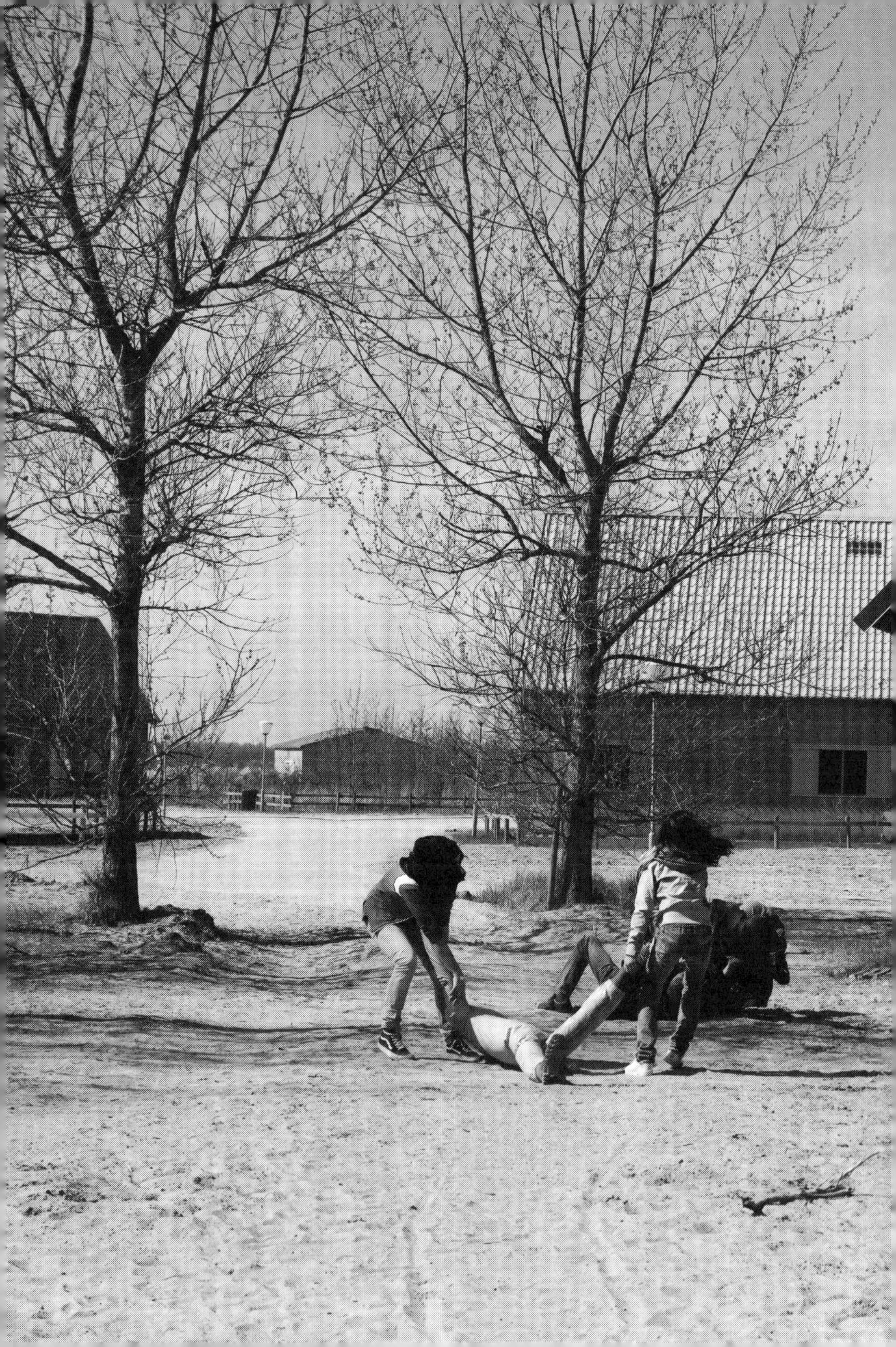

# Political Art as an Interesting Gesture? Counterbalancing Political Fear with Artistic 'Interesse'

Henk Oosterling

'Say fear's a man's best friend.' (John Cale, *Fear*, 1974)

On the early morning of Tuesday 2 November 2004, Dutch-Moroccan Mohammed Bouyeri assassinated film director and media provocateur Theo van Gogh in broad daylight in the streets of Amsterdam. After eight bullets from a HS 2000 had entered the body, Bouyeri slit Van Gogh's throat, stabbed him in the chest and, with one of two knives, pinned a letter to his body. In this five-page note, western governments, Jews and Somali-born, Kenya raised, Dutch politician Ayaan Hirsi Ali were threatened. Three months before, Hirsi Ali had given Van Gogh the script for a ten-minute movie titled *Submission* – the literal meaning of Islam. This movie deals with violence against Muslim women who, veiled with semi-transparent shrouds as they kneel in prayer, tell their stories of abuse and violence as if they are speaking to Allah. Like the protagonists in Peter Greenaway's *The Pillow Book* these women are covered all over with texts: this time not with Japanese *kanji*, but with Arabic Koranic verses unfavourable to women. Van Gogh shot the film with his characteristic nonchalance in one day, proclaiming it art. The movie was released in 2004 and shown on national television in the context of an extensive autobiographical interview with Hirsi Ali.

Although the assassination of the Dutch politician Pim Fortuyn in 2002 aroused an even fiercer reaction, the brutal murder of the rebellious Van Gogh struck different chords: as with the Khomeini fatwa on Salman Rushdie, his freedom of speech directly involved art. Van Gogh stated explicitly that he had made an artistic movie of Hirsi Ali's political statement. The avant-garde inspired provocation of Van Gogh, this *parrhesia* or 'fearless speech', had overstretched the thin texture that enveloped politics and art. Aestheticizing politics, as Walter Benjamin argued during the interbellum, is a highly explosive reduction. Van Gogh's absurdist TV performances furiously mocking crypto-Nazism warrant no analogy and artists venting anti-bourgeois sentiments have always been the avant-garde's imperative. But in a totally aestheticized media society Van Gogh's retro-avant-gardism has lost its context and sense. His absurdism got caught between Hirsi Ali's political radicalism and Bouyeri's religious fundamentalism. Unwillingly, his provocative attitude served a deep-rooted feminist anger and frustrated socio-religious ambition, both guided by an overpowering will to purify and mobilize public opinion and action for their righteous cause.

### The fear-factor

Terrorists like Bouyeri strive to create chaos in order to take advantage of the momentary loss of sense, i.e. of meaning and direction, that becomes manifest in panicked crowds. The first attack on sense and sensibility, however, is discursive: through polarization. The fundamentalist's mindset thrives on dichotomies: us and them, good and bad, the West and the rest. Being forced to choose sides, the spectrum of individual choices is reduced to rigid polarities. Every sense of differences is destroyed. But this is only the most comforting side of the coin of fear that is tossed once people are forced to decide: the side portraying the head to be hunted. The other side of the coin, the tail, brings the opponent into play: the state with its duality-based identity politics and biopolitics. Nation-states too, use fear as an instrument for mobilizing populations, reiterating time and again a human, all too human xenophobia. From the days of Thomas Hobbes to our times of terror different strategies have been applied. The Leviathan used fear of death to pacify and mobilize its people, seventeenth-century despotic terror inspired Montesquieu to formulate his political philosophy, nineteenth-century anxiety of the masses was used to mobilize them for nationalist purposes and the Cold War configured a balance of terror.[1] Solely referring to totalitarian and fascist regimes is therefore too simple an argument to safeguard modern democracy against 'fear management'.

### I. Affect-ontological sediments of fear

Fear as a human affect is psycho-geologically stratified. It takes an archaeo-genealogist like Michel Foucault to unearth its scattered foundations and schizoanalysts like Gilles Deleuze and Félix Guattari to trace, map, diagram and find the programme within these fixed stratifications. Making sense of fear asks for percepts,[2] i.e. collectively bred and historically staged images of the Enemy, beyond individual perceptions, transferred over generations. The most virulent ones, as current immigration politics shows, are invasive percepts: 'they' are coming. The threatened communities in the West were constantly reminded of the devastating ravaging hordes of Mongols, Huns, Vandals and Turks. Modern nation-states updated these fears in cultivating archenemies. Once the industrializing nation-state got caught in the paradoxes of its own technology, once a blessing turned into a curse and faith in technology became fate, these fears were contextualized by apocalyptic percepts.

Social life of leisure has engendered its own fear paradoxes. Status anxiety arises when individuals become obsessed and possessed by their possessions.[3] This fear turns the gaze to oneself through the eyes of others. The bottom line of this self-reflection is existential: fear of one's own death. The percepts that bind this specific affect in a secular world vary from the late-nineteenth-century fear of being buried alive[4]

[1] Corey Robin, *Fear. The History of a Political Idea*. (Oxford: Oxford University Press, 2004).

[2] Deleuze and Guattari use this neologism to explain the second constituent of a sensation that is reception-aesthetic element of a affects and percepts. A percept is residue of individual perceptions. See Gilles Deleuze and Félix Guattari, *What is Philosophy?* (London/New York: Verso 1994), 164.

[3] Alain De Botton, *Status Anxiety* (London: Hamish Hamilton, 2004).

[4] Joanna Bourke, *Fear. A Cultural History*. (London: Virago, 2005), 3.

to the late-twentieth-century fear of falling prey to a serial killer. The horror genre thrives on these fears. Being afraid of a specific threat triggers a fight, a flight or freezing. But fear can also become an amorphous, unidentifiable, omnipresent anxiety: Martin Heidegger's Being-toward-Death. Precepts are no longer available. This unbridled, haunting mood or *Angst* colours the world of man as a relational being, as *Dasein*. According to Alexis de Tocqueville's psycho-sociological analysis of modernity, this pure affectivity comes to the fore in the process of modernization, in which western individuals are being uprooted. Having lost their religious and communal roots, most are too weak to rely on themselves in facing their finitude. Paraphrasing Erich Fromm, they no longer fear their fear, but fear their freedom. For De Tocqueville, passive submission of the masses to state terror was therefore an onto-political implication of the democratic process: pursuing freedom and striving for equality produced terrified, but willing masses.

*II. Fear as a political affect*
In order to understand the logic of terrorism we have to take into account this complex layering of fear. However, like freedom, fear is both an individual asset and a collective habitat. Fear as an affect is a relational concept, although *ex negativo*. That is why fear and anxiety perfectly suit the aims of a threatened identity politics, since it includes exclusively. In the current totally mediated spectacle society, percepts are constantly furnished by the media for 'policing' populations. Since fear is relational, it is a micropolitical, bipolar phenomenon: it is 'a people's apprehension of some harm to their collective well-being ... or the intimidation wielded over men and women by governments or groups.'[5]

obin, *Fear. The History of a cal Idea*, 2.

Governing by surveillance is the articulation of a nation-state's biopolitics that aims at enhancing and channelling the productive life forces of the community by anticipating and projecting their ultimate limit: indiscriminate arbitrary violence. This biopolitical governance has its roots in the Greek *polis*. Within the spectrum of *pathoi* or affects, fear turns out to be the principal affect that focuses man's politics. According to Aristotle, man becomes a *zoon politikon* once he fears the right things, for the right motive, in the right manner and at the right time. Aristotle is primarily interested in one specific reaction: neither frozen fright nor frantic flight, but the 'ruse of the pathos', i.e. fighting back. This makes the fearful citizen a courageous, but tragic hero. In transcending our fears we could be heroes, be it just for one day.

This politically productive intuition was shared by generations of philosophers. Channelling its free flows – through collective precepts –

in rigid identities, fear was forged as an effective political instrument. At the very start of political modernity in the early sixteenth century, Machiavelli already conceived fear as an *instrumentum regni*, yet its first self-reflective, psychological articulation – its subjectifying potential – is articulated by Montaigne in *Essais* (1580): 'The fear I fear most is fear.' Feeding back fear on itself closes the circular space of interiority that Descartes called the *cogito*. This was politically rephrased in *Leviathan* (1651). Hobbes realized that 'fear and I are twin brother'. However, for the population it was fear of death instrumentalized by the sovereign to pacify the beast in man and force him to a contract with the state. With this double articulation of fear – micro- and macropolitically – the political creed was formulated: systematic cultivation of fear not only tames the wolf in man – *homo homini lupus est* – but also guarantees the socio-political survival of the sovereign state.

### III. Self-reflective quality of fear: terror and banality

Fear always has been a productive force, migrating on all strata of the human condition. John Locke and other heroes of liberalism conceived fear as an 'uneasiness' of the mind that nevertheless requires appreciation and cultivation because it is the chief, if not the only spur to human industry and action. Once fear takes itself as an object – fear of fear – it gets a reflective quality, filling modern man's interiority with nihilistic emptiness, destroying its relational potential. The loop folds subjectivity back upon itself, making oneself the ultimate reference for reality. At the peak of the Second World War psycho(patho)logy, politics and economics are rhetorically combined in Franklin D. Roosevelt's famous speech of 1942. In order to persuade the isolationists to help the European allies breaking the Axis of Evil he asked his fellow Americans whether they preferred to fear the fearing and be immobilized by frozen fright over taking action and fighting back. Implicitly Roosevelt's appeal struck the right chord: the real threat of the American god-fearing soul is nihilism. Paradoxical as it may sound, this nihilistic condition, this shaken state of being, is also the bottom line of terror. Violence is just its limit figure. Roosevelt's appeal however showed that fear management was not only part and parcel of the totalitarian regimes that had to be defeated.

During the Cold War Hannah Arendt, a Jewish intellectual, student of Heidegger, refugee and American citizen, shifted the attention from totalitarian terror to a less spectacular, but all the more effective terror. The total terror of Nazism – and in later variations, Stalinism – analysed in *The Origins of Totalitarianism* (1951) was radical evil. The inert masses needed anxiously to be sensed, i.e. signified, directed and mobilized. But after having witnessed the trial of Adolf Eichmann – one of Hitler's bureaucratic administrators of the *Endlösung* (final solution) – in 1961, Arendt reviewed her theses on the dynamics of political fear by concluding that terror was finally conditioned by active banality. Eichmann's careerism was beyond radical evil. It revealed the banality of evil. Confirming Adorno's study on fascism, Arendt's study on Eichmann located a microfascism in the soul of every virtuous citizen.

**Normalization as radical mediocrity**

Do macropolitics and micropolitics still coincide after the fall of the Wall in 1989? Does political terrorism under the guise of a 'clash of fundamentalisms' still have a counterpart in man's soul, in the human condition of the *homo sapiens*? And how do these relate to recent adaptations of fear management within globalization? After the production of subjectivity, in post-war consumer society excess had to be implemented in this self-disciplined existence. After 1980 virtuous citizens had to become proactive consumers; in risk society after 1990, accountable clients. Through aestheticization and mediatization yet another human condition unfolds: *homo informans*. Being fully embedded in media milieus, I prefer to coin the present condition of *homo informans* as *radical mediocrity*.

*I. Discipline and punish: transformation of violence into secular asceticism*

Foucault has explained how modern self-consciousness – subjectivity – was the product of disciplining micropolitics. Since approximately 1800, institutions like family, school, work, prison and hospital 'formatted' docile bodies by normalizing their behaviour, implementing the advice of public health officers and professional educators trained in human sciences discourse: power-knowledge (*pouvoir-savoir*) produced the subject. Enforcing social behaviour in the child's body eventually resulted, after a necessary transitory period of resistance – crisis and critique always being encouraged as core business of subjectivation – in the desire to develop and realize one's Self in disciplined behaviour. In this biopolitical transformation sovereign violence was internalized, constituting modern man's autonomy. Between the end of the eighteenth century and the Second World War, daily life was micropolitically reorganized with a focus on accumulating seriality, *Bildung* (education) and progression. The surplus value of human labour was no longer dissipated in grandiose projects for the pleasure of the sovereign who punished transgressions of his Law with public executions of outlaws. Nation-state democracy started to focus on biopolitics: channelling productive forces to enhance collective life. Imprisonment and resocialization replaced public execution. Formerly transgressive violence was reinvested in individual empowerment and collective emancipation.

But secularisation, democratization and emancipation had their price too: 'the death of God' and anxiety as self-reflective fear. The emptiness of man's radicalized finitude replaced hell; his unconscious drives, the devil. Although violence was checked in and as self-discipline, periodic transgressions to experience pseudo-sacral roots remained necessary. In practices of dissipation, extensively theorized by Georges Bataille, one of Foucault's main sources of inspiration, modern individuals craved for ever more spectacular thrills, paradoxically anticipating a controlled loss of control in gambling, prostitution, porn, carnival, sports, using the media as alcohol, drugs, fast cars and hard bodies. Twentieth-century avant-garde art, beginning with Dada and Duchamp who shocked the wits out of their bourgeois audiences, but more specifically with body art – Chris Burden, Gina Pane, Orlan, Stelarc, Ulay & Abramovic, Viennese Actionists, etc. – both radically affirmed and critically exposed[6] this vio-lent undertow of socio-political normalization. Van Gogh's provocative abusive language, chain smoking and obesity-promoting media perfor-mances still remind us of this once highly valued avant-gardism. His life was a great performance. Nowadays thrills, kicks and hits are more than available in spectacle society. As Jean Baudrillard argued, individual excess replaced collective transgression. Institutionalized addictions are promoted, not in the least because they are biopolitically unavoid-able, but mainly because they are economically profitable. However, they no longer serve a collective goal as tribal rituals and feudal cere-monies once did. In objectifying anxiety, these practices ambiguously enhance and destroy individual freedom.

[6] Terms like exposure and exposition are used by Jean-Luc Nancy to stress the deconstructiv intention of art practices.

## II. Surveillance and aestheticization: Dasein is design

Once facilitating leisure becomes a primary productive force in a society of consumers, the whole picture changes. In late capitalism, Deleuze has shown, self-discipline is recast in other mechanisms of control. The avant-garde's urge to connect art and life – and thus develop a critical biopolitics – is popularized: gradually daily life and public space get aestheticized. Unwillingly art becomes a strategy of repressive biopoli-tics. Once Dasein becomes design, self-reflection becomes foremost a matter of aesthetics: the reflections in the mirror at home are enhanced by shop windows.

Focusing on status anxiety, consumption appeared far more effective a mobilizing force than the disciplining practices Foucault described.

After commodities changed into goods and goods into services, after the Second World War, services were extended beyond the point of instrumentalization: services became experiences and finally lifestyles.[7] The medium turned into a message. By customizing 'branded' lifestyles, mass-produced products transformed into unique individual assets. Biopolitical and economic interests once more converge. In interweaving Locke's fear management and Alain De Botton's status anxiety, neoliberal politics gradually turned into corporate business as usual, with the market as a religious icon,[8] profit being the real prophet. This explains not so much the clash as the bond between Muslim fundamentalism and market fundamentalism.

### III. Homo informans: radical mediocrity as human condition

The most recent strategy of control and surveillance is cyberspatialization, underpinning globalization. If panic is one of the main targets of terror, this target is fully met in daily interactions and transactions. Over the last decades all life processes have been sped up and accelerated exponentially. Life has become ecstatic. Physical death is replaced by deadlines. A second life is available. In spite of infrastructural immobilizations – traffic jams, terrorist threats, tsunamis, physical and digital viruses – automobility has become an integral part of our being. Individuals strive to realize Aristotle's *Demiurges*: the ultimate self (Greek: *autos*) mover (Latin: *mobilis*). Though in panic, they seem hectically busy: physically travelling around the globe as tourists, traders or terrorists, virtually reallocating themselves, communicating telepresence to others via e-mail, SMS, MSN and MMS. This mode of being – virtual, actual *and* real – is beyond oppositions: it is presence *and* absence, global *and* local, private *and* public. Public space has become a transitory vector that is privatized by cars and mobile phones, while at the same time all private interactions and transactions are public, due to GPS registration and digital storage by providers. The subject is no longer a trace of traces, but a provided and registered trajectory, continuously anticipating a future presence. Life is a scenario.

As Peter Sloterdijk rightly states, the issue is no longer time, but vectoral displacement. To counter the current panic and dispersion Sloterdijk 'unearths' a concept that still binds and bridges: spherical ambiance. His neo-Heideggerian ontology no longer refers to atomic individuals, but – having both Heidegger and Deleuze in mind – to relational arrangements.[9] *Dasein* becomes being-in-media, that is reflected upon in his spherology. Media being extensions of bodies, automobile man is omnipresent. Media, conditioning his milieu, have become indispensable, self-evident, transparent and therefore nearly invisible. Like a fish

Joseph Pine II and James H.
re, *The Experience Economy*
on: Harvard Business School
, 1999), 72.

rk Baecker, ed., *Kapitalismus als*
*on* (Berlin: Kulturverlag Kadmos,
.

e Peter Sloterdijk, *Sphäre I,II,III.*
kfurt am Main: Suhrkamp,
1999/2004).

in the water, man is conditioned by mediascape. Once transport media, communication media but also artistic media, psychedelic means and pharmaceutics and medical devices, once all these become means of subsistence defining man's basis needs and conditioning his sociability, these media factually rule (Greek: *kratein*). Man's present condition has become radical mediocrity.

The avant-garde aim to expose the mediocrity of the bourgeoisie is outdated. Ideologically present aestheticization annihilates the opposition between art and life. In a psycho-technological sense mediocrity is also fully realized as an overall mediatization. The alliance between media and politics is both macropolitical (CNN) and micropolitical (provider), both geopolitical (GPS) and biopolitical (from the 'hands-free' cell phone to the brain chip). Moreover, this mediocrity is radical: not only are we rerouted by media, being outside the media implies social death. Biopolitically man no longer has to be controlled by spies. Everyone has become a spy in his own house. The radical mediocre *homo sapiens* is a *homo informans*.

### IV. State of exception and the homo sacer

The present 'war on terror' with its surveillance imperative is only one tactic of the modernist politico-economic strategy to control the masses by mobilizing their desire. Normalization is now being appropriated by neoliberal governments in their collaborationist policies to combat the war on terror. Normalization is, in these terms, creating the idea of threat and terrorism as normal conditions that have to be dealt with on a daily basis rather than exceptional and temporary moments of (inter)national alert. Such an ideology allows the suspension of inconvenient democratic or collective rights in the name of upholding democracy. This suspension is no longer exceptional, Giorgio Agamben claims in *Homo sacer* (1998), but the state of exception has become the rationale of present governance. He connects this observation with the seemingly marginal life conditions of the concentration camp where individual lives are stripped to 'bare life': 'The camp is the space that is opened when the state of exception begins to become the rule'.(168–69) Refugees are denied any politico-juridical status. They can be killed without sanction. This killing is not even a sacrifice for a greater cause. This is the life of *homo sacer*, captured in the sovereign ban as a *conditio inhumana*. It is not hard to imagine what Agamben is aiming at: the current state of emergency is an enduring state of exception. The camp, Agamben states in *Means Without End: Notes on Politics* (1996) is 'a space in which power confronts nothing other than pure biological life without any mediation',(41) the most absolute biopolitical space.

# Art and Politics: Art of the State, State of the Art

Is this too bleak an analysis? Most of us are inclined to say yes. But imagine the following absurdity.

*I. Art and politics: Kurtz vs the US*

On 11 May 2004, Steve Kurtz, assistant professor at the University of Buffalo (New York) and member of the Critical Art Ensemble (CAE), woke in the middle of the night. His 46-year-old wife Hope had suffered a heart attack. Kurtz rang 911 for assistance (sic!), but by the time the ambulance arrived his wife had died. The paramedic noticed some laboratory equipment in the room, including a few Petri dishes containing bacterial cultures, which proved to be *bacillus globigii*, *serratia marcenschens* and *e.coli*. Materials like this are to be found in practically any secondary school biology lab. Kurtz used them for a new CAE installation in *The Interventionists. Art in the Social Sphere*, a group exhibition that was to open at MASS MoCA on 30 May 2004. With their project, *Free Range Grains*, CAE wanted to draw attention to the genetic manipulation of foodstuffs. The installation included a mobile DNA analysis laboratory that museum visitors could use to test their food for the presence of genetically modified organisms.

The paramedic put two and two together: a dead woman plus a suspicious-looking bacterial culture. He phoned the police, who then warned the Joint Terrorism Task Force. The Task Force raided Kurtz's home together with the FBI. Kurtz was arrested on suspicion of bioterrorism under the US Patriot Act as amended after 9/11. His experimental apparatus was seized together with his wife's corpse and all his computers, papers and books. Kurtz and later the other CAE members received summonses, as did several other colleagues, to appear in court. CAE's publisher, Autonomedia, was also served a writ. On 16 June 2004, Kurtz and the CAE had to appear before a Federal Grand Jury in Buffalo. The bioterrorism charge proved to be overreaching. On 29 June, the defendants were arraigned on counts of 'wire and mail fraud' (because the bacterial source cultures were allegedly illegally procured), a crime for which the Patriot Act prescribes a penalty of twenty years jail. While still awaiting trial, Kurt has to present himself to the police at regular intervals.[10]

It is hard to deny that art and politics have entered a new liaison under the ongoing state of exception. Kurtz's case is the flipside of the coin of fear, the tail with Bush's head on it, with the head of Van Gogh's murderer or bin Laden on the other side. Both sides raise the question as to the current art of the state and state of the art. Media-directed xenophobia seems the ultimate art of the state, while MTV and TV ads are the

See Henk Oosterling, '*The Public ‌nce of Homo informans. On art in of terror*', in (In) Visibility, *OPEN. ‌r on Art and the Public Domain*, (2005), NAi Publishers.

state of the art. Since the overwhelming success of aesthetics in spectacle society, the great divide between high art, low art and lifestyle aesthetics can easily be crossed. The end of Art, once Arthur Danto's big issue, is the result of art's overwhelming success. But if this means that art has realized itself in serving the fear management of the state, a redefinition of the relation between art and politics beyond retro-avant-gardism or sterile entertainment is unavoidable. What should be at stake in art practices that position themselves in media society?

*II. Gesture: means without end as radical mediocrity?*
Does Agamben's philosophy allow us to expose public aestheticization and mediatization, the two current strategies of biopolitics? Phrased affirmatively: how can the positive relationality that, in spite of all negativity, is implied in both fear and radical mediocrity be thematized? In *The Man Without Content* (1994) Agamben criticizes aesthetics, especially Immanuel Kant's definition of the beautiful as disinterested pleasure. He shifts the emphasis from *aisthesis* as 'the sensory involvement of the spectator' to 'the creative experience of the artist'.(2) Art's beauty is not defined by the disinterestedness of the spectator. It is better served by the viewpoint of the interested artist. Although a spectator may simply experience a work of art as merely *interesting*, for its maker, 'what is at stake seems to be not in any way the production of a beautiful work but instead the life and death of the author.'(5) Art turns out to be affirmative fear management, making the artist a threat for the state, once he transforms his attitude into a collective experience. Is that why Plato expelled artists from his Republic? Agamben critically concludes that aesthetics isn't as innocent a way of looking at art. In fact, 'nothing is more urgent – if we really want to engage the problem of art in our time – than a *destruction* of aesthetics'.(6)

In *Means Without End* he turns to cinema as the realm of ethics and politics. What is at stake in cinema is the gesture. With a gesture, nothing is *made,* i.e. there is no production in view of an end; nothing is *acted,* i.e. it is not an end in itself beyond the means; but something is *carried on,* i.e. supported and endured. Action films are a *contradictio in terminis.* As for dance, this too is a gesture: 'It is nothing more than the endurance and the exhibition of the media character of corporal movements.'(58) The gesture exposes unreflected radical mediocrity: it '*is the exhibition of a mediality: it is the process of making a means visible as such.* It allows the emergence of the being-in-the-medium of human beings and thus it opens the ethical dimension for them.'(58)

The gesture shows how people are mediated. However, this communicability cannot be phrased in another medium. It cannot be explained, just shown. As such it is meaningless, senseless, lacking any direction, but not panic. It happens on the spot as an event. As 'communication of a communicability'(59), placed against the background of radical mediocrity, one can say that cinematic or choreographic gestures break the spell of an aestheticization in showing the very fact of relating, of interacting without any finality. It is interactive reflectivity *pur sang*. Or even stricter: it shows the activity of an *inter*. For Agamben this is the domain of speech, but from a semiotic point of view all artistic and even cultural interactions are involved. But even more instructive is Agamben's conclusion that 'politics is the sphere of pure means, that is, of the absolute and complete gesturality of human beings'.(60)

This short text is interwoven with texts of other thinkers. Agamben's affinity with Guy Debord's diagnosis of late capitalist spectacle society and his appraisal of the Situationist's *constructed situation*, defined as a 'point of indifference between life and art', containing 'a politics that is finally adequate to its tasks', reminds us of Arendt's definition of politics in *The Promise of Politics* (2005): 'Politics arises *between men*, and so quite *outside* of *man*. There is therefore no real political substance. Politics arises in what lies *between men* and is established as relationships.'(95) Although Arendt discerns between labour, work and action and relates politics solely to action, while Agamben does not include action in the gesture, both agree on one crucial point: politics coincides with relationality and speech. What they both emphasize, be it in different wordings – natality and creativity respectively, be it as a matter of life and death – is the primacy of mediality as an in-between, or to be more precise: an *inter*.

### Intermedial art, art as public space, art as *interesse*

When we are prepared to recontextualize the present war on terror in these terms, one question concerning contemporary art arises: can this situation artistically be resisted? Or must artists only serve spectacle society's fear management by entertaining the *homo informans*? Have artists become a fake *homo sacer* who can only survive by amusing and entertaining their *capo* and administrators? Using Art for political goals is a very ambiguous project. Stalinism proved this. This reduction is as ambiguous as the aestheticization of politics in fascism. The total reduction to either side destroys precisely the tension that both artists and spectators need in order to reflect and project what they experience in self-reflective art practices. Avant-garde art as an experiment with its own artistic media and forms has always preserved this tension and

Agamben's 'gesture' seems to extend, but also problematize this medial self reflectivity: 'What hinders communication, therefore, is communicability itself: human beings are being separated by what unites them',(115) he states in *Means Without End*.

I disagree with Agamben's exclusive focus on the artist's creativity. Over the past decade an international discourse has been articulated on intermediality. This concerns art practices that combine interdisciplinarity, multimedia and interactivity. Here the former avant-garde experiment is more explicitly focused on the audience's *aesthesis* aiming to sensitize its spectators for the *inter*.[11] The problematization of the *inter* in public space due to recent fear management through aestheticization and mediatization has forced artists to become interventionists creating new public space. They are no longer working *in* public space, but present their art practice *as* public space, explicating the transparency of current communicability. Both intermedial art and this 'public' art take the *inter* simultaneously as a working space, a medium, a sensibility and an object of research.[12]

From the aforementioned we can at least conclude that nowadays the focus of 'political' art practices is an ambiguous clarification of binding and bridging, the substance of which is an in-between. The transparency of mediality and the lack of reflection within radical mediocrity demands artistic clarification. Foucault once defined art fiction after modernity as follows: 'fiction . . . does not mean making the invisible visible, but of showing just how invisible the invisibility of the visible really is', and he added, '[fictions] are not so much images as transformations, alterations, neutral intermediate instances, spaces between images.'[13]

But the invisible cannot be 'exposed', as Jean-Luc Nancy explained time and again. For him Agamben's 'means without end' is an impossible centre of the political community, an '*être-en-commun*', '*avec*' or '*cum*'. Other neo-Heideggerians such as Sloterdijk coined this originary relationality as a spherical 'being-in-media' that tends towards a *Gesamtkunstwerk* (total work of art). Behind all these articulations of the *inter* a crucial Heideggerian concept scintillates: the concept of '*Interesse*', to be interested in: 'Interest, *interesse*, means to be among and in the midst of things, or to be at the centre of a thing and to stay with it. But today's interest accepts as valid only what is interesting.'[14] In this sense *interesse* surpasses art philosophy and becomes an ethic, as Agamben claims, but eventually even an ontology: a being (esse) of the in between (inter). In *The Human Condition* Arendt takes Heidegger's notion one

[11] See Henk Oosterling, 'Sens(a Intermediality and Interesse. Tow on Ontology of the In-Between', *Intermédialités*, no. 1 (Spring 2003 CRI Montreal, 29–46.

[12] See note 9.

[13] Michel Foucault and Maurice Blanchot, *Maurice Blanchot: The Thought from Outside and Fouca I imagined him* (New York: Zone Books, 1987), 14.

[14] Martin Heidegger, 'What Cal Thinking', in *Basic Writing. Heide David Farrell Krell, ed. (London: Routledge & Kegan, 1978), 347. Se also: *Being and Time*, 124.

step further: 'These interests constitute, in the words of the most literal significance, something which *inter-est*, which lies between people and therefore can relate and bind them together. Most action and speech is concerned with this in-between. . . . (182) *Interesse* appears to be synonymous with 'politics'. In order to locate its everyday meaning and to show what this concept micropolitically implies for criticizing the present human condition – radical mediocrity – one last player in this field has to be referred to: Friedrich Nietzsche. His 'revaluation of all values' has been referred to by all other players who have been mentioned. Not in the least because on the most basic level of human interaction the current culture of fear with its anxiety loop can only be countered by a simple gesture: being interested without any fearful prejudice. Whatever the final product, art first and foremost creates space where this great adventure of the human soul can be explored. Nowadays being interested – *interesse* – is the most radical gesture.

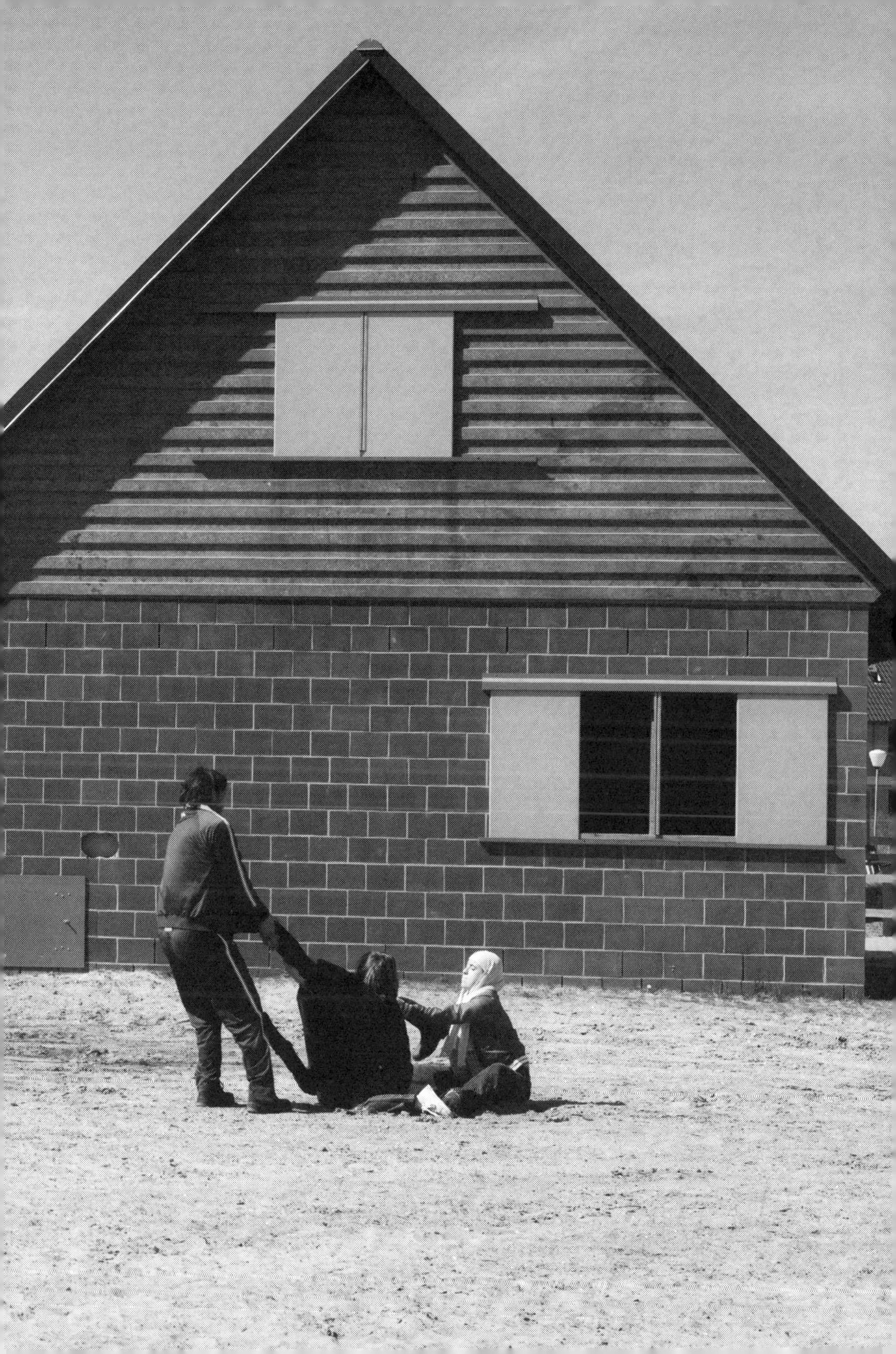

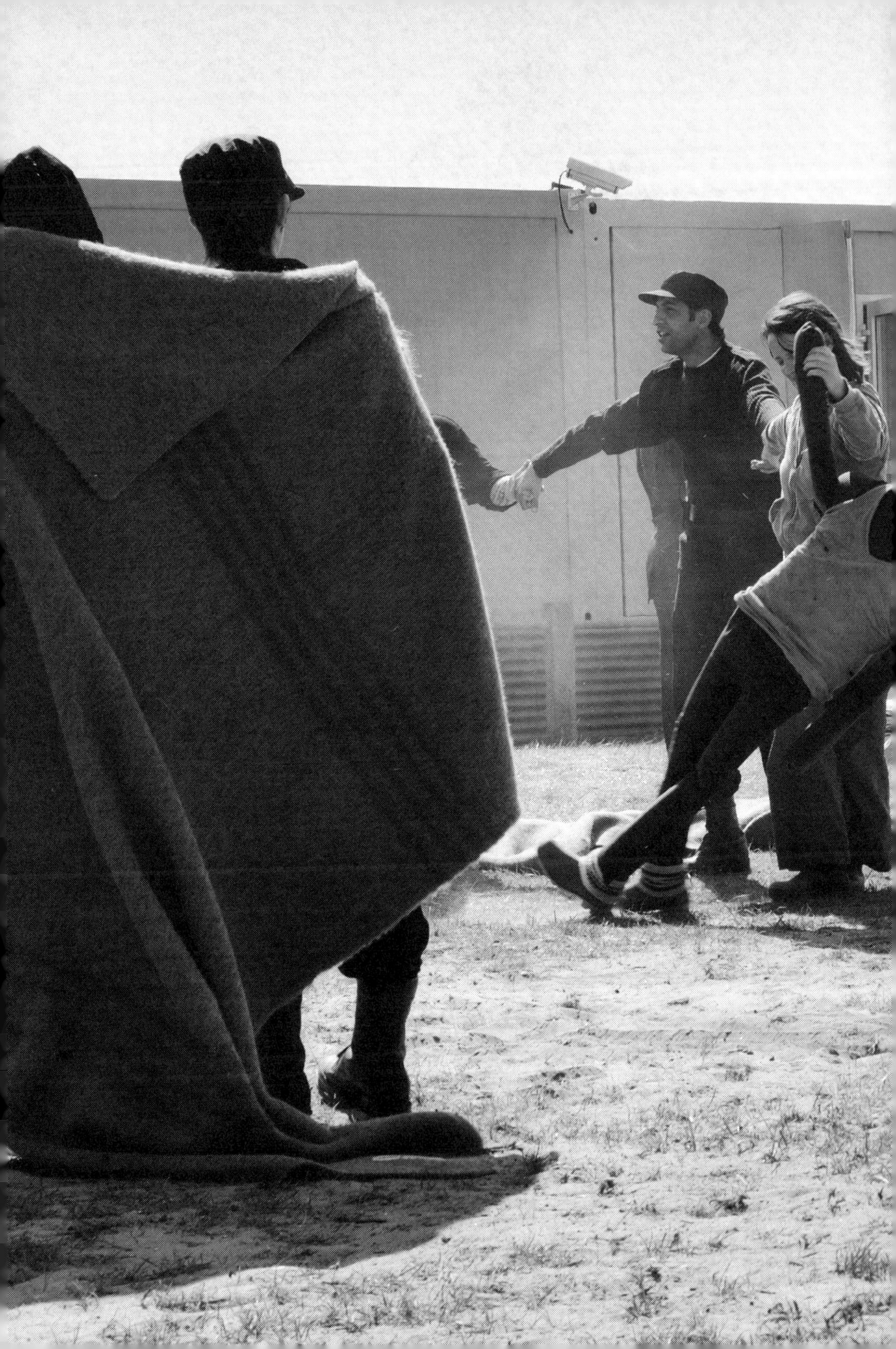

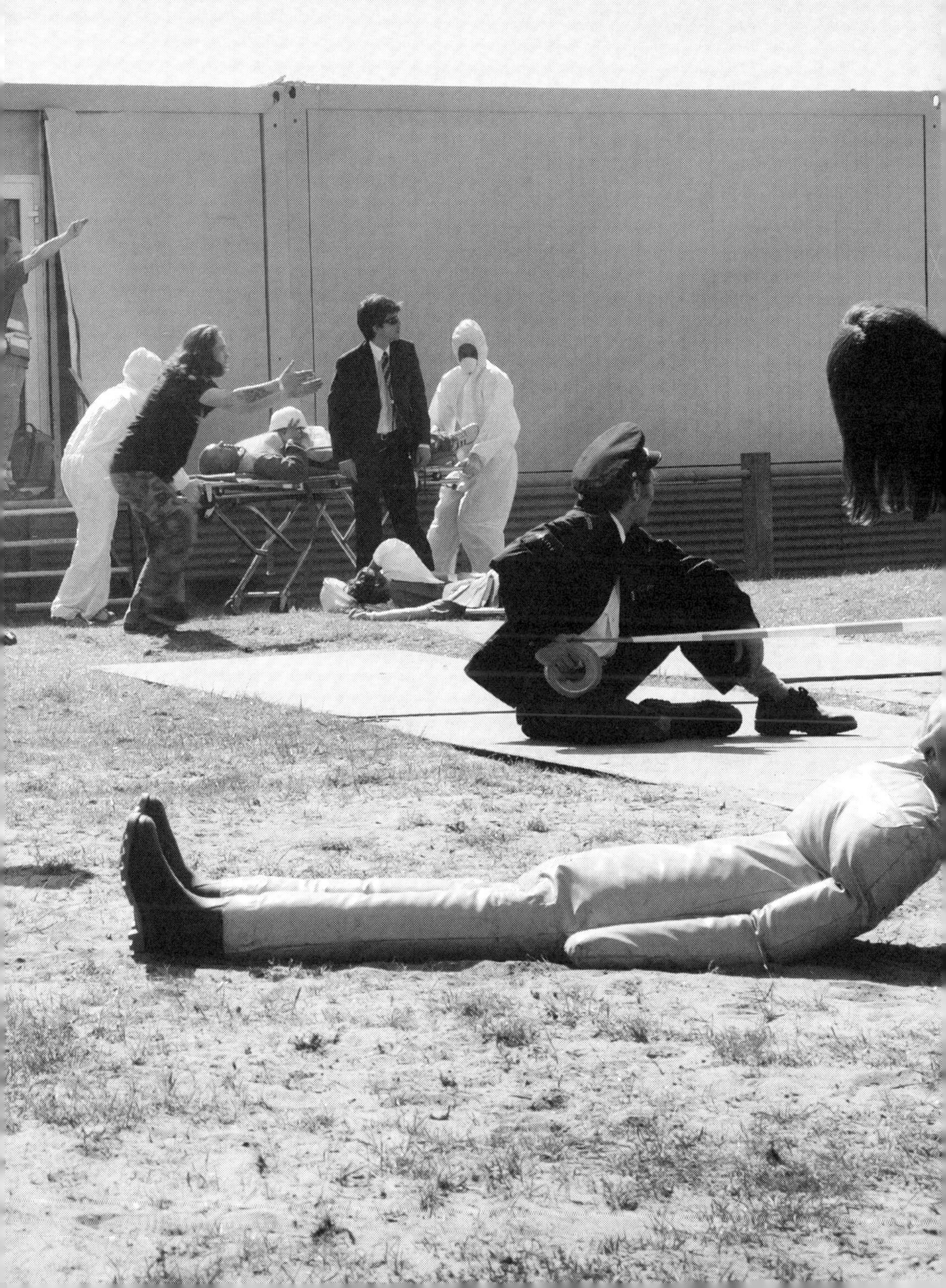

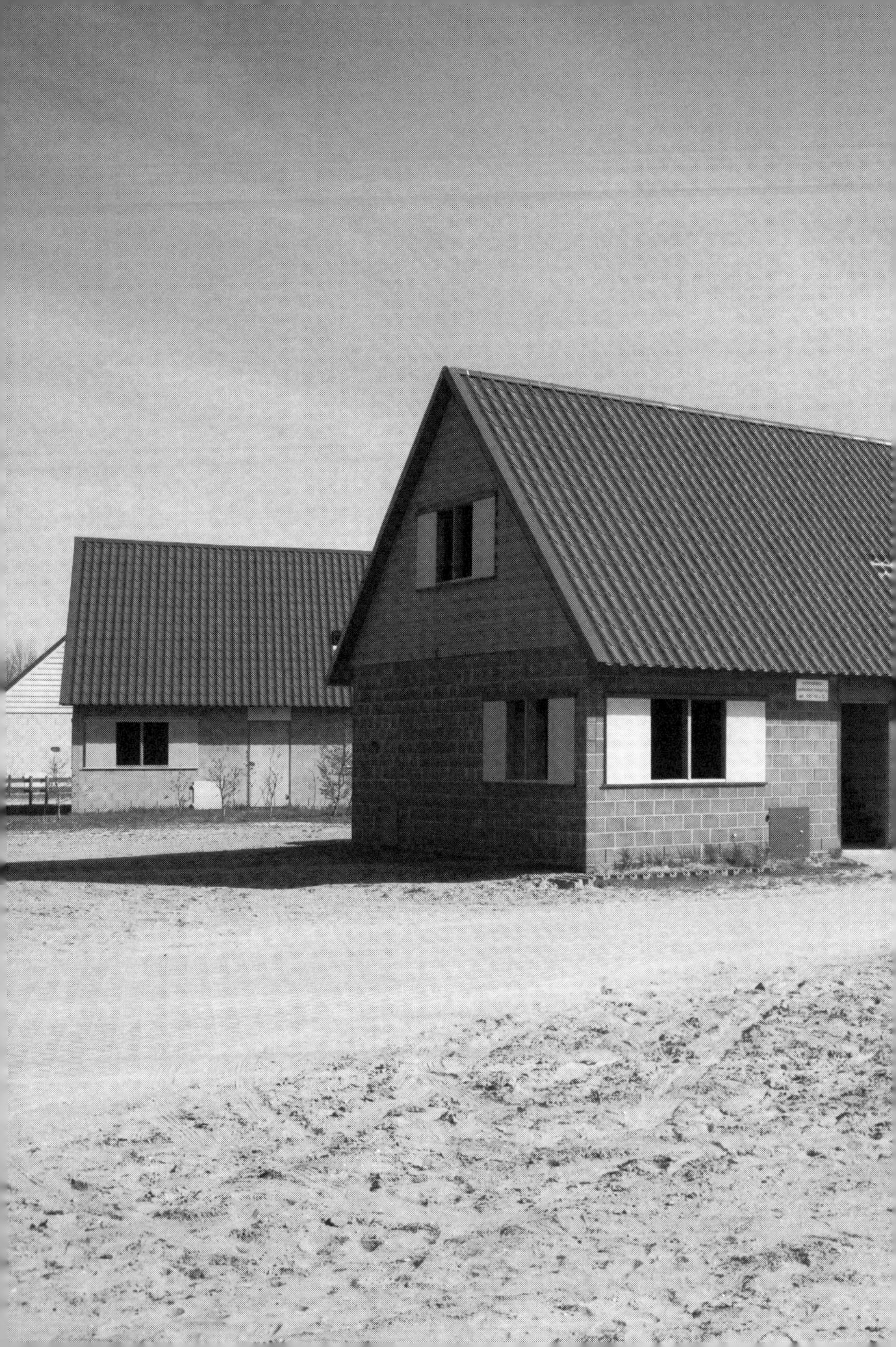

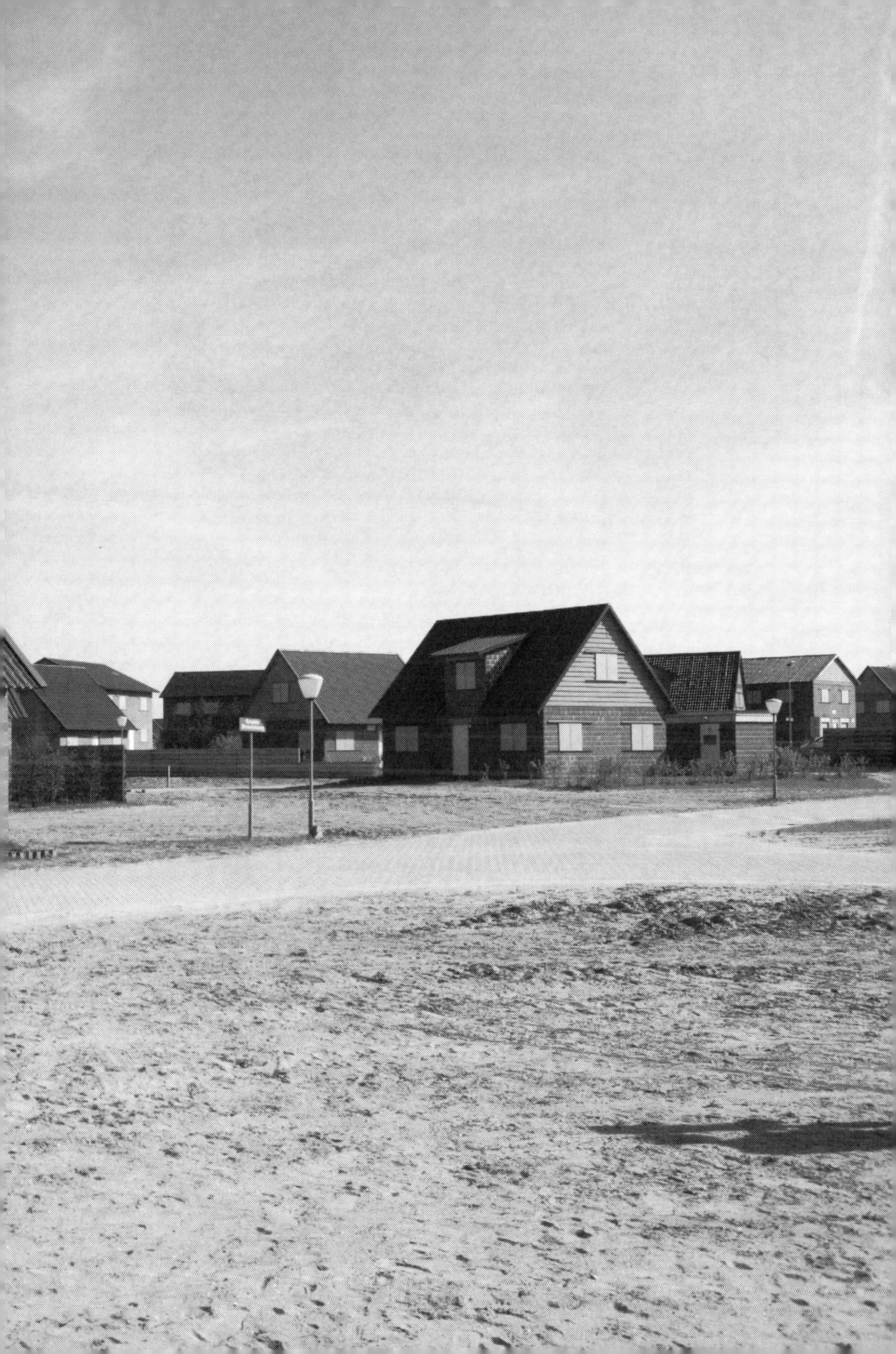

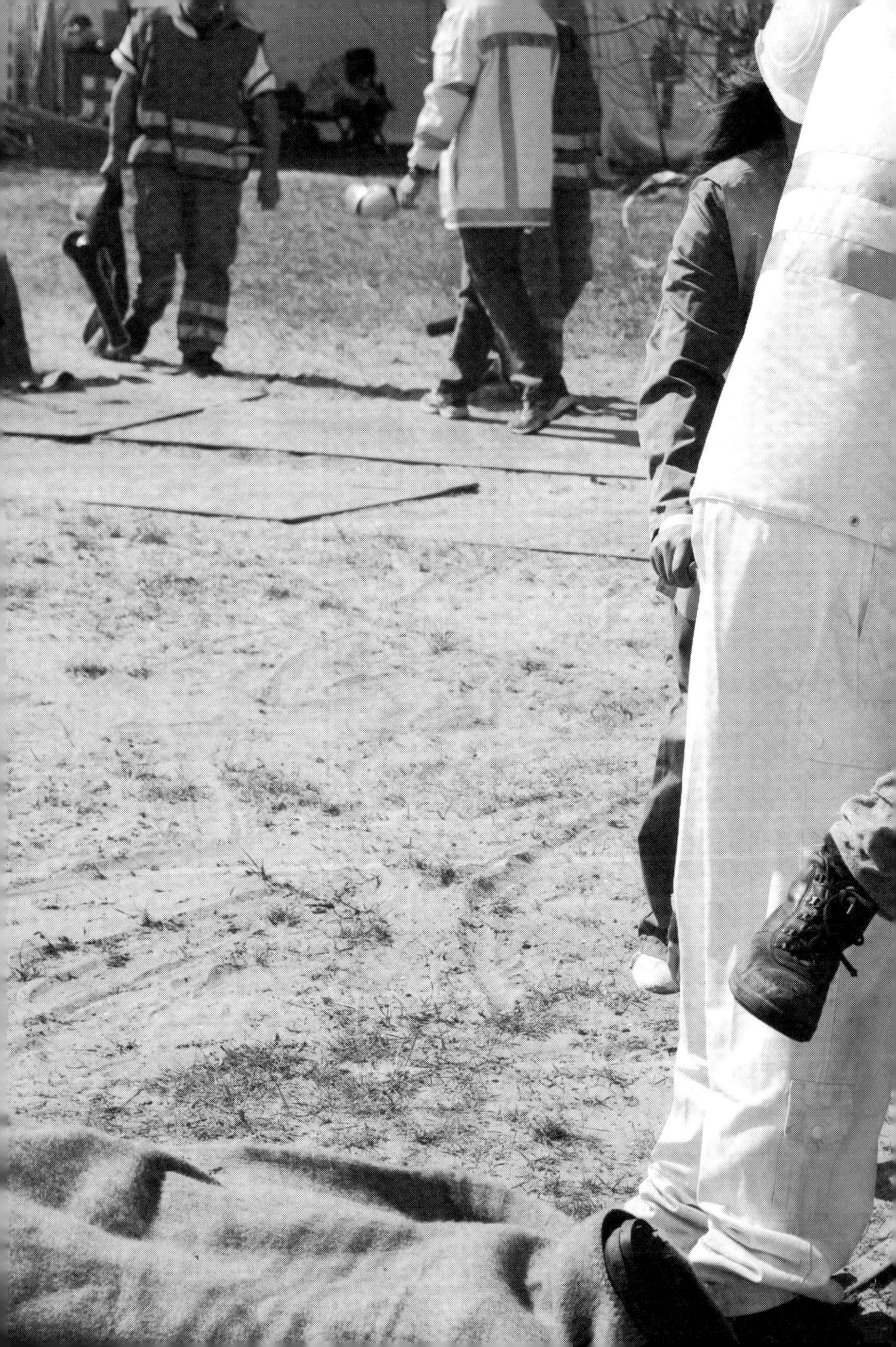

---

# Indecisiveness as a Mode of Being
A Conversation with Pages (Nasrin Tabatabai & Babak Afrassiabi)

---

---

**Charles Esche** As artists and cultural producers based in the
Netherlands you initiated the project Pages. I think it would be
good at the start to talk simply about what Pages is, and more
specifically about *Pages* magazine, which you publish in Farsi
and English. What do you think its position is – in Iran and in
Europe and who is your readership? What was the impetus
behind it and what are your hopes for the project?

**Pages** We started our activities as Pages in 2004, when we
published the first issue of the magazine. Later we initiated
other kinds of collaborative projects to be able to focus on
particular subjects and issues. Coming from Iran and maintaining an active connection to the country, a great part of
Pages' activities starts precisely from there. Yet the specificity
of the Iranian situation has triggered discussions of a broader
context. Addressing issues with regard to their locally specific
conditions brings one closer to the reality of the issues,
problematizing their common notions and triggering their
re-articulation.

If we would try to shortly describe what we hope to do with
Pages, it is to circulate critical notions of artistic and cultural
practices, on a scale from the personal micro-level to the
larger context. That said, with each issue of the magazine
or new project, we articulate the objectives anew, not on the
level of rhetoric but also based on our encounters with the
participatory practices in which we are interested.

In sync with this mode of working, the *Pages* magazine is
published irregularly. This is because of many factors, mostly
due to practical reasons like the financial and working
conditions connected to each issue. The process of editing,
publishing and distributing has changed constantly since we
started publication. Our aim has never been to be a regular art
and culture magazine that sends information to Iran or vice
versa. On the other hand we see that we've been constantly
busy with Pages as an ongoing research project. In that sense
it's as if we just started with the first issue every time. This
structure defines the kind of readership or the public for
*Pages*, which is never vast but specific and network based.
Our website and its forum also help to focus this readership
and at the same time expand it through direct discussion and
contact.

**CE** As editors of *Pages*, you are dealing all the time with the question of the translation of contexts and languages. How do you understand the responsibilities of translation and the limitations it has? What do the two languages each permit and disallow?

**Pages** Translation is something that starts with the magazine and is passed onto the reader – so there is a shared responsibility between us as editors and those who engage in reading and interpreting it. The bilingualism of the magazine was a clear choice for us. The question is if and in what ways the space of translation is a social and political space. Or is it a space where these traits are suspended for the sake of a 'responsible' translation? For us it is clearly a space of conflict, negotiations and re-articulations. Since the very beginning, we always tried to search for ways of expanding the space of translation into the content of the magazine and to the readership. In short, the responsibility of translation is actually taken on only once the circumstances of a discourse within a language are also passed on. Through this process, various points of identification within each of the linguistic spaces and its different readerships are put into question.

In general most of the modern terminology in art and criticism is western and many of these have not gained a proper equivalence in the Farsi language, or have not yet completely integrated into the language. This is a challenge for us and for everyone working in these fields. There are sometimes different translations for a single term and also words referring to different terms. Often to transfer a text fully one has to include the English origin of the terms in front of its translation in brackets. Many Farsi writers already do this in their own texts, in fact, to indicate clearly which term they mean exactly. The interesting part of the challenge is when one has to translate these terms 'back' into English.

Translation truly becomes an issue when it starts to involve complexities beyond language – when you have to translate a term that has gained a lot of weight beyond its initial meaning. To give an example, the term 'conceptual art' started to resonate more in the art context in Iran after an exhibition called *The First Iranian Conceptual Art Exhibition* at the Tehran Museum of Contemporary Art in 2001. But the context and the language of these works are different from what we know of conceptual art in the West. In fact, there is little in common between the two. When this term is simply translated 'back' into English it does not at all reflect the true nature of the works to which it refers. In other words, one sometimes has to 'de-translate' as it were in order to convey the real connotations of terms or words within different contexts.

Besides the fact that translation tries to bring one closer to a particular meaning, it also introduces a kind of 'interval' in terms of the ambiguity of relationships. You could say that translation is the interval. As such it necessitates ambivalence in order to maintain within it the possibility of meaning. In this sense, it is not about maintaining distance, but about provoking a space of participation beyond fixed subjectivities. However, what we see happening is the filling up of this prolonged vacuum of meaning with predefined words, because we tend to see this vacuum as a threat to our being in relation to the 'other'. We tend to explain the other through agendas irrelevant to the reality. So translation, in its political meaning, can be seen as an interval that is introduced into the circulation of these preconceived agendas.

**CE** How do you see this understanding of translation playing out in the Netherlands, where it seems that demands for pragmatic solutions and effectiveness limit space for reflection? And in relation to that, could you describe why you decided to work here and what the social and cultural structures this country offers that you would not find elsewhere?

**Pages** The situation in Holland is quite complicated. On the one hand there is this pragmatism with a slight lean towards hard-to-define nationalist sentiments, and on the other hand an interest in what is different. The latter is increasingly the case, and is the result of a wider trend in Western European countries to know the other. This attempt is not necessarily one of understanding other contexts and conditions in different parts of the world. What has happened is that the complexities and conflicts often associated with non-western countries now seem to find themselves in the heart of the western world. So in the end, the will to understand the other outside is a pragmatic attempt to understand the other within. But this is a mistake, we are afraid, because of the disparate circumstances in which these phenomena appear. One is almost tempted to say that associating the stranger inside

with an exterior context is an (unconscious) attempt to
dissociate them from or deny them access to the community
here. In any case there remains a misinterpretation, if not
misrepresentation on both levels.

There are also sometimes unexpected coincidences that bring
the two situations in very different cultural climates quite close
to one another. For instance, the first issue of *Pages* was about
the experience of public and private spaces in Iran. There is
a common notion that in a religious society, or a religiously
defined system of governance like that of Iran, the division of
public and private is heavily defined by unchallengeable codes
and regulations. Even when the private space is depicted in a
film, its protagonists have to follow the codes that pertain to
public space, since the film is being shown in public. At this
moment of obsessive protectiveness against the infiltration of
privacy into the public, the boundaries between the two start to
blur. You can only define one within the domain of the other,
and this is what we explored in the issue. But doesn't this tell us
something about recent features of public space in the Netherlands, too? Recently a brochure was distributed on our street in
Rotterdam encouraging us to keep the neighbourhood clean.
On the last two pages, there was a series of signs indicating
things that are not allowed – among which was a satellite dish.
On that same page there were various snapshots of our street,
including one in particular 'casually' depicting the satellite dish
of our neighbour attached on the inside of his balcony. Another
image next to this was of a sign hanging on our street since last
year. It read: '*Je hebt rust, zolang als je buren het je gunnen –
Nederland*' (You can only have peace if your neighbours allow it –
Netherlands).

Yet it is also hard to say if Holland is fundamentally different
than other Western European countries. Artists often
manoeuvre through different cultural structures, especially
when one is active in more than one context and always has
a foot somewhere else, with different social and cultural
anatomies. What we mean to say is that you try to let these
differences overlap and somehow affect one another, at least
within the boundaries of your own practice as an artist. It is as
such that you try to create a space of reflection for yourself
that is not geographically bound. In this sense the Netherlands
does offer the possibility of defining one's own space of

practice to some degree; there is a certain flexibility here that is missing in a great part of the world.

**CE** In what sense, if any, do you think you could be understood as Dutch artists? Do national designations hold any cultural meaning for you?

**Pages** To answer this question one should first define what it means to be a Dutch artist and what Dutch art is. If we look at our work with Pages, it is undeniable that there has been a significant effect on the project from living in Holland for many years, and therefore having to deal with both where we come from and where we are. We can never know how we would have worked if we had never left Iran but it would surely have been different.

The flow of émigré artists to European countries has greatly influenced the art context of these countries. Art is no longer defined purely by the works of artists born in a particular place. The art context in many of these countries has itself been expanded with different notions and codes coming from elsewhere – codes that require different readings. It is the same in a broader social context. Immigrants living in Holland from all over the world each introduce a different series of codes into the social fabric. What kind of definition of 'Dutchness' would we then get if we were to put all these different subjectivities together?

We know an Iranian woman who had moved to Holland some years ago. Until recently we knew her by a name that we found out only recently was not her real name, the one she was called back in Iran. When we asked her why she had hidden her true name, her reply was quite interesting. She said from the moment she entered Holland that became her name. To examine one's true identity is to experiment with the boundaries that define it, and most probably at the moment of this experimentation, definitions of identity become quite irrelevant, because there, at the excess of this experimentation, you may find relationships you never expected to encounter. We could say national designation gains a cultural significance exactly at the moment of this experimentation, when notions of identity and nationhood are constantly put into question.

**CE** So does your multiple identity allow you to stay outside
these designations, a neither/nor position? If so, what do you
observe about the rest of the Dutch art scene? Do you think
there are characteristics that define Dutch art?

> **Pages** It's hard to say something really concrete about Dutch
> art, unlike what you would be able to say about Iranian art. In
> Iran there is a struggle with identity and the imagery of self-
> representation. Artists are caught in the predicament of
> cultural and political conditions and deal with that. This is not
> at all the case here in the Netherlands. There is a lack of a
> collective concern among artists here; they are more involved
> in their individual urgencies, something that also applies to
> many of the art institutions. This is why here in the
> Netherlands there are only moments and occasions that one
> might find interesting or to which one can relate closely.
> Moments like a particular exhibition, a specific work of an
> artist or period in the history of an art institution.

**CE** Have there been changes in your engagement with the
Netherlands over time? How do you read the recent changes
in the political landscape here, and have they affected your
work in any way?

> **Pages** Unfortunately the recent political climate in the
> Netherlands has forced most debates into a deadlock of overt
> self-indulgence, often disguised as good old-fashioned self-
> criticism in the most banal form. A good example of this is the
> endless variety of TV programmes dedicated to issues of
> national identity and foreignness. What holds this deadlock in
> place is not only a political indifference towards the other, but
> most of all a kind of disinterestedness to specify a clear stand
> in regard to positions outside of recognizable (socially and
> culturally pre-defined) boundaries.
>
> Inevitably these characteristics have found their way into the
> art world as well. Whether you want to or not, you become
> a part of these debates, especially as foreign artists. The
> question is on what level you would want to engage in them.
> When we started Pages, we were aware of the kind of
> connotations it may have in relation to the current political
> climate. By focusing on different social and political circum-
> stances, we search to consider the relevance of these debates

on a wider scope than the national. It is the very specificity of the things encountered that force one to take a stand beyond generalizations. In this sense you could say that the peculiarity of the political climate in the Netherlands has given us an awareness of a possible place we can have within it.

**CE** Besides editing *Pages* you are also artists working independently. How do you think the activities of editor and artist feed each other? It often seems to me that immigrants in general have an easier time maintaining multiple identities than people educated within the Dutch pragmatic tradition. Do you recognize this, or do you find that people in the Netherlands or Western Europe are wary of an artist who is also something else?

> **Pages** Maintaining multiple identities still requires you to clearly define what each of these identities are, which for us has never been an issue. One important effect that our activities as editors and artists have had on our practice in general is a certain open-endedness. It is increasingly becoming a trend among artists to be active in different fields at the same time. Educational systems in art hardly teach you ways of working in multiple fields. It is something that you learn as you go along. It is what comes from the necessity one feels as an artist. Therefore it is not so much a question of identity (multiple or singular) but rather of a willingness to participate in something that is not predefined in its social and political form; something that requires intimacy in the face of constant indecisiveness. The issue of translation we spoke of earlier is in fact a part of this. Finally, if being an artist is also being something else, the 'else' is something that you repeatedly become as a result of such involvement.

**CE** The notion of 'indecisiveness' that you just mentioned is something that you have dealt with. You wrote about the notion of 'indecisive discourse' to describe what cultural practitioners have at our disposal to undermine the discourses of power. How does this play out in your work?

> **Pages** Indecisiveness, as explained more extensively in our text *Practice of Indecisiveness*, refers to conditions – like those in Iran – where life is lived in the discrepancy between true realities of social life and their totalizing political representation.

Discourses of power try to hide this discrepancy because it threatens their validity. Yet indecisiveness as a mode of being can have agency and a voice, because it constantly refers to this gap and the irresoluteness of political identification. In the case of Iran for example, rumours circulate critical, often-revealing stories while remaining free of inhibitions and control due to their very indecisiveness.

The crucial question for us was how cultural practice may channel such agency and voice to undermine discourses of power. How can indecisiveness become a mode of practice, opening spaces for negotiation and rearticulation. Indecisiveness for us was not something we approached on a theoretical level. It was first of all something that we were truly affected by during our early engagements working with Iran. It required us to encounter situations through long processes of involvement, and thus offered us the possibility to address them within their complexities.

**CE** Yet such indecisivness seems at least superficially absent from the secure Netherlands. Do you find it in your adopted homeland or only in situations like Iran at this moment?

**Pages** If we see indecisiveness as something conditioned by a gap between the reality of life and its political articulation, then we do see it here in the Netherlands too. This is especially the case regarding religion, immigration, integration, etc. Having both lived here now for about twenty years, we have never experienced life being so defined by terms and signs as in the last few years. What is sought for is not an understanding of reality itself, but rather the absolute meaning of terms that are thought to define reality. The notion of tolerance, for example, forces the tolerating subjects to define their relation to the other only under such definition. The result is that they are either tolerant or racist; there remains no option in between. In reality one is suspended in the gap between one's real desire and its articulation by these terms. You become foreign to your own desires. The same goes for the notion of security. The neighbour-hood articulated under such a term is never a place in which one is actually living day by day. Again it is defined as either secure or unsafe and, in the end, this definition turns the given neigh-bourhood itself into somewhere that is unrecognizable for everyone, whether the definition applied is secure or unsafe.

*This conversation took place via e-mail in spring 2007.*

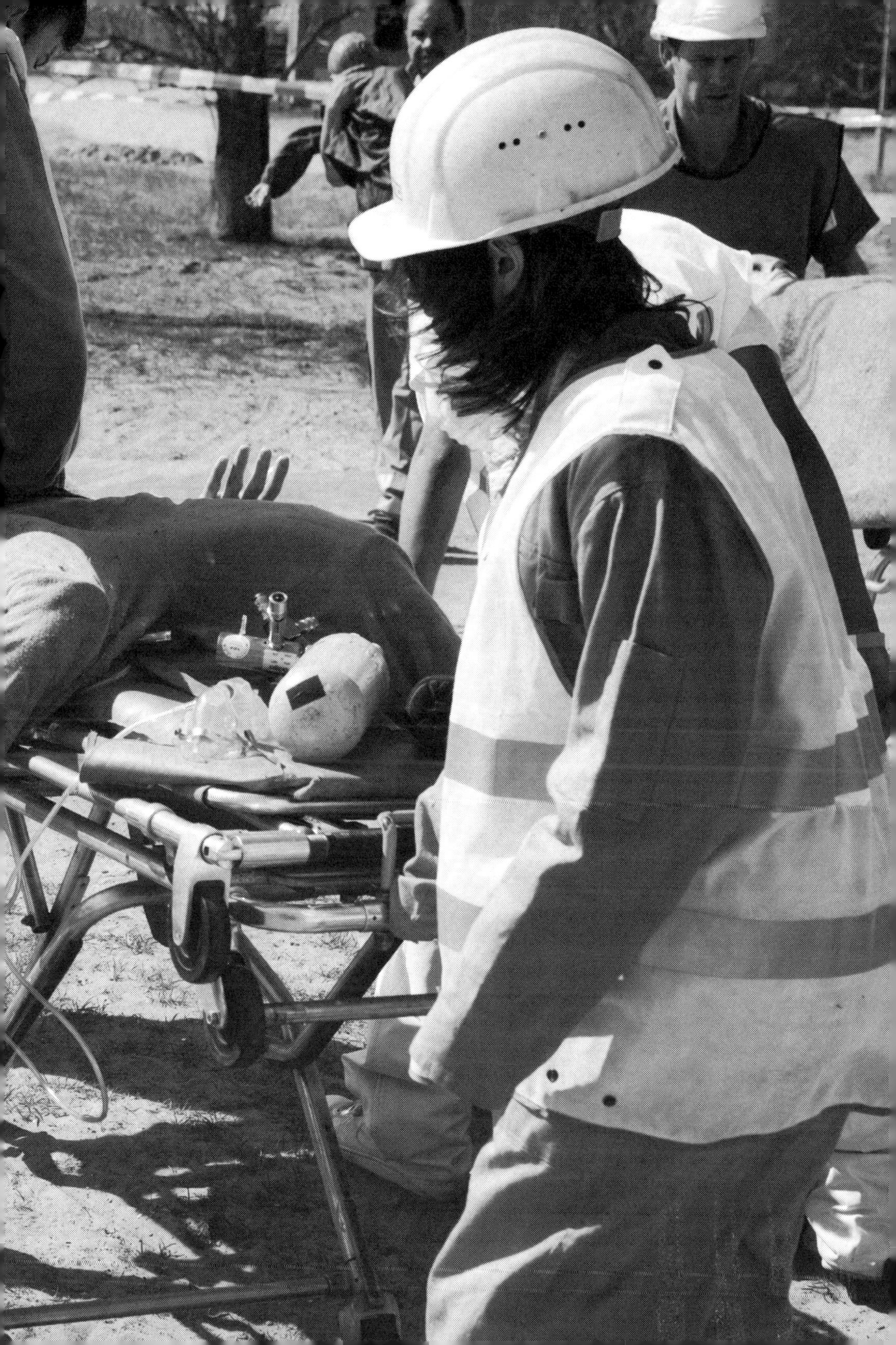

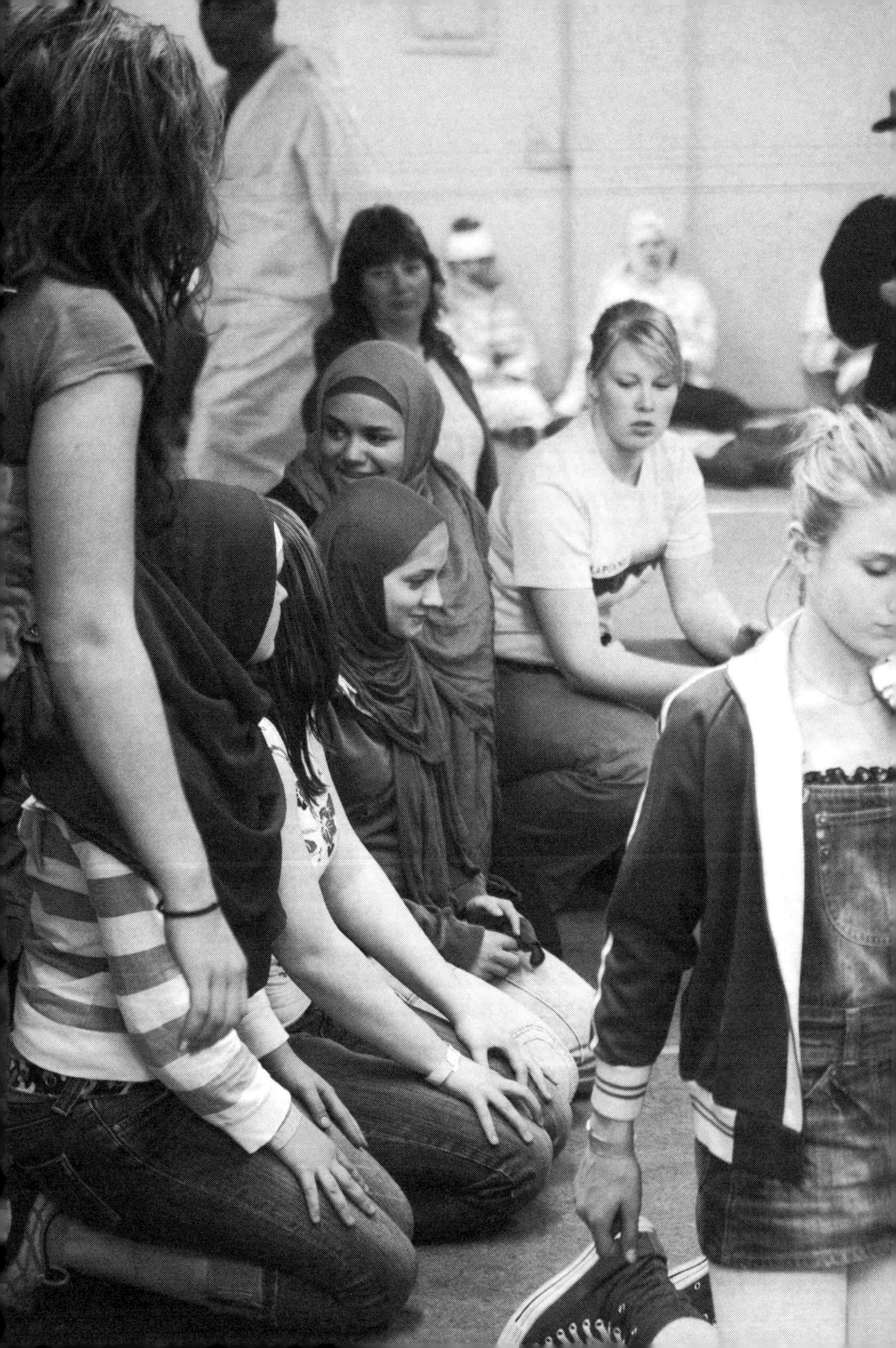

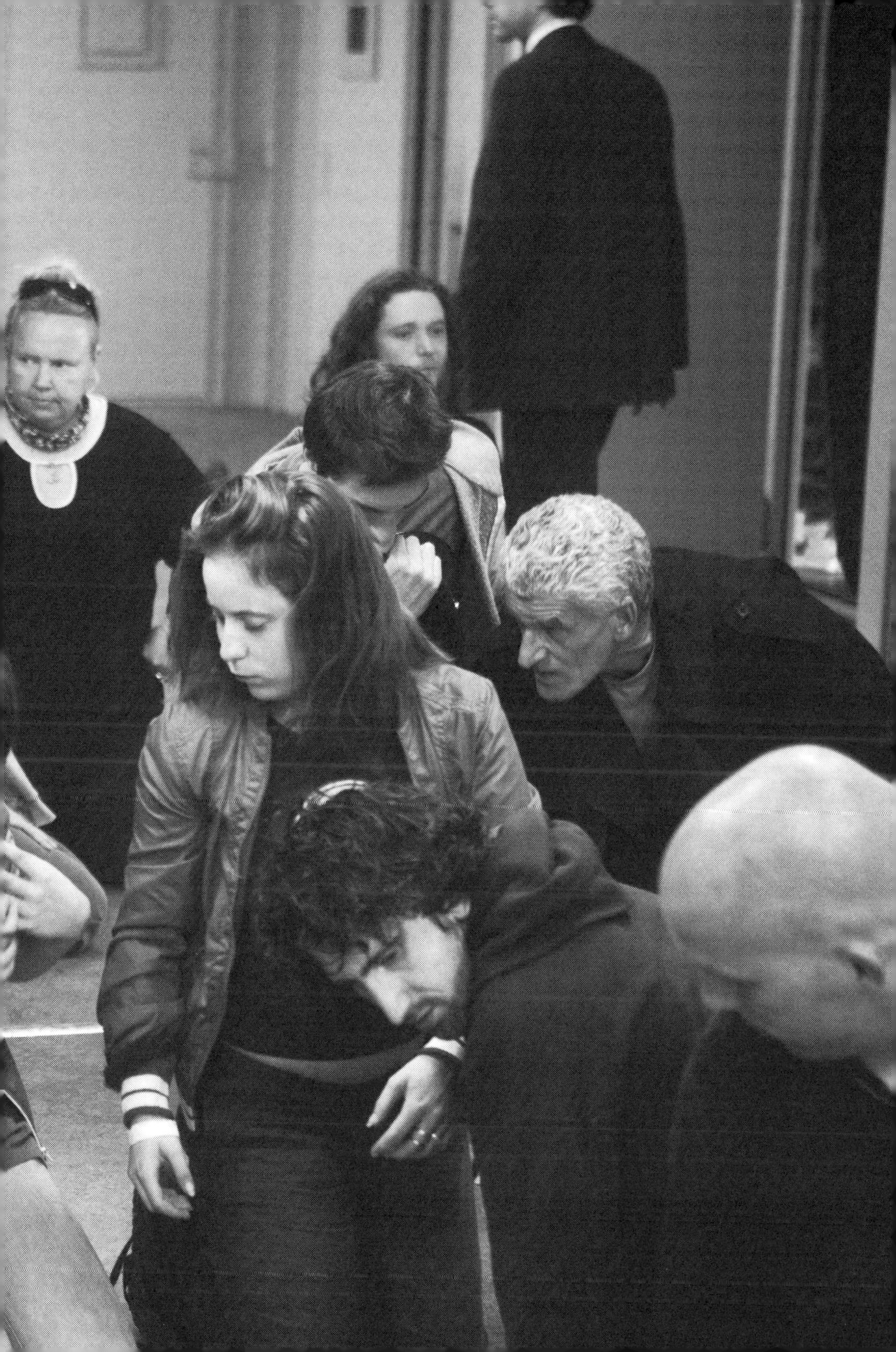

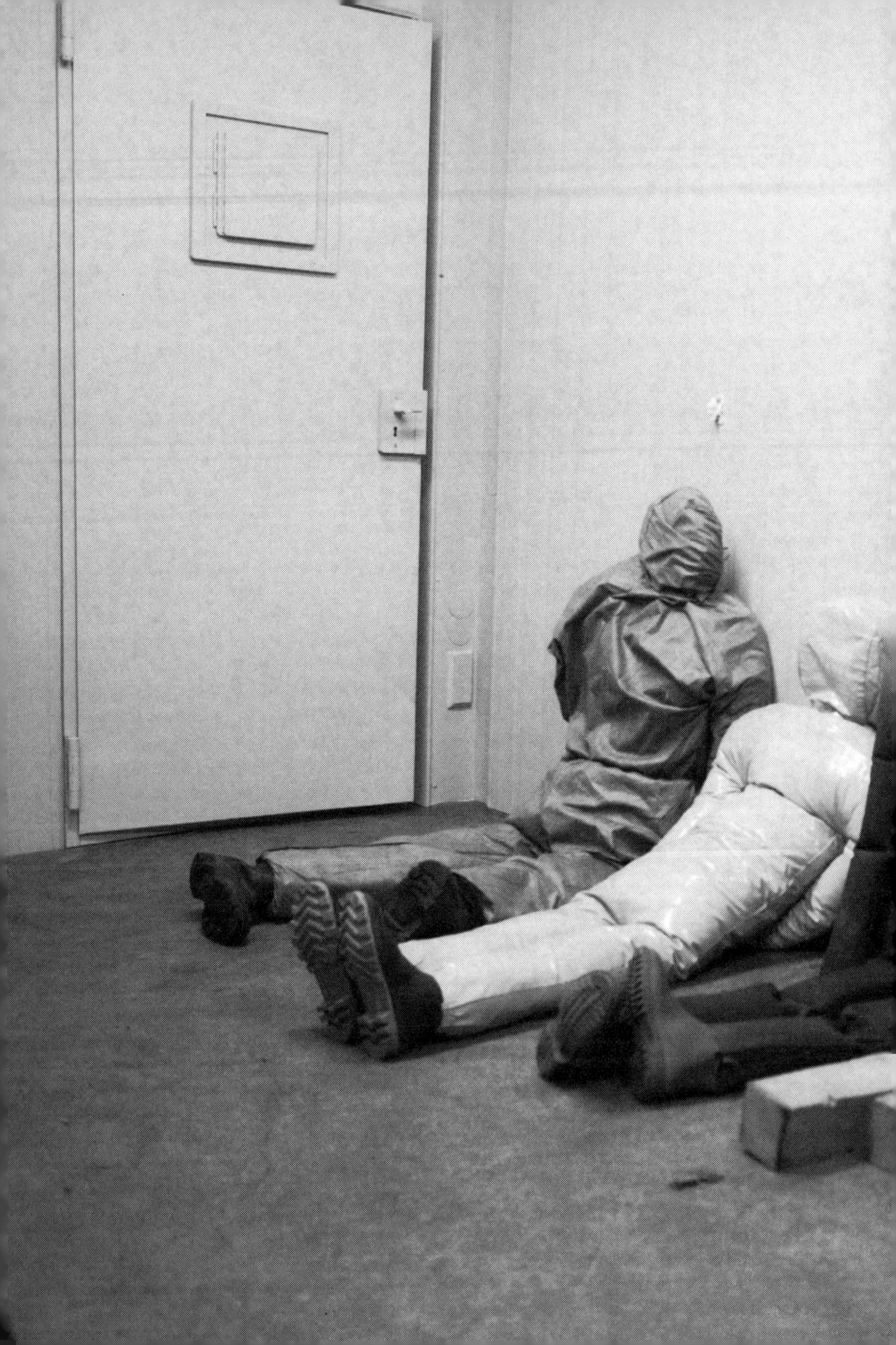

# Beyond Innocence:
# The Genre of New Realism and Its Contenders

## Baukje Prins

Was this the stuff of a classic Greek tragedy or of a postmodern soap opera? During the dramatic clash in May 2006 between Ayaan Hirsi Ali and Rita Verdonk, two notorious Dutch politicians and fellow party members, many in the Dutch audience who watched the spectacle must have asked themselves this question. Until this affair, Hirsi Ali, a Somali-Dutch member of parliament for the conservative-liberal party (VVD),[1] and Verdonk, Minister of Integration and Immigration, had supported each other wholeheartedly in their uncompromizing approach to Muslim migrants and asylum seekers, which made both women extremely popular among the Dutch population.

lkspartij voor Vrijheid en
cratie, or the People's Party for
om and Democracy.

Verdonk prided herself on following an unequivocal and impartial style of ruling, not surrendering to emotional considerations or subjective reasoning. When, during a meeting with a group of imams, one of them politely refused her hand because his faith did not allow him to touch a woman, she ostentatiously held her hand outstretched, put an amazed expression on her face and asked: 'But man and woman are equal in this country, aren't they?', thus making it crystal clear that he had not yet understood the Dutch (i.e. civilized) way of paying respect. Verdonk also regularly emphasized that asylum seekers should not primarily be perceived as victims: many of them were not really political refugees, but economic 'fortune hunters'. If rejection of an application for asylum resulted in the deportation of children born and raised in the Netherlands, she claimed that the parents had chosen to have the children and therefore their ordeal was their responsibility, not that of the Dutch government.

Hirsi Ali had always agreed with Verdonk that integration into Dutch society required immigrants to express full loyalty to liberal values and to the Dutch nation. Muslim women should distance themselves from their religious and cultural background, as only a conversion to western liberalism could truly emancipate them. And she agreed that asylum seekers should not be handled with too much pity – especially Somali refugees were prone to fraudulent practices. Yet Hirsi Ali had been an asylum seeker herself. Moreover, it was a public secret that she had committed fraud when applying for asylum back in 1992. Already in her first interviews she mentioned how she had given a false name and a false date of birth, that she had lied about the country from which she had fled and the reasons for her flight. However, when a television documentary broadcast in May 2006 supposedly 'revealed' those lies, a member of parliament asked critical questions regarding the legal status of his colleague. Within just a few days Minister Verdonk, true to her adage that 'rules are rules', announced that Hirsi Ali had, formally speaking, never acquired Dutch citizenship. Hirsi Ali immediately held a press conference where she announced that she was leaving the Netherlands to take up a position at the American Enterprise Institute, a conservative Washington D.C. think tank with close ties to the Bush administration.

The tragic irony of the story was that both heroines fell on their own swords: the sword of the blind Lady of Justice, who in the end was forced to return to Hirsi Ali her Dutch passport and the sword of the unflinching Somali war lord (as Hirsi Ali once called herself) who was expelled from the country she held so dear because it gave her freedom. However, while the entire Cabinet and Parliament fiercely attacked the Minister for her context-insensitive and overly rash application of the rules, a majority of the Dutch audience stood squarely behind Verdonk, and felt that Hirsi Ali had better leave the country.

Hirsi Ali and Verdonk are two particularly outspoken representatives of what I call the genre of *new realism* in the current Dutch discourse on immigration and ethnic minorities. New realism has gradually emerged in the Dutch public debates since the early 1990s. It reached its first culmination point when in autumn 2001, just after the September 11 attacks, Pim Fortuyn entered the Dutch political stage. Fortuyn was notorious for the revolt he instigated in Dutch political culture by posing as the man who had the guts to break 'politically correct' taboos on immigrants and Islam. After his murder, the first political murder in the Netherlands since 1672, Dutch politics made a radical turn from a relatively 'soft' and cosmopolitan outlook to a tough and inward-looking nationalistic approach. The fate of some of Fortuyn's followers, notably Hirsi Ali and Theo van Gogh, put the Netherlands on the international map as a real-life experiment of immigrant integration: exemplary to some, a spectre to others.

### Politically correct: the genres of denunciation, empowerment and report

Our speech is neither epistemologically nor politically innocent: something said is something done. I focus here not so much on the extent to which the standpoints in the Dutch discourse are in accordance with reality, but on the different rhetorical strategies that seduce readers into going along with their account. The focus is on the performative effects of particular utterances and discourses, i.e. on the ways in which they (co)produce rather than represent social realities.

In the 1970s and 1980s, the Dutch public discourse on ethnic and racial minorities was infused with the collective memory of the persecution and mass murder of Jewish citizens during the Second World War. Anti-racism equalled anti-fascism. Action groups and journalists exposed the exploitation of foreign guest workers by big industries and the racism of the white lower classes vis-à-vis postcolonial migrants. The (desired) performative effect of this genre was *denunciation*: the white Dutch narrator acted as the more articulate spokesperson for the victims of exploitation and discrimination who were assumed not (yet) able to speak or fight for themselves. The narrator's role was like that of the plaintiff in a court of justice. Just like the prosecutor, who as a 'professional' accuser is more skilled in the juridical language game than her clients, narrators in the denunciatory genre posed as 'professional' knowers, more articulate than the guest workers, immigrants and illegal residents they represented. They brought their cases before a forum of right-minded citizens, supposedly capable of putting themselves in an impartial position and assessing the reliability of the accounts. The genre of denunciation appealed to the value of *solidarity*. Its views were structured by the normative political frameworks of Marxism and socialist-feminism, which perceived society as structured by social antagonisms between victims and perpetrators.

At the end of the 1980s, Black and immigrant spokespersons entered the public arena to struggle out of the 'narrator's guardianship' of the denunciators. While the latter were the ones who 'knew better' than their protagonists, within this genre the roles were reversed: Blacks and immigrants now were the real experts, very capable of speaking for themselves. The narrator had receded into the background as the modest mediator between protagonists and the public. The inscribed audience were members of ethnic minority groups themselves. This genre of texts and speech aimed at their *empowerment*. The protagonists were pioneers: the living proof that against all odds, with much hard work and faith in yourself, you could achieve something as an immigrant. And they were role models also because, despite their careers, they remained loyal to their own (ethnic, racial) group. The core value in the genre of empowerment was (cultural) diversity. On the one hand, diversity was to be embraced for its intrinsic worth, for its enrichment of Dutch society. On the other hand, diversity was to be applauded because of its instrumental value: a diverse body of workers, for instance, would foster creativity, flexibility and efficiency, and could therefore enhance a company's profit. The ideological frameworks underlying the genre of empowerment were Black activism, radical multiculturalism and feminism; the antagonisms characterizing society were those between dominant and marginalized groups.

Throughout the 1980s and 1990s, however, the hegemonic genre of speech was the genre of the *report*. Most of these texts were studies by sociologists, psychologists and anthropologists carried out at the government's request. They concentrated on the problems of particular immigrant groups and concluded with recommendations on how to improve their socio-economic position. The inscribed readers were policy makers, politicians, social workers and the like. Reports were conveyed by an impersonal narrator; their protagonists were the representatives of a particular (ethnic, racial, cultural) category. However, apart from the wish to formulate general and valid conclusions concerning the group studied, they also attempted to convey a sense of the uniqueness of each individual case. Many reports oscillated between a scientific and a literary purpose: they appealed both to the cognitive capacities of the reader, and to faculties like empathy and imagination. Sometimes they presented the problems of immigrants as generated by social injustices that could be undone, at other times they appeared as the inevitable tragic effects of living 'between two cultures'. The underlying normative political framework of the genre of the report was social democracy, a framework within which the emancipation of subordinated groups is one of the most important values.

Until quite recently, the master dichotomy in most reports was the opposition between 'traditional' and 'modern' ways of life. One assumed that immigrants held on to their traditional habits and values because of social and economic deprivation. If their socio-economic situation improved, integration into modern Dutch society would naturally follow. In order to achieve that aim, governmental support was needed, mainly through measures in the fields of education and employment. Hence, it was socio-economic deprivation, not traditional culture or Islamic religion that hampered the integration of immigrants.

In the last decade, however, several scholars have challenged this refusal to problematize culture. They claimed that the reluctance to make a causal connection between culture and criminality, for instance, was dictated by an irrational fear of lapsing into the pitfalls of 'blaming the victim' and the affirmation of stereotypes. Such politically correct motivations should be put aside in order to reveal a reality that, however unpleasant, had to be faced in order to address the problematics at hand. In these more recent reports, minority cultures are not so much perceived from the perspective of *deprivation*, but from the perspective of *deviancy*. By implication, the government was not asked to help minority groups with their emancipation, but to press individual members to assume *responsibility*.

### New realism

This latest trend shows affinity with a fourth genre of discourse, the genre of new realism. Since the early 1990s, against the assumed political correctness of the genres of denunciation, empowerment and report, new realism has become ever more dominant in Dutch public debates on immigration and integration. Its main (desired) performative effect is to make the public face (the harsh) reality again. One of the first public expressions of new realism came from the then leader of the Conservative Liberals, Frits Bolkestein. In its eagerness to help migrants emancipate, he claimed, Dutch government had become too lenient and permissive. Mottos based on the Dutch tradition of religious pillarisation, such as 'identity with the preservation of identity' and 'emancipation within one's own circle first', should be replaced by a policy that dared to present western values as superior, and to handle the integration of Muslim migrants 'with guts'. His supporters spoke of Dutch political culture as a 'culture of pitifulness' which was 'hugging migrants to death'.

The genre of new realism has five distinctive rhetorical features. Firstly, the narrator is someone who dares to face the facts, who speaks frankly about 'truths' that the dominant discourse has supposedly covered up. Furthermore, a new realist sets himself up as the mouthpiece for the 'ordinary people', i.e. (in Dutch usage) the *autochthonous*, or ethnically Dutch, population. On the one hand, ordinary people deserve to be represented because they are realists *par excellence*: they know from daily experience what is really going on, especially in the poor neighbourhoods of big cities, and they are not blinded by politically correct ideas. On the other hand, one should take their complaints seriously in order to channel the underlying emotions in the right direction. Thirdly, realism is assumed to be a characteristic feature of national identity: being Dutch equals being frank, straightforward and realistic. Moreover, a new realist challenges the power of the progressive establishment that, with its 'politically correct' sensibilities, has dominated the public realm for too long. This supposedly left-wing censorship is also criticized because it is assumed to be accompanied by a relativistic approach to cultures. Finally, the discourse of new realism is highly gendered. Narrators prove their point by referring to issues of gender and sexuality such as the headscarf, arranged or forced marriage, female genital mutilation, honour killing, the cult of virginity, domestic violence and homophobia. For new realists, the equality between men and women is an obvious and uncontested part of western culture in general and Dutch liberal democracy in particular. Many new realists therefore reserve their 'guts' for challenging Muslim men to leave their ('backward') values behind, while they pose as the chivalrous protector of the safety and happiness of Muslim women. The underlying normative political frameworks of new realism are neoliberalism and conservative communitarianism, with their core value of individual responsibility. Present-day relationships are perceived in terms of the antagonism between the West and Islam, often represented as a clash between 'civilized' and 'backward' cultures.

That new realism had gained ground not only among politicians but also among intellectuals was confirmed by the huge affirmative response elicited by an essay published in January 2000 by the sociologist and commentator Paul Scheffer. Scheffer castigated the Dutch elite for closing their eyes to the 'multicultural drama' developing right before their eyes. Although rates of unemployment, criminality and school dropouts among ethnic minorities were extremely high, the Dutch mistakenly held onto their good old strategies of peaceful coexistence through deliberation and compromise. Islam, Scheffer argued, with its refusal to accept the separation of church and state, could not be compared to modernized Christianity. Ethnic youngsters were accumulating feelings of frustration and resentment. To foster their integration, he claimed, teaching Dutch language, culture and history should be taken much more seriously again.

### Pim Fortuyn and the turn to hyperrealism

The powerful rhetoric of Pim Fortuyn showed all the characteristics of new realism. On one occasion, his face appeared on the cover of a magazine, his mouth tied up with his necktie, accompanied by the caption: 'Are you allowed to say everything you think? Dutch taboos'. Fortuyn prided himself on knowing what was going on in the poor neighbourhoods and fully understanding the concerns of the 'ordinary people'. On the one hand, the ordinary Dutchman was a new realist like himself: 'The poor are not at all the pitiful people the left church wants them to be. Most of them are just like us: emancipated, individualized, independent citizens.' On the other hand, the Dutch were in need of a true leader, someone who, like himself, could act as their father and mother at the same time: 'the father as the one who lays down the law, the mother as the binding element of the herd.' Against the expanding influence of the European Union he insisted on the preservation of national sovereignty, and warned against the imminent 'Islamization' of Dutch society. Contempt for the progressive elite ('the left church') pervaded almost every aspect of his writings. Finally, gender and sexuality figured as a somewhat noisy subtext throughout his public performances. He made no secret of his homosexuality and stood up to accusations of racism by stating that he had slept with Moroccan boys often enough – for him the threat of Islamization also referred to the homophobia among Muslim youngsters. Fortuyn was no stranger to ironic gender role play either: when an interviewer once asked about his ultimate ambition, he confessed that as a boy he had wanted to become the pope (because everything you say then is considered infallible truth), but that nowadays he would love to become queen – of the Netherlands, obviously ...

Fortuyn further radicalized the new realist discourse. Freedom of opinion, whether for a jester like Van Gogh who had spoken carelessly about Muslims as 'goat-fuckers' and imams as 'pygmies', or an imam who deemed homosexuals lower than pigs, was more important than legal protection against discrimination. As 'a man who says what he thinks and does what he says', Fortuyn had no qualms stating that Holland was a 'full country', Islam 'a backward culture' and proposing the abolition of 'that weird article of the Constitution: Thou shalt not discriminate'. People were asked to put their trust in him more on account of his new realist rhetoric than on the basis of his political programme. And so they did, as was evident in the massive outburst of grief and anger after his murder.

Fortuyn's particular style, this odd mixture of aristocratic appearance and tough talk, turned out to be his strongest political weapon. New realism, which was initially about having the guts to speak freely about problems and how they should be solved, was turned into simply having guts, i.e. venting one's gut feelings. Fortuyn thus managed to radicalize the genre of new realism such that it turned into its very opposite, into a kind of hyperrealism. Frankness was no longer practised for the sake of truth, but for its own sake. References to reality and the 'hard facts' became mere indicators of the strong personality of the speaker, proof that a 'real leader' had entered the stage who dared migrants to shoulder their responsibility rather than wait for help.

### *Submission*, Part I

Like Fortuyn, Hirsi Ali is a charismatic and charming person who showed the new realist knack for provoking and breaking taboos. Within just couple of months she became an immensely popular public figure and in January 2003 was elected a member of parliament for the conservative-liberal party (VVD). Her apostasy was underlined by statements that Mohammed was a 'tyrant' and a 'perverse man', while Islam was denounced as an authoritarian and inherently violent religion, irreconcilable with the principles of liberal democracy. Her trenchant interventions caused much more commotion than similar statements by Fortuyn.

For this time, the speaker was someone who 'fouled her own nest'. Her total identification with Dutch culture and history and her espousal of western values as the only guarantee for a happy and fulfilling life led to accusations of her being 'bounty', a traitor of her 'own' people. This was only aggravated by claims to the effect that Islam condemned women to a life of obedience and subordination, and that the only way to free themselves was to remove the shackles of religion, of which the veil was only the most visible sign. She calmly maintained this position, indifferent to the voices of Muslim women who did not recognize themselves in this absolutist view, and who were striving to emancipate themselves while remaining in touch with their community.

In the summer of 2004, Hirsi Ali wrote the script of a short movie, *Submission* (Part 1), and engaged filmmaker Theo van Gogh as director. The film, first broadcast on national television, was a dramatic staging of the fate of Muslim women in the form of a prayer to Allah. The text of the prayer shows remarkable similarities to the rhetorical strategies used in the genre of denunciation. The main protagonist, Amina, stands upright, dressed in a see-through veil that covers all but her eyes, but under which we can see her nearly naked body. She acts as the spokesperson for the four silent women surrounding her. Through her voice, each of them begs Allah to explain why she has to suffer so much violence and injustice while she has always obeyed His commands. Texts from the Koran suggesting that violence and the oppression of women is legitimated by Islam are inscribed on the skin of the women, whose bodies shiver from the wounds inflicted upon them by being beaten up, flogged and raped.

It soon became clear that to some, this movie had exceeded all bounds. In November 2004, Van Gogh was brutally slaughtered in the streets of Amsterdam. His murderer, a 26-year-old Dutch-Moroccan, pinned a letter on Van Gogh's body with a knife, the contents of which made it clear that his deed was actually meant as a warning to Hirsi Ali. She was forced to go underground for the second time in her short career. Upon her return she expressed determination to hold on to her mission to stimulate Muslims to make a 'shortcut to Enlightenment'. However, while this affair established her fame abroad, at home her star was gradually fading.

### Moving

Before 2002 it was widely believed (also by ourselves . . . ) that the Dutch cherished no nationalistic sentiments outside politically innocent happenings like football matches, skating championships and Queen's Day.

Only a couple of years and two political murders later, a majority of the population has rejected the European Constitution, Dutch intellectuals have developed a new canon of Dutch history and culture, and the Netherlands have been condemned by the European Council and Human Rights Watch for violating the basic human rights of asylum seekers and migrants.

However much the clash between Hirsi Ali and Verdonk had the appearance of a grand finale signalling the downfall of two heroines of Dutch new realism, nothing is further from the truth. Hirsi Ali's expulsion from the Netherlands was only an overture to a new episode in her successful mission as a champion of individual liberty and a fighter against a 'backward' Islam. And although in the Netherlands the national elections of November 2006 led to the formation of a moderate Social Democratic–Christian government, the winners were the extreme-right Freedom Party, the extreme-left Socialist Party, and ('not right, not left, but straight ahead') Rita Verdonk, who drew more than half a million votes for the Conservative Liberals. Although the socialists did not brand immigrants as scapegoats, these were the parties that, in line with new realism, tapped into the fears of the 'ordinary people' regarding Dutch sovereignty and identity. New realism reached a further all-time low when, in March 2007, Geert Wilders of the Freedom Party (PVV) publicly questioned the loyalty of two (newly appointed) ministers and a senior member of parliament of Turkish and Moroccan descent. His motion demanding that they either hand in their 'other' passports or resign was rejected by a large majority. But Wilders, triumphant because of the many Dutch who welcomed his debating style, coolly announced: 'They should prepare for the worst, I haven't even started yet. It will become even more heated. Whoever cannot stomach it, should look for another profession. Actually, I don't care one bit what the other parties think.'

How can we counter the hegemony of new realism? How can we subvert this forceful rhetoric that appeals to a desire for moral and political innocence, for a position from which we, freed from all ideological blinders, can perceive reality as it really is? The most effective counter-strategies can be perceived in accounts that, for want of a better term, could be subsumed under the heading of 'heterogeneity'. Heterogeneous accounts cut across the binary oppositions that play a constitutive role in the previous genres. Heterogeneous works do not offer us certainty in the sense that they confront us with reality as it truly is. Their (desired) performative effect is not so much to confront as to *move* us, in the double sense of the word: to affect and to mobilize.

The genre of heterogeneity can be, and already is practised by a motley crew of 'storytellers' and 'image makers'. Some of them are academic scholars and journalists, but it is especially the domains of contemporary art and culture that are open to multilayered and multiperspectival accounts of the world that is our habitat today. That goes for the literary as well as visual arts, for specimens of 'high' as well as popular culture. Whether in the esoteric form of an installation, the popular form of a sitcom or the classic form of a painting or novel, art can be a site where mirrors are held up to us – not the flat mirror of a square confrontation with reality, but ever so many distorting mirrors that offer us our realities in an altered, processed, stylized form. They may make us smile about ourselves, and provide us with new angles and fresh food for thought.

It might be objected that this espousal of heterogeneity endows each perspective with equal validity, leaving us empty handed when it comes to everyday politics: when we are confronted with a problem we cannot simply muse on the complexities and ambiguities of the world – we have to act. Such a line of criticism, I would argue, rests on the mistaken assumption that epistemic perspectivism equals moral relativism, a posture of 'anything goes' that is indifferent to the fundamental values of liberal democracy. Nothing could be further from the stakes of heterogeneous accounts as I envision them. If it is to live up to its credentials, a liberal democratic regime gives ample room for articulating dissent and differences, for cherishing practices and ways of life that are open to alternative perspectives, even if they touch upon our most fundamental convictions. Heterogeneous works of art and culture may be beneficial in fostering democratic forms of life that leave behind politically damaging and exclusionary claims to innocence or purity, and strive for truly inclusive and universally accessible negotiations of our differences.

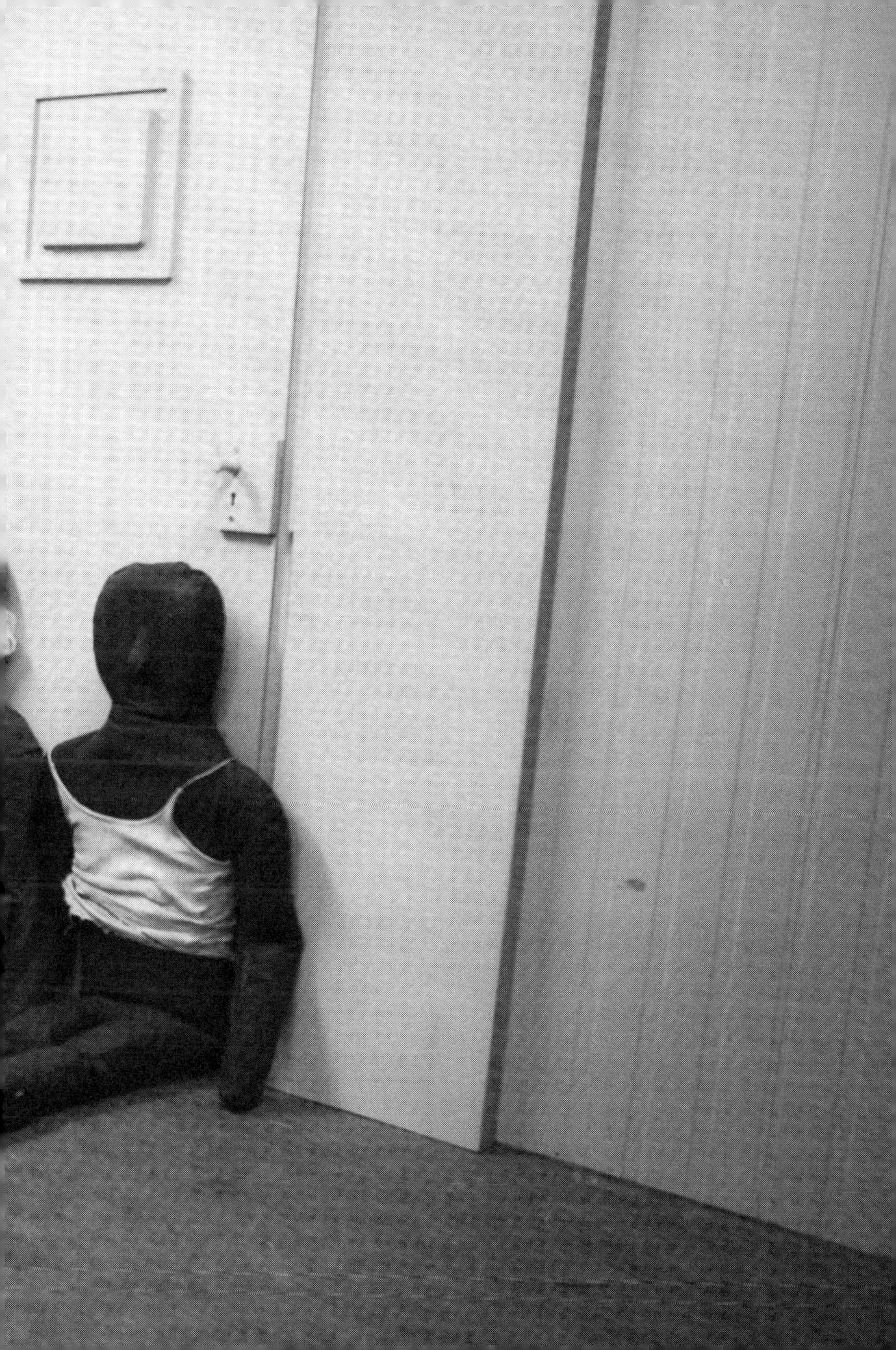

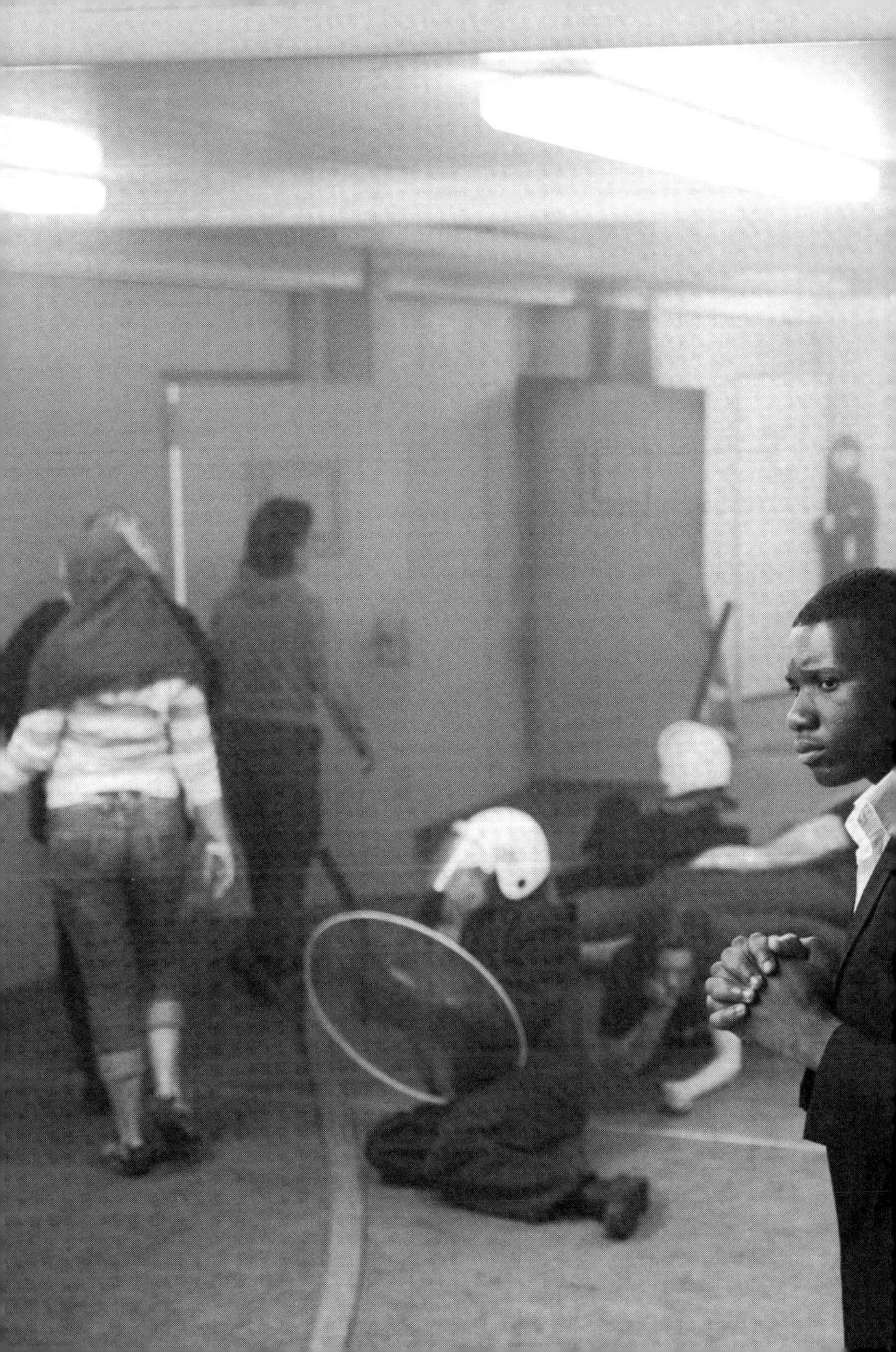

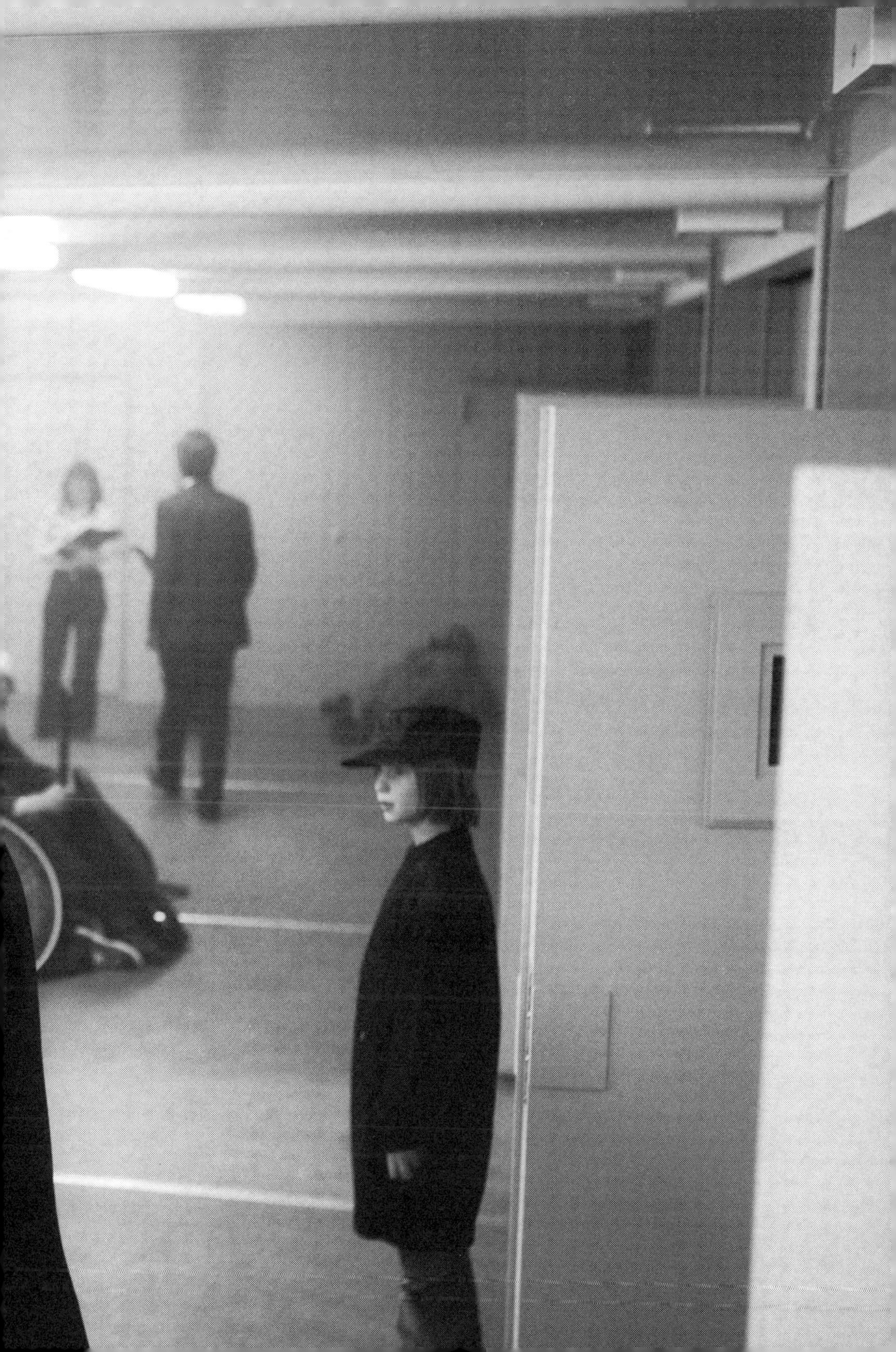

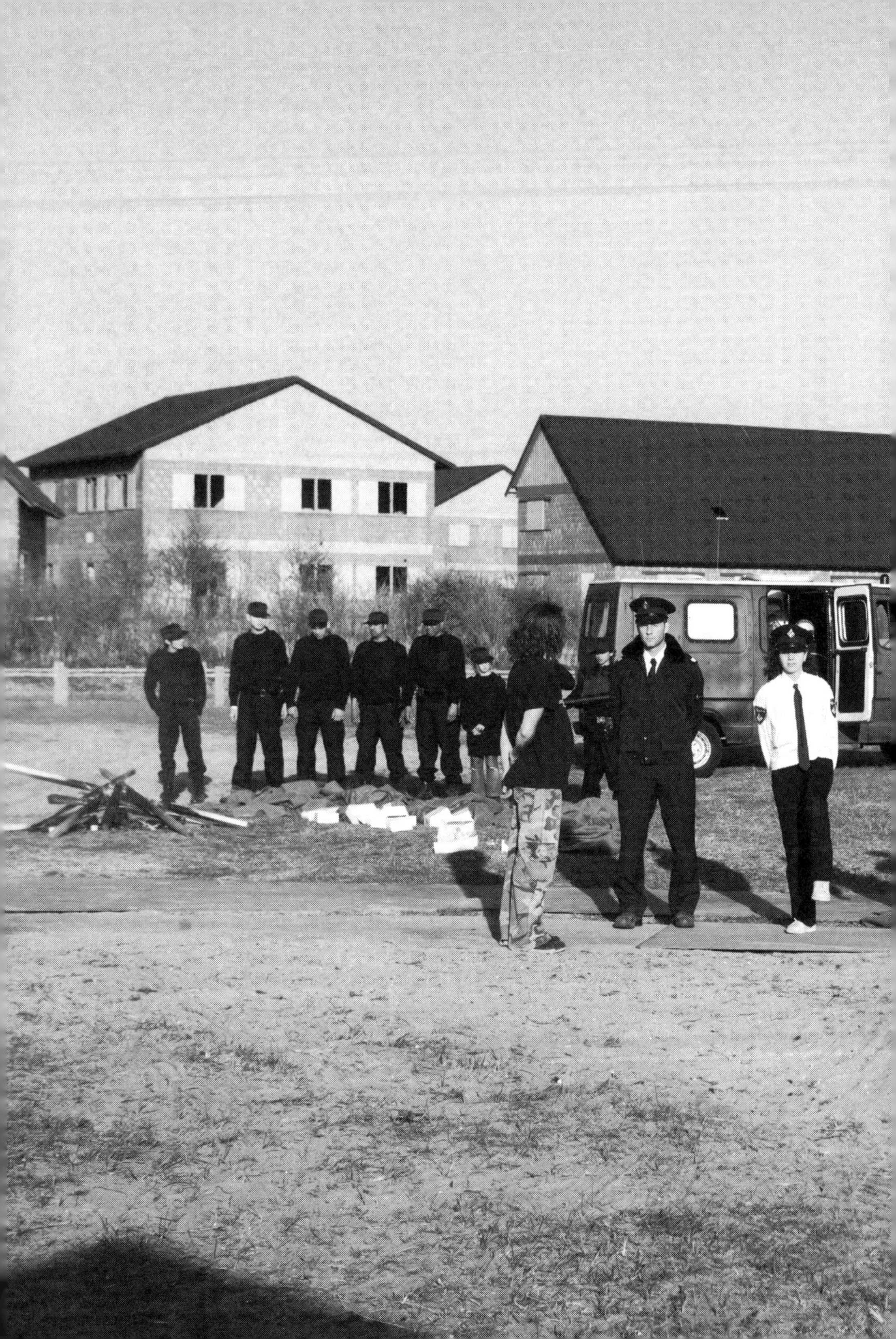

# The 'Droste Effect' or What Comes after Being Critical?

## A Conversation with Willem de Rooij

utscher Akademischer
usch Dienst (German Academic
nge Service)

**Maria Hlavajova** You've been in Berlin on a DAAD[1] scholarship for almost a year. What's the story of you leaving the Netherlands for Germany?

**Willem de Rooij** DAAD's generous invitation came at the right time. I've been trying to plan an extended stay outside of the Netherlands for a long time, but for practical reasons it was never really possible. And although my scholarship ends soon, I'll stay in Berlin for now. I never considered Berlin as a possible hometown, and it's been extremely pleasant to move to a city that I had no expectations about.

**MH** So what is it that is so attractive for artists like you to live here?

**WdR** Since Berlin is bankrupt, the galleries mainly cater to markets outside of the city. Most artists who live here are not economically bound to the city. So maybe it's not great for art, but it's very good for artists. It's quiet, very quiet. There is a lot of physical and social space and there is a lot of time. But there is also another sort of quietness here for me: as a non-local you simply do not understand everything you see and hear. A lot of unnecessary (as well as necessary) information is filtered out that way. Being able to interpret and contextualize everything I read, heard or witnessed increasingly became problematic for me in Amsterdam. I guess Dutch culture has a certain tendency for navel-gazing, and I started to feel like I got trapped in a house of mirrors. Think of the 'Droste effect'.[2] The current political climate added to my claustrophobia. Of course the recent rise of nationalist and populist sentiments is not confined to the Netherlands, but for me it became unbearable to live in a place where I could interpret the finest fibres of its xenophobia and the ways it is expressed, institutionalized and instrumentalized. On top of this it's hard to discuss these issues in the Netherlands because the Dutch see politicality as something separate from the rest of life. In Germany, and maybe in other countries too, everything one does has a political component. It's something that is part of the fabric of everyday life, and this applies to all layers of the population at all levels of discourse.

e 'Droste effect' is a Dutch term
articular recursive picture. A
e with the Droste effect depicts
ller version of itself in a place
a similar picture would be
ted to appear. This smaller
n then depicts an even smaller
n of itself in the same place,
o on. One can easily create an
ole of the Droste effect by
g two mirrors in front of each
The term was coined by the
nd columnist Nico Scheep-
r at end of the 1970s and is
d after Droste, a Dutch cocoa
as a picture of a nurse carrying
ing tray with a cup and a box of
me brand of hot chocolate on
.

**MH** With regard to what you describe, I'd like to discuss a few of your works that deal with the current xenophobia that you

mentioned and the western condition of today, so to speak.
You realized these works in collaboration with Jeroen de Rijke,
who unexpectedly passed away a year ago. Is it possible for
you to speak about these pieces?

> **WdR** Jeroen and I were working in a continuous flux. We both
> felt that each work was produced in reaction to the one before,
> and that we were creating a family of works in the process.
> These works are as much part of my past as they are part of my
> present and future, so I am happy to discuss them with you.

**MH** I would like to begin with a 'family of works', as you call it,
which consists of three films: *Of Three Men* (1998), *Bantar
Gebang* (2000) and *Untitled* (2001). Each of these works
contains a set of aesthetic and political propositions: an
exploration of the interior and the light in an Amsterdam
church-turned-mosque; a picturesque twilight in
confrontation with life in a slum in Indonesia; and a view of an
Islamic cemetery enveloped in the absurd context of a
booming contemporary monumental urban site near Jakarta,
respectively. In my opinion, these works have a lot in common,
as to me they speak about the contemporary western
condition – or perhaps about the much more concrete case of
the Netherlands – that we tend to experience today through
immigration, for example, which is somewhat automatically
associated with Islam and not unrelated to the colonial past (as
Indonesia is a former Dutch colony). Furthermore, you introduced Islamic imagery – or rather its iconoclastic associations –
into your work well ahead of the explosion of such images in
the western media in the last five to seven years. I would like to
ask, what actually prompted you to realize these works and
how did you choose the locations for filming?

> **WdR** We started looking at mosques after we came back from
> Greenland, where we'd been shooting a film about an iceberg
> (*I'm Coming Home in Forty Days*, 1997). While producing that
> film we were thinking about emptiness, about images that are
> figurative, but appear abstract. About how abstraction and
> spirituality could actually meet. We looked at Pasolini's
> *Teorema*, at Barnett Newman and at Minimalist sculpture. We
> had not made many films and had not yet found a mode of
> presentation that fit our pieces. We had screened earlier works
> in traditional cinema settings and were disappointed: our

films never met the expectations of the viewers who attended those screenings. We started to position our films in the physical context of art. For the presentation of *I'm Coming Home in Forty Days* we started looking at the white cube as a model for presentation. At the same time we were looking at mosques. We saw both as spaces with a more or less square orientation in which figuration is not allowed, so the mosque and the white cube started to merge in our fantasy. We always promoted the capacity of film to be absent – that's one of the reasons we never wanted to produce loops. We became interested in the Islamic tradition of image production, which focuses on other strategies than those of figuration. Out of these interests we developed a presentation model we were able to elaborate on in the years that followed, as well as *Of Three Men*.

**MH** So your motivation was mainly aesthetic?

**WdR** Only partly. The context was pregnant with issues of immigration and integration related (mainly) to the Muslim population in Amsterdam when we filmed in Fatih Mosque in 1998. Islamophobia was not invented on 9/11. There are several influences at work in *Of Three Men*: the notion of iconoclastic tendencies in the Islamic tradition, as well as our own investigations into the possibility of the 'absence' of image as artistic strategy. We also looked at the works of Pieter Saenredam, mainly for ideas about composition.

**MH** And the works filmed in Indonesia?

**WdR** We did not primarily go to Jakarta because it was in a former Dutch colony, but we were obviously interested in the possibilities the historical context provided us with. However, we did not feel that being Dutch automatically entitled us to comment on a past we had not physically been a part of. We were thinking about what a 'political image' might be. How it could look. So we asked each other: what was the first image we ever thought of as political?

**MH** So what did you think?

**WdR** Interestingly, we both remembered the same image, probably from a 1970s primary school textbook. It was an image that combined a slum area and a corporate tower in the same frame, an illustration that taught children how the wealth of the world is divided.

**MH** So that image of a slum was from Indonesia? That makes me curious how those types of images, namely, images of Dutch colonial history, are dealt with in Dutch school.

**WdR** We were taught about the heroic conquests of the VOC[3] and its positive consequences for the seventeenth-century Dutch economy and the development of the arts. There was no notion of the 'other's' experience of colonialism, or slavery. Similarly, for instance, we were only told one side of the story in terms of the role of the Netherlands and the Dutch in the Second World War. But we didn't want to get involved in a discussion of the colonial past. We were more interested in investigating our role as image producers within our neocolonial present.

More generally we were interested in images we can tell each other about. Archetypal constructs of sorts. If I say 'Eiffel Tower', or 'Palm Beach', chances are you'll think of an image that to a large extent matches the one that I am thinking of. I guess that's how texts and descriptions became important in some of our later works. These pieces investigate the relationship between an image or object and a text, and at the same time respond to larger frameworks, such as history, or how it is being transmitted through education.

**MH** How about the second grouping of works, the four 'bouquets' you have made since 2002. *Bouquet II* (2003) was the first of your works, if I am not mistaken, accompanied by a text written by you. What was the text about?

**WdR** The text reflected the positions of four women in connection to the events surrounding the Miss World pageant in Nigeria in 2000. Maybe you recall how that beauty contest stirred up massive religious riots. The resulting killings and violence became so threatening that the competition had to be relocated to England. The text investigates possible connections to the ambiguous position of Ayaan Hirsi Ali, who at that moment was not yet a member of the Dutch Parliament, but a self-appointed spokesperson for – or against – Muslim



[3] The colonial *Verenigde Oost-Indische Compagnie* (VOC) (Dutch East India Company)

women in the Netherlands. In the end the pageant was won by Miss Turkey Azra Akin, who grew up in the Netherlands and did not speak a word of Turkish. She was, as a matter of fact, a Dutch girl, but as the daughter of Turkish parents she was considered fit to symbolize Turkish national identity. In the text Akin serves as a metaphor for migration and integration. It's these areas of cultural ambiguity that I'm particularly interested in.

**MH** *Bouquet III* (2004) consists of flowers, a vase, a wooden pedestal, and a wall text and image – a kind of collage.

**WdR** The newspaper photograph and the text focus on events that took place on 5 May 2004, when Dutch troops in Iraq celebrated the 1945 liberation of the Netherlands. *Bouquet III* was first shown at the Biennale of Sydney, and it is supposed to be constructed of Australian native flowers only.

**MH** And *Bouquet* number four?

**WdR** This *Bouquet* (2005) was an investigation of how colour translates into black and white and vice versa. We made a piece that was constructed in such a way that if you photographed it in black and white, all the colours would more or less translate into the same shade of grey. It thus excludes extremes, or clear 'positions', and is devoid of contrast. It's an egalitarian bouquet.

**MH** A mainstream bouquet . . .

**WdR** To some extent, popular culture inspires my work. I see the concept of 'mainstream' as representative of populism in the field of arts. In populist rhetoric there is no space for details, ambiguities and subtleties. The larger the desired audience, the less space there is for ambiguities. The growing unwillingness of Dutch voters to constructively make use of their electoral possibilities (during the 2006 elections there were ten political parties listed) is telling in this respect. It has been said Dutch voters inherently strive towards a two-party system. In our field, the increasing dominance of visitor counts and the dictates of the majority lead to spectacle-driven art practices. Alternative voices are so called because they alternate from the mainstream. The essence of mainstream is, however, that is strives to incorporate anything that does not belong to the mainstream. Telling in this respect is the emergence of a sub-branch of Warner Brothers called 'Warner Independent'. They produced among others, George Clooney's *Good Night and Good Luck*, an intensely codified and unthreatening critique of the Patriot Act. The incorporation of 'Independent' by Warner implies the artistic submission of the former to the latter. The majority is by its nature traditional and not inclined towards innovation or change. Its impulses, in other words, are contrary to those of art.

**MH** What really interests me is the relationship between the work and the text, which you use as a type of extended label for the work. But you could also read it simply as a part of the work. This has been commented upon numerous times in relation to your work, that these elements of the same work have a mimetic relationship, explaining one another. I disagree with this interpretation. Let's point to your installation *Orange* (2004) to discuss this further. The work consists of eighty-one monochrome slides projected in succession on a white wall, presenting a variety of shades of the colour orange, and a text on the wall.

> **WdR** I do not really think about an image and a text in the work in a hierarchical way. Both elements have the same value to me. I see these works rather as collages of different elements. I feel that the visual and the textual are not there to explain each other, but to inform each other.

**MH** In the text for *Orange*, as a part of this work, you first discuss the optical qualities of the colour in relation to photographic material. Only then do you reveal what your initial aim was, 'to approach the colour of overalls worn by prisoners at Guantanamo Bay'. Then, as you elaborate on this further, you touch upon the 'nationalist sentiments in post-populist neoconservative Holland' and the incomprehensibly high approval rating of the Dutch monarchy (the House of Orange) in these politically complex times. Yet, as a viewer one can choose to sit down and enjoy monochrome orange projected on a white wall in front of you, to view a formal experimentation with the succession of light, or read it in the political context you offer.

**WdR** We were testing the possibilities of referentiality. In *Mandarin Ducks* (2005), which we produced for the Dutch Pavilion during the last Venice Biennale, we actually wanted to saturate the piece, the form, with so many multiple references that the system would blow up. We were thinking of pieces that exist only by the grace of their references. Pieces that make viewers believe they'll be able to 'crack the code' when they get all the references right. Pieces that make viewers feel all good about themselves, and good about the artist who made them feel so good. That is precisely the mechanism we intended to question in *Mandarin Ducks*.

**MH** Was *Mandarin Ducks* also referring to the particularities of the Dutch situation? Things like having the actors speak English, bad English I mean, as a metaphor of the Dutch pretending to be international but in fact failing in that respect? Or when the first scene opens with this claustro-phobic feeling of too many people in too small a room?

**WdR** Yes, we intentionally left the actors little space within most of the frames we composed, as a reference to the narrow physical and social space we experienced in our daily lives. We never intended this film to deal explicitly with 'Dutchness', but rather with the condition of the West in general.

I don't really know what 'bad English' is. Is that English that doesn't sound like British English? Which British English? We were not interested in making similar choices, but we also did not want to thematize the Dutch language. Pidgin English is our daily reality. In my professional life, it's a more prominent reality then Dutch. Funnily enough, *Mandarin Ducks*' pidgin English was often discussed in pidgin English.

**MH** Speaking of which . . . Do you think of yourself as a Dutch artist?

**WdR** I'm not sure what that means. However, I felt forced into a particular reading of the role of the 'Dutch Artist' when we inaugurated the Dutch Pavilion at the Venice Biennale. This was jut a few days after the Dutch collectively voted 'no' in a referendum on the European Constitution. Instead of the Dutch flag we wanted to raise a European Union flag over the Pavilion, but we were not allowed – the organizers did not

want to upset the Ministry of Culture. In general I was shocked
to find out how strongly many Dutch viewers feel about the
National Pavilion and the notion of national representation.
But to answer your question properly: although I tend to resist
that notion, I know I am a Dutch artist.

**MH** How do you know?

**WdR** For one because of the financial privileges I enjoy as a
Dutch artist. Many of my international presentations would not
have happened had the Mondriaan Foundation not supported
them. Being born in the Netherlands as a white male, even a
gay white male, makes me one of the most fortunate people on
earth. My passport is like a worldwide VIP-pass. Wherever
I go people smile at me. I'm not kidding. I was provided with
possibilities artists from most other countries will never have.
And given the system and the context in which I grew up, I know
I can afford not even having to conceptualize that position.

I have no national sentiments, but Dutch art history always
provided important referential parameters for my work. In
London or Paris, a young child can get acquainted with actual
works of Velasquez and Da Vinci. My first encounters with
historical art took place in the Rijksmuseum in Amsterdam,
where primarily Dutch art is collected.

**MH** One could indeed trace many references of that kind in
your work. But what about our contemporaries? About the
Dutch art scene? Is it taking pride in your achievements?

**WdR** That's hard to say.

**MH** What about the notion of solidarity?

**WdR** You know it yourself. In general I never experienced the
Dutch cultural *Umfeld* (environment) as supportive, rather the
opposite. I guess Dutch culture always had a strong ambition
towards egalitarianism, so individual success is not respected,
or stimulated. That said, I have a few very loyal and supportive
friends and colleagues in the Netherlands, whom I deeply
respect and value. But I never really felt there was an art scene
in the Netherlands. I always felt we were all working alone, by
ourselves.

**MH** In the catalogue that accompanied your presentation at the last Venice Biennale, I read in a note in Dario Gamboni's text that you wondered 'what comes after being critical'. Can I reformulate this remark into a question to you?

> **WdR** I've been thinking about this question a lot. It is a difficult one, which is also why it remains rhetorical in the catalogue you mention. I am actually thinking about what forms of criticality there are in the first place. What bothers me is the ease with which pieces, or artists, are labelled (or label themselves) as critical. It is too easy to say: 'George Bush lied', or 'Dog shit should not cover the sidewalk.' Everyone will agree. These are complaints mistaken for criticism. The only aim seems to be for the artist to be proven right. Maybe the empowerment of the opinionated citizen that facilitated the bloom of populism also gave birth to this type of quasi-critical art practice. Some Dutch artists work in studios subsidized by the government, claiming their work is critical of the subsidy system. But critical impulses of this nature provide no risk to the critic.

**MH** What does this mean in concrete terms in the realm of art? Do you believe you've dealt with it this way in *Mandarin Ducks*, for example?

> **WdR** Yes, we gave it a try. We gave it a good shot, I think. We made an effort to step out of what to a great extent became predictable, from what worked as a successful formula. I'm really uninterested in art claiming a style or a territory. One cannot be critical of imperialist politics and at the same time be territorial about the programmatic parameters of one's own artistic practice.
>
> I started to believe that what comes 'after being critical' has to do with one's own responsibility. As I said, I believe criticality must also apply to the critic. In that respect, *Mandarin Ducks* was meant as a portrait of those who are enjoying the same social, political and economical privileges as you and I are, in the Netherlands, in Europe and in the West. But is was also a piece that was actively constructed (as a piece of fiction) and thus it tried to propose a new form. A more 'documentary' approach, through which the world is solely observed, would have left the status quo untouched.

**MH** I would still like to know what you think art has got to do with all these political issues, if anything. Or to rephrase, why should we discuss issues such as immigration or war, to name two examples, in art?

> **WdR** Artists are part of the world like all others, and immigration is a pivotal issue in many societies today. I would want everyone to be aware of these issues, whether it's my doctor, my grocer or my artist. That would be an easy answer to your question, but an example comes to my mind. I remember watching the Academy Awards ceremony, I think in 2003, when Michael Moore won a prize for *Bowling for Columbine*. Once on stage Moore gave a laboured, emotional speech about the corruption of the Bush administration and the illegitimacy of the occupation of Iraq. After some time a section of the visibly confused and divided audience started booing, and Moore was basically forced off the stage when the organizers interrupted his speech with music. Half an hour later, Adrian Brody walked on stage to accept his Oscar for best male performance in *The Pianist*, in which he played a Holocaust victim. He looked gorgeous and calm and said something along the lines of, 'Thank you for the award; I wish everyone in the world could live in peace'. After which the entire audience, suddenly unified, gave him a standing ovation. His abstract statement moved people to tears, because of its openness, and because of the way it was presented. And of course there was all this integrity projected on Brody because of the role he played in the film. Moore's clear assessment of current affairs was unsuccessful because he was too direct, and too ugly.

**MH** Do you refer to what you wrote previously, about a 'moral split' that 'defines the dilemma of most socially and politically engaged art', i.e. that the form is what art needs to deal with primarily in order to make the content legible?

> **WdR** Exactly. Form matters.

**MH** Do you believe that art can actually propose other ways of dealing with such issues, and ways of opening up new possibilities?

**WdR** In my understanding and experience, art is not something that large crowds of people are willing to interact with. I think the majority of people are choosing not to interact with art and I think that's all right. I invest in producing interesting art. In return I expect my viewers to invest in becoming interesting viewers. I think art can change thoughts and attitudes, but only for those who are willing to actively interact with art. Being a viewer is not the same as being a consumer.

*This conversation took place on 17 February 2007 in Berlin.*

 **The 'Droste Effect' or What Comes after Being Critical?**
A Conversation with Willem de Rooij

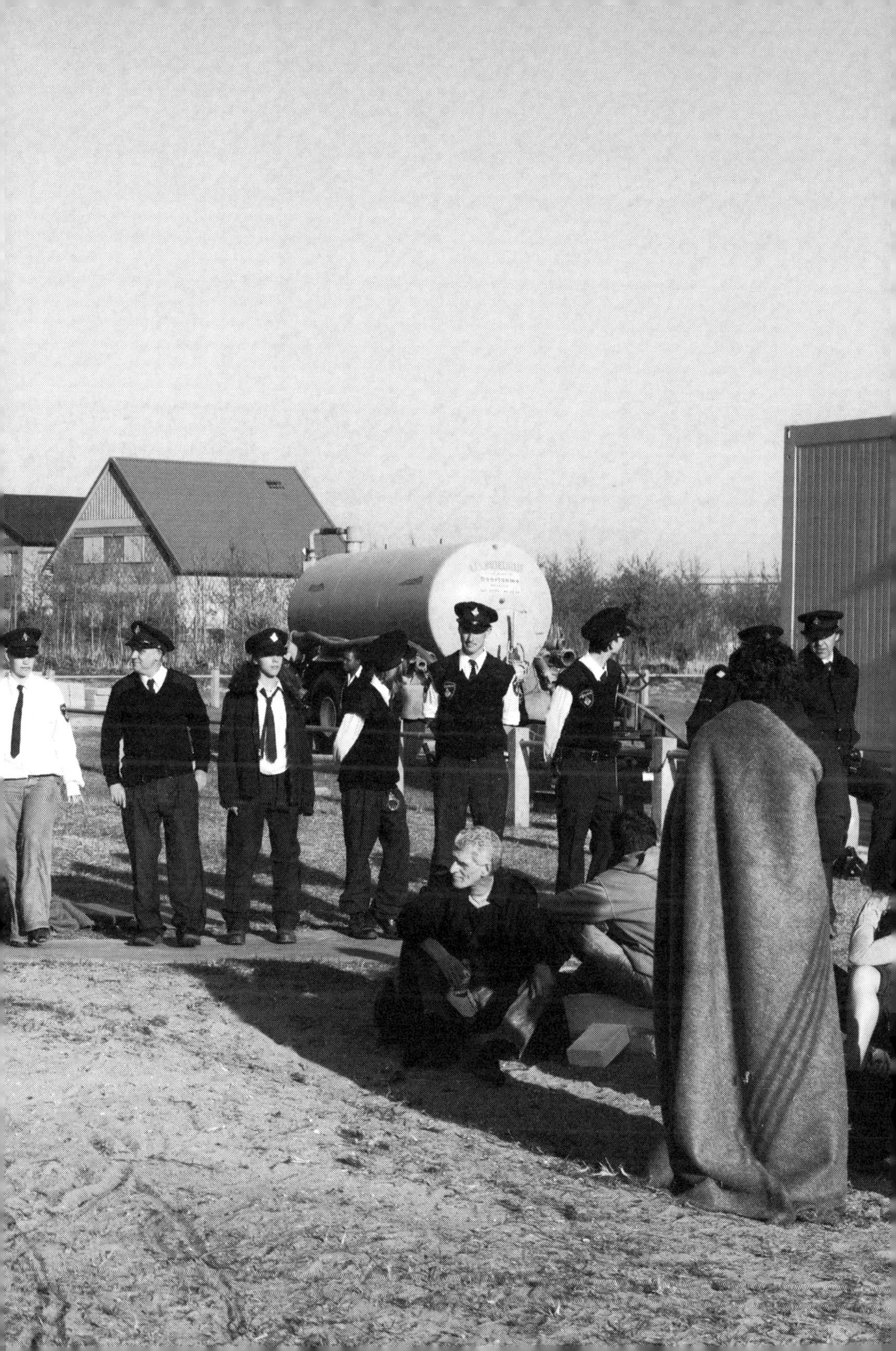

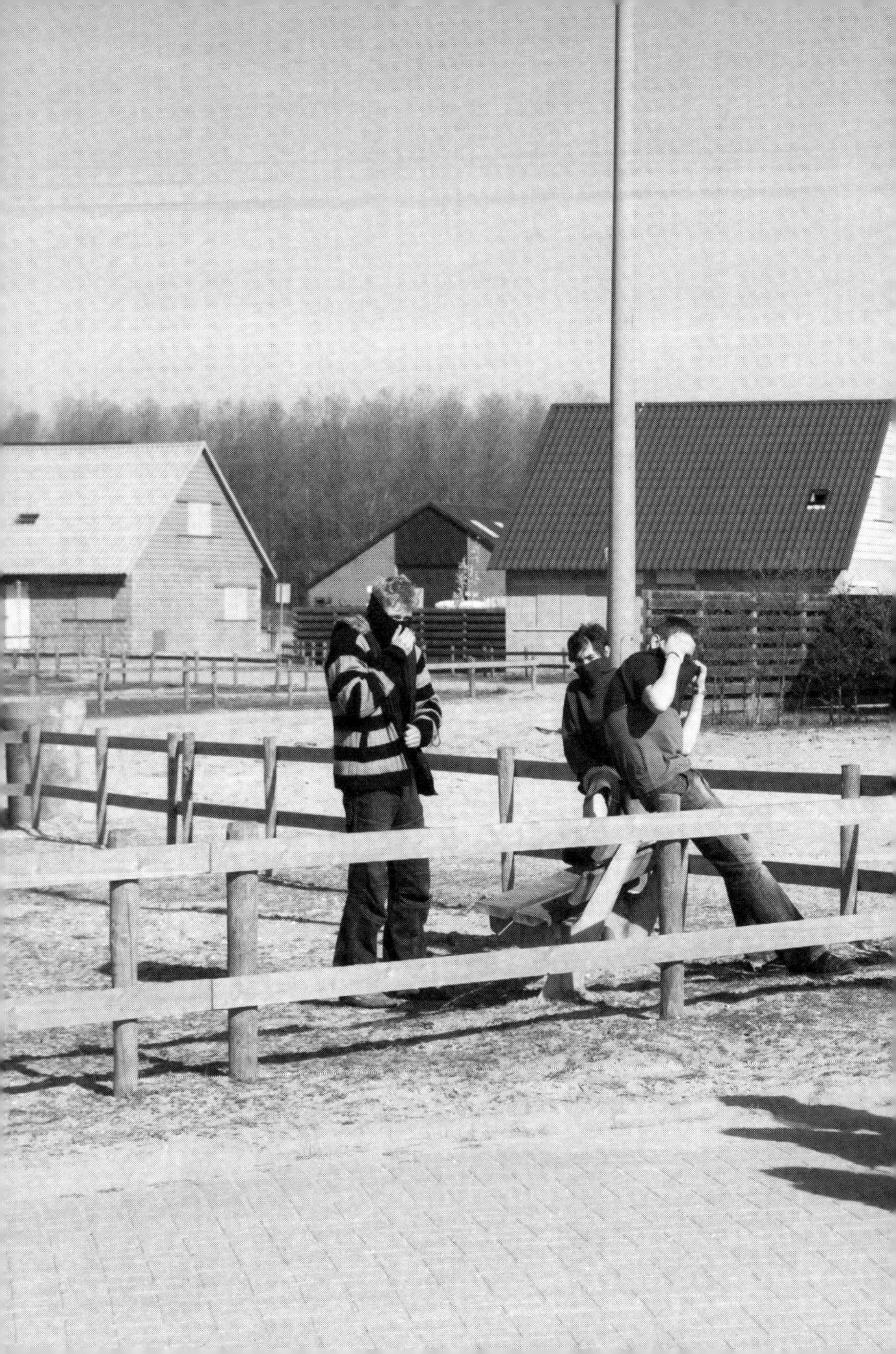

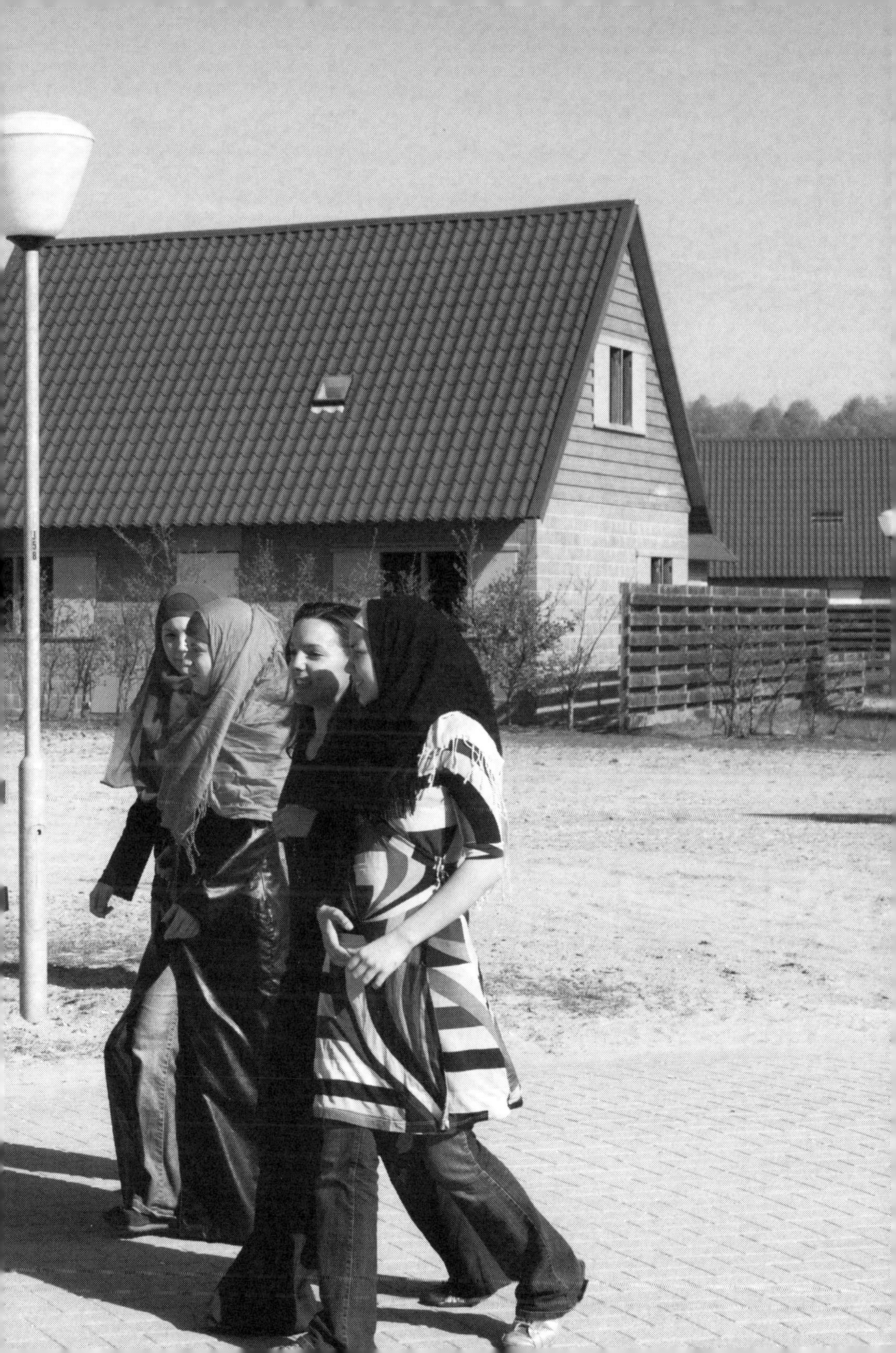

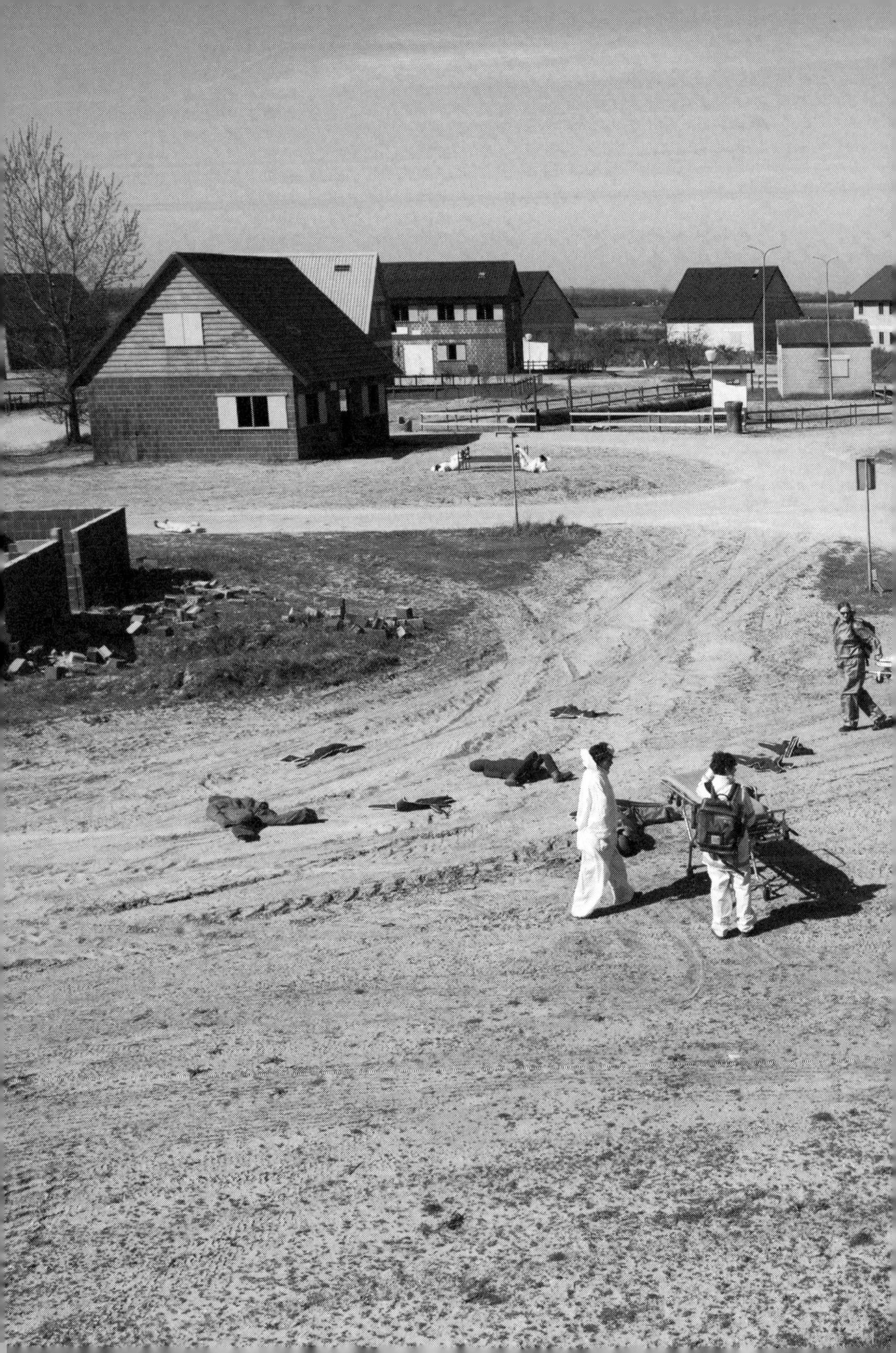

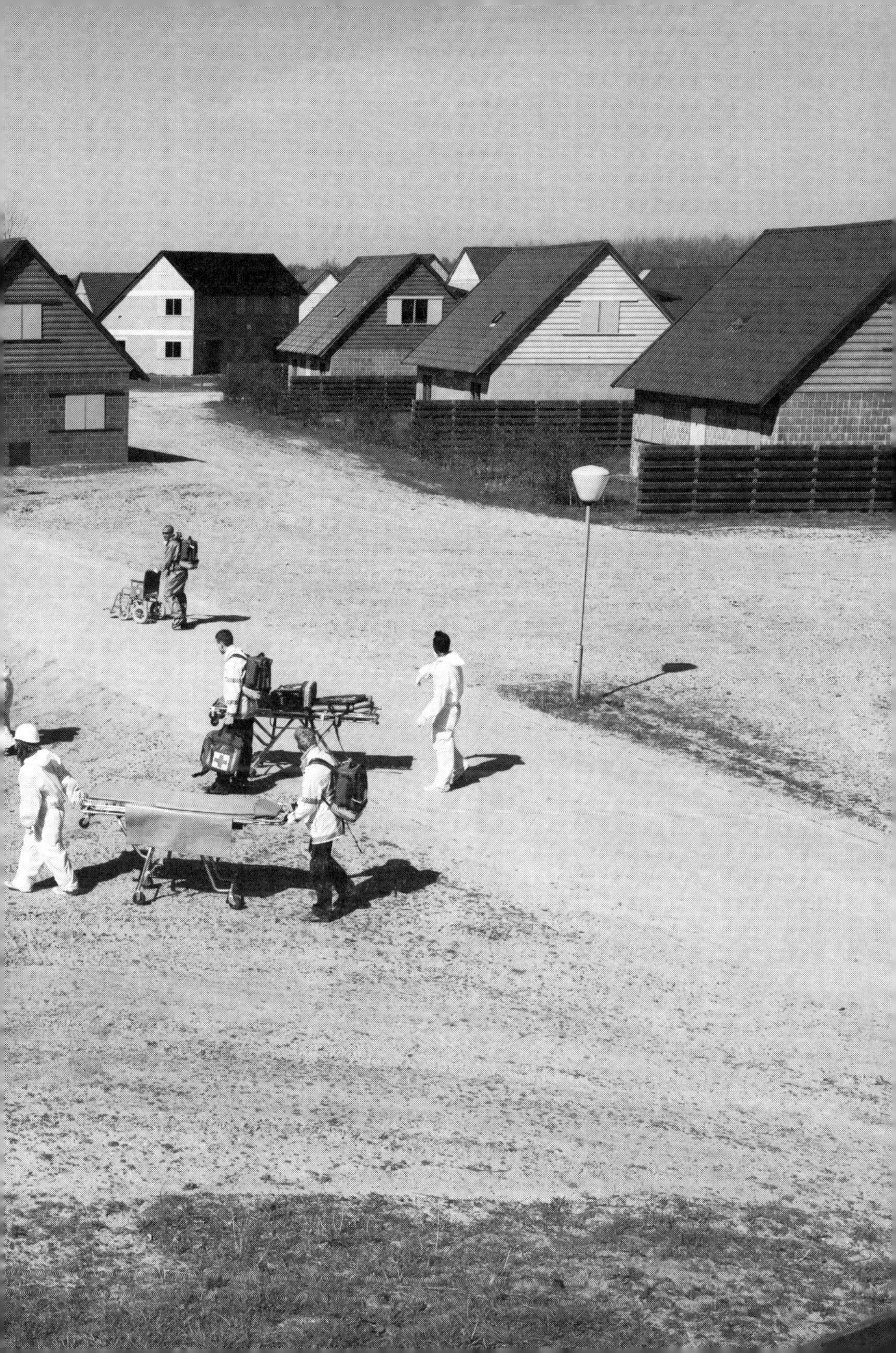

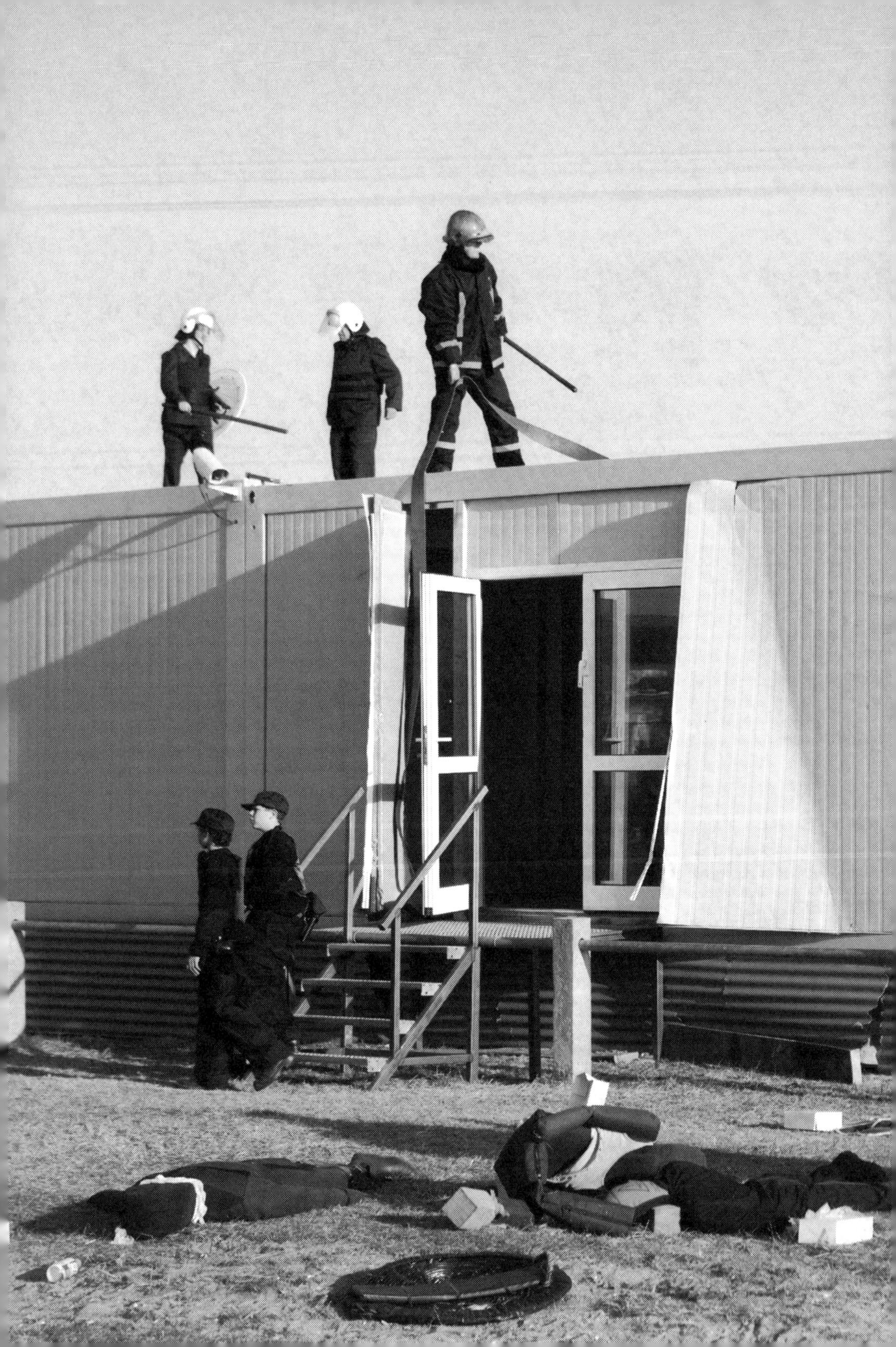

# Generational Othering and the Dutch Obsession with the Here and Now

Iris van der Tuin

In the commentaries of Dutch right-wing authors, immigrants and refugees are predominantly referred to in terms of their own or their (grand) parent's place of birth – their so-called country of origin. They are often not discussed in terms of their nationality – many 'others' have a Dutch passport, but are labelled Surinamese or Antillean, Moroccan, Turkish, Somali, Polish, etc. 'Origin' as in 'the country of origin' suggests an external cause to which one can refer in case of problems or conflicts. Moreover, the problematic effect is often singled out as its *logical* consequence. The insinuation is that the social effects – religious/Islamic fundamentalism, women as second-class citizens, homophobia, bad school results for boys, good school results for girls – have come about *by necessity*.

'The country of origin' has a spatial (there versus here) and a temporal (past versus present) dimension. Researchers and journalists generally employ time and space as independent and stable 'variables' rather than as phenomena having their own, sometimes erratic, dynamics. Time and space are considered to be *pre*-determined rather than determined *by*. This overlooks the fact that boundaries are actually drawn rather than found.[1] This is not to say that one should ignore the fact that these practices of 'cutting' lead to sedimentation. What binds the different layers of the process together is 'sticky signs'.[2] This concept refers to the histories that have become stuck to signs and to the signs that have become stuck to bodies. The sign 'immigrant' for instance has undergone changes on the basis of the historical events of decolonization, the fall of the Berlin Wall, European enlargement and war. But it has come to refer to *certain* subjects in the Netherlands (non- or Eastern-Europeans) despite the fact that many of these subjects have been born here. Thus, ignoring practices of 'cutting' *naturalizes* boundaries and linguistic conventions. This is problematic because migrants are assigned supposedly unchangeable characteristics, meanings, roles and places in the process. The only way out is through 'transcendence' (of the country of origin) into 'Dutchness'.

The cause and effect relation used with regard to immigrants and refugees in the Netherlands is based on fixed times and spaces, but also on causal linearity, and this is equally questionable. A 'causal theory of time'[3] isolates the past; the past is given *fixed meaning*. This fixed past then determines or constrains the present and the future: the past gets to define the present, and the present gets to define the future. Here, *chronos* locks into *logos*, generating a structure of entitlements that honours the authority of the past by freezing it in social practices and discourses. This framework leaves no room for the indeterminate;

aren Barad, 'Re(Con)Figuring :e, Time, and Matter', in *Feminist tions: Global and Local, Theory Practice*, ed. Marianne DeKoven Brunswick: Rutgers University s, 2001), 75–109.

ara Ahmed, *The Cultural Politics notion* (Edinburgh/New York: ledge/Edinburgh University s, 2004).

izabeth Grosz, 'Thinking the Of Futures Yet Unthought', *loke* 6.1 (1998), 55.

nothing can 'spring from' the past in a surprising manner. Allowing for the undefined does not mean to say that one should ignore the working of sticky signs. I want to argue that migrants can only lose when they and their actions are judged based upon a fixed past that either constrains them or has to be transcended. In both cases negotiation becomes almost impossible.

An alternative approach that involves a more dynamic and less linear relationship to time and a more playful conceptualization of space is needed. What if present-day conditions can redefine the past? What if we imagine the 'past' as a trickster,[4] as multiple and multilayered and open for reinterpretation? What if the coordinates of spaces are flexible[5] and we conceptualize them as heterogeneous and open for various interpretations?[6] This is not just a quantitative change towards a kind of epistemological pluralism, but rather a *qualitative* shift[7] that transforms the cutting-off points themselves and hence also the way we think about time as well as generations.

Instead, I propose thinking of 'generationality' as an embodied and embedded social axis (along with gender, ethnicity and religion) when it comes to the current Dutch attitude vis-à-vis immigrants and refugees. The elections of 22 November 2006 showed that we can generalize about right-wing approaches to the subject, not least because the political centre as well as parts of the left wing have gradually taken over the more conservative rhetoric surrounding the issue. In the debate about migrants 'the country of origin' is often accompanied by the signifiers 'first', 'second' or 'third generation'. These are sticky signs that have far-reaching consequences. We need to account for processes of 'generational othering' and their damaging effects, and suggest an alternative conceptualization of generation along with an alternative theory of time.

### Generations

Generationality is used as a sociological factor in the classification of immigrants and refugees. A generation then refers to a clearly definable group on the basis of fixed coordinates in time and space. Time and space co-constitute generationality, but often one variable prevails over the other. Dates are 'boundary objects'[8] as seen in the case of the baby boomers and Generation X. Here place plays a less important role; baby boomers were born on several continents affected by the Second World War, and the label Gen X could easily be exported to Europe. Naturalization of boundaries is the lurking danger here and it is concrete, not theoretical. Being 'cut off' from one's origins and confined to a spatially

[4] Donna J. Haraway, 'Situated Knowledges: The Science Question Feminism and the Privilege of Partial Perspective', *Feminist Studies* vol. no. 3 (1988), 575–599.

[5] Neil Smith, 'Contours of a Spatialized Politics: Homeless Vehicles and the Production of Geographical Scale', *Social Text* no. 33 (1992), 54–81.

[6] See Aernout Mik, *Echt Onecht* (Amsterdam: Heineken Prizes and KNAW, 2002).

[7] Rosi Braidotti, *Transpositions: Nomadic Ethics* (Cambridge: Polity, 2006), 6.

[8] Haraway, 'Situated Knowledges', 595.

and temporally static social structure, immigrants and refugees experience a systematic form of marginalization. Along with the acquisition of a Dutch passport, often at the expense of one's 'original' passport, 'naturalization' has a restricting effect because it often assigns specific (low-paying) jobs, (bad) neighbourhoods and (negative) connotations to migrants of specific generations.

Of course, this need not be the case. In so far as the 'first' generation refers to an *event*, namely the actual migration, the rise of 'guest work' or the seeking of asylum the term could be employed in a less sociological manner. A focus on the ways in which events are experienced and remembered makes one less susceptible to the naturalization of boundaries. Conceptualizing experiences, memories and even the events themselves as *produced* means that time and space are no longer naturally applicable variables. In other words, practices of 'cutting' can be accounted for. What happens in the Netherlands, however, is that the potential for rethinking how these terms are used is not being utilized. The notion of 'generation' circulating in current debates on immigration and refugees is used in the narrowest possible sense, whereas critical theory since post-structuralism has taught us that 'generation is neither an innocent empirical model nor an accurate assessment of a historical reality'.[9]

As a result, public debate on these issues is stifled. Events such as immigration or the seeking of asylum are not understood as experiences that both constrain and free subjects. The negative and the positive are not held in any balanced perspective; on the contrary, the negative aspects are allowed to run wild in public debates. The event of migration is not allowed to travel from the past, through the present and into the future, or to change along the way and form a creative potential. The event is fixed with reference to the past, and its fixed meaning haunts the present and future of the subjects in question. It is seen as a constraint for 'them', which 'we' can point at. This rigid approach hinders both dialogue and the flow of information across the many ethnic communities in Dutch society today because it entails new forms of compartmentalization.

Moreover, the strict usage of the term 'generation' has a certain teleological twist to it that reinforces assumptions assigned to immigrants or asylum seekers. It is presumed, therefore, that members of 'the third generation' have become more 'Dutch' and less attached to the so-called norms, values, culture and religion of their grandparents' country of origin. The assumptions made about this generation ('more Dutch'

udith Roof, 'Generational
culties; or, the Fear of a Barren
ory', in *Generations: Academic
nists in Dialogue*, eds. Devony
er and E. Ann Kaplan
neapolis/London: University of
esota Press, 1997), 69–87.



**Generational Othering and the Dutch
Obsession with the Here and Now**
Iris van der Tuin

translates as 'less backward') show that non-Dutch and/or non-Western-European family histories are assumed to have trapped and blocked the subject. Furthermore, this discussion gets structured as a one-way track, which parallels the linear flow of chronological time. Thus, the full responsibility for the present situation is assigned to 'them', whereas 'we' are expecting to be left untouched and unchallenged. Consequently, nothing is added to our understanding or conceptualization of Dutchness. Dutchness remains something 'pure' and it forms some sort of apotheosis. In this context, the suggestion that third-generation subjects are to a greater or lesser extent free(d) from the norms and values of their family's country of origin is constraining rather than liberating, because these subjects are left no space for negotiating their family history in the present. Family histories of migration authored by the migrants themselves have to be kept out of the public sphere, because mainstream Dutch culture determines cultural memory according to the rigid concepts of both history and time. These assumptions can and must be challenged in order for alternative, more dynamic and interactive approaches to emerge in contemporary Dutch debates.

### Narcissism and nostalgia

According to politicians, policy makers and commentators from the right wing, the umbilical cord between migrants' past/there and present/here has to be cut. They call this 'integration'. Any resistance or objection to this cutting-off exercise is attributed to a nostalgic longing on the part of the migrants for the time and space *preceding* the migration or for a situation still *untouched* by what caused the need for seeking asylum. Dutch right-wing commentators argue that migrants hold on to backward norms and values, which they would be better off forgetting. The commentators prefer a (narcissistic) 'obsession with the here and now'. The thing is, however, that both approaches freeze 'the past' of migrants. In other words, what right-wingers fear (non-integration caused by the nostalgia of migrants) is predicated on the same principles as the narcissism of the commentators themselves!

Dutch politics suffers from a self-referential twist, which is linked to populism and to an over-simplified approach to the age-old history of immigration in the Netherlands. Right-wing commentators do not allow for the study of the common ground between their own claims and the claims that are assigned to immigrants and refugees. The common opinion about migrants is predicated on a schism between Dutch and non-Dutch approaches. Ironically this dialectical approach (us versus them) is precisely what *constitutes* the schism. What the nostalgia commentators ascribe to immigrants and refugees is *not* radically different from their own narcissism, because in both cases it rests on rigid chronology. The narcissism of the right wing is informed by an equally nostalgic vision of Dutchness as it relies upon a core set of norms and values (individualism, tolerance, democracy, secularism) that leaves out most societal trends both in the past (strict Christian Calvinist fundamentalism, the oppression and exclusion of women, cultural provincialism) and in the present. Thus, this nostalgic approach actively conceals developments in Dutch society, such as the current reinforcement of Christian norms and values within Dutch governing bodies, and the connected questioning of rights such as abortion, euthanasia and gay marriage, among others. A great deal of the Dutch public debate has therefore lost touch with 'reality'. Within this constellation, the voices of immigrants and refugees are most clearly heard when a certain form of nostalgia can be read into their accounts. This is a situation offering no prospects of progress or development – the Dutch debate about immigrants and refugees has come to a dead end when viewed from the perspective of generationality.

### Time

In debates about immigrants and refugees in the Netherlands, time and consequently generation are utilized in such a restrictive way that *discarding* the whole notion of generationality seems the only way out of the cul-de-sac. However, I prefer to explore the creative potential of generation as a multilayered and nonlinear concept that should never be approached in a dialectical and oppositional manner. Reconceptualizing time as other than causal linearity starts from understanding the past, present and future as co-constitutive and interlocked rather than successive and isolatable. The past is not merely something that defines or constrains us; it is something to take with us, and to cherish and criticize along the way. We need to allow for a *deterritorialization*[10] from a past, which is comprised of both constraint and undecidability.[11] Deterritorialization does away with the past as fully *defining, constraining and determining* present and future. While acknowledging the (constraining) influence of the past on present and future, the theory of deterritorialization simultaneously allows for surprising connections between past, present and future that can lead to unexpected outcomes. Thinking through the present condition one needs to include the past, because cutting off the past leads to a seductive apotheosis that has damaging effects for (individual) migrants, and forecloses the possible lessons we can learn from the past. Time as constraining *and* liberating brings together the legacies of the past and the potentials of the future. Utilizing this approach, one is neither seduced by a fantasy (working towards pure Dutchness) nor paralysed by an isolatable cause (backward otherness).

Claire Colebrook, *Gilles Deleuze* [London/New York: Routledge, 2002).

Grosz, 'Thinking the New', 40.

### Generation as generative

I propose conceptualizing the potentiality of 'generation' by starting from generation as *generative*. The first step is to disconnect this discussion from the tyranny of chronology. One's engagement with a generational standpoint does not necessarily derive from one's actual and 'truthful' experience or memory of a historical reality isolated in the past. Nor do immigrants, refugees and others belong to generations on the basis of sociological quantification. A generation can be created for specific goals ('third-wave feminism') and can be relived and reinvented in a specific situation at a later date ('activist feminism' in the twenty-first century.[12] Generational standpoints can also travel through time and in space (take third-generation Moroccans (temporarily) living according to the norms and values they ascribe to their parent's childhood, for example). Generative patterns are 'neither random nor arbitrary'.[13] Third-generation migrants will always be restricted by their family history of migration and the (virtual) departure from a country and/or continent, but at the same time their specific knowledge and skills (for instance adaptability and bilingualism) and their paradoxical, post-secular subject positions have enormous potential. I am not arguing for a pluralistic strategy in which the constraints of migration are exchanged for surprising, affirmative outcomes. Rather it is essential to incorporate the *full meaning* of deterritorialization, to take into account the constraining *and* undecidable aspects of a non-linear practice of time.

### Conclusion

The 'generative' potential of generationality lies in its ability to unblock the Dutch public debate on immigrants and refugees, which is currently predicated on the dialectical oppositions us versus them, past versus present and here versus there. The potentiality of generation rests in a non-linear notion of time that does away with 'chronology is power'. It also holds a privileged link to creative experiments in art practice, where non-linearity constitutes the starting point for attacking narcissism and nostalgia, and practices of othering. The incorporation of deterritorializing strategies such as rethinking, recitals and intertextuality in these practices avoids generational othering. In this way critical artistic practices generate insight into time, space and generation(s) as boundary projects through an inquiry of the material and discursive forces involved.


[12] Rosalyn Deutsche, 'Not-Forgetting: Mary Kelly's *Love Son Grey Room* no. 24 (2006), 26–37.

[13] Braidotti, *Transpositions*, 5.

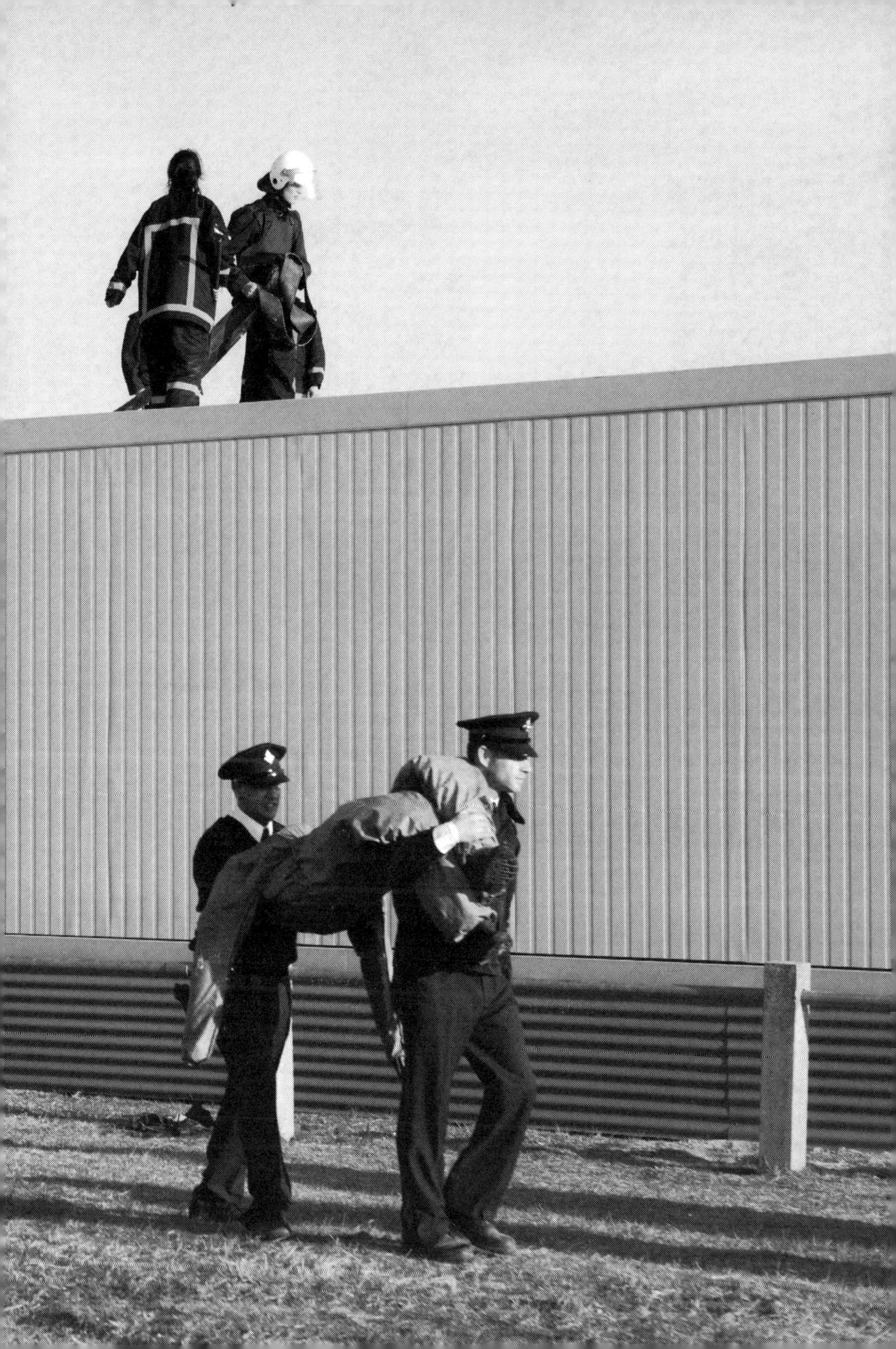

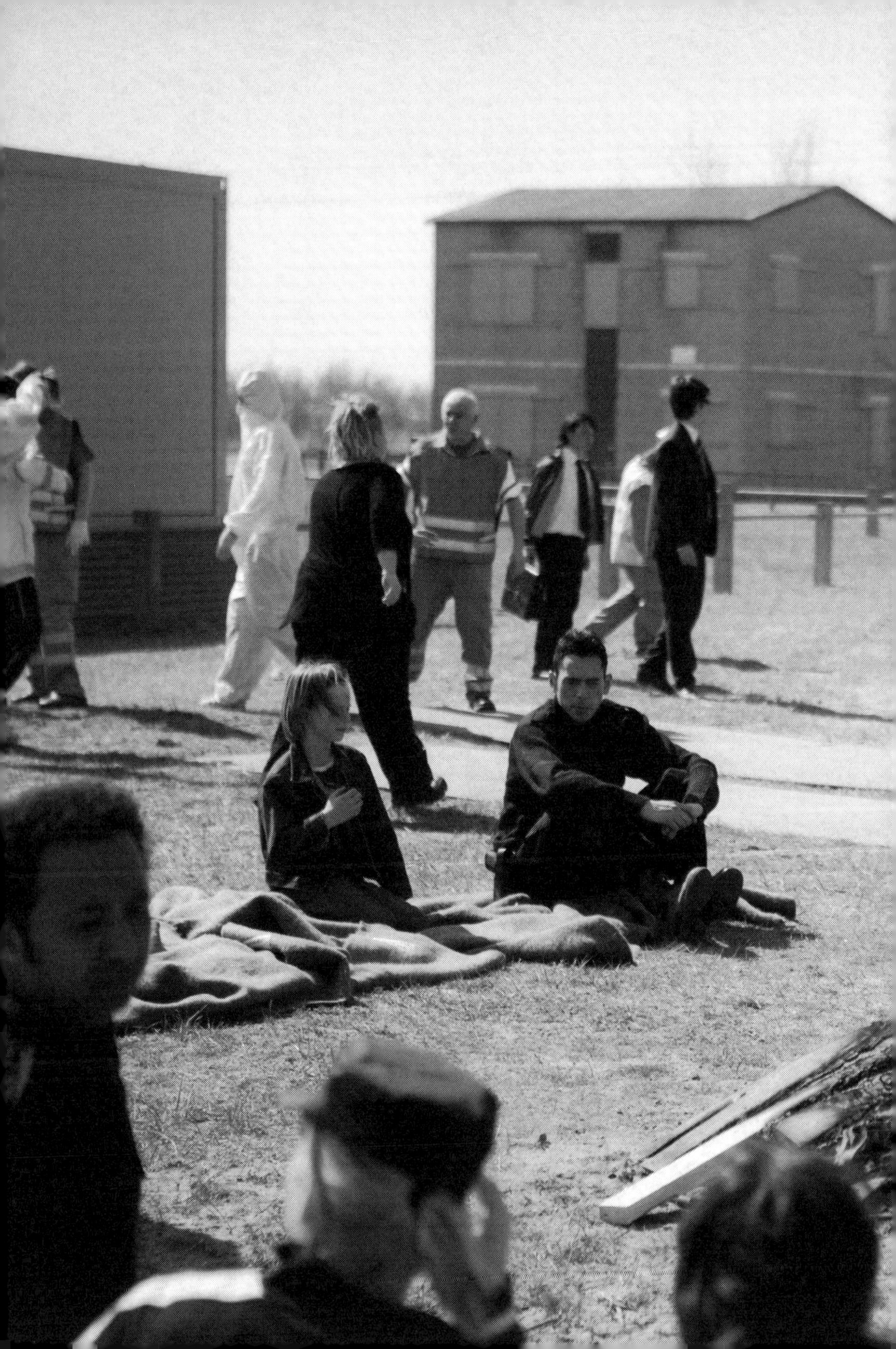

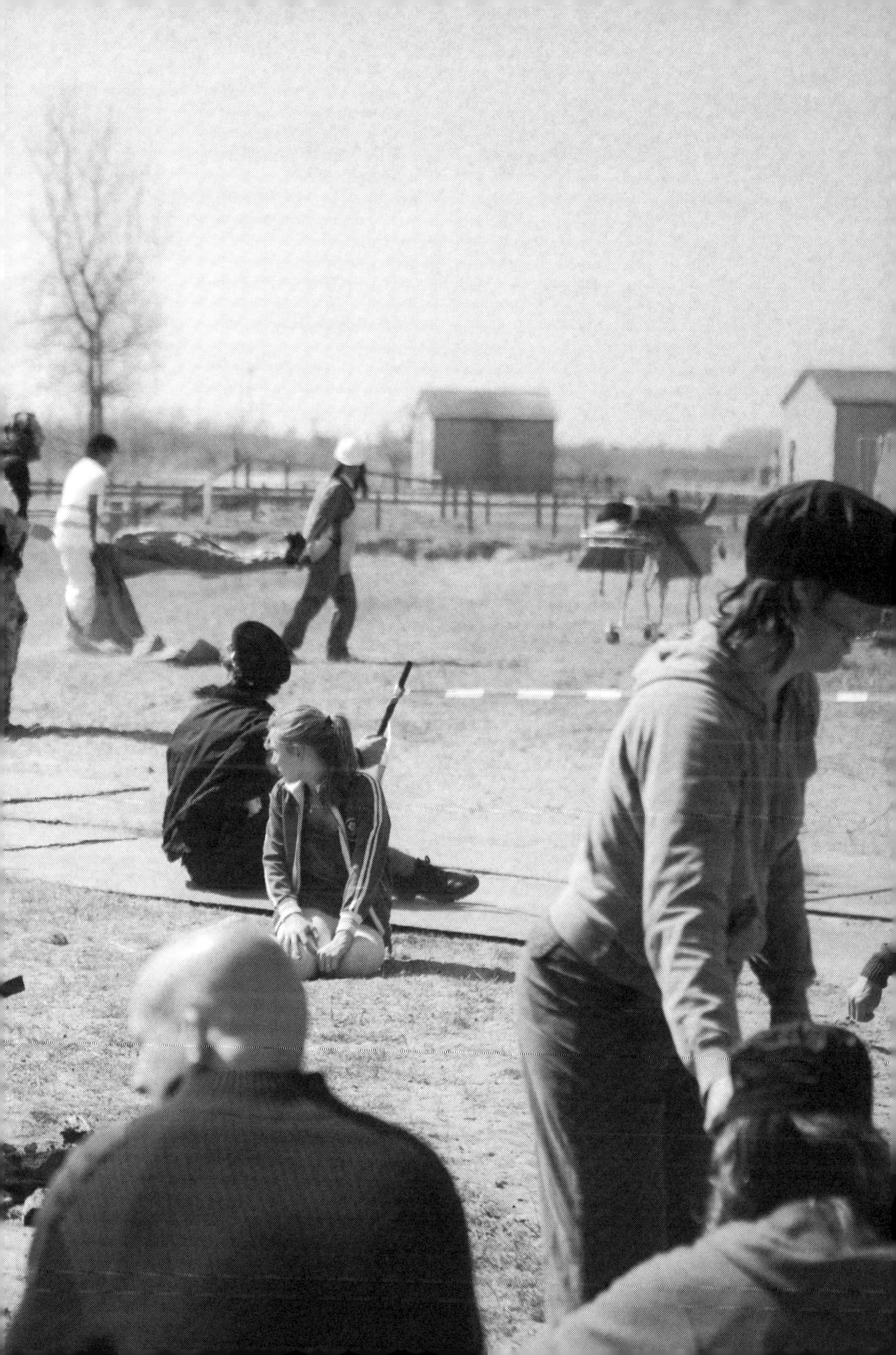

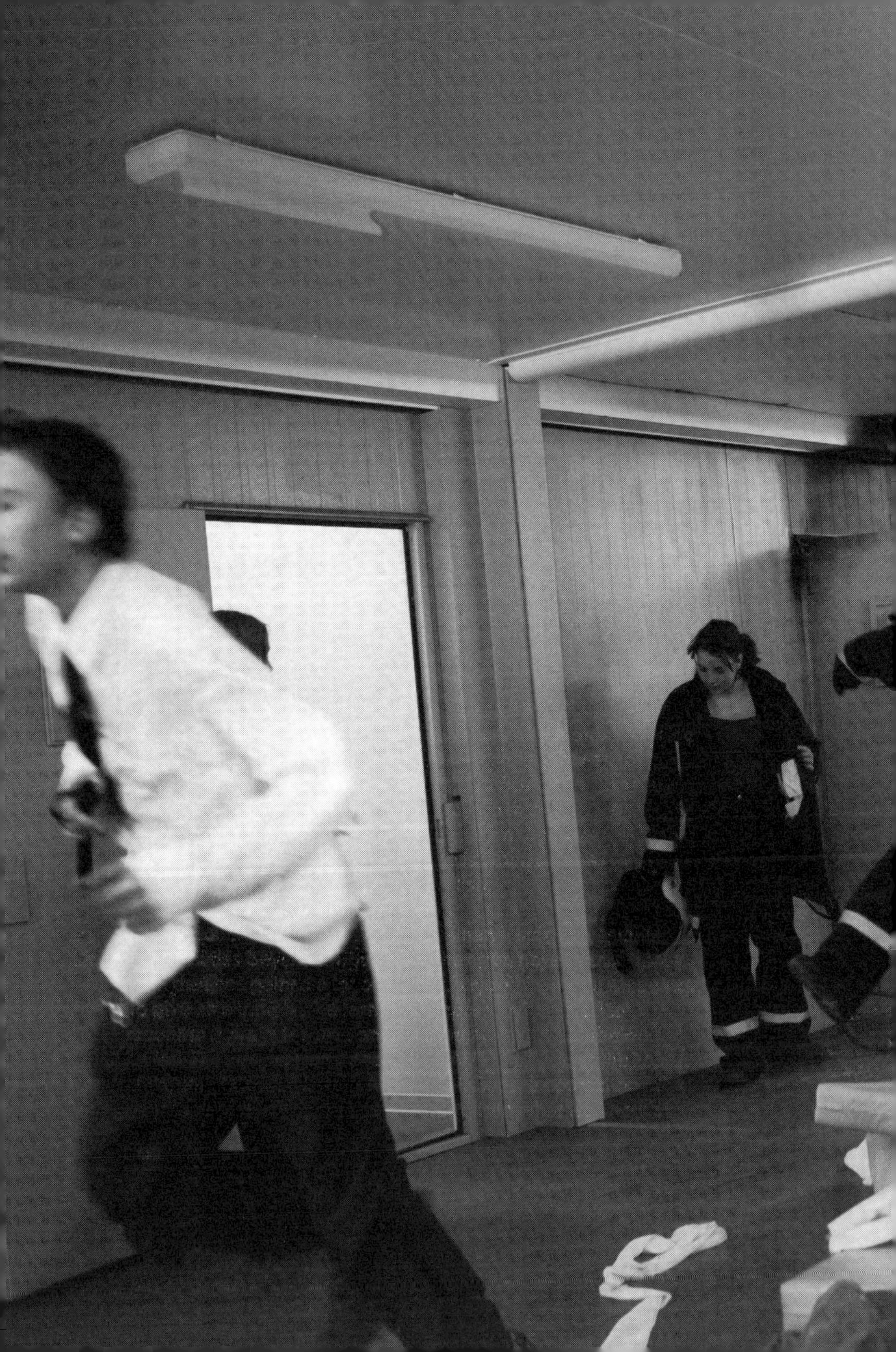

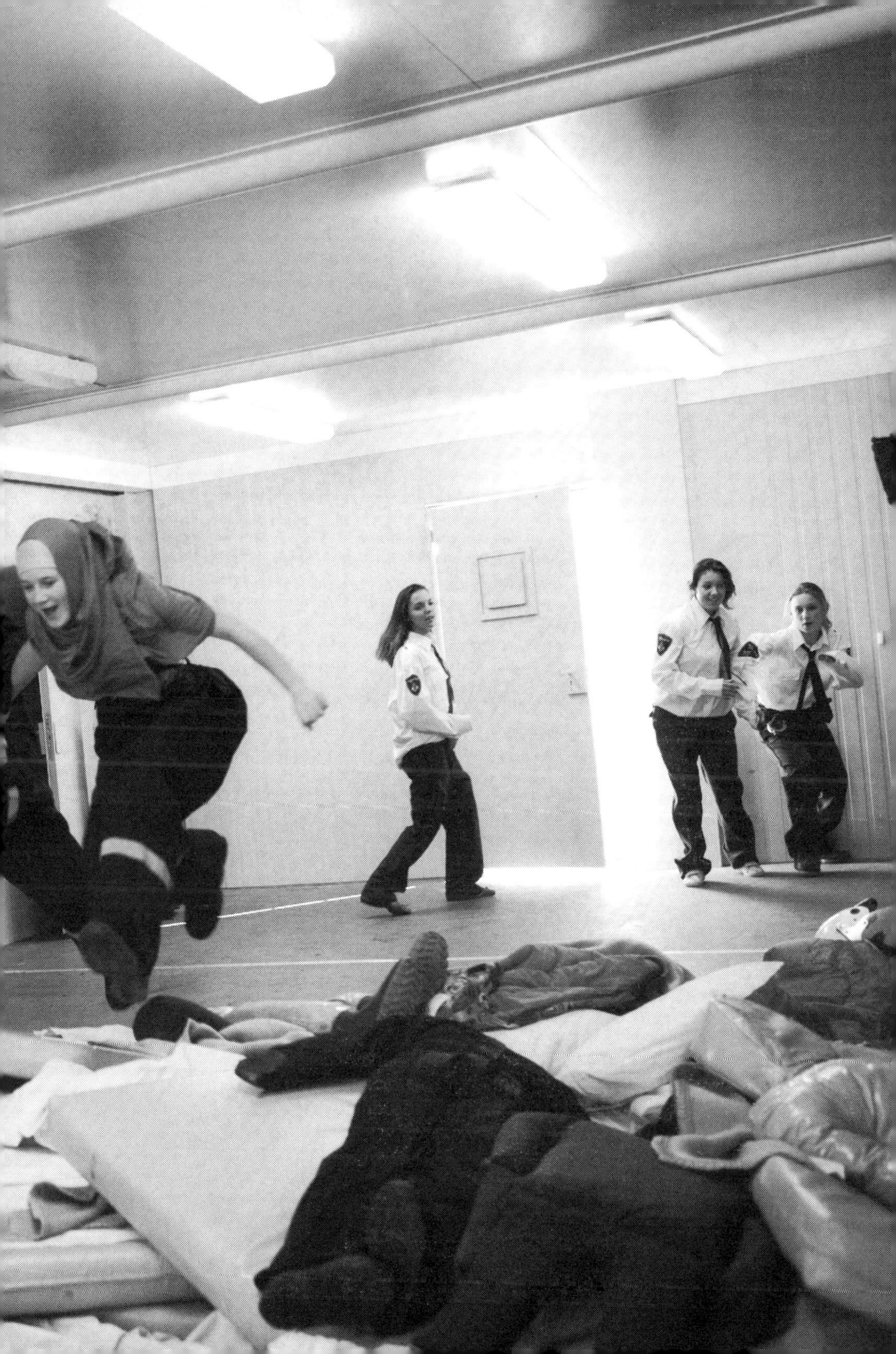

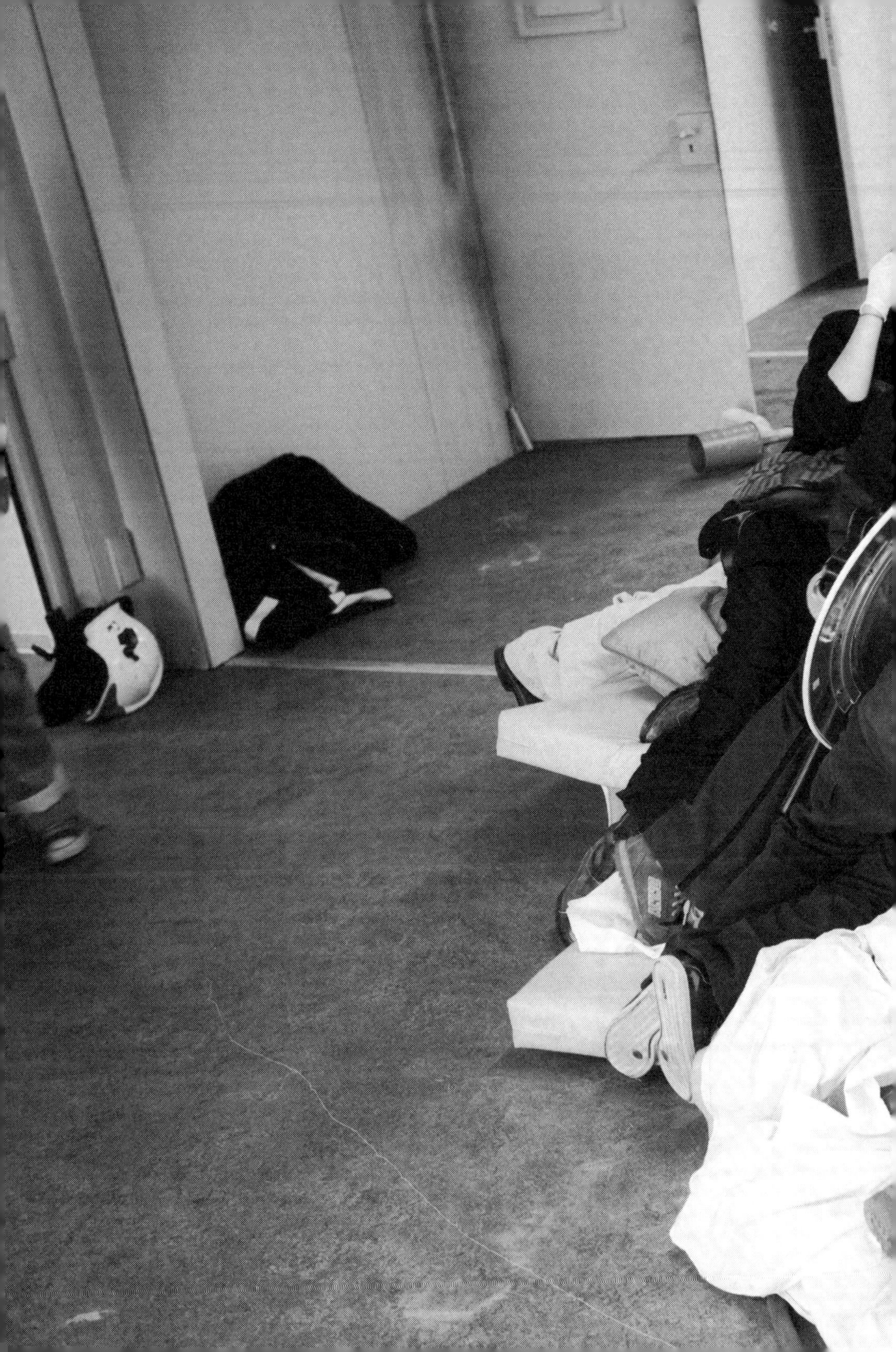

# Art Is about We
## A Conversation with Lawrence Weiner

**Maria Hlavajova** It is my own experience, but I often hear it also from friends and colleagues coming from abroad and living and working in the Netherlands, that from the outside the country appears to be something completely different than what you get to know from (relatively) within. You have chosen, if I am not mistaken, to maintain both positions simultaneously, that of an outsider and insider. I would like to start by asking in general, what is your relationship to the Netherlands? When did you first come to the country? How much do you feel connected to the Dutch art scene? And what did/does the Netherlands offer you? To me, Lawrence Weiner somehow stands for the Netherlands that no longer is. Do you think the country has changed in the years you have been visiting it, or living here?

**Lawrence Weiner** My primary response to the Netherlands was in the early 1960s when I visited it in search of … At the same time I visited other points of unrest, Paris, Copenhagen, etc. I seem to have retained a positive sensual response to the Netherlands (Amsterdam). In the late 1960s, opportunities for showing presented themselves, Art & Project, the Stedelijk Museum, *Op Losse Schroeven*, the lifestyle and the internationality of Amsterdam continued to attract me. When Alice and I decided that we would attempt to raise our child with one foot in the new world and one foot in the old, Amsterdam provided an atmosphere conducive to that aspiration. We've stayed with our feet floating on the boat since 1970. I feel connected to the Dutch art scene as much as any artist feels connected to any art scene anywhere. The Netherlands offers intense fruitful relationships, both within and without the art world.

**MH** How has the art world developed here in your view?

**LW** It went from an aspirational, at times charmingly naive hope to involve itself with the entire world to the advent of an extremely paternalistic nationalism that seems to have dampened the initial enthusiasm. It went from a post-Galilean world that was aware that it revolved around the sun, to that of a pre-Galilean concept of a world revolving only around itself, much as what happened worldwide. Comfortable as it may have been for some I must admit that my refusal to join in has allowed me to maintain my affection for the Netherlands.

**MH** Would it be possible to grasp that moment of change, the
turning point when the worldly aspiration became just a
routine management of local matters, if I understand you well?
And then, is there a way to reiterate the kind of hope you
address, to nourish a new yet comparable aspiration in our day
and age?

> **LW** When the stream of life begins to eddy into small pools
> and those pools begin to resemble a team and when the team
> of some pool in the north goes up against the team of a
> southern pool and the phenomenon seemed to be worldwide
> – the games began. My culture can whop your culture.  My
> culture is accredited by Sotheby's. By Christie's. By Philips de
> Pury. There didn't seem to be terribly much other than the
> carnage to be of interest. As this conversation is about the
> Netherlands, perhaps I became disappointed. This was the
> Netherlands of the Hanseatic League reduced down to
> looking for football ratings, not that any other country is any
> different. But you've engaged me in a conversation
> concerning the Netherlands. I'm not addressing any hope, I'm
> not addressing any grievance. Sometimes a conversation
> would be nice.

**MH** When you have somebody look at your art or have a
conversation with it, do you give them an (national) identity?
Does the Netherlands differ from other places in its forms of
reception?

> **LW** My aspiration would be that it does not have a national tag
> on it. But in the Netherlands, the same as every place else, the
> inclusion of the English language (even in tandem with the
> language of the place where it is being shown) connotes that
> perhaps it came from an English-speaking place.

**MH** I wonder if living partially in Holland gave you a certain
freedom or ability to make work that did not fit the rubric of
American art?

> **LW** Absolutely. One of the reasons for my choice of the
> Netherlands was the exquisite light. I specifically fight for time
> to spend in the Netherlands in order to be able to draw within
> that light.

Having chosen to live in a harbour and having a propensity
for many of the materials used on the sea, it is a necessary and
highly substantial component of what makes me me.

**MH** The idea of the involvement of art with the world you're
mentioning is something I would like to consider. It seems to
be on top of Dutch art world's agenda nowadays to debate
about the conflict between art that is autonomous versus art
that is in the world, involved, and engaged – art (and artists)
that acknowledge being part of the world. I wonder what your
thoughts are about this?

**LW** Art ain't about you. Art ain't about me. Art is about we.
There is no autonomous art. Each artist functions in society
in a non-proscribed manner. Art in itself is engaged in its
pondering not only of its position, but as well of its propositions. The only requirement of art is that it is public. In being
public, the question of autonomous is obviated. I don't see
where this so-called conflict could even exist because
sociological and material art exist simultaneously – at the
same time and the same place. A disadvantage for the
sociological art is the inevitable problem of finding a use for
yesterday's newspapers.

**MH** You once said, 'All Art as it becomes known becomes
Political regardless of the intent of the Artist.' Could you say
a bit more about your ideas of the political in art?

**LW** Politics as a process involves implementation of a logic
pattern – the implementation of a logic pattern that brings
about a desired cultural result. Art presents a logic pattern
that promises no goal but is useful on a temporal level – the
idea that even within an idealistic socialism idiosyncrasies
become a virtue rather than a fault. Art, by its very nature
and by its function, becomes at all times a questioning of
implementation. If that ain't political, I don't know what is.

**MH** With this project, we are looking at the Netherlands as
'the example' of the western condition, defined nowadays in
large by fear and anxiety. I can imagine your first-hand
experience with these concepts is nurtured by the reality of
the United States. Yet, the example in this context (Agamben)
is both particular and universal, and I would be interested to

hear how you personally experience the current reality, and
mainly the processes of normalization that constitute it?
I mean, how fear has become a political tool and one of the
governing control mechanisms in our time?

**LW** We must admit that fear and exclusion are mainstays of
national cultures and have been since the advent of national
cultures. My own personal experience, slight as it was being
blue-eyed, was the slight change in temperament within the
art structure when it became obvious I intended to stay and to
stay apart. I remember my astonishment in the 1970s to
discover there were as many studies of Dutch culture in Dutch
as new novels in Dutch. It is the nature of mercantile cultures
to basically look at themselves in terms of their adventures.
Fear and loathing, while I am as susceptible as the next
person, in the Netherlands, my legal status as one who walks
alongside allows one a sense of ambivalence. All adapting
cultures present dangers within the situation they choose to
adapt within.

**MH** Is it then nothing more than our sensitivity that has
changed? If you say that fear and exclusion have always been
part of the social contract, I agree. Yet, in my eyes the
consensus about what the social contract is has been broken
recently – just look at the dismantling of the western welfare
state that continues to happen all over Europe. In simple
terms, one could view the current situation in the Netherlands
as a troubled negotiation of new possibilities. I keep asking
myself, how can art contribute to this change? To avoid
misunderstanding, I do not have in mind art that should be
'useful' to these processes, but wonder about a space of
thinking that art can contribute to.

**LW** It's not a question of sensitivity. It is a question of
grammar. The use of the term 'Welfare State' to illustrate the
basic rights of human beings to shelter, education, medical
maintenance is to accept a grammar of a ruling class that
takes those basic human rights for granted. When the artist
accepts that grammar as a means of communication, the art
itself, which at its inception was a theory concerning the
relationship of human beings to objects, must present itself
as a theorem precluding its usefulness as art. Art in its
questioning role must assess the times as they are at the time.

Not in relation to what has been, and certainly not in relation
to what could be in the future. Art is not only in the present.
It is the present.

**MH** But what about art as a tool for making propositions – the
idea that art could predict a new world or cater to an imagined
world, which has its roots in modernism. Is this not a way for
art to speak about the future?

**LW** *WAT OP DE TAFEL STAAT STAAT OP DE TAFEL.* (What's on
the table is on the table.) All we can do is set together patterns
of relationships of human beings to objects that take into
consideration the continuing development of the destiny of
human beings and objects. As I previously noted, we are not in
the business of predicting the future and would not want to
take away the ability to look at the present and try to maintain
a relationship with that.

**MH** You once said that you realized you made art because you
were unsatisfied with the configuration that you saw before
you: 'The reason I make art is to try and present another
configuration to fuck up the one that I'm living in now.' I wonder,
is this what you believe art is capable of doing vis-à-vis the
current social, political, cultural and economic frameworks?
Presenting other configurations? Is there a way to formulate
what kind of imaginary you strive for?

**LW** When confronted by a configuration (overall culture)
that is not functioning in the manner that you would choose,
art is one of the only means of presenting a logic structure
concerning the relationship of human beings to objects that
imbues both parties with perhaps another sense of dignity.
Work and class hierarchies diffuse when the materials
involved, stone steel wood water, are connected in a logic
pattern with those who use them. Perhaps it does not turn the
world on its head, but it does change those who accept the
logic patterns as presented. It's the best I can do.

*This conversation took place via e-mail in spring 2007.*

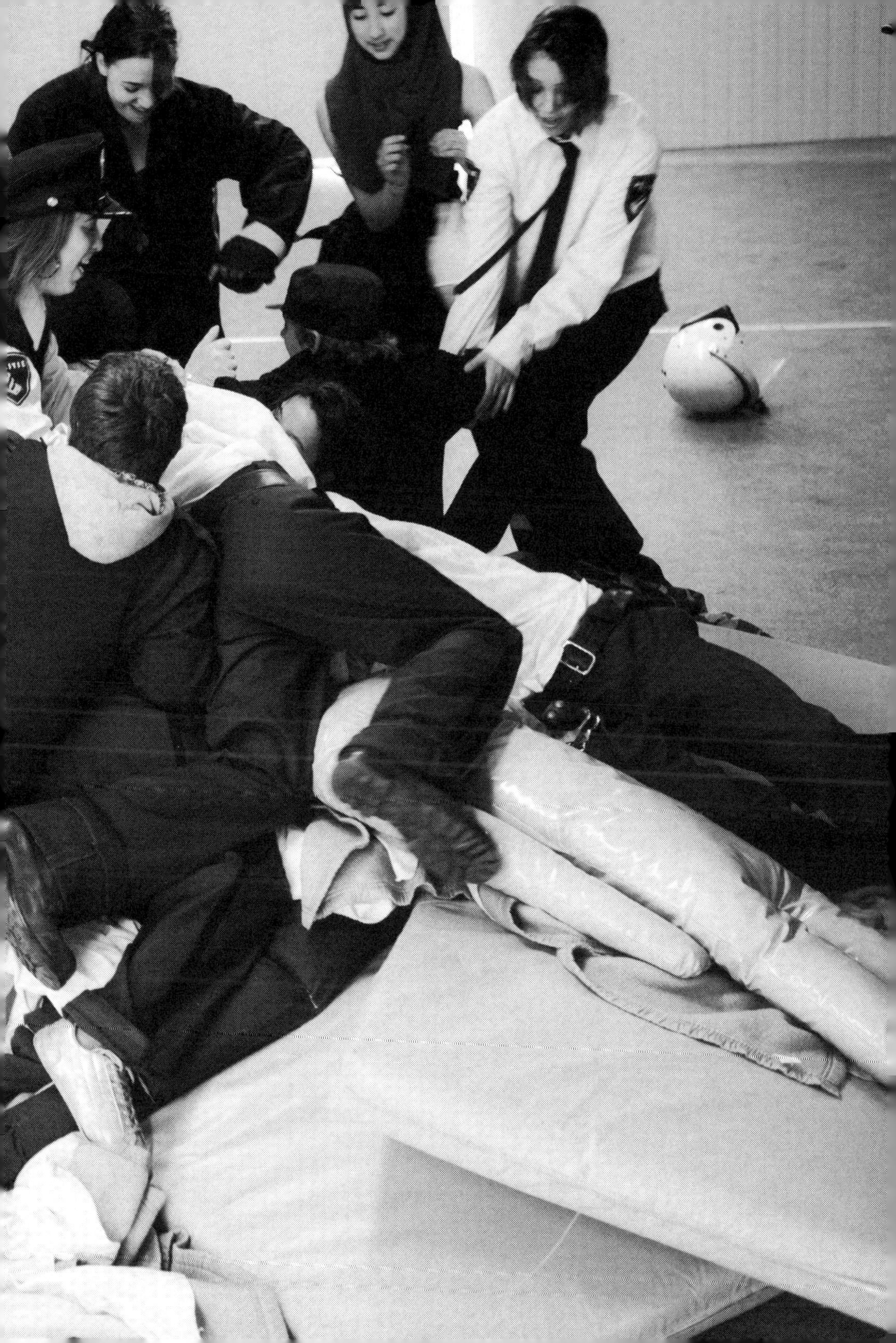

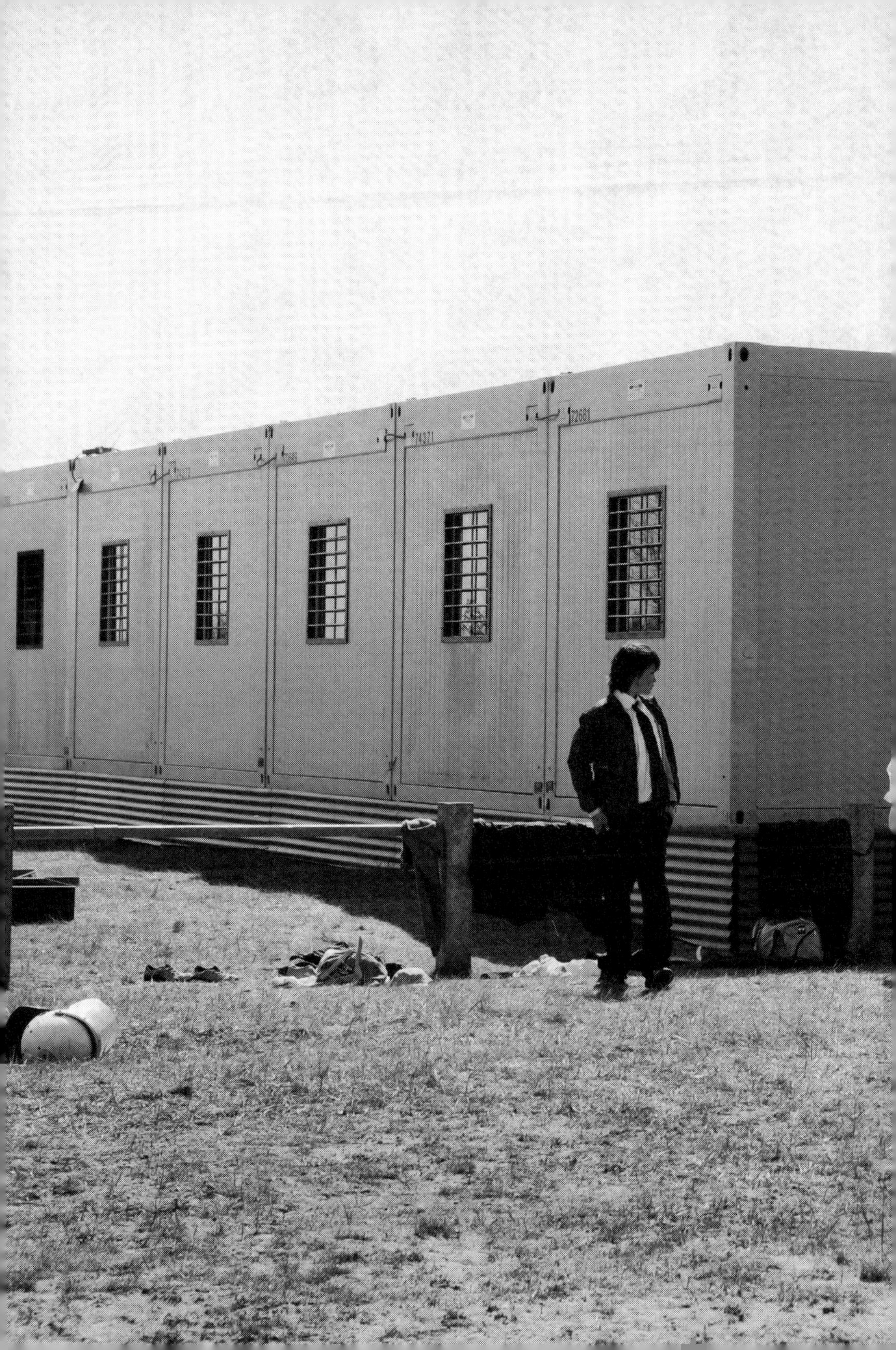

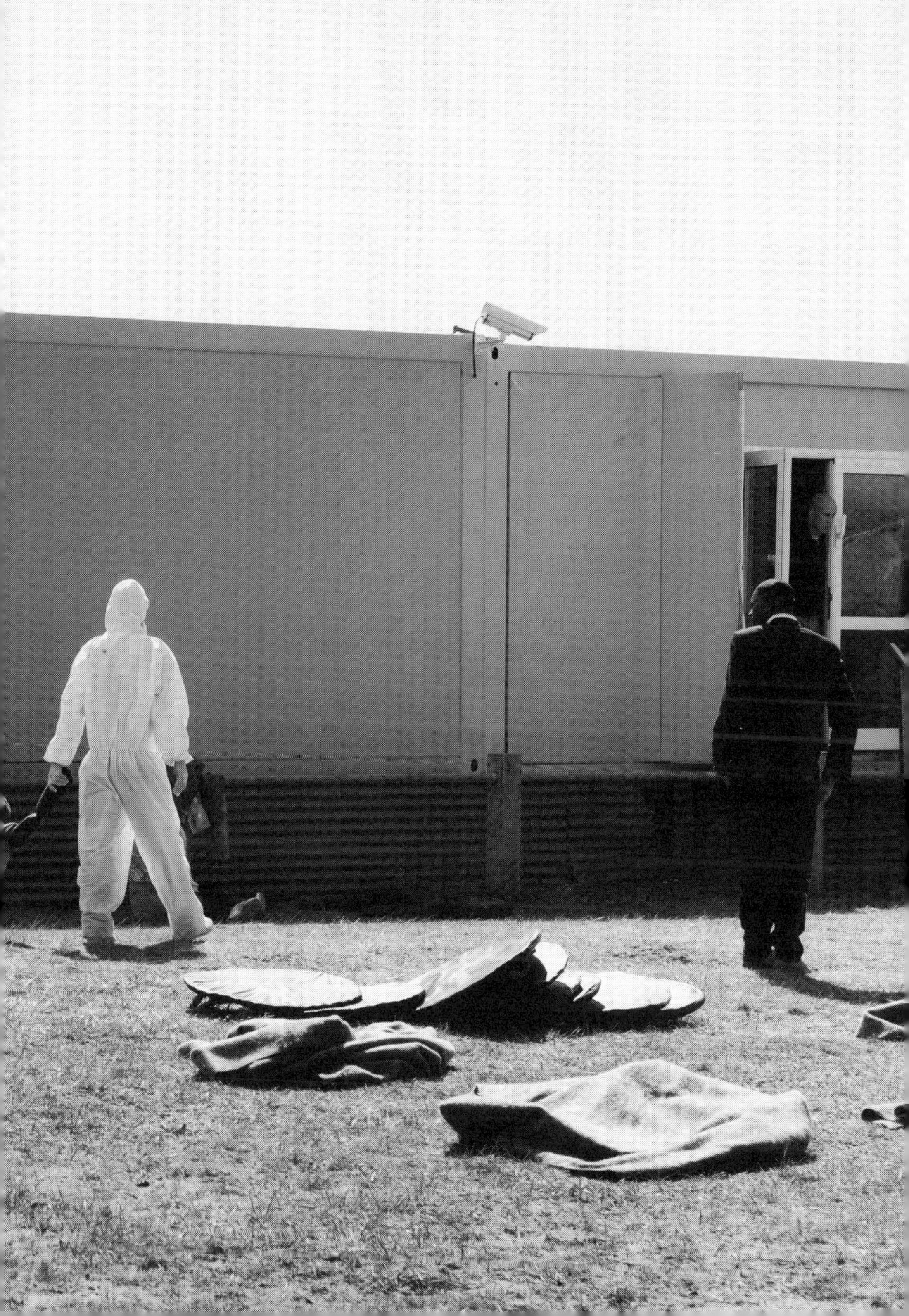

# ntributors

**VO** is a research team consisting of **Gideon
ie** (born 1975) and **Matthias Pauwels** (born
5), who are both trained in architecture and
losophy. Their work focuses on the politi-
dimension of art, architecture and urban-
. BAVO has organized several debates,
nposia and conferences and published
ny articles in a diverse array of media
luding *Archis/Volume, De Groene
sterdammer, Metropolis M, Architectura
rator, Stereo, Cut-up, Andere Sinema,
V* and *Omagiu*. They were guest editors
*Andere Sinema* no. 176 entitled *Spectres
vant-garde* (2006), and published the
ok *The Undivided City and its Willing
cutioners* in 2003. Boie and Pauwels live
d work in Rotterdam.

rah **Bracke** (born 1971) holds a postdoctoral
rie Curie Fellowship at Utrecht University
nder Studies) and is affiliated with the
iversity of California Santa Cruz (Anthro-
ogy). Her work explores questions of
gion, modernity, secularism, subjectivity
d gender in a European context. She has
blished in, among others, *Tijdschrift voor
nderstudies, Tijdschrift voor Humanistiek,
iek en Maatschappij, Yang, Andere
ema, European Journal of Women's
dies* and *Multitudes*. She participates
various feminist groups and networks,
luding the transnational European
ninist research and activism network
xtGeneration. Bracke lives and works in
ssels, Utrecht and Santa Cruz.

si **Braidotti** (born 1954) is distinguished
fessor in the Humanities in a Globalised
rld in the Arts Faculty at Utrecht University.
idotti is especially interested in poststruc-
alism and psychoanalysis, theories of
sexual difference and the history of feminist
ideas. Her research and writing deals mainly
with issues of feminist philosophy and cultural
studies, and more recently, biopower and
bioethics. In addition to her work as co-editor
of this reader, she has published numerous
books including: *Transpositions: On Nomadic
Ethics* (2006); *Feminismo, diferencia sexual y
subjetividad nomade* (2004); *Op doorreis:
nomadisch denken in de 21ste eeuw* (2004)
and *Matamorphoses: Towards a Materialist
Theory of Becoming* (2002). Braidotti lives and
works in Utrecht.

**Esther Captain** (born 1968) and **Guno Jones**
(born 1969) co-wrote the forthcoming article
'The Enrichment of the Netherlands. Dutch
Colonial Rule and Decolonization in East and
West' in Robert Aldridge (ed.), *Overseas
Empires in the Early Modern and Modern
World* (2007). Captain is a historian and project
manager Dutch-Indies Heritage of the
Department Victims and Remembrance WW II
at the Ministry of Health, Welfare and Sports
in The Hague. She is a researcher at Utrecht
University and teaches at the Vrije Universiteit
in Amsterdam. Captain is the author of *Traces
of War. Survivors of the Burma and Sumatra
Railways* (with Jan Banning) (2005); *Achter het
kawat was Nederland: Indische oorlogservar-
ingen en -herinneringen 1942–1995* (2002) and
editor of *Vertrouwd en vreemd: ontmoetingen
tussen Nederland, Indië en Indonesië* (with
Marieke Hellevoort and Marian van der Klein)
(2000). Jones is a cultural anthropologist and
lecturer/researcher at the Vrije Universiteit in
Amsterdam. His current research interest is
the postcolonial migration from the (former)
Dutch colonies to the Netherlands. Jones's
Ph.D. thesis *Rijksgenoten, onderdanen en
Nederlanders* is forthcoming. He has published on a variety of subjects, such as Dutch
ethnic identity, postcolonial migration and the

legacy of slavery. Captain lives and works in Utrecht and The Hague. Jones lives and works in Utrecht and Amsterdam.

**Marlene Dumas** (born 1953) is an internationally renowned artist whose works examine ethnic, sexual and political norms. In 2006 she held the Alex Katz Chair in Painting at The Cooper Union School of Art in New York, and participated in the Nexus Conference *New Notes Towards the Definition of Western Culture*. Her upcoming and recent exhibitions include: *Marlene Dumas—Broken White*, Metropolitan Museum of Contemporary Art, Tokyo, 2007; *Global Feminism*, Brooklyn Museum, Brooklyn, 2007; *The Painting of Modern Life*, Howard Gallery, London/Castello di Rivoli, Torino, 2007 and *Drawing from the Modern, 1975–2005*, MOMA, New York, 2006. Dumas lives and works in Amsterdam.

**Charles Esche** (born 1963) is a curator and writer, currently director of the Van Abbemuseum in Eindhoven. Esche has curated and co-curated numerous exhibitions including: 9th Istanbul Biennial, Istanbul, 2005; the project *Cork Caucus*, Cork, 2005; Gwangju Biennale, Gwangju, 2002; *Intelligence: New British Art*, Tate Gallery, London, 2000 and *Amateur: Variable Research Initiatives*, Konstmuseum and Konsthall, Göteborg, 2000. He is editor of *AFTERALL*, an art journal based at Central St. Martins College of Art and Design, London and CalArts, Los Angeles. In addition to co-editing this reader, Esche has written for numerous catalogues and magazines and published an edited volume of his writings in Turkish and English, *Modest Proposals* (2005). Esche lives and works in Eindhoven.

**Halleh Ghorashi** (born 1962) holds the PaVEM Chair in Management of Diversity and Integration in the Department of Culture, Organization and Management at the Vrije Universiteit in Amsterdam since September 2005. She was born in Iran and came to the Netherlands in 1988. In 1994, she completed her MA degree in Anthropology at the Vrije Universiteit. She received her Ph.D. in 2001 from the University of Nijmegen. She is the author of *Ways to Survive, Battles to Win: Iranian Women Exiles in the Netherlands and the US* (2003) and several articles on questions of identity, Diaspora and the Iranian women's movement. Ghorashi lives and works in Amsterdam.

**Maria Hlavajova** (born 1971) is artistic director of BAK, basis voor actuele kunst, Utrecht since 2000. She curated the three-part project *Citizens and Subjects* for the Dutch Pavilion at the 52nd Venice Biennale and is a co-editor of this reader. Hlavajova has organized numerous exhibitions and projects at BAK including *Roman Ondák: The Day After Yesterday*, 2006; *Concerning 'Knowledge Production': Practices in Contemporary Art*, 2006; *Adrian Paci*, 2006; *Concerning War*, 2005; *Gerrit Dekker: About no below, no above, no sides*, 2005; *Cordially Invited*, episode 3, *Who if not we...?*, 2004 and *Now What? Dreaming a better world in six parts*, 2003. In 2004, Hlavajova curated *Who if not we...?*, an international collaborative project across Europe. She is co-director of the tranzit network, a foundation that supports exchange and contemporary art practices in Austria, Czech Republic, Hungary and Slovakia. Hlavajova was a faculty member at the Center for Curatorial Studies, Bard College, New York from 1998–2002, co-curator of Manifesta 3, Ljubljana (2000) and director of the Soros Center for Contemporary Arts in Bratislava from 1994–1999. Hlavajova lives and works in Amsterdam and Utrecht.

han Kinoshita** (born 1960) is an interdisci-
ary artist whose work is a combination of
formance and installation that focuses on
vement, space and time. She studied
temporary music at the Cologne University
Music and is involved in the performing
. In addition, Kinoshita was an advising
earcher in the Fine Art Department at Jan
Eyck Academy, Maastricht. Her upcoming
recent exhibitions include: Skulptur
jekte Münster 07, Münster, 2007; 8th
arjah Biennial, Sharjah, 2007; *Travelin'
ht*, Bonnefanten Museum, Maastricht, 2006
*Ensemble!*, MuHKA, Museum voor
dendaagse Kunst Antwerpen, Antwerp,
5. Kinoshita lives and works in Maastricht.

**n Lütticken** (born 1971) is an art and film
ic, editor and writer who teaches modern
contemporary art history at the Vrije
versiteit Amsterdam. He was the editor of
journal *De Witte Raaf* from 2000 till 2004
has written extensively on the central role
istorical theory in contemporary art and
dia. He published *Secret Publicity. Essays
contemporary art* in 2005 and is currently
earching and writing a book on contempo-
art, idolatry and iconoclasm. Recent
atorial projects include: *Life, once more:
ns of reenactment in contemporary art*,
te de With, Rotterdam (2005) and *In This
ony*, Kunstfort Vijfhuizen, Vijfhuizen (2005).
ticken lives and works in Amsterdam.

**nout Mik** (born in 1962) is an artist who
rks predominantly in the medium of video
tallation. He often combines video and
hitecture to transform exhibition spaces
vivid, unsettling tableaux of irrational
nan behavior. Recent exhibitions include:
*zens and Subjects: Aernout Mik*, Dutch
ilion, 52nd Venice Biennale, Venice, 2007;
*fting, Shifting*, Camden Arts Centre,

London, 2007; *Raw Footage/Scapegoats*, BAK,
basis voor actuele kunst, Utrecht, 2006; *Under
the Skin*, Universal Studios-beijing, Beijing,
2006; *A Short History of Performance – Part IV*,
Whitechapel Art Gallery, London, 2006; *post_
modelism*, Bergen Kunsthall, Bergen, 2006;
*Refraction*, New Museum of Contemporary
Art, New York, 2005; *Soft Target. War as a
Daily, First-Hand Reality*, BAK, basis voor
actuele kunst, Utrecht, 2005; *Vacuum Room*,
Argos, Brussels and Centre pour l'image
Contemporaine, Geneva, 2005; *The Gravity in
Art*, De Appel, Amsterdam, 2005; *Ensemble!*,
Museum van Hedendaagse Kunst Antwerpen,
Antwerp, 2005; *InSite_05*, San Diego/Tijuana,
2005; *Whatever Happened to Social Demo-
cracy?* Rooseum, Malmö, 2005; *Irreducible*,
CCA Wattis Institute for Contemporary Arts,
San Francisco, 2005; 26th São Paulo Biennial,
São Paulo, 2004; *Aernout Mik*, Museum
Ludwig, Cologne, 2004 and *Dispersions*, Haus
der Kunst, Munich, 2004. Mik lives and works
in Amsterdam.

**Melvin Moti** (born 1977) is an artist whose
films could be described as conceptual
documentaries, which move between fiction
and reality, history and present. He partici-
pated in the postgraduate course at De
Ateliers in Amsterdam and won the Charlotte
Köhler Prize and Van Lanschot Prize in 2006.
Recently Moti has been a resident at
Künstlerhaus Bethanien in Berlin. His recent
exhibitions include: 2nd Moscow Biennale of
Contemporary Art, Moscow, 2007; *The magic
manual*, Künstlerhaus Bethanien, Berlin;
*Prophets of Deceit*, CCA Wattis Institute for
Contemporary Arts, San Francisco, 2006 and 7.
Werkleitz Biennale – *Happy Believers*,
Werkleitz Biennale, Halle (Saale), 2006. Moti
lives and works in Rotterdam and Berlin.

**Soheila Najand** (born 1957) is an artist and
co-founder and director of InterArt in Arnhem,
the Netherlands. InterArt, founded in 1997, is
a cultural institution that brings social challenges to the public's attention using multi-
disciplinary art projects that aim to promote
social commitment and cohesion. Najand
was born in Iran and came to the Netherlands
in 1989 as a refugee. Upon her arrival, she
attended the graphic design study programme at the Hogeschool voor de Kunsten
(Institute of the Arts) in Arnhem and subsequently the advanced study programme in
visual art at De Ateliers in Amsterdam. She is
also a mentor at DasArts in Amsterdam and
the Frank Mohr Institute in Groningen. Najand
lives and works in Arnhem.

**Henk Oosterling** (born 1952) is associate
professor at the Department of Philosophy
of the Erasmus University in Rotterdam. He
teaches dialectical method, French philosophy of differences, intercultural philosophy
and aesthetics. He is secretary of the Dutch-
Flemish Association of Intercultural
Philosophy, chairman of the Dutch Federation
of Aesthetics, director of Platform Political
Philosophy (PPP) and co-editor of the series
*Studies in Intercultural Philosophy*. As director
of the Center for Philosophy & Arts (CFK) he
initiated and supervized the research programme *Intermediality. On the borders between
philosophy, arts and politics* (1997–2002). This
summer his co-edited volume *Intermediali-
ties. Philosophy, Arts, Politics* will be published by Rowman & Littlefield. Oosterling lives
and works in Rotterdam.

**Pages** was initiated in 2004 by Iranian-born
artists **Nasrin Tabatabai** (born 1961) and
**Babak Afrassiabi** (born 1969). Pages began
its activities by publishing a bilingual Farsi/
English periodical and developing collabora-

tive projects with practitioners in different
cultural fields with critical views on art,
culture, urbanism and social issues. Pages
examines specific social-political condition
that surround artistic practice in order to
'surpass predefined and geographically
bound discourses of subjectivity and locali
Pages recently participated in the Documer
12 magazines project (2007). Tabatabai and
Afrassiabi live and work in Rotterdam and
Tehran.

**Baukje Prins** (born 1956) is Assistant Profes
of Social Philosophy in the Department of
Practical Philosophy at the University of
Groningen. She is the author of *Voorbij de
onschuld. Het debat over integratie in
Nederland* (Beyond Innocence. The Debate
Integration in the Netherlands) (2nd rev. ed
(2004). Prins is an active participant in the
Dutch public debate on integration and
multiculturalism. She is currently working c
book entitled *Accidental Classmates*, in wh
she investigates the history and dynamics c
interethnic relationships through the life
stories of her former classmates at a Dutch
multiethnic school in the 1960s. Prins lives
works in Amsterdam and Groningen.

**Willem de Rooij** (born 1969) is an artist who
studied at the Rijksacademie in Amsterdam
and worked together with Jeroen de Rijke
(1970–2006) since 1994. Their films aim to
bring together the aesthetic and engageme
in art. De Rijke and De Rooij represented th
Netherlands at the Venice Biennale in 2005
with their film *Mandarin Ducks*. De Rooij's
recent exhibitions include: *Jenseits des Kin
– Die Kunst der Projektion*, Hamburger
Bahnhof, Berlin, 2007; *Information/Transforr
tion*, Extra City – Center for Contemporary A
Antwerp, 2005 and *Populism*, Frankfurter
Kunstverein, Frankfurt am Main/Stedelijk

seum Amsterdam, Amsterdam, 2005.
Rooij lives and works in Berlin.

van der Tuin (born 1978) is a Ph.D. candi-
e and junior teacher in Gender Studies at
echt University. Her Ph.D. dissertation is on
w feminist epistemologies and European
men's Studies. She has coined the terms
rd-wave materialism' and 'jumping gen-
tions' to account for the co-constitution of
w feminist materialist epistemologies and
third feminist wave. She teaches courses
using on feminist classics and feminist
ory. With Professor Rosemarie Buikema
e is editing the book *Gender in Media,
nst en Cultuur* (2007). Van der Tuin lives and
rks in Amsterdam and Utrecht.

wrence Weiner (born 1942) is considered
be one of the pioneers of Conceptual art.
is best known for his text pieces and wall
tallations, but works in a variety of media.
work has been widely exhibited all over
world. Weiner and his family have spent
e on a houseboat docked at Westerdoks-
k, Amsterdam since 1970. Recent exhibi-
ns include: *INTO ME/OUT OF ME*, Kunst
rke, Berlin, 2007/P.S.1 Contemporary Art
nter, Long Island, 2006; 27th São Paulo
nnial, São Paulo, 2006 and *Made To
duce A Spark*, Museo D'Arte Contem-
anea, Rivoli, Torino, 2006. Weiner lives and
rks in New York and Westerdoksdijk,
sterdam.

Winder (born 1975) is a writer and editor.
e studied Political Theory and has an MA
Curatorial Studies from the Center of
ratorial Studies, Bard College, New York.
nder has worked as an editor at BAK, basis
r actuele kunst since 2003. In addition to
ing as associate editor of this reader, she
co-edited (with Maria Hlavajova):

*Concerning War: A Critical Reader* (2006),
*World Question Center (Reloaded)* (2005) *and
Who if not we should at least try to imagine
the future of all this? 7 episodes on
(ex)changing Europe* (2004). From 2004–2006,
she was writing fellow of the Institute of
Current World Affairs in Berlin. Winder lives
and works in Berlin and Utrecht.

**ect Credits**

**zens and Subjects** is a three-
 project consisting of new work
 rtist Aernout Mik in the Dutch
 ilion, 52nd International Art
 ibition – La Biennale di Venezia;
 itical reader, *Citizens and
 jects: The Netherlands, for
 mple*; and an 'extension' of
 Pavilion taking place in the
 herlands in autumn 2007.


 nmissioned by:
 driaan Foundation
 cept, Curator: Maria Hlavajova
 ect Realization: BAK, basis voor
 ele kunst, Utrecht
 ect Development and
 agement: Arjan van Meeuwen
 ect Research: Danila Cahen,
 anne Tiemersma
 or: Jill Winder
 ect Production: Marente
 mheuvel, Suzanne Tiemersma
 lic Relations and Communication:
 te Barner, Hanna Sohier


**zens and Subjects: Aernout Mik
ch Pavilion, 52nd International
Exhibition – La Biennale di
ezia
June–21 November 2007**

 ibition Realization: Anything Is
 sible, Amsterdam
 hnical Equipment and Installation:
 AV Art, Espoo
 rdinator Venice: Ankie
 ellekens


*ning Ground*, 2007, two-channel
 eo installation, courtesy
 ier | gebauer, Berlin and The
 ject, New York
 duction: Dirk Tolman
 ier & Schaaf), Anca Munteanu
 ady-Cam: Benito Strangio,
 Vermaercke
 Direction: Marjoleine Boonstra
 Direction: Elsje de Bruijn

Costumes: Elisabetta Pian
Fight Instructor: Rik Wiessenhaan
Casting: Anca Munteanu
Art Department: Josche Allwardt
Photography on Set: Florian Braun

*Convergencies*, 2007, two-channel
video installation, courtesy
carlier | gebauer, Berlin and The
Project, New York
Research: Danila Cahen, Barbara Kist,
Gerard Nijssen, Suzanne Tiemersma
Mixage/Sound Engineering: Hugo
Dijkstal
Online: Joke Treffers
Images from Found Documentary
Material: AP Archive, Brainwave,
Reuters & ITN (ITN Source), RNN7
and various other sources

*Mock Up*, 2007, four-channel
video installation, courtesy
carlier | gebauer, Berlin
Production: Dirk Tolman, Jelier &
Schaaf
Director of Photography: Benito
Strangio
Steady Cam Operator: Jo
Vermaercke, Istvan Imreh
Camera: Danila Cahen
Co-Direction: Marjoleine Boonstra
Art Direction: Elsje de Bruijn
Casting: Hans Kemna and Kemna
Casting
Costumes: Sylvia Huijerman
Camera Equipment: Cam-a-lot
Production Manager: Wikke van der
Burg
Make-Up: Niels Wahler
Special Effects: Rik Wiessenhaan
Set Photography: Florian Braun
Post Production: Ultimate

*Citizens and Subjects:
The Netherlands, for example
A Critical Reader*

For credits, see the colophon in this
volume.

*Citizens and Subjects:
Practices and Debates
September–November 2007*

Realized as collaboration among
the following partners: BAK, basis
voor actuele kunst, Utrecht
(www.bak-utrecht.nl) and the
Dutch Pavilion, 52nd International
Art Exhibition – La Biennale di
Venezia; Utrecht University; Vrede
van Utrecht; Van Abbemuseum,
Eindhoven (www.vanabbemuseum.
nl) and the project *Be(com)ing
Dutch*; Witte de With, Rotterdam
(www.wdw.nl) and the German
Pavilion, 52nd International Art
Exhibition – La Biennale di Venezia.
Conceived by: Rosi Braidotti, Binna
Choi, Charles Esche, Annie Fletcher,
Maria Hlavajova, Melanie Peters,
Nicolaus Schafhausen

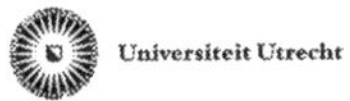


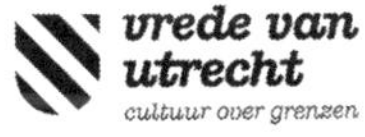


vanabbemuseum

Witte de With
Center for Contemporary Art

## Acknowledgments

**We wish to thank all artists who contributed to the research for the Dutch Pavilion, and the writers, curators and other art practitioners involved in the realization of *Citizens and Subjects* as well as the individuals listed below, who have contributed generously in a variety of ways to make this project possible:**

Annet Gelink Gallery, Amsterdam
Rachida Azough, Foundation Kosmopolis, the Netherlands
Andreas Bunte, carlier | gebauer, Berlin
Marius Babias, Berlin
Han Bakker, Amsterdam
Bart de Baere, Antwerp
Peter Baren, Luka and Samo Barendse, Amsterdam
Harry J. van den Bergh, Onno Yska and VluchtelingenWerk Nederland
Manon Berendse, Rabobank, Eindhoven
Dirk Jan Blikkendaal, Amsterdam
Alex Blauw and Hulpverleningsdienst Kennermeland
Wilma Blom, Adjudant Mekkring, Anne Visser and Ministry of Defence, The Hague
Ole Bouman, Netherlands Architecture Institute (NAI), Rotterdam
Bernard Brosi, Nieuwegein
Annie Brouwer-Korf, Mayor of Utrecht
Galerie Daniel Buchholz, Cologne
Willem Burmanje, Forbo Flooring, the Netherlands
Cam-a-lot, Amsterdam
Massimo de Carlo, Milan
Sara Casolari, Modena
Mels Crouwel and Ministry of Housing, Spatial Planning and the Environment (Ministry of VROM), The Hague
De Brakke Grond, Amsterdam
Antonio Denti and Reuters Rome
Rob Docter, Foundation Rietveld Pavilion, Rotterdam
Chantal van Doorn, Province of Utrecht

Willem Duivestein, Rotterdam
Bregje van Eekelen, Amsterdam/ Santa Cruz
Cees van Eijck, Alderman for Culture, Municipality of Utrecht
Franka Faase, Utrecht
Leigh Foster and The UN Refugee Agency UNHCR, Geneva
Galerie Fons Welters, Amsterdam
Galerie Paul Andriesse, Amsterdam
Ulrich Gebauer and Marie-Blanche Carlier, carlier | gebauer, Berlin
Floris de Gelder, Utrecht
Tom van Gestel, Amsterdam
Esther Gotschalk, Amsterdam
Uta Grosenick, Cologne
Vít Havránek, tranzit, Prague
Arthur Haijer and Stichting OOV-Support, Wateringen
Sirine Haidar and INA – Institut National de l'Audiovisuel, Paris
Christian Haye, The Project, New York
Jozef Hey, BeamSystems, Amsterdam
Sofia Hilden and Reuters Denmark
Annelies van der Horst, Utrecht
Peter van Ingen, Amsterdam
Martin Janda, Vienna
Nancy Jouwe, Foundation Kosmopolis, Utrecht
Corrie Kars, Police Department Amsterdam – Amstelland
David Kat, Amsterdam
Marte Kappert and Municipality of Utrecht
Matthew Keene and ITN Independent Television News, London
James Kennedy, Amsterdam
Martin Kievit and Fire Department Hollands Midden
Ralph Kits, Utrecht
Bernadette Klein Douwel, Municipality of Utrecht
Diederik Kramers and The UN Refugee Agency UNHCR, Brussels
Svebor Kranjc and Reuters, Amsterdam
Debrah Kyvrikosaios and Reuters, Athens
Ine Legerstee, Mestre
Gitta Luiten, Mondriaan Foundation, Amsterdam
Gabriele Mazzariol, Ponte di Piave

Steve McQueen, Amsterdam
Simone Merati, Venice
Emile Miedema, Utrecht
Akiko and Eva Yuki Mik
Marcus Muraro, Dumont, Cologne
Ruud Natrop and Brainwave, Rotterdam
Taco de Neef, Mondriaan Foundat, Amsterdam
Martijn van Nieuwenhuijzen, Stedelijk Museum, Amsterdam
Willem Nijkerk, Amsterdam
Sophie von Olfers, Witte de With, Rotterdam
Nadine Orth, Utrecht
Hans Ouwerling, Gerlach, Schipol
Jolanda Prinsen, Haarlem
Dennis Polak, Amsterdam
Carine Portengen and Korps Landelijke Politiediensten, the Netherlands
Betty Post, Kemma Casting, Amsterdam
Kathrin Rhomberg, Vienna
Roberto Rosolen, La Biennale di Venezia, Venice
Jorma Saarikko, Pro AV Art, Espoo
Jelena Samancje, Belgrade
Brigitte van der Sande, Amsterdam
Jeff Schaeffer and Associated Pres, Paris
Nicolaus Schafhausen, Witte de W, Rotterdam
Paul Scheffer, Amsterdam
Dennis and Debra Scholl, Miami
Georg Schöllhammer, Vienna
Oliver Sertić, Zagreb
Raymond Sienot and Municipality Amsterdam
Jeremy Smith and Reuters, London
Eric Sondervan, Gerdo Elzinga, Racida Riffi and Police Academy, Amsterdam
Stedelijk Museum, Amsterdam
Roger Strijland, Paris
David van Traa and Municipality of Amsterdam
Marina Turko and T.G.S. Tele Giorn di Sicilia Spa, Palermo
Gijs van Tuyl, Stedelijk Museum, Amsterdam
Rudi van der Valk, Utrecht

ns van de Veen, Fire Department,
sterdam
bara Vanderlinden, Brussels
rand van Veelen, Amsterdam
hael van der Velden, Andersson
ers Felix, Utrecht
x de Vries, Amsterdam
van Werkhoven, Utrecht
rlie Wu and Associated Press,
don
ius Zaharia and Reuters Romania
van Zanten, Rabobank,
dhoven
bert Ziher, Nieuwegein


nout Mik and Maria Hlavajova
uld like to specially thank
ter Braak and the Netherlands
ndation for Visual Arts, Design
Architecture for their generosity,
erstanding and commitment.

**ncial Partners**

project *Citizens and Subjects*
been commissioned and funded
he Mondriaan Foundation,
sterdam.

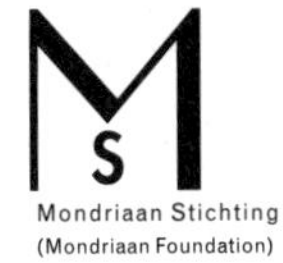

Mondriaan Stichting
(Mondriaan Foundation)

Municipality of Utrecht kindly
ported *Citizens and Subjects:*
*ctices and Debates,* the 'extension'
he Pavilion in Utrecht in autumn
7. This part of the project has
n realized with an additional
tribution from Utrecht University
Vrede van Utrecht.

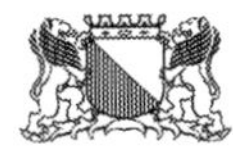

Gemeente Utrecht

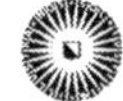

Universiteit Utrecht

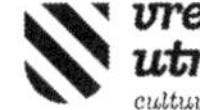

ier | gebauer, Berlin has
erously provided financial and
duction assistance to the
ect.

carlier | gebauer

ther financial or in-kind support
been provided by:
bo Flooring, the Netherlands
bo Art Collection, the Netherlands
ependent Television News,
don
ociated Press, London

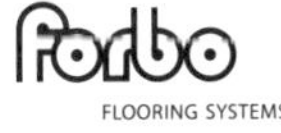

FLOORING SYSTEMS

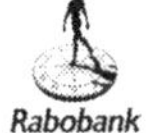

Rabobank

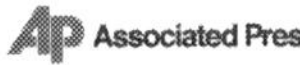

Associated Press

**Index**

111, 127–128, 131–133, 151, 262, 273,
296, 312
ure industry 161, 167, 169
ure wars 161, 173
ação 90

D (Deutscher Akademischer
tausch Dienst) 273
a 222
ish cartoon riots 161, 165
to, Arthur 226
Vinci, Leonardo 170, 280
ord, Guy 168–169, 172, 227
olonization 94–95, 293
wars of 93
euze, Gilles 22, 218, 222–223
ocracy 53, 201, 218, 221, 258–259,
264, 297
accountability in 21
culture of 131–132
rights in 21, 224
deren, Ad van 116
illarisation (ontzuiling) 74, 128–129
cartes, René 202, 220
ention centres 39
erritorialization 297–298
tsche Oper 161
Volkskrant 151
ersity 22, 90–91, 114, 130–133, 201–
, 257
umentary footage 37–38, 41–42
ble nationality See citizenship,
l
ste effect 273
champ, Marcel 222
nas, Marlene 107–108, 111, 115–117
ch Antilles 91, 93–95
ch Constitution 74, 261
ch East India Company 57, 89, 276
ch East Indies 90, 92–95
See also Indonesia
ch Empire 90–93
colonial subjects of 90–93,
183–186
ch Guyana See Suriname
ch monarchy See House of
nge
ch Parliament 57, 93, 95, 114, 255–
, 261, 263, 276
ch Pavilion (Venice)
architecture of 40
work of Aernout Mik in 10–11, 19,
33–43
work of Jeroen de Rijke & Willem
de Rooij in 279–281

Dutch West Indies 89–90, 92–95
See also Suriname
'Dutchness' 131–132, 243, 279, 293,
296–297
Dwaallicht (Van Heeswijk) 59–60

Eastern Europe 39
education 185, 204–205, 218, 221, 258,
276, 312
Egypt 162
Eichmann, Adolf 220–221
Eindhoven 10, 12, 19
11 September See 9/11
Elspeet 73
emancipation 24, 38, 133, 222, 258
as aim of pillarisation 74, 129, 259
of Muslim women 129–130
social 19
embedded cultural practice 60–62
Emerald Belt 92–93
See also Dutch East Indies
empowerment 21, 222, 256–257, 281
Endlösung (final solution) 221
England 185, 276
Enlightenment, the 161, 164–165, 167–
168, 173
'shortcut' to 262
Enlightenment fundamentalism 75,
163–164
ethics 226
ethnic minorities 256, 260
Etüde (Kinoshita) 146
Eurasians 93–95
Europe 35, 39, 56, 89, 130, 162, 164, 168,
239, 241–243, 245, 281, 294, 312
European civilization 75, 117
European Council 263
European enlargement 293
European Union 260, 279
Constitution 279
flag of 279
exceptionalism 151
exclusion 21, 75, 93, 95, 131, 264, 297,
312

fascism 109, 167, 221, 227, 257
Fatih Mosque 168, 274–275
fatwas 171, 217
fear 10, 21, 23, 37, 40, 43, 90, 107, 128,
130, 166, 170, 172, 188, 201–202
use in politics 11, 38, 56–57,
217–223, 226–229, 263
feminism 257, 298
fetishism 167
Figures (Killaars) 162–163, 173

Flanders 113
The Fog of War (Dumas) 115
former Communist bloc 53, 56
Fortuyn, Pim 75, 113, 129
homosexual identity of 260–261
murder of 89, 217, 256
new realism of 260–261
Foucault, Michel 20, 221–222, 228
freedom 22, 79, 164, 202, 219, 222, 256,
310
freedom of expression 75, 127, 201, 261
Free Range Grains (CAE) 225
French Guyana 185
Fromm, Erich 219
Fukuyama, Francis 53
fundamentalism 202, 221
Calvinist 297
Christian 173
Islamic 161, 173, 217, 223, 293

Gamboni, Dario 281
gender 21, 74, 152, 259–260, 294
genealogy 91
generationality 294–298
generation as generative 298
Gerbrandy, Pieter 93
German Pavilion (Venice) 10
Germany 110, 132, 273
Gérôme, Jean-Léon 167
Gesamtkunstwerk (total work of art)
228
Ghana 35, 132
globalization 149, 201–202, 221, 223
God 73–77, 113, 166–167
death of 222
Gogh, Theo van 164, 222, 225, 261–262
murder of 89, 161, 163, 217, 262
See also Submission
Granin, Daniil 189
Greenaway, Peter 217
Greenberg, Clement 169
Greenland 274
Guantanamo Bay 117, 278
Guattari, Félix 218
Gubchevsky, Pavel 188–189
guest workers 95, 127, 183–186, 257,
295
See also labour migrants
guilt 109
Gulf War 110

Hall, Stuart 188
Hanseatic League 310
Hauka cult 35
Heeswijk, Jeanne van 59–60